ACT: Full Study Guide and Test Strategies for the ACT Exam

Smart Edition Media
36 Gorham Street
Suite 1
Cambridge, MA 02138
800-496-5994

Email: info@smarteditionmedia.com

Library of Congress Cataloging-in-Publication Data
Smart Edition Media.
ACT: Full Study Guide and Test Strategies for the ACT
ISBN: Print: 978-1-949147-01-8, 1st edition

1. ACT Exam
2. Study Guides
3. American College Test
4. College Preparation
5. Careers

Disclaimer:

The opinions expressed in this publication are the sole works of Smart Edition Media and were created independently from any National Evaluation Systems or other testing affiliates. Between the time of publication and printing, specific standards as well as testing formats and website information may change that are not included in part or in whole within this product. Smart Edition Media develops sample test questions, and they reflect similar content as on real tests; however, they are not former tests. Smart Edition Media assembles content that aligns with exam standards but makes no claims nor guarantees candidates a passing score.

Printed in the United States of America

ACT: Full Study Guide and Test Strategies for the ACT/Smart Edition Media.

ISBN: Print: 978-1-949147-01-8
Ebook: 978-1-949147-26-1

Print and digital composition by Book Genesis, Inc.

ACT PRACTICE ONLINE

Smart Edition Media's Online Learning Resources allow you the flexibility to study for your exam on your own schedule and are the perfect companion to help you reach your goals! You can access online content with an Internet connection from any computer, laptop, or mobile device.

Online Learning Resources

Designed to enable you to master the content in quick bursts of focused learning, these tools cover a complete range of subjects, including:

- English Language Arts
- Reading
- Math
- Science
- Writing

Our online resources are filled with test-taking tips and strategies, important facts, and practice problems that mirror questions on the exam.

Online Sample Tests & Flashcards

Access additional full-length practice tests online!

Use these tests as a diagnostic tool to determine areas of strength and weakness before embarking on your study program or to assess mastery of skills once you have completed your studies.

FLASHCARDS 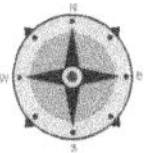 **GAMES** 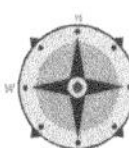 **QUIZZES** 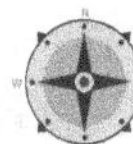 **TESTS**

Go to the URL: **https://smarteditionmedia.com/pages/act-online-resources** and follow the password/login instructions.

TABLE OF CONTENTS

INTRODUCTION

AN OVERVIEW OF THE ACT EXAM

The ACT is a national college admissions examination that assesses college readiness in English, Mathematics, Reading, and Science. An optional Writing assessment is also offered. The ACT is accepted by all four-year colleges and universities in the United States, and can help determine mastery of high school level subject areas as well as predict a student's ability to handle first-year college courses. The ACT is administered on seven test dates within the United States, U.S. territories, and Puerto Rico.

ABOUT THIS BOOK

This book provides you with an accurate and complete representation of the ACT test and includes instructional content on the four core sections on the exam, plus a chapter on the optional Writing exam with practice essay prompts. The reviews in this book are designed to provide the information and strategies you need to do well on the exam. The full-length practice test in the book is based on the ACT and contains questions similar to those you can expect to encounter on the official test. A detailed answer key follows each practice quiz and test. These answer keys provide explanations designed to help you completely understand the test material. Each explanation references the book chapter to allow you to go back to that section for additional review, if necessary.

ONLINE SAMPLE TESTS

The purchase of this book grants you access to two additional full-length practice tests online. You can locate these exams on the Smart Edition Media website.

Go to the URL: https://smarteditionmedia.com/pages/act-online-resources and follow the password/login instructions.

HOW TO USE THIS BOOK

Studies show that most people begin preparing for college-entry exams approximately 8 weeks before their test date. If you are scheduled to take your test in sooner than 8 weeks, do not despair! Smart Edition Media has designed this study guide to be flexible to allow you to concentrate on areas where you need the most support.

Whether you have 8 weeks to study – or much less than that – we urge you to take one of the online practice tests to determine areas of strength and weakness, if you have not done so already. These tests can be found in your online resources.

Once you have completed a practice test, use this information to help you create a study plan that suits your individual study habits and time frame. If you are short on time, look at your diagnostic test results to determine which subject matter could use the most attention and focus the majority of your efforts on those areas. While this study guide is organized to follow the order of the actual test, you are not required to complete the book from beginning to end, in that exact order.

HOW THIS BOOK IS ORGANIZED

Take a look at the Table of Contents. Notice that each **Section** in the study guide corresponds to a subtest of the exam. These sections are broken into **Chapters** that identify the major content categories of the exam.

Each chapter is further divided into individual **Lessons** that address the specific content and objectives required to pass the exam. Some lessons contain embedded example questions to assess your comprehension of the content "in the moment." All lessons contain a bulleted list called "**Let's Review.**" Use this list to refresh your memory before taking a practice quiz, test, or the actual exam. A **Practice Quiz**, designed to check your progress as you move through the content, follows each chapter.

Whether you plan on working through the study guide from cover to cover, or selecting specific sections to review, each chapter of this book can be completed in one sitting. If you must end your study session before finishing a chapter, try to complete your current lesson in order to maximize comprehension and retention of the material.

ONLINE SAMPLE TESTS

The purchase of this book grants you access to two additional full-length practice tests online. You can locate these exams on the Smart Edition Media website.

Study Strategies and Tips

MAKE STUDY SESSIONS A PRIORITY.

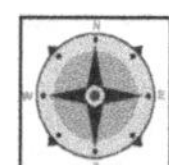

- Use a calendar to schedule your study sessions. Set aside a dedicated amount of time each day/week for studying. While it may seem difficult to manage, given your other responsibilities, remember that in order to reach your goals, it is crucial to dedicate the time now to prepare for this test. A satisfactory score on your exam is the key to unlocking a multitude of opportunities for your future success.
- Do you work? Have children? Other obligations? Be sure to take these into account when creating your schedule. Work around them to ensure that your scheduled study sessions can be free of distractions.

> **TIPS FOR FINDING TIME TO STUDY.**
>
> - Wake up 1-2 hours before your family for some quiet time
> - Study 1-2 hours before bedtime and after everything has quieted down
> - Utilize weekends for longer study periods
> - Hire a babysitter to watch children

TAKE PRACTICE TESTS

- Smart Edition Media offers practice tests, both online and in print. Take as many as you can to help be prepared. This will eliminate any surprises you may encounter during the exam.

KNOW YOUR LEARNING STYLE

- Identify your strengths and weaknesses as a student. All students are different and everyone has a different learning style. Do not compare yourself to others.
- Howard Gardner, a developmental psychologist at Harvard University, has studied the ways in which people learn new information. He has identified seven distinct intelligences. According to his theory:

  "we are all able to know the world through language, logical-mathematical analysis, spatial representation, musical thinking, the use of the body to solve problems or to make things, an understanding of other individuals, and an understanding of ourselves. Where individuals differ is in the strength of these intelligences - the so-called profile of intelligences -and in the ways in which such intelligences are invoked and combined to carry out different tasks, solve diverse problems, and progress in various domains."

- Knowing your learning style can help you to tailor your studying efforts to suit your natural strengths.
- What ways help you learn best? Videos? Reading textbooks? Find the best way for you to study and learn/review the material.

WHAT IS YOUR LEARNING STYLE?

- **Visual-Spatial** – Do you like to draw, do jigsaw puzzles, read maps, daydream? Creating drawings, graphic organizers, or watching videos might be useful for you.
- **Bodily-kinesthetic** – Do you like movement, making things, physical activity? Do you communicate well through body language, or like to be taught through physical activity? Hands-on learning, acting out, role playing are tools you might try.
- **Musical** – Do you show sensitivity to rhythm and sound? If you love music, and are also sensitive to sounds in your environments, it might be beneficial to study with music in the background. You can turn lessons into lyricsor speak rhythmically to aid in content retention.
- **Interpersonal** – Do you have many friends, empathy for others, street smarts, and interact well with others? You might learn best in a group setting. Form a study group with other students who are preparing for the same exam. Technology makes it easy to connect, if you are unable to meet in person, teleconferencing or video chats are useful tools to aid interpersonal learners in connecting with others.
- **Intrapersonal** – Do you prefer to work alone rather than in a group? Are you in tune with your inner feelings, follow your intuition and possess a strong will, confidence and opinions? Independent study and introspection will be ideal for you. Reading books, using creative materials, keeping a diary of your progress will be helpful. Intrapersonal learners are the most independent of the learners.
- **Linguistic** – Do you use words effectively, have highly developed auditory skills and often think in words? Do you like reading, playing word games, making up poetry or stories? Learning tools such as computers, games, multimedia will be beneficial to your studies.
- **Logical-Mathematical** – Do you think conceptually, abstractly, and are able to see and explore patterns and relationships? Try exploring subject matter through logic games, experiments and puzzles.

CREATE THE OPTIMAL STUDY ENVIRONMENT

- Some people enjoy listening to soft background music when they study. (Instrumental music is a good choice.) Others need to have a silent space in order to concentrate. Which do you prefer? Either way, it is best to create an environment that is free of distractions for your study sessions.
- Have study guide – Will travel! Leave your house: Daily routines and chores can be distractions. Check out your local library, a coffee shop, or other quiet space to remove yourself from distractions and daunting household tasks will compete for your attention.
- Create a Technology Free Zone. Silence the ringer on your cell phone and place it out of reach to prevent surfing the Web, social media interactions, and email/texting exchanges. Turn off the television, radio, or other devices while you study.
- Are you comfy? Find a comfortable, but not *too* comfortable, place to study. Sit at a desk or table in a straight, upright chair. Avoid sitting on the couch, a bed, or in front of the TV. Wear clothing that is not binding and restricting.
- Keep your area organized. Have all the materials you need available and ready: Smart Edition study guide, computer, notebook, pen, calculator, and pencil/eraser. Use a desk lamp or overhead light that provides ample lighting to prevent eye-strain and fatigue.

HEALTHY BODY, HEALTHY MIND

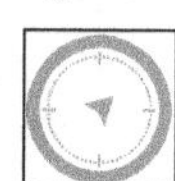

- Consider these words of wisdom from Buddha, "To keep the body in good health is a duty – otherwise we shall not be able to keep our mind strong and clear."

KEYS TO CREATING A HEALTHY BODY AND MIND:

- Drink water – Stay hydrated! Limit drinks with excessive sugar or caffeine.
- Eat natural foods – Make smart food choices and avoid greasy, fatty, sugary foods.
- Think positively – You can do this! Do not doubt yourself, and trust in the process.
- Exercise daily – If you have a workout routine, stick to it! If you are more sedentary, now is a great time to begin! Try yoga or a low-impact sport. Simply walking at a brisk pace will help to get your heart rate going.
- Sleep well – Getting a good night's sleep is important, but too few of us actually make it a priority. Aim to get eight hours of uninterrupted sleep in order to maximize your mental focus, memory, learning, and physical wellbeing.

FINAL THOUGHTS

- Remember to relax and take breaks during study sessions.
- Review the testing material. Go over topics you already know for a refresher.
- Focus more time on less familiar subjects.

Exam Preparation

In addition to studying for your upcoming exam, it is important to keep in mind that you need to prepare your mind and body as well. When preparing to take an exam as a whole, not just studying, taking practice exams, and reviewing math rules, it is critical to prepare your body in order to be mentally and physically ready. Often, your success rate will be much higher when you are *fully* ready.

Here are some tips to keep in mind when preparing for your exam:

SEVERAL WEEKS/DAYS BEFORE THE EXAM

- Get a full night of sleep, approximately 8 hours
- Turn off electronics before bed
- Exercise regularly
- Eat a healthy balanced diet, include fruits and vegetable
- Drink water

THE NIGHT BEFORE

- Eat a good dinner
- Pack materials/bag, healthy snacks, and water

- Gather materials needed for test: your ID and receipt of test. You do not want to be scrambling the morning of the exam. If you are unsure of what to bring with you, check with your testing center or test administrator.
- Map the location of test center, identify how you will be getting there (driving, public transportation, uber, etc.), when you need to leave, and parking options.
- Lay your clothes out. Wear comfortable clothes and shoes, do not wear items that are too hot/cold
- Allow minimum of ~8 hours of sleep
- Avoid coffee and alcohol
- Do not take any medications or drugs to help you sleep
- Set alarm

THE DAY OF THE EXAM 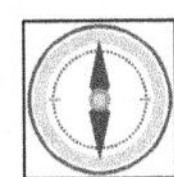

- Wake up early, allow ample time to do all the things you need to do and for travel
- Eat a healthy, well-rounded breakfast
- Drink water
- Leave early and arrive early, leave time for any traffic or any other unforeseeable circumstances
- Arrive early and check in for exam. This will give you enough time to relax, take off coat, and become comfortable with your surroundings.

<u>Take a deep breath, get ready, go! You got this!</u>

SECTION I. LANGUAGE

Chapter 1 Conventions of Standard English

Spelling

Spelling correctly is important to accurately convey thoughts to an audience. This lesson will cover (1) vowels and consonants, (2) suffixes and plurals, (3) homophones and homographs.

Vowels and Consonants

Vowels and **consonants** are different speech sounds in English.

The letters A, E, I, O, U and sometimes Y are **vowels** and can create a variety of sounds. The most common are short sounds and long sounds. Long **vowel** sounds sound like the name of the letter such as the *a* in late. Short **vowel** sounds have a unique sound such as the *a* in cat. A rule for **vowels** is that when two vowels are walking, the first does the talking as in pain and meat.

Consonants include the other twenty-one letters in the alphabet. **Consonants** are weak letters and only make sounds when paired with **vowels**. That is why words always must have a **vowel**. This also means that **consonants** need to be doubled to make a stronger sound like sitting, grabbed, progress. Understanding general trends and patterns for **vowels** and **consonants** will help with spelling. The table below represents the difference between short and long **vowels** and gives examples for each.

	Symbol	Example Words
Short a	a	Cat, mat, hat, pat
Long a	ā	Late, pain, pay, they, weight, straight
Short e	e	Met, said, bread
Long e	ē	Breeze, cheap, dean, equal
Short i	i	Bit, myth, kiss, rip
Long i	ī	Cry, pie, high
Short o	o	Dog, hot, pop
Long o	ō	Snow, nose, elbow
Short u	u	Run, cut, club, gum
Long u	ū	Duty, rule, new, food
Short oo	oo	Book, foot, cookie
Long oo	ōō	Mood, bloom, shoot

Suffixes and Plurals

A **suffix** is a word part that is added to the ending of a root word. A **suffix** changes the meaning and spelling of words. There are some general patterns to follow with **suffixes**.

- Adding -er, -ist, or -or changes the root to mean *doer* or *performer*
    - Paint → Painter
    - Abolition → Abolitionist
    - Act → Actor
- Adding -ation or -ment changes the root to mean *an action* or *a process*
    - Ador(e) → Adoration
    - Develop → Development
- Adding -ism changes the root to mean *a theory or ideology*
    - Real → Realism
- Adding -ity, -ness, -ship, or -tude changes the root to mean *a condition, quality, or state*
    - Real → Reality
    - Sad → Sadness
    - Relation → Relationship
    - Soli(tary) → Solitude

Plurals are similar to suffixes as letters are added to the end of the word to signify more than one person, place, thing, or idea. There are also general patterns to follow when creating **plurals**.

- If a word ends in -s,-ss,-z,-zz,-ch, or -sh, add -es.
    - Bus → Buses
- If a word ends in a -y, drop the -y and add -ies.
    - Pony → Ponies
- If a word ends in an -f, change the f to a v and add -es.
    - Knife → Knives
- For all other words, add an -s.
    - Dog → Dogs

Homophones and Homographs

A **homophone** is a word that has the same sound as another word, but does not have the same meaning or spelling.

- To, too, and two
- There, their, and they're
- See and sea

A **homograph** is a word that has the same spelling as another word, but does not have the same sound or meaning.

- Lead (to go in front of) and lead (a metal)
- Bass (deep sound) and bass (a fish)

Let's Review!

- Vowels include the letters A, E, I, O, U and sometimes Y and have both short and long sounds.
- Consonants are the other twenty-one letters and have weak sounds. They are often doubled to make stronger sounds.
- Suffixes are word parts added to the root of a word and change the meaning and spelling.
- To make a word plural, add -es, -ies, -ves, or -s to the end of a word.
- Homophones are words that have the same sound, but not the same meaning or spelling.
- Homographs are words that have the same spelling, but not the same meaning or sound.

Capitalization

Correct capitalization helps readers understand when a new sentence begins and the importance of specific words. This lesson will cover the capitalization rules of (1) geographic locations and event names, (2) organizations and publication titles, (3) individual names and professional titles, and (4) months, days, and holidays.

Geographic Locations and Event Names

North, east, south, and west are not capitalized unless they relate to a **definite region**.

- Go north on I-5 for 200 miles.
- The West Coast has nice weather.

Words like northern, southern, eastern, and western are also not capitalized unless they describe **people or the cultural and political activities of people**.

- There is nothing interesting to see in eastern Colorado.
- Midwesterners are known for being extremely nice.
- The Western states almost always vote Democratic.

These words are not capitalized when placed before a name or region unless it is part of the **official name**.

- She lives in southern California.
- I loved visiting Northern Ireland.

Continents, countries, states, cities, and **towns** need to be capitalized.

- Australia has a lot of scary animals.
- Not many people live in Antarctica.
- Albany is the capital of New York.

Historical events should be capitalized to separate the specific from the general.

- The bubonic plague in the Middle Ages killed a large portion of the population in Europe.
- The Great Depression took place in the early 1930s.
- We are living in the twenty-first century.

Organizations and Publication Titles

The **names of national organizations** need to be capitalized. Short prepositions, articles, and conjunctions within the title are not capitalized unless they are the first word.

- The National American Woman Suffrage Association was essential in passing the Nineteenth Amendment.
- The House of Representatives is one part of Congress.

- The National Football League consists of thirty-two teams.

The **titles of books, chapters, articles, poems, newspapers, and other publications** should be capitalized.

- Her favorite book is *A Wrinkle in Time.*
- I do the crossword in *The New York Times* every Sunday.
- *The Jabberwocky* by Lewis Carroll has many silly sounding words.

Individual Names and Professional Titles

People's names as well as their **familial relationship title** need to be capitalized.

- Barack Obama was our first African American president.
- Uncle Joe brought the steaks for our Memorial Day grill.
- Aunt Sarah lives in California, but my other aunt lives in Florida.

Professional titles need to be capitalized when they precede a name, or as a direct address. If it is after a name or is used generally, titles do not need to be capitalized.

- Governor Cuomo is trying to modernize the subway system in New York.
- Andrew Cuomo is the governor of New York.
- A governor runs the state. A president runs the country.
- Thank you for the recommendation, Mr. President.
- I need to see Doctor Smith.
- I need to see a doctor.

Capitalize the **title of high-ranking government officials** when an individual is referred to.

- The Secretary of State travels all over the world.
- The Vice President joined the meeting.

With **compound titles**, the prefixes or suffixes do not need to be capitalized.

- George W. Bush is the ex-President of the United States.

Months, Days, and Holidays

Capitalize **all months of the year** (January, February, March, April, May, June, July, August, September, October, November, December) and **days of the week** (Sunday, Monday, Tuesday, Wednesday, Thursday, Friday, Saturday).

- Her birthday is in November.
- People graduate from college in May or June.
- Saturdays and Sundays are supposed to be fun and relaxing.

Holidays are also capitalized.

- Most kids' favorite holiday is Christmas.
- The new school year usually starts after Labor Day.
- It is nice to go to the beach over Memorial Day weekend.

The **seasons** are not capitalized.

- It gets too hot in the summer and too cold in the winter.
- The flowers and trees bloom so beautifully in the spring.

Let's Review!

- Only capitalize directional words like north, south, east, and, west when they describe a definite region, people, and their political and cultural activities, or when it is part of the official name.
- Historical periods and events are capitalized to represent their importance and specificity.
- Every word except short prepositions, conjunctions, and articles in the names of national organizations are capitalized.
- The titles of publications follow the same rules as organizations.
- The names of individual people need to be capitalized.
- Professional titles are capitalized if they precede a name or are used as a direct address.
- All months of the year, days of the week, and holidays are capitalized.
- Seasons are not capitalized.

PUNCTUATION

Punctuation is important in writing to accurately represent ideas. Without correct punctuation, the meaning of a sentence is difficult to understand. This lesson will cover (1) periods, question marks, and exclamation points, (2) commas, semicolons, and colons, and (3) apostrophes, hyphens, and quotation marks.

Terminal Punctuation Marks: Periods, Question Marks, and Exclamation Points

Terminal punctuation is used at the end of a sentence. Periods, question marks, and exclamation points are the three types of terminal punctuation.

Periods (.) mark the end of a declarative sentence, one that states a fact, or an imperative sentence, one that states a command or request). Periods can also be used in abbreviations.

- Doctors save lives.
- She has a B.A. in Psychology.

Question Marks (?) signify the end of a sentence that is a question. Where, when, who, whom, what, why, and how are common words that begin question sentences.

- Who is he?
- Where is the restaurant?
- Why is the sky blue?

Exclamation Points (!) indicate strong feelings, shouting, or emphasize a feeling.

- Watch out!
- That is incredible!
- I hate you!

Internal Punctuation: Commas, Semicolons, and Colons

Internal punctuation is used within a sentence to help keep words, phrases, and clauses in order. These punctuation marks can be used to indicate elements such as direct quotations and definitions in a sentence.

A **comma** (,) signifies a small break within a sentence and separates words, clauses, or ideas.

Commas are used before conjunctions that connect two independent clauses.

- I ate some cookies, and I drank some milk.

Commas are also used to set off an introductory phrase.

- After the test, she grabbed dinner with a friend.

Short phrases that emphasis thoughts or emotions are enclosed by **commas**.

- The school year, thankfully, ends in a week.

Commas set off the words yes and no.

- Yes, I am available this weekend.
- No, she has not finished her homework.

Commas set off a question tag.

- It is beautiful outside, isn't it?

Commas are used to indicate direct address.

- Are you ready, Jack?
- Mom, what is for dinner?

Commas separate items in a series.

- We ate eggs, potatoes, and toast for breakfast.
- I need to grab coffee, go to the store, and put gas in my car.

Semicolons (;) are used to connect two independent clauses without a coordinating conjunction like *and* or *but*. A **semicolon** creates a bond between two sentences that are related. Do not capitalize the first word after the **semicolon** unless it is a word that is normally capitalized.

- The ice cream man drove down my street; I bought a popsicle.
- My mom cooked dinner; the chicken was delicious.
- It is cloudy today; it will probably rain.

Colons (:) introduce a list.

- She teaches three subjects: English, history, and geography.

Within a sentence, **colons** can create emphasis of a word or phrase.

- She had one goal: pay the bills.

More Internal Punctuation: Apostrophes, Hyphens, and Quotation Marks

Apostrophes (') are used to indicate possession or to create a contraction.

- Bob has a car - Bob's car is blue.
- Steve's cat is beautiful.

For plurals that are also possessive, put the **apostrophe** after the s.

- Soldiers' uniforms are impressive.

Make contractions by combining two words.

- I do not have a dog - I don't have a dog
- I can't swim.

Its and it's do not follow the normal possessive rules. Its is possessive while it's means "it is."

- It's a beautiful day to be at the park.
- The dog has many toys, but its favorite is the rope.

Hyphens (-) are mainly used to create compound words.

- The documentary was a real eye-opener for me.
- We have to check-in to the hotel before midnight.
- The graduate is a twenty-two-year-old woman.

Quotation Marks (") are used when directly using another person's words in your own writing. Commas and periods, sometimes question marks and exclamation points, are placed within **quotation marks**. Colons and semicolons are placed outside of the **quotation marks**, unless they are part of the quoted material. If quoting an entire sentence, capitalize the first word. If it is a fragment, do not capitalize the first word.

- Ernest Hemingway once claimed, "There is nothing noble in being superior to your fellow man; true nobility is being superior to your former self."
- Steve said, "I will be there at noon."

An indirect quote which paraphrases what someone else said does not need **quotation marks**.

- Steve said he would be there at noon.

Quotation marks are also used for the titles of short works such as poems, articles, and chapters. They are not italicized.

- Robert Frost wrote "The Road Not Taken."

Let's Review!

- **Periods (.)** signify the end of a sentence or are used in abbreviations.
- **Question Marks (?)** are also used at the end of a sentence and distinguish the sentence as a question.
- **Exclamation Points (!)** indicate strong feelings, shouting, or emphasis and are usually at the end of the sentence.
- **Commas (,)** are small breaks within a sentence that separate clauses, ideas, or words. They are used to set off introductory phrases, the words yes and no, question tags, indicate direct address, and separate items in a series.
- **Semicolons (;)** connect two similar sentences without a coordinating conjunctions such as and or but.
- **Colons (:)** are used to introduce a list or emphasize a word or phrase.
- **Apostrophes (')** indicate possession or a contraction of two words.
- **Hyphens (-)** are used to create compound words.
- **Quotation Marks (")** are used when directly quoting someone else's words and to indicate the title of poems, chapters, and articles.

Chapter 1 Conventions of Standard English
Practice Quiz

1. **Which word(s) in the following sentence should NOT be capitalized?**

   Can You Speak German?

   A. You and Speak
   B. Can and German
   C. Can, You, and Speak
   D. You, Speak, and German

2. **Fill in the blank with the correctly capitalized form.**

   Every week, they get together to watch ______.

   A. *the bachelor*
   B. *The Bachelor*
   C. *The bachelor*
   D. *the Bachelor*

3. **Choose the correct sentence.**

   A. They used to live in the pacific northwest.
   B. They used to live in the Pacific northwest.
   C. They used to live in the pacific Northwest.
   D. They used to live in the Pacific Northwest.

4. **What is the sentence with the correct use of punctuation?**

   A. Offcampus apartments are nicer.
   B. Off campus apartments are nicer.
   C. Off-campus apartments are nicer.
   D. Off-campus-apartments are nicer.

5. **Which of the following sentences is correct?**

   A. I asked Scott, How was your day?
   B. Scott said, it was awesome.
   C. He claimed, "My history presentation was great!"
   D. I said, That's wonderful!

6. **What is the mistake in the following sentence?**

   The highestranking officer can choose his own work, including his own hours.

   A. *Highestranking* needs a hyphen.
   B. There should be a comma after *officer*.
   C. There should be no comma after *work*.
   D. There should be a semicolon after *work*.

7. **Which of the following spellings is correct?**

   A. Busines
   B. Business
   C. Buseness
   D. Bussiness

8. **What is the correct plural of morning?**

   A. Morning
   B. Mornings
   C. Morninges
   D. Morningies

9. **On Earth, ______ are seven continents.**

   A. their
   B. there
   C. theer
   D. they're

Chapter 1 Conventions of Standard English
Practice Quiz — Answer Key

1. A. *You and Speak.* Can is the first word in the sentence and needs to be capitalized. German is a nationality and needs to be capitalized. The other two words do not need to be capitalized. **See Lesson: Capitalization.**

2. B. *The Bachelor.* The names of TV shows are capitalized. *The* is capitalized here because it is the first word in the name. **See Lesson: Capitalization.**

3. D. *They used to live in the Pacific Northwest.* Specific geographic regions are capitalized. **See Lesson: Capitalization.**

4. C. *Off-campus apartments are nicer.* Hyphens are often used for compound words that are placed before the noun to help with understanding. **See Lesson: Punctuation.**

5. C. *He claimed, "My history presentation was great!"* Quotation marks enclose direct statements. **See Lesson: Punctuation.**

6. A. *Highestranking needs a hyphen.* Hyphens are used for compound words that describe a person or object. **See Lesson: Punctuation.**

7. B. *Business* is the only correct spelling. **See Lesson: Spelling.**

8. B. For most words ending in consonants, just add -s. **See Lesson: Spelling.**

9. B. *There* describes a place or position and is correctly spelled. **See Lesson: Spelling.**

Chapter 2 Parts of Speech

Nouns

In this lesson, you will learn about nouns. A noun is a word that names a person, place, thing, or idea. This lesson will cover (1) the role of nouns in sentences and (2) different types of nouns.

Nouns and Their Role in Sentences

A **noun** names a person, place, thing, or idea.

Some examples of nouns are:

- Gandhi
- New Hampshire
- garden
- happiness

A noun's role in a sentence is as **subject** or **object**. A subject is the part of the sentence that does something, whereas the object is the thing that something is done to. In simple terms, the subject acts, and the object is acted upon.

Look for the nouns in these sentences.

1. The Louvre is stunning. (subject noun: The Louvre)
2. Marco ate dinner with Sara and Petra. (subject noun: Marco; object nouns: dinner, Sara, Petra)
3. Honesty is the best policy. (subject noun: honesty; object noun: policy)
4. After the election, we celebrated our new governor. (object nouns: governor, election)
5. I slept. (0 nouns)

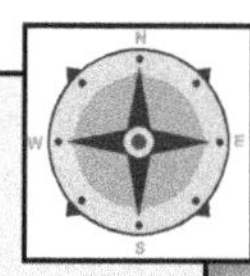

KEEP IN MIND . . .
The subjects *I* and *we* in the two sentences to the left are pronouns, not nouns.

Look for the nouns in these sentences.

1. Mrs. Garcia makes a great pumpkin pie. (subject noun: Mrs. Garcia; object noun: pie)
2. We really need to water the garden. (object noun: garden)
3. Love is sweet. (subject noun: love)
4. Sam loves New York in the springtime. (subject noun: Sam; object nouns: New York, springtime)
5. Lin and her mother and father ate soup, fish, potatoes, and fruit for dinner. (subject nouns: Lin, mother, father; object nouns: soup, fish, potatoes, fruit, dinner)

Why isn't the word *pumpkin* a noun in the first sentence? *Pumpkin* is often a noun, but here it is used as an adjective that describes what kind of *pie*.

Why isn't the word *water* a noun in the second sentence? Here, *water* is an **action verb**. To *water the garden* is something we do.

How is the word *love* a noun in the third sentence and not in the fourth sentence? *Love* is a noun (thing) in sentence 3 and a verb (action) in the sentence 4.

How many nouns can a sentence contain? As long as the sentence remains grammatically correct, it can contain an unlimited number of nouns.

BE CAREFUL!

Words can change to serve different roles in different sentences. A word that is usually a noun can sometimes be used as an adjective or a verb. Determine a word's function in a sentence to be sure of its part of speech.

Types of Nouns

Singular and Plural Nouns

Nouns can be **singular** or **plural**. A noun is singular when there is only one. A noun is plural when there are two or more.

- The book has 650 pages.

Book is a singular noun. *Pages* is a plural noun.

Often, to make a noun plural, we add *-s* at the end of the word: *cat/cats*. This is a **regular** plural noun. Sometimes we make a word plural in another way: *child/children*. This is an **irregular** plural noun. Some plurals follow rules, while others do not. The most common rules are listed here:

KEEP IN MIND . . .

Some nouns are countable, and others are not. For example, we eat *three blueberries*, but we **do not** drink *three milks*. Instead, we drink *three glasses of milk* or *some milk*.

Singular noun	Plural noun	Rule for making plural
star	stars	for most words, add *-s*
box	boxes	for words that end in *-j*, *-s*, *-x*, *-z*, *-ch* or *-sh*, add *-es*
baby	babies	for words that end in *-y*, change *-y* to *-i* and add *-es*
woman	women	irregular
foot	feet	irregular

Common and Proper Nouns

Common nouns are general words, and they are written in lowercase. **Proper nouns** are specific names, and they begin with an uppercase letter.

Examples:

Common noun	Proper noun
ocean	Baltic Sea
dentist	Dr. Marx
company	Honda
park	Yosemite National Park

Concrete and Abstract Nouns

Concrete nouns are people, places, or things that physically exist. We can use our senses to see or hear them. *Turtle, spreadsheet,* and *Australia* are concrete nouns.

Abstract nouns are ideas, qualities, or feelings that we cannot see and that might be harder to describe. *Beauty, childhood, energy, envy, generosity, happiness, patience, pride, trust, truth,* and *victory* are abstract nouns.

Some words can be either concrete or abstract nouns. For example, the concept of *art* is abstract, but *art* that we see and touch is concrete.

- We talked about *art.* (abstract)
- She showed me the *art* she had created in class. (concrete)

Let's Review!

- A noun is a person, place, thing, or idea.
- A noun's function in a sentence is as subject or object.
- Common nouns are general words, while proper nouns are specific names.
- Nouns can be concrete or abstract.

PRONOUNS

A pronoun is a word that takes the place of or refers to a specific noun. This lesson will cover (1) the role of pronouns in sentences and (2) the purpose of pronouns.

Pronouns and Their Role in Sentences

A **pronoun** takes the place of a noun or refers to a specific noun.

Subject, Object, and Possessive Pronouns

A pronoun's role in a sentence is as **subject, object,** or **possessive**.

Subject Pronouns	Object Pronouns	Possessive Pronouns
I	me	my, mine
you	you	your, yours
he	her	his
she	him	her, hers
it	it	its
we	us	ours
they	them	their, theirs

In simple sentences, subject pronouns come before the verb, object pronouns come after the verb, and possessive pronouns show ownership.

Look at the pronouns in these examples:

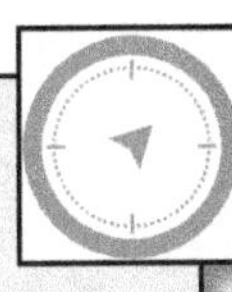

BE CAREFUL!

It is easy to make a mistake when you have multiple words in the role of subject or object.

- She forgot her coat. (subject: she; possessive: her)
- I lent her mine. (subject: I; object: her; possessive: mine)
- She left it at school. (subject: she; object: it)
- I had to go and get it the next day. (subject: I; object: it)
- I will never lend her something of mine again! (subject: I; object: her; possessive: mine)

Correct	Incorrect	Why?
John and I went out.	*John and me* went out.	*John and I* is a subject. *I* is a subject pronoun; *me* is not.
Johan took *Sam and me* to the show.	Johan took *Sam and I* to the show.	*Sam and me* is an object. *Me* is an object pronoun; *I* is not.

Relative Pronouns

Relative pronouns connect a clause to a noun or pronoun.

These are some relative pronouns:

who, whom, whoever, whose, that, which

- Steve Jobs, *who founded Apple,* changed the way people use technology.

The pronoun *who* introduces a clause that gives more information about Steve Jobs.

- This is the movie *that Emily told us to see.*

The pronoun *that* introduces a clause that gives more information about the movie.

Other Pronouns

Some other pronouns are:

this, that, what, anyone, everything, something

DID YOU KNOW?
Pronouns can sometimes refer to general or unspecified things.

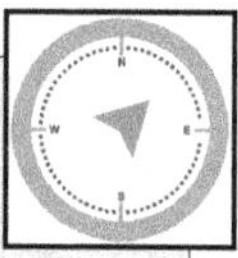

Look for the pronouns in these sentences.

- What is that?
- There is something over there!
- Does anyone have a pen?

Pronouns and Their Purpose

The purpose of a pronoun is to replace a noun. Note the use of the pronoun *their* in the heading of this section. If we did not have pronouns, we would have to call this section *Pronouns and Pronouns' Purpose.*

What Is an Antecedent?

A pronoun in a sentence refers to a specific noun, and this noun called the **antecedent**.

- John Hancock signed the Declaration of Independence. He signed it in 1776.

The antecedent for *he* is John Hancock.
The antecedent for *it* is the Declaration of Independence.

BE CAREFUL!
Look out for unclear antecedents, such as in this sentence:

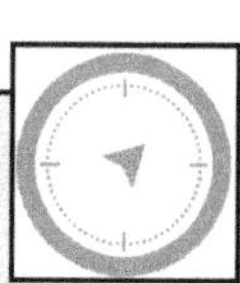

- Take the furniture out of the room and paint *it*.

What needs to be painted, the furniture or the room?

Find the pronouns in the following sentence. Then identify the antecedent for each pronoun.

Erin had an idea *that she* suggested to Antonio: "*I*'ll help *you* with *your* math homework if *you* help *me* with *my* writing assignment."

Pronoun	Antecedent
that	idea
she	Erin
I	Erin
you	Antonio
your	Antonio's
you	Antonio
me	Erin
my	Erin's

What Is Antecedent Agreement?

A pronoun must agree in **gender** and **number** with the antecedent it refers to. For example:

- Singular pronouns *I, you, he, she,* and *it* replace singular nouns.
- Plural pronouns *you, we,* and *they* replace plural nouns.
- Pronouns *he, she,* and *it* replace masculine, feminine, or neutral nouns.

Correct	Incorrect	Why?
Students should do their homework every night.	A student should do their homework every night.	The pronoun *their* is plural, so it must refer to a plural noun such as *students.*
When an employee is sick, he or she should call the office.	When an employee is sick, they should call the office.	The pronoun *they* is plural, so it must refer to a plural noun. *Employee* is not a plural noun.

Let's Review!

- A pronoun takes the place of or refers to a noun.
- The role of pronouns in sentences is as subject, object, or possessive.
- A pronoun must agree in number and gender with the noun it refers to.

Adjectives and Adverbs

An **adjective** is a word that describes a noun or a pronoun. An **adverb** is a word that describes a verb, an adjective, or another adverb.

Adjectives

An **adjective** describes, modifies, or tells us more about a **noun** or a **pronoun**. Colors, numbers, and descriptive words such as *healthy, good,* and *sharp* are adjectives.

KEEP IN MIND . . .

Adjectives typically come **before the noun** in English. However, with **linking verbs** (non-action verbs such as *be, seem, look*), the adjective may come **after the verb** instead. Think of it like this: a linking verb **links** the adjective to the noun or pronoun.

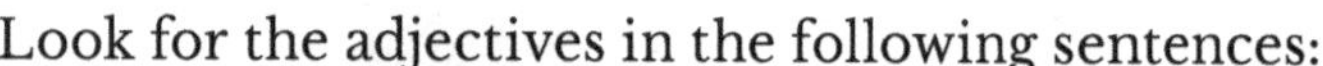

Look for the adjectives in the following sentences:

	Adjective	Noun or pronoun it describes
I rode the blue bike.	blue	bike
It was a long trip.	long	trip
Bring two pencils for the exam.	two	pencils
The box is brown.	brown	box
She looked beautiful.	beautiful	she
That's great!	great	that

Multiple adjectives can be used in a sentence, as can multiple nouns. Look at these examples:

	Adjectives	Noun or pronoun it describes
The six girls were happy, healthy, and rested after their long beach vacation.	six, happy, healthy, rested; long, beach	girls; vacation
Leo has a good job, but he is applying for a better one.	good; better	job; one

KEEP IN MIND . . .

Note comparative and superlative forms of adjectives, such as:

fast, faster, fastest

far, farther, farthest

good, better, best

bad, worse, worst

Articles: *A, An, The*

Articles are a unique part of speech, but they work like adjectives. An article tells more about a noun. *A* and *an* are **indefinite** articles. Use *a* before a singular **general** noun. Use *an* before a singular general noun that begins with a vowel.

The is a **definite** article. Use *the* before a singular or plural **specific** noun.

Look at how articles are used in the following sentences:

- I need *a* pencil to take *the* exam. (any pencil; specific exam)
- Is there *a* zoo in town? (any zoo)
- Let's go to *the* zoo today. (specific zoo)
- Can you get me *a* glass of milk? (any glass)
- Would you bring me *the* glass that's over there? (specific glass)

Adverbs

An **adverb** describes, modifies, or tells us more about a **verb**, an **adjective**, or another **adverb**. Many adverbs end in *-ly*. Often, adverbs tell when, where, or how something happened. Words such as *slowly, very,* and *yesterday* are adverbs.

Adverbs that Describe Verbs

Adverbs that describe verbs tell something more about the action.

Look for the adverbs in these sentences:

	Adverb	Verb it describes
They walked quickly.	quickly	walked
She disapproved somewhat of his actions, but she completely understood them.	somewhat; completely	disapproved; understood
The boys will go inside if it rains heavily.	inside; heavily	go; rains

Adverbs that Describe Adjectives

Adverbs that describe adjectives often add intensity to the adjective. Words like *quite, more*, and *always* are adverbs.

Look for the adverbs in these sentences:

	Adverb	Adjective it describes
The giraffe is very tall.	very	tall
Do you think that you are more intelligent than them?	more	intelligent
If it's really loud, we can make the volume slightly lower.	really; slightly	loud; lower

Adverbs that Describe Other Adverbs

Adverbs that describe adverbs often add intensity to the adverb.

Look for the adverbs in these sentences:

	Adverb	Adverb it describes
The mouse moved too quickly for us to catch it.	too	quickly
This store is almost never open.	almost	never
Those women are quite fashionably dressed.	quite	fashionably

Adjectives vs. Adverbs

Not sure whether a word is an adjective or an adverb? Look at these examples.

	Adjective	Adverb	Explanation
fast	You're a *fast* driver.	You drove *fast*.	The adjective *fast* describes *driver* (noun); the adverb *fast* describes *drove* (verb).
early	I don't like *early* mornings!	Try to arrive *early*.	The adjective *early* describes *mornings* (noun); the adverb *early* describes *arrive* (verb).
good/well	They did *good* work together.	They worked *well* together.	The adjective *good* describes *work* (noun); the adverb *well* describes *worked* (verb).
bad/badly	The dog is *bad*.	The dog behaves *badly*.	The adjective *bad* describes *dog* (noun); the adverb *badly* describes *behaves* (verb).

Let's Review!

- An **adjective** describes, modifies, or tells us more about a **noun** or a **pronoun**.
- An **adverb** describes, modifies, or tells us more about a **verb**, an **adjective**, or another **adverb**.

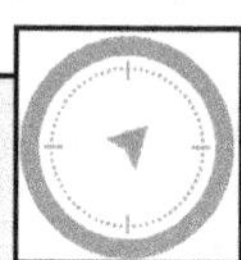

BE CAREFUL!

When an adverb ends in *-ly*, add *more* or *most* to make comparisons.

Correct: The car moved *more slowly*.

Incorrect: The car moved *slower*.

Conjunctions and Prepositions

A **conjunction** is a connector word; it connects words, phrases, or clauses in a sentence. A **preposition** is a relationship word; it shows the relationship between two nearby words.

Conjunctions

A **conjunction** connects words, phrases, or clauses.

And, so, and *or* are conjunctions.

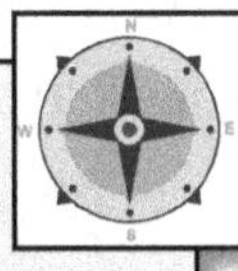

KEEP IN MIND . . .

A clause is a phrase that has a subject and a verb.

Some clauses are **independent**. An independent clause can stand alone.

Some clauses are **dependent**. A dependent clause relies on another clause in order to make sense.

Types of Conjunctions

- **Coordinating** conjunctions connect two words, phrases, or independent clauses. The full list of coordinating conjunctions is: *and, or, but, so, for, nor, yet.*
- **Subordinating** conjunctions connect a main (independent) clause and a dependent clause. The conjunction may show a relationship or time order for the two clauses. Some subordinating conjunctions are: *after, as soon as, once, if, even though, unless.*
- **Correlative** conjunctions are pairs of conjunctions that work together to connect two words or phrases. Some correlative conjunctions are: *either/or, neither/nor, as/as.*

Example	Conjunction	What it is connecting
Verdi, Mozart, **and** *Wagner* are famous opera composers.	and	three nouns
Would you like *angel food cake, chocolate lava cake,* **or** *banana cream pie* for dessert?	or	three noun phrases
I took the bus to work, **but** *I walked home.*	but	two independent clauses
It was noisy at home, **so** *we went to the library.*	so	two independent clauses
They have to clean the house **before** *the realtor shows it.*	before	a main clause and a dependent clause
Use **either** *hers* **or** *mine.*	either/or	two pronouns
After *everyone leaves,* make sure you lock up.	after	a main clause and a dependent clause
I'd **rather** *fly* **than** *take the train.*	rather/than	two verb phrases
As soon as *they announced the winning number,* she looked at her ticket and shouted, "Whoopee!"	as soon as	a main clause and a dependent clause

DID YOU KNOW?

In the last example above, "*Whoopee!*" is an interjection. An **interjection** is a short phrase or clause that communicates emotion.

Some other interjections are:

- *Way to go!*
- *Yuck.*
- *Hooray!*
- *Holy cow!*
- *Oops!*

Prepositions

A **preposition** shows the relationship between two nearby words. Prepositions help to tell information such as direction, location, and time. *To, for,* and *with* are prepositions.

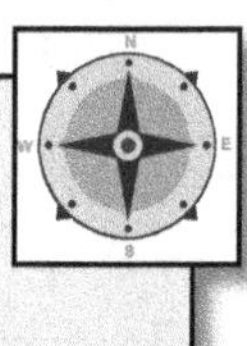

KEEP IN MIND . . .

Some prepositions are more than one word. *On top of* and *instead of* are prepositions.

Example	Preposition	What it tells us
The desk is in the classroom.	in	location
We'll meet you at 6:00.	at	time
We'll meet you at the museum.	at	place
The book is on top of the desk.	on top of	location

Prepositional Phrases

A preposition must be followed by an **object of the preposition**. This can be a noun or something that serves as a noun, such as a pronoun or a gerund.

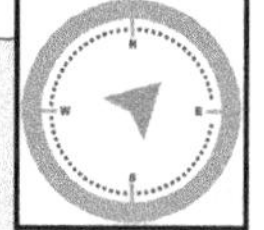

DID YOU KNOW?

A gerund is the *-ing* form a verb that serves as a noun. *Hiking* is a gerund in this sentence:

I wear these shoes for *hiking*.

A **prepositional phrase** is a preposition plus the object that follows it.

Look for the prepositional phrases in the following examples. Note that a sentence can have more than one prepositional phrase.

Example	Preposition	Object of the preposition
The tiny country won the war *against all odds.*	against	all odds
Look *at us*!	at	us
Why don't we go swimming *instead of sweating in this heat?*	instead of; in	sweating; this heat
Aunt Tea kept the trophy *on a shelf of the cabinet between the sofas in the living room.*	on; of; between; in	a shelf; the cabinet; the sofas; the living room

BE CAREFUL!

Sometimes a word looks like a preposition but is actually part of the verb. In this case, the verb is called a phrasal verb, and the preposition-like word is called a particle. Here is an example:

- *Turn on* the light. (*Turn on* has a meaning of its own; it is a phrasal verb. *On* is a particle here, rather than a preposition.)
- Turn *on that street*. (*On that street* shows location; it is a prepositional phrase. *On* is a preposition here.)

Let's Review!

- A **conjunction** connects words, phrases, or clauses. *And, so,* and *or* are conjunctions.
- A **preposition** shows the relationship between two nearby words. *To, for,* and *with* are prepositions.
- A **prepositional phrase** includes a preposition plus the object of the preposition.

VERBS AND VERB TENSES

A **verb** is a word that describes a **physical or mental action** or a **state of being**. This lesson will cover the role of verbs in sentences, verb forms and tenses, and helping verbs.

The Role of Verbs in Sentences

A verb describes an action or a state of being. A complete sentence must have at least one verb.

Verbs have different tenses, which show time.

Verb Forms

Each verb has three primary forms. The **base form** is used for simple present tense, and the **past form** is used for simple past tense. The **participle form** is used for more complicated time situations. Participle form verbs are accompanied by a helping verb.

Base Form	Past Form	Participle Form
end	ended	ended
jump	jumped	jumped
explain	explained	explained
eat	ate	eaten
take	took	taken
go	went	gone
come	came	come

Some verbs are **regular**. To make the **past** or **participle** form of a regular verb, we just add *-ed*. However, many verbs that we commonly use are **irregular**. We need to memorize the forms for these verbs.

In the chart above, *end, jump,* and *explain* are regular verbs. *Eat, take, go,* and *come* are irregular.

Using Verbs

A simple sentence has a **subject** and a **verb**. The subject tells us who or what, and the verb tells us the action or state.

Example	Subject	Verb	*Explanation/Time*
They ate breakfast together yesterday.	They	ate	*happened yesterday*
I walk to school.	I	walk	*happens regularly*
We went to California last year.	We	went	*happened last year*
She seems really tired.	She	seems	*how she seems right now*
The teacher is sad.	teacher	is	*her state right now*

You can see from the examples in this chart that **past tense verbs** are used for a time in the past, and **present tense verbs** are used for something that happens regularly or for a state or condition right now.

Often a sentence has more than one verb. If it has a connector word or more than one subject, it can have more than one verb.

- The two cousins live, work, and vacation together. (3 verbs)
- The girls planned by phone, and then they met at the movies. (2 verbs)

BE CAREFUL!
When you have more than one verb in a sentence, make sure both verb tenses are correct.

Helping Verbs and Progressive and Perfect Tenses

Helping Verbs

A **helping verb** is a supporting verb that accompanies a main verb.

Questions, negative sentences, and certain time situations require helping verbs.

forms of helping verb "to be"	forms of helping verb "to have"	forms of helping verb "to do"	some modals (used like helping verbs)
am, are, is, was, were, be, being, been	have, has, had, having	do, does, did, doing	will, would, can, could, must, might, should

Here are examples of helping verbs in questions and negatives.

- Where *is* he *going*?
- *Did* they *win*?
- I *do*n't *want* that.
- The boys *can*'t go.

Progressive and Perfect Tenses

Helping verbs accompany main verbs in certain time situations, such as when an action is or was ongoing, or when two actions overlap in time. To form these tenses, we use a **helping verb** with the **base form plus *-ing*** or with the **participle form** of the main verb.

The **progressive tense** is used for an action that is or was ongoing. It takes base form of the main verb plus *-ing*.

Example sentence	Tense	*Explanation/Time*
I am taking French this semester.	Present progressive	*happening now, over a continuous period of time*
I was working when you stopped by.	Past progressive	*happened over a continuous period of time in the past*

The **perfect tense** is used to cover two time periods. It takes the *participle* form of the main verb.

Example sentence	Tense	*Explanation/Time*
I have lived here for three years.	Present perfect	*started in the past and continues to present*
I had finished half of my homework when my computer stopped working.	Past perfect	*started and finished in the past, overlapping in time with another action*

Sometimes we use both the **progressive** and **perfect** tenses together.

Example sentence	Tense	*Explanation/Time*
I have been walking for hours!	Present perfect progressive	*started in the past, took place for a period of time, and continues to present*
She had been asking for a raise for months before she finally received one.	Past perfect progressive	*started in the past, took place for a period of time, and ended*

Let's Review!

- A verb describes an action or state of being.
- Each verb has three primary forms: base form, past form, and participle form.
- Verbs have different tenses, which are used to show time.
- Helping verbs are used in questions, negative sentences, and to form progressive and perfect tenses.

Chapter 2 Parts of Speech Practice Quiz

1. **Select the part of speech of the underlined word in the following sentence.**

   She did <u>quite</u> well on the exam.

   A. Noun
   B. Adverb
   C. Adjective
   D. Preposition

2. **Select the noun that the underlined adjectives describe.**

   Two weeks after his surgery, Henry felt <u>strong</u> and <u>healthy</u>.

   A. weeks
   B. his
   C. surgery
   D. Henry

3. **Which word is an adverb that describes the underlined verb?**

   The man <u>spoke</u> to us wisely.

   A. man
   B. to
   C. us
   D. wisely

4. **Identify the conjunction in the following sentence.**

   He is sick, yet he came to work.

   A. is
   B. yet
   C. came
   D. to

5. **Which is <u>not</u> a prepositional phrase?**

   Keep me informed about the status of the problem throughout the day.

   A. Keep me informed
   B. about the status
   C. of the problem
   D. throughout the day

6. **How many prepositions are in the following sentence?**

   The athletes traveled from Boston to Dallas for the competition.

   A. 0
   B. 1
   C. 2
   D. 3

7. **Which words in the following sentence are proper nouns?**

   Matthew had a meeting with his supervisor on Tuesday.

   A. Matthew, meeting
   B. Matthew, Tuesday
   C. meeting, supervisor
   D. supervisor, Tuesday

8. **How many plural nouns are in the following sentence?**

   Marie's father's appendix was taken out.

   A. 0
   B. 1
   C. 2
   D. 3

9. **Which of the following words is an abstract noun?**

   A. Car
   B. Tent
   C. Ruler
   D. Health

10. **Which word in the following sentence is a pronoun?**

    To whom should the applicant address the letter?

    A. To
    B. the
    C. whom
    D. should

11. **Which pronoun correctly completes the following sentence?**

    Nigel introduced Van and ____ to the new administrator.

    A. I
    B. me
    C. she
    D. they

12. **Select the noun to which the underlined pronoun refers.**

    Greta Garbo, <u>who</u> performed in both silent and talking pictures, is my favorite actress.

    A. actress
    B. pictures
    C. performed
    D. Greta Garbo

13. **How many verbs are in the following sentence?**

    They toured the art museum and saw the conservatory.

    A. 0
    B. 1
    C. 2
    D. 3

14. **Which word in the following sentence is a helping verb?**

    They did not ask for our help.

    A. did
    B. ask
    C. for
    D. our

15. **Select the correct verb form to complete the following sentence.**

    William didn't think he would enjoy the musical, but he ____.

    A. do
    B. did
    C. liked
    D. would

Chapter 2 Parts of Speech Practice Quiz – Answer Key

1. B. *Quite* is an adverb that describes the adverb *well.* **See Lesson: Adjectives and Adverbs.**

2. D. These adjectives describe *Henry.* **See Lesson: Adjectives and Adverbs.**

3. D. *Wisely* is an adverb that describes the verb *spoke.* **See Lesson: Adjectives and Adverbs.**

4. B. *Yet* is a conjunction. **See Lesson: Conjunctions and Prepositions.**

5. A. *Keep me informed* does not contain a preposition. *About, of,* and *throughout* are prepositions. **See Lesson: Conjunctions and Prepositions.**

6. D. *From, to,* and *for* are prepositions. **See Lesson: Conjunctions and Prepositions.**

7. B. *Matthew* and *Tuesday* are proper nouns. **See Lesson: Nouns.**

8. A. *Marie's* and *father's* are possessive; neither is plural. *Appendix* is a singular noun. **See Lesson: Nouns.**

9. D. *Health* is an abstract noun; it does not physically exist. **See Lesson: Nouns.**

10. C. *Whom* is a pronoun. **See Lesson: Pronouns.**

11. B. An object pronoun must be used here. **See Lesson: Pronouns.**

12. D. *Who* is a relative pronoun that refers to the subject *Greta Garbo.* **See Lesson: Pronouns.**

13. C. *Toured* and *saw* are verbs. **See Lesson: Verbs and Verb Tenses.**

14. A. *Did* is a helping verb; *ask* is the main verb. **See Lesson: Verbs and Verb Tenses.**

15. B. *Did* can be used here, for a shortened form of *did enjoy it.* **See Lesson: Verbs and Verb Tenses.**

CHAPTER 3 KNOWLEDGE OF LANGUAGE

TYPES OF SENTENCES

Sentences are a combination of words that communicate a complete thought. Sentences can be written in many ways to signal different relationships among ideas. This lesson will cover (1) simple sentences (2) compound sentences (3) complex sentences (4) parallel structure.

Simple Sentences

A **simple sentence** is a group of words that make up a **complete thought**. To be a complete thought, simple sentences must have one **independent clause.** An independent clause contains a single **subject** (who or what the sentence is about) and a **predicate** (a **verb** and something about the subject.)

Let's take a look at some simple sentences:

Simple Sentence	Subject	Predicate	Complete Thought?
The car was fast.	car	was fast (verb = was)	Yes
Sally waited for the bus.	Sally	waited for the bus (verb = waited)	Yes
The pizza smells delicious.	pizza	smells delicious (verb = smells)	Yes
Anton loves cycling.	Anton	loves cycling (verb = loves)	Yes

It is important to be able to recognize what a simple sentence is in order to avoid **run-ons** and **fragments**, two common grammatical errors.

A **run-on** is when two or more independent clauses are combined without proper punctuation:

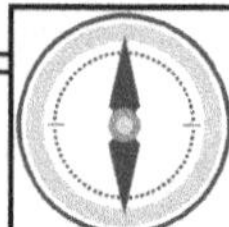

FOR EXAMPLE

Gregory is a very talented actor he was the lead in the school play.

If you take a look at this sentence, you can see that it is made up of 2 independent clauses or simple sentences:

1. *Gregory is a very talented actor*
2. *he was the lead in the school play*

You <u>cannot</u> have two independent clauses running into each other without proper punctuation.

You can fix this run-on in the following way:

Gregory is a very talented actor. He was the lead in the school play.

A **fragment** is a group of words that looks like a sentence. It starts with a capital letter and has end punctuation, but when you examine it closely you will see it is not a complete thought.

Let's put this information all together to determine whether a group of words is a simple sentence, a run-on, or a fragment:

Group of Words	Category
Mondays are the worst they are a drag.	Run-On: These are two independent clauses running into one another without proper punctuation. FIX: *Mondays are the worst. They are a drag.*
Because I wanted soda.	Fragment: This is a dependent clause and needs more information to make it a complete thought. FIX: *I went to the store because I wanted soda.*
Ereni is from Greece.	Simple Sentence: YES! This is a simple sentence with a subject (*Ereni*) and a predicate (*is from Greece*), so it is a complete thought.
While I was apple picking.	Fragment: This is a dependent clause and needs more information to make it a complete thought. FIX: *While I was apple picking, I spotted a bunny.*
New York City is magical it is my favorite place.	Run-On: These are two independent clauses running into one another without proper punctuation. FIX: *New York City is magical. It is my favorite place.*

Compound Sentences

A **compound sentence** is a sentence made up of two independent clauses connected with a **coordinating conjunction**.

Let's take a look at the following sentence:

Joe waited for the bus, but it never arrived.

If you take a close look at this compound sentence, you will see that it is made up of two independent clauses:

1. *Joe waited for the bus*
2. *it never arrived*

The word *but* is the coordinating conjunction that connects these two sentences. Notice that the coordinating conjunction has a comma right before it. This is the proper way to punctuate compound sentences.

Here are other examples of compound sentences:

FOR EXAMPLE

I want to try out for the baseball team, and I also want to try out for track.

Sally can play the clarinet in the band, ***or*** *she can play the violin in the orchestra.*

Mr. Henry is going to run the half marathon, ***so*** *he has a lot of training to do.*

All these sentences are compound sentences since they each have two independent clauses joined by a comma and a coordinating conjunction.

The following is a list of **coordinating conjunctions** that can be used in compound sentences. You can use the mnemonic device "FANBOYS" to help you remember them:

For

And

Nor

But

Or

Yet

So

Think back to Section 1: Simple Sentences. You learned about run-ons. Another way to fix run-ons is by turning the group of words into a compound sentence:

RUN-ON:	*Gregory is a very talented actor he was the lead in the school play.*
FIX:	*Gregory is a very talented actor,* so *he was the lead in the school play.*

Complex Sentences

A **complex** sentence is a sentence that is made up of an independent clause and one or more dependent clauses connected to it.

Think back to Section 1 when you learned about fragments. You learned about a **dependent clause**, the part of a sentence that cannot stand by itself. These clauses need other information to make them complete.

You can recognize a dependent clause because they always begin with a **subordinating conjunction**. These words are a key ingredient in complex sentences.

Here is a list of **subordinating conjunctions:**

after	although	as	because	before
despite	even if	even though	if	in order to
that	once	provided that	rather than	since
so that	than	that	though	unless
until	when	whenever	where	whereas
wherever	while	why		

Let's take a look at a few complex sentences:

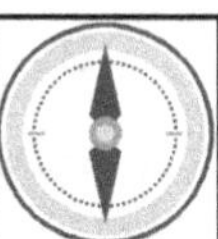

FOR EXAMPLE

Since the alarm clock didn't go off, I was late for class.

This is an example of a complex sentence because it contains:

A dependent clause: *Since the alarm clock didn't go off*
An independent clause: *I was late for class*
A subordinating conjunction: *since*

Sarah studied all night for the exam even though she did not receive an A.

This is an example of a complex sentence because it contains:

A dependent clause: *even though she did not receive an A*
An independent clause: *Sarah studied all night*
A subordinating conjunction: *even though*

****NOTE:** To make a complex sentence, you can either start with the dependent clause or the independent clause. When beginning with the dependent clause, you need a comma after it. When beginning with an independent clause, you do not need a comma after it.*

Parallel Structure

Parallel structure is the repetition of a grammatical form within a sentence to make the sentence sound more harmonious. Parallel structure comes into play when you are making a list of items. Stylistically, you want all the items in the list to line up with each other to make them sound better.

Let's take a look at when to use parallel structure:

1. Use parallel structure with verb forms:

   In a sentence listing different verbs, you want all the verbs to use the same form:

   Manuel likes hiking, biking, and mountain climbing.

   In this example, the words *hiking, biking* and *climbing* are all gerunds (having an -ing ending), so the sentence is balanced since the words are all using the gerund form of the verb.

   Manuel likes to hike, bike, and mountain climb.

In this example, the words *hike, bike* and *climb* are all infinitives (using the basic form of the verb), so the sentence is balanced.

You do not want to mix them up:

Manuel likes hiking, biking, and to mountain climb.

This sentence **does not** use parallel structure since *hiking* and *biking* use the gerund form of the verb and *to mountain climb* uses the infinitive form.

2. Use parallel structure with active and passive voice:

   In a sentence written in the **active voice**, the subject performs the action:

   Sally kicked the ball.

   Sally, the subject, is the one doing the action, kicking the ball.

   In a sentence written in the **passive voice**, the subject is acted on by the verb.

   The ball was kicked by Sally.

   When using parallel structure, you want to make sure your items in a list are either all in **active voice**:

   Raymond baked, frosted, and decorated the cake.

   Or all in **passive voice**:

   The cake was baked, frosted, and decorated by Raymond.

   You do not want to mix them up:

   The cake was baked, frosted, and Raymond decorated it.

   This sentence **does not** use parallel structure because it starts off with passive voice and then switches to active voice.

3. Use parallel structure with the length of terms within a list:

   When making a list, you should either have all short individual terms or all long phrases.

   Keep these consistent by either choosing short, individual terms:

   Cassandra is bold, courageous, and strong.

   Or longer phrases:

   Cassandra is brave in the face of danger, willing to take risks, and a force to be reckoned with.

   You do not want to mix them up:

   Cassandra is bold, courageous, and a force to be reckoned with.

This sentence **does not** use parallel structure because the first two terms are short, and the last one is a longer phrase.

Let's Review!

- A simple sentence consists of a clause, which has a single subject and a predicate.
- A compound sentence is made up of two independent clauses connected by a coordinating conjunction.
- A complex sentence is made up of a subordinating conjunction, an independent clause and one or more dependent clauses connected to it.
- Parallel structure is the repetition of a grammatical form within a sentence to make the sentence sound more harmonious.

Types of Clauses

There are four types of clauses that are used to create sentences. Sentences with several clauses, and different types of clauses, are considered complex. This lesson will cover (1) independent clauses, (2) dependent clauses and subordinate clauses, and (3) coordinate clauses.

Independent Clause

An **independent clause** is a simple sentence. It has a subject, a verb, and expresses a complete thought.

- Steve went to the store.
- She will cook dinner tonight.
- The class was very boring.
- The author argues that listening to music helps productivity.

Two **independent clauses** can be connected by a semicolon. There are some common words that indicate the beginning of an **independent clause** such as: moreover, also, nevertheless, however, furthermore, consequently.

- I wanted to go to dinner; however, I had to work late tonight.
- She had a job interview; therefore, she dressed nicely.

Dependent and Subordinate Clauses

A **dependent clause** is not a complete sentence. It has a subject and a verb but does not express a complete thought. **Dependent clauses** are also called **subordinate clauses**, because they depend on the **independent or main clause** to complete the thought. A sentence that has both at least one **independent clause** and one **subordinate clause** are considered complex.

Subordinate clauses can be placed before or after the **independent clause**. When the **subordinate clause** begins the sentence, there should be a comma before the **main clause**. If the **subordinate clause** ends the sentence, there is no need for a comma.

Dependent clauses also have common indicator words. These are often called **subordinating conjunctions** because they connect a **dependent clause** to an **independent clause**. Some of these include: although, after, as, because, before, if, once, since, unless, until, when, whether, and while. Relative pronouns also signify the beginning of a **subordinate clause**. These include: that, which, who, whom, whichever, whoever, whomever, and whose.

- When I went to school...
- Since she joined the team...
- After we saw the play...
- *Because she studied hard*, she received an A on her exam.
- *Although the professor was late*, the class was very informative.
- I can't join you *unless I finish my homework*.

Coordinate Clause

A **coordinate clause** is a sentence or phrase that combines clauses of equal grammatical rank (verbs, nouns, adjectives, phrases, or independent clauses) by using a coordinating conjunction (and, but, for, nor, or so, yet). **Coordinating conjunctions** cannot connect a **dependent or subordinate clause** and an **independent clause.**

- She woke up, and he went to bed.
- We did not have cheese, so I went to the store to get some.
- Ice cream and candy taste great, but they are not good for you.
- Do you want to study, or do you want to go to Disneyland?

Let's Review!

- An **independent clause** is a simple sentence that has a noun, a verb, and a complete thought. Two **independent clauses** can be connected by a semicolon.
- A **dependent or subordinate clause** depends on the main clause to complete a thought. A **dependent or subordinate clause** can go before or after the **independent clause** and there are indicator words that signify the beginning of the **dependent or subordinate clause.**
- A **coordinate clause** connects two verbs, nouns, adjectives, phrases, or **independent clauses** using a **coordinating conjunction** (and, but, for, nor, or, so, yet).

Subject and Verb Agreement

Every sentence must include a **subject** and a **verb**. The subject tells **who or what**, and the verb describes an **action or condition**. Subject and verb agree in number and person.

Roles of Subject and Verb

A complete sentence includes a **subject** and a **verb**. The verb is in the part of the sentence called the **predicate**. A predicate can be thought of as a verb phrase.

Simple Sentences

A sentence can be very simple, with just one or two words as the **subject** and one or two words as the **predicate**.

BE CAREFUL!

It's is a contraction of *it is*.

Its (without an apostrophe) is the possessive of the pronoun *it*.

Sometimes, in a command, a subject is "understood," rather than written or spoken.

Look at these examples of short sentences:

Sentence	Subject	Predicate, with main verb(s) underlined
I ate.	I	ate
They ran away.	They	ran away
It's OK.	It	is OK
Go and find the cat!	(You)	go and find the cat

Complex Sentences

Sometimes a subject or predicate is a long phrase or clause.

Some sentences have more than one subject or predicate, or even a predicate within a predicate.

Sentence	Subject(s)	Predicate(s), with main verb(s) underlined
My friend from work had a bad car accident.	My friend from work	had a bad car accident
John, his sister, and I plan to ride our bikes across the country this summer.	John, his sister, and I	plan to ride our bikes across the country this summer
I did so much for them, and they didn't even thank me.*	I; they	did so much for them; didn't even thank me
She wrote a letter that explained the problem.**	She	wrote a letter that explained the problem

*This sentence consists of two clauses, and each clause has its own subject and its own predicate.

**In this sentence, *that explained the problem* is part of the predicate, and it is also a relative clause with own subject and predicate.

Subject and Verb Agreement

Subjects and verbs must agree in **number** and **person**. This means that different subjects take different forms of a verb.

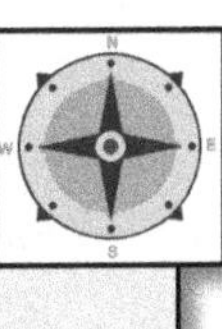

KEEP IN MIND . . .

The third person singular subject takes a different verb form than other subjects.

With **regular** verbs, simply add ***-s*** to the singular third person verb, as shown below:

	Singular		Plural	
	Subject	**Verb**	**Subject**	**Verb**
(first person)	I	play	we	play
(second person)	you	play	you	play
(third person)	he/she/it	plays	they	play

Some verbs are **irregular**, so simply adding *-s* doesn't work. For example:

Verb	Form for Third Person Singular Subject
have	has
do	does
fix	fixes

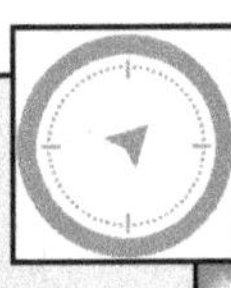

BE CAREFUL!

The verbs *be, have,* and *do* can be either main verbs or helping verbs.

Look for subject-verb agreement in the following sentences:

- *I* usually eat a banana for breakfast.
- *Marcy* does well in school.
- The *cat* licks its fur.

Subject-Verb Agreement for the Verb *Be*

Present		Past	
I am	we are	I was	we were
you are	you are	you were	you were
he/she/it is	they are	they were	they were

BE CAREFUL!

The verb ***be*** is very irregular. Its forms change with several subjects, in both present and past tense.

Things to Look Out For

Subject-verb agreement can be tricky. Be careful of these situations:

- **Sentences with more than one subject:** If two subjects are connected by *and,* the subject is **plural**. When two singular subjects are connected by *neither/nor,* the subject is **singular**.

Sandra and Luiz shop. (plural)
Neither Sandra nor Luiz has money. (singular)

- **Collective nouns:** Sometimes a noun stands for a group of people or things. If the subject is **one group**, it is considered **singular**.

Those students are still on chapter three. (plural)
That class is still on chapter three. (singular)

- ***There is* and *there are*:** With pronouns such as *there, what,* and *where,* the verb agrees with the noun or pronoun that follows it.

There's a rabbit! (singular)
Where are my shoes? (plural)

- **Indefinite pronouns:** Subjects such as *everybody, someone,* and *nobody* are **singular**. Subjects such as *all, none,* and *any* can be either **singular or plural**.

Everyone in the band plays well. (singular)
All of the students are there. (plural)
All is well. (singular)

Let's Review!

- Every sentence has a subject and a verb.
- The predicate is the part of the sentence that contains the verb.
- The subject and verb must agree in number and person.
- The third person singular subject takes a different verb form.

Modifiers

A modifier is a word, phrase, or clause that adds detail or changes (modifies) another word in the sentence. Descriptive words such as adjectives and adverbs are examples of modifiers.

The Role of Modifiers in a Sentence

Modifiers make a sentence more descriptive and interesting.

Look at these simple sentences. Notice how much more interesting they are with modifiers added.

Simple sentence	With Modifiers Added
I drove.	I drove my family along snowy roads to my grandmother's house.
They ate.	They ate a fruit salad of blueberries, strawberries, peaches, and apples.
The boy looked.	The boy in pajamas looked out the window at the birds eating from the feeder.
He climbed.	He climbed the ladder to fix the roof.

Look at the modifiers in bold type in the following sentences. Notice how these words add description to the basic idea in the sentence.

	Modifier	Word It Modifies	Type
The hungry man ate **quickly.**	1. the; 2. hungry; 3. quickly	1. man 2. man; 3. ate	1. article 2. adjective; 3. adverb
The small child, **who had scraped his knee,** cried **quietly.**	1. the; 2. small; 3. who had scraped his knee; 4. quietly	1. child; 2. child; 3. child; 4. cried	1. article; 2. adjective; 3. adjective clause; 4. adverb
The horse **standing near the fence** is **beautiful.**	1. the; 2. standing near the fence; 3. beautiful	1. horse; 2. horse; 3. horse	1. article; 2. participle phrase; 3. adjective
Hana and Mario stood **by the lake** and watched **a gorgeous** sunset.	1. by the lake; 2. a; 3. gorgeous	1. stood; 2. sunset; 3. sunset	1. prepositional phrase; 2. article; 3. adjective
They tried **to duck out of the way as the large spider dangled from the ceiling.**	1. to duck out of the way; 2. as the large spider dangled; 3. from the ceiling	1. tried; 2. duck; 3. dangled	1. infinitive phrase; 2. adverb clause; 3. prepositional phrase

DID YOU KNOW?

Adjectives and adverbs are not the only modifiers. With a participle phrase, **an -ing verb** can act as a modifier. For example, *eating from the feeder* modifies *the birds*. With an infinitive, ***to* plus the main form of a verb** can act as a modifier. For example, *to fix the roof* modifies *climbed*.

Misplaced and Dangling Modifiers

A **misplaced modifier** is a modifier that is placed incorrectly in a sentence, so that it modifies the wrong word.

A **dangling modifier** is a modifier that modifies a word that should be included in the sentence but is not.

> **BE CAREFUL!**
> Sometimes there is a modifier within a modifier. For example, in the clause *as the large spider dangled, the* and *large* are words that modify *spider.*

Look at these examples.

- First, notice the modifier, in bold.
- Next, look for the word it modifies.

Incorrect	Problem	How to Fix It	Correct
Sam wore his new shirt to school, **which was too big for him.**	Misplaced modifier. Notice the placement of the modifier ***which was too big for him.*** It is placed after the word *school*, which makes it seem like *school* is the word it describes. However, this was not the writer's intention. The writer intended for ***which was too big for him*** to describe the word *shirt*.	The modifier needs to be placed after the word *shirt*, rather than after the word *school.*	Sam wore his new shirt, **which was too big for him**, to school.
Running down the hallway, Maria's bag of groceries fell.	Dangling modifier. The modifier ***running down the hallway*** is placed before the phrase *Maria's bag of groceries*, which makes it seem this is what it describes. However, this was not the writer's intention; the *bag of groceries* cannot run! The correct reference would be the noun *Maria*, which was omitted from the sentence completely.	The modifier must reference *Maria*, rather than *Maria's bag of groceries.* This can be fixed by adding the noun *Maria* as a subject.	**Running down the hallway,** Maria dropped her bag of groceries.
With a leash on, my sister walked the dog.	Misplaced modifier. The modifier ***with a leash on*** is placed before *my sister*, which makes it seem like she is wearing a leash.	Move the modifier so that it is next to *the dog*, rather than *my sister.*	My sister walked the dog, **who had a leash on.**

Let's Review!

- A modifier is a word, phrase, or clause that adds detail by describing or modifying another word in the sentence.
- Adverbs, adjectives, articles, and prepositional phrases are some examples of modifiers.
- Misplaced and dangling modifiers have unclear references, leading to confusion about the meaning of a sentence.

> **BE CAREFUL!**
> A modifier should be placed next to the word it modifies. Misplaced and dangling modifiers lead to confusion about the meaning of a sentence.

DIRECT OBJECTS AND INDIRECT OBJECTS

A direct or indirect object has a relationship with the action verb that precedes it. A direct object directly receives the action of the verb. An indirect object indirectly receives the action.

Direct and Indirect Objects in a Sentence

An **object** in grammar is something that is acted on. The **subject** does the action; the **object** receives it.

An object is usually a noun or a pronoun.

There are three types of objects:

- direct object
- indirect object
- object of the preposition

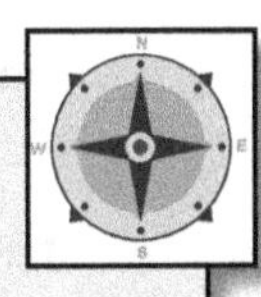

KEEP IN MIND . . .

When there is an **indirect object**, it will be placed between the verb and the direct object.

Many sentences have a direct object. Some sentences also have an indirect object.

Look at these examples:

- Kim threw *the ball*. *The ball* is the direct object. *Ask yourself:* What did she throw?
- Kim threw *Tommy* the ball. *Tommy* is the indirect object. *Ask yourself:* Who did she throw it to?

Look for the objects in the sentences below.

Sentence	Direct Object	Indirect Object	Be Careful!
Her mom poured her a glass of milk.	a glass of milk (*ask:* what did she pour?)	her (*ask:* who did she pour it for?)	The indirect object, when there is one, can be found between the verb and the direct object.
They work hard.			Not all sentences have objects. Here, *hard* is not an object. It is not the recipient of *work*. Instead, it is a modifier; it describes the work.
Kazu bought Katrina a present.	a present (*ask:* what did he buy?)	Katrina (*ask:* whom did he buy it for?)	
Kazu bought a present for Katrina.	a present (*ask*: what did he buy?)		Don't confuse indirect objects with prepositional phrases. *For* is a preposition, so *Katrina* is the object of the preposition; it is not an indirect object.

BE CAREFUL!

Some verbs can never take **direct objects**. These are:

- **Linking verbs** such as *is* and *seem*.
- **Intransitive verbs** such as *snore, go, sit*, and *die*.
- *Ask yourself:* Can you *snore* something? No. Therefore, this verb cannot take a direct object.

Let's Review!

- A direct object directly receives the action of the verb.
- An indirect object indirectly receives the action of the verb.
- An indirect object comes between the verb and the direct object.

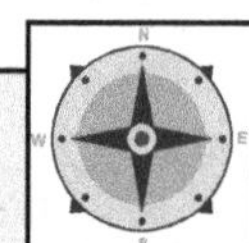

KEEP IN MIND . . .

If there is a preposition, the object is the **object of the preposition** rather than an **indirect object**.

Compare these two sentences:

- She made *me* dinner. (*Me* is an indirect object.)
- She made dinner *for me*. (*For me* is a prepositional phrase.)

Chapter 3 Knowledge of Language Practice Quiz

1. **Identify the direct object in the following sentence.**

   Paulo accidentally locked his keys in his car.

   A. Paulo
   B. accidentally
   C. his keys
   D. his car

2. **Select the word that is an object of the underlined verb.**

   The graduates held lit candles.

   A. The
   B. graduates
   C. lit
   D. candles

3. **Select the verb that acts on the underlined direct object in the following sentence.**

   We have no choice but to sit here and wait for these cows to cross the road!

   A. have
   B. sit
   C. wait
   D. cross

4. **Which modifier, if any, modifies the underlined word in the following sentence?**

   We always visit the bakery on the corner when we are in town.

   A. always
   B. on the corner
   C. when we are in town
   D. No modifier describes it.

5. **Identify the dangling or misplaced modifier, if there is one.**

   Having been repaired, we can drive the car again.

   A. Having been repaired
   B. we can drive
   C. the car again
   D. There is no dangling or misplaced modifier.

6. **Which ending does not create a sentence with a dangling modifier?**

   Trying to earn some extra money, ____.

   A. the new position paid more
   B. he got a second job
   C. the job was difficult
   D. it was an extra shift

7. **Select the "understood" subject with which the underlined verb must agree.**

   Watch out!

   A. You
   B. He
   C. I
   D. Out

8. **How many verbs must agree with the underlined subject in the following sentence?**

   Kareem Abdul-Jabbar, my favorite basketball player, dribbles, shoots, and scores to win the game!

   A. 0
   B. 1
   C. 2
   D. 3

9. **Select the correct verb to complete the following sentence.**

   Our family ____ staying home for the holidays this year.

   A. is
   B. be
   C. am
   D. are

10. **Fill in the blank with the correct subordinating conjunction.**

    You cannot go to the movies with your friends _____ you finish your homework.

    A. if
    B. once
    C. since
    D. unless

11. **Identify the dependent clause in the following sentence.**

    We decided to take our dog to the park although it was hot outside.

    A. We decided to take our dog
    B. to the park
    C. although it was hot outside
    D. to take our dog

12. **Identify the independent clause in the following sentence.**

    After eating dinner, the couple went on a stroll through the park.

    A. After eating dinner
    B. the couple went on a stroll through the park
    C. through the park
    D. went on a stroll

13. **Which of the following is an example of a simple sentence?**

    A. Tamara's sporting goods store.
    B. Tamara has a sporting goods store in town.
    C. Tamara has a sporting goods store it is in town.
    D. Tamara's sporting goods store is in town, and she is the owner.

14. **Which of the following uses a conjunction to combine the sentences below so the focus is on puppies requiring a lot of work?**

    Puppies are fun-loving animals. They do require a lot of work.

    A. Puppies are fun-loving animals; they do require a lot of work.
    B. Puppies are fun-loving animals, so they do require a lot of work.
    C. Since puppies are fun-loving animals they do require a lot of work.
    D. Although puppies are fun-loving animals, they do require a lot of work.

15. **Which of these options would complete the following sentence to make it a compound sentence?**

    The class of middle school students ______________________.

    A. served food at
    B. served food at a soup kitchen
    C. served food at a soup kitchen, and they enjoyed the experience
    D. served food at a soup kitchen even though they weren't required to

Chapter 3 Knowledge of Language Practice Quiz – Answer Key

1. C. *His keys* is the direct object of the verb *locked.* **See Lesson: Direct Objects and Indirect Objects.**

2. D. *Candles* is the direct object of the verb *held.* **See Lesson: Direct Objects and Indirect Objects.**

3. D. *The road* is a direct object of the verb *cross.* **See Lesson: Direct Objects and Indirect Objects.**

4. B. *On the corner* modifies *bakery.* **See Lesson: Modifiers.**

5. A. *Having been repaired* is placed where it references *we,* but it should reference *the car.* **See Lesson: Modifiers.**

6. B. Of these choices, *trying to earn some extra money* can only reference *he.* **See Lesson: Modifiers.**

7. A. In a command like this one, the "understood" subject is *you.* **See Lesson: Subject and Verb Agreement.**

8. D. The verbs *dribbles, shoots,* and *scores* must agree with the subject *Kareem Abdul-Jabbar.* **See Lesson: Subject and Verb Agreement.**

9. A. The subject *family* is singular and takes the verb *is.* **See Lesson: Subject and Verb Agreement.**

10. D. The word "unless" signifies the beginning of a dependent clause and is the only conjunction that makes sense in the sentence. **See Lesson: Types of Clauses.**

11. C. *Although it was hot outside* is dependent because it does not express a complete thought and relies on the independent clause. The word "although" also signifies the beginning of a dependent clause. **See Lesson: Types of Clauses.**

12. B. The couple went on a stroll through the park. It is independent because it has a subject, verb, and expresses a complete thought. **See Lesson: Types of Clauses.**

13. B. This is a simple sentence since it contains one independent clause consisting of a simple subject and a predicate. **See Lesson: Types of Sentences.**

14. D. The subordinate conjunction "although" combines the sentences and puts the focus on puppies requiring a lot of work. **See Lesson: Types of Sentences.**

15. C. This option would make the sentence a compound sentence. **See Lesson: Types of Sentences.**

Chapter 4 Vocabulary Acquisition

Root Words, Prefixes, and Suffixes

A root word is the most basic part of a word. You can create new words by: adding a prefix, a group of letters placed before the root word; or a suffix, a group of letters placed at the end of a root word. In this lesson you will learn about root words, prefixes, suffixes, and how to determine the meaning of a word by analyzing these word parts.

Root Words

Root words are found in everyday language. They are the most basic parts of words. Root words in the English language are mostly derived from Latin or Greek. You can add beginnings (prefixes) and endings (suffixes) to root words to change their meanings. To discover what a root word is, simply remove its prefix and/or suffix. What you are left with is the root word, or the core or basis of the word.

At times, root words can be stand-alone words.

Here are some examples of stand-alone root words:

Stand-Alone Root Word	Meaning
dress	*clothing*
form	*shape*
normal	*typical*
phobia	*fear of*
port	*carry*

Most root words, however, are **not** stand-alone words. They are not full words on their own, but they still form the basis of other words when you remove their prefixes and suffixes.

Here are some common root words in the English language:

Root Word	Meaning	Example
ami, amic	*love*	amicable
anni	*year*	anniversary
aud	*to hear*	auditory
bene	*good*	beneficial
biblio	*book*	bibliography
cap	*take, seize*	capture
cent	*one hundred*	century
chrom	*color*	chromatic

Root Word	Meaning	Example
chron	*time*	chronological
circum	*around*	circumvent
cred	*believe*	credible
corp	*body*	corpse
dict	*to say*	dictate
equi	*equal*	equality
fract; rupt	*to break*	fracture
ject	*throw*	eject
mal	*bad*	malignant
min	*small*	miniature
mort	*death*	mortal
multi	*many*	multiply
ped	*foot*	pedestrian
rupt	*break*	rupture
sect	*cut*	dissect
script	*write*	manuscript
sol	*sun*	solar
struct	*build*	construct
terr	*earth*	terrain
therm	*heat*	thermometer
vid, vis	*to see*	visual
voc	*voice; to call*	vocal

Prefixes

Prefixes are the letters added to the **beginning** of a root word to make a new word with a different meaning.

Prefixes on their own have meanings, too. If you add a prefix to a root word, it can change its meaning entirely.

Here are some of the most common prefixes, their meanings, and some examples:

Prefix	Meaning	Example
auto	*self*	autograph
con	*with*	conclude
hydro	*water*	hydrate
im, in, non, un	*not*	unimportant
inter	*between*	international
mis	*incorrect, badly*	mislead

Prefix	Meaning	Example
over	*too much*	over-stimulate
post	*after*	postpone
pre	*before*	preview
re	*again*	rewrite
sub	*under, below*	submarine
trans	*across*	transcribe

Let's look back at some of the root words from Section 1. By adding prefixes to these root words, you can create a completely new word with a new meaning:

Root Word	Prefix	New Word	Meaning
dress (*clothing*)	un (*remove*)	**un**dress	*remove clothing*
sect (*cut*)	inter (*between*)	**inter**sect	*cut across or through*
phobia (*fear*)	hydro (*water*)	**hydro**phobia	*fear of water*
script (*write*)	post (*after*)	**post**script	*additional remark at the end of a letter*

Suffixes

Suffixes are the letters added to the **end** of a root word to make a new word with a different meaning.

Suffixes on their own have meanings, too. If you add a suffix to a root word, it can change its meaning entirely.

Here are some of the most common suffixes, their meanings, and some examples:

Suffix	Meanings	Example
able, ible	*can be done*	agreeable
an, ean, ian	*belonging or relating to*	European
ed	*happened in the past*	jogged
en	*made of*	wooden
er	*comparative (more than)*	stricter
est	*comparative (most)*	largest
ful	*full of*	meaningful
ic	*having characteristics of*	psychotic
ion, tion, ation, ition	*act, process*	hospitalization
ist	*person who practices*	linguist
less	*without*	artless
logy	*study of*	biology

Let's look back at some of the root words from Section 1. By adding suffixes to these root words, you can create a completely new word with a new meaning:

Root Word	Suffix	New Word	Meaning
aud (*to hear*)	logy (*study of*)	audio**logy**	*the study of hearing*
form (*shape*)	less (*without*)	form**less**	*without a clear shape*
port (*carry*)	able (*can be done*)	port**able**	*able to be carried*
normal (*typical*)	ity (*state of*)	normal**ity**	*condition of being normal*

Determining Meaning

Knowing the meanings of common root words, prefixes, and suffixes can help you determine the meaning of unknown words. By looking at a word's individual parts, you can get a good sense of its definition.

If you look at the word *transportation*, you can study the different parts of the word to figure out what it means.

If you were to break up the word you would see the following:

PREFIX: *trans = across*	ROOT: *port = carry*	SUFFIX: *tion = act or process*

If you put all these word parts together, you can define transportation as: *the act or process of carrying something across.*

Let's define some other words by looking at their roots, prefixes and suffixes:

Word	Prefix	Root	Suffix	Working Definition
indestructible	in (*not*)	struct (*build*)	able (*can be done*)	Not able to be "un" built (torn down)
nonconformist	non (*not*) con (*with*)	form (*shape*)	ist (*person who practices*)	A person who can not be shaped (someone who doesn't go along with the norm)
subterranean	sub (*under, below*)	terr (*earth*)	ean (*belonging or relating to*)	Relating or belonging to something under the earth

Let's Review!

- A root word is the most basic part of a word.
- A prefix is the letters added to beginning of a root word to change the word and its meaning.
- A suffix is the letters added to the end of a root word to change the word and its meaning.
- You can figure out a word's meaning by looking closely at its different word parts (root, prefixes, and suffixes).

CONTEXT CLUES AND MULTIPLE MEANING WORDS

Sometimes when you read a text, you come across an unfamiliar word. Instead of skipping the word and reading on, it is important to figure out what that word means so you can better understand the text. There are different strategies you can use to determine the meaning of unfamiliar words. This lesson will cover (1) how to determine unfamiliar words by reading context clues, (2) multiple meaning words, and (3) using multiple meaning words properly in context.

Using Context Clues to Determine Meaning

When reading a text, it is common to come across unfamiliar words. One way to determine the meaning of unfamiliar words is by studying other context clues to help you better understand what the word means.

Context means the other words in the sentences around the unfamiliar word.

You can look at these other words to find **clues** or **hints** to help you figure out what the word means.

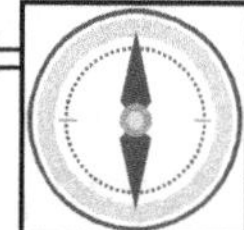

FOR EXAMPLE

Look at the following sentence:

Some of the kids in the cafeteria *ostracized* Janice because she dressed differently; they never allowed her to sit at their lunch table, and they whispered behind her back.

If you did not know what the word *ostracized* meant, you could look at the **other words** for **clues** to help you.

Here is what we know based on the clues in the sentence:

- Janice dressed differently
- Some kids did not allow her to sit at their table
- They whispered behind her back

We know that the kids **never allowed her to sit at their lunch** table and that they **whispered behind her back**. If you put all these clues together, you can conclude that the other students were **mistreating** Janice by **excluding** her.

Therefore, based on these context clues, *ostracized* means "excluded from the group."

Here's another example:

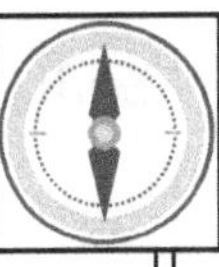

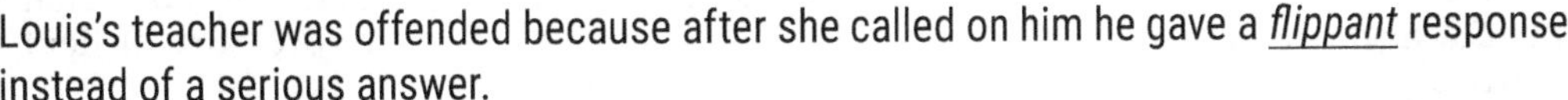

EXAMPLE 2

Look at this next sentence:

Louis's teacher was offended because after she called on him he gave a *flippant* response instead of a serious answer.

If you did not know what the word *flippant* meant, you could look at the **other words** for **clues** to help you.

Here is what we know based on the clues in the sentence:

- Louis's teacher was offended
- He gave a flippant response instead of a serious answer

We know that Louis said something that **offended** his teacher. Another keyword in this sentence is the word **instead**. This means that **instead of a serious answer** Louis gave the **opposite** of a serious answer.

Therefore, based on these context clues, *flippant* means "lacking respect or seriousness."

Multiple Meaning Words

Sometimes when we read words in a text, we encounter words that have **multiple meanings.**

Multiple meaning words are words that have **more than one definition** or meaning.

FOR EXAMPLE

The word **current** is a multiple meaning word. Here are the different definitions of *current:*

CURRENT:

1. adj: happening or existing in the present time

   Example: *It is important to keep up with current events so you know what's happening in the world.*

2. noun: the continuous movement of a body of water or air in a certain direction

   Example: *The river's current was strong as we paddled down the rapids.*

3. noun: a flow of electricity

   Example: *The electrical current was very weak in the house.*

Here are some other examples of words with multiple meanings:

Multiple Meaning Word	Definition #1	Definition #2	Definition #3
Buckle	noun: a metal or plastic device that connects one end of a belt to another	verb: to fasten or attach	verb: to bend or collapse from pressure or heat
Cabinet	noun: a piece of furniture used for storing things	noun: a group of people who give advice to a government leader	-
Channel	noun: a radio or television station	noun: a system used for sending something	noun: a long, narrow place where water flows
Doctor	noun: a person skilled in the science of medicine, dentistry, or one holding a PhD	verb: to change something in a way to trick or deceive	verb: to give medical treatment
Grave	noun: a hole in the ground for burying a dead body	adj: very serious	-
Hamper	noun: a large basket used for holding dirty clothes	verb: to slow the movement, action, or progress of	-
Plane	noun: a mode of transportation that has wings and an engine and can carry people and things in the air	noun: a flat or level surface that extends outward	noun: a level of though, development, or existence
Reservation	noun: an agreement to have something (such as a table, room, or seat) held for use at a later time	noun: a feeling of uncertainty or doubt	noun: an area of land kept separate for Native Americans to live an area of land set aside for animals to live for protection
Season	noun: one of the four periods in which a year is divided (winter, spring, summer, and fall)	noun: a particular period of time during the year	verb: to add spices to something to give it more flavor
Sentence	noun: a group words that expresses a statement, question, command, or wish	noun: the punishment given to someone by a court of law	verb: to officially state the punishment given by a court of law

From this chart you will notice that words with multiple meanings may have different **parts of speech**. A part of speech is a category of words that have the same grammatical properties. Some of the main parts of speech for words in the English language are: nouns, adjectives, verbs, and adverbs.

Part of Speech	Definition	Example
Noun	a person, place, thing, or idea	*Linda, New York City, toaster, happiness*
Adjective	a word that describes a noun or pronoun	*adventurous, young, red, intelligent*
Verb	an action or state of being	*run, is, sleep, become*
Adverb	a word that describes a verb, adjective, or other adverb	*quietly, extremely, carefully, well*

For example, in the chart above, *season* can be a **noun** or a **verb**.

Using Multiple Meaning Words Properly in Context

When you come across a **multiple meaning word** in a text, it is important to discern which meaning of the word is being used so you do not get confused.

You can once again turn to the **context clues** to clarify which meaning of the word is being used.

Let's take a look at the word coach. This word has several definitions:

COACH:

1. noun: a person who teaches and trains an athlete or performer
2. noun: a large bus with comfortable seating used for long trips
3. noun: the section on an airplane with the least expensive seats
4. verb: to teach or train someone in a specific area
5. verb: to give someone instructions on what to do or say in a certain situation

Since *coach* has so many definitions, you need to look at the **context clues** to figure out which definition of the word is being used:

The man was not happy that he had to sit in coach on the 24-hour flight to Australia.

In this sentence, the context clues **sit in** and **24-hour flight** help you see that *coach* means the least expensive seat on an airplane.

Let's look at another sentence using the word *coach*:

The lawyer needed to coach her witness so he would answer all the questions properly.

In this sentence, the context clues **so he would answer all the questions properly** help you see that the lawyer was giving the witness instructions on what to say.

Let's Review!

- When you come across an unfamiliar word in a text you can use context clues to help you define it.
- Context clues can also help you determine which definition of a multiple meaning word to use.

SYNONYMS, ANTONYMS, AND ANALOGIES

In order to utilize language to the best of your ability while reading, writing, or speaking, you must know how to interpret and use new vocabulary words, and also understand how these words relate to one another. Sometimes words have the same meaning. Sometimes words are complete opposites of each other. Understanding how the words you read, write, and speak with relate to each other will deepen your understanding of how language works. This lesson will cover (1) synonyms, (2) antonyms, and (3) analogies.

Synonyms

A **synonym** is a word that has the same meaning or close to the same meaning as another word. For example, if you look up the words *irritated* and *annoyed* in a dictionary, you will discover that they both mean "showing or feeling slight anger." Similarly, if you were to look up *blissful* and *joyful*, you will see that they both mean "extremely happy." The dictionary definition of a word is called its **denotation**. This is a word's literal or direct meaning.

When you understand that there are multiple words that have the same **denotation**, it will broaden your vocabulary.

It is also important to know that words with similar meanings have **nuances**, or subtle differences.

One way that words have nuances is in their **shades of meanings.** This means that although they have a similar definition, if you look closely, you will see that they have slight differences.

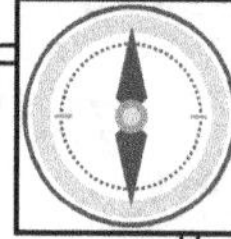

FOR EXAMPLE

If you quickly glance at the following words, you will see that they all have a similar meaning. However, if you look closely, you will see that their meanings have subtle differences. You can see their differences by looking at their various **levels** or **degrees**:

LEAST ⟶ MOST

nibble	bite	eat	devour
upset	angry	furious	irate
wet	soggy	soaked	drenched
good	great	amazing	phenomenal

Another way that words have nuance are in their **connotations.** A word's connotation is its **positive** or **negative** association. This can be the case even when two words have the same **denotations**, or dictionary definitions.

For example, the words *aroma* and *stench* both have a similar dictionary definition or **denotation**: "a smell." However, their **connotations** are quite different. *Aroma* has a **positive connotation** because it describes a *pleasant* smell. But *stench* has a **negative connotation** because it describes an unpleasant smell.

FOR EXAMPLE

Look at the following words. Although they have the same denotation, their connotations are very different:

Denotation	Positive Connotation	Negative Connotation
CLIQUE and *CLUB* both mean "a group of people."	*CLUB* has a positive connotation because it describes a group of people coming together to accomplish something.	*CLIQUE* has a negative connotation because it describes a group of people who exclude others.
INTERESTED and *NOSY* both mean "showing curiosity."	*INTERESTED* has a positive connotation because it means having a genuine curiosity about someone or something.	*NOSY* has a negative connotation because it describes who tries to pry information out of someone else to gossip or judge.
EMPLOY and *EXPLOIT* both mean "to use someone."	*EMPLOY* has a positive connotation because it means to use someone for a job.	*EXPLOIT* has a negative connotation because it means to use someone for one's own advantage.

Seeing that synonymous words have different **shades of meaning** and **connotations** will allow you to more precisely interpret and understand the nuances of language.

Antonyms

An **antonym** is a word that means the opposite or close to the opposite of another word. Think of an antonym as the direct opposite of a **synonym**. For example, *caring* and *apathetic* are antonyms because *caring* means "displaying concern and kindness for others" whereas *apathetic* means "showing no interest or concern."

Antonyms can fall under three categories:

Graded Antonyms:	Word pairs whose meanings are opposite and lie on a spectrum or continuum; there are many other words that fall between the two words. If you look at *hot* and *cold*, there are other words on this spectrum: *scalding*, ***hot***, *warm*, *tepid*, *cool*, ***cold***
Relational Antonyms:	Word pairs whose opposites make sense only in the context of the relationship between the two meanings. These two words could not exist without the other: ***open - close***
Complementary Antonyms:	Word pairs that have no degree of meaning at all; there are only two possibilities, one or the other: ***dead - alive***

Here are some more examples of the three types of antonyms:

Graded Antonyms	Relational Antonyms	Complementary Antonyms
hard - soft	front - back	day - night
fast - slow	predator - prey	sink - float
bad - good	top - bottom	input - output
wet - dry	capture - release	interior - exterior
big - small	on - off	occupied - vacant

There are also common **prefixes** that help make antonyms. The most common prefixes for antonyms of words are: **UN**, **NON**, and **IN**. All these prefixes mean "not" or "without."

FOR EXAMPLE

UN:	**IN:**	**NON:**
likely – **un**likely	tolerant – **in**tolerant	conformist – **non**conformist
fortunate – **un**fortunate	excusable – **in**excusable	payment – **non**payment

Analogies

An **analogy** is a simple comparison between two things. Analogies help us understand the world around us by seeing how different things relate to one another.

In looking closely at words, analogies help us understand how they are connected.

In word analogies, they are usually set up using colons in the following way:

Pleasure: Smile :: Pain: ______________________________

This can be read as: Pleasure **IS TO** Smile **AS** Pain **IS TO** ______________________________

The answer: "grimace"

Sometimes you see analogies written out like this:

Pleasure is to Smile as Pain is to ______________________________

These are the common types of word analogies that illustrate how different words relate to one another:

Type of Analogy	Relationship	Example
Synonyms	Two words with the same meaning	Beginner : Novice:: Expert : Pro
Antonyms	Two words with the opposite meaning	Hot : Cold :: Up : Down
Part/Whole	One word is a part of another word	Stars : Galaxy :: Pages : Book
Cause/Effect	One word describes a condition or action, and the other describes an outcome	Tornado : Damage :: Joke : Laughter
Object/Function	One word describes something, and the other word describes what it's used for	Needle : Sew :: Saw : Cut

Category/Type	One word is a general category, and the other is something that falls in that category	Music : Folk :: Dance : Ballet
Performer/Related Action	One word is a person or object, and the other words is the action he/she/it commonly performs	Thief : Steal :: Surgeon : Operate
Degree of Intensity	These words have similar meanings, but one word is stronger or more intense than the other	Glad : Elated :: Angry : Furious

By recognizing the type of analogy two words have, you then can explore how they are connected.

Let's Review!

- Synonyms are words that have the same meaning. Synonyms also have nuances.
- Analogies are words that have an opposite meaning. There are three types of antonyms.
- Analogies show how words relate to each other. There are different types of analogy relationships to look for.
- Understanding how words relate to each other will help you better understand language, pull meaning from texts, and write and speak with a wider vocabulary.

Chapter 4 Vocabulary Acquisition Practice Quiz

1. **Select the word from the following sentence that has more than one meaning.**

   Cassandra's voice has a much different pitch than her brother's, so they sound great when they sing together.

   A. Voice
   B. Different
   C. Pitch
   D. Sing

2. **Select the correct definition of the underlined word that has multiple meanings in the sentence.**

   When the young boy saw his angry mother coming toward him, he made a bolt for the door.

   A. A large roll of cloth
   B. A quick movement in a particular direction
   C. A sliding bar that is used to lock a window or door
   D. A bright line of light appearing in the sky during a storm

3. **Select the meaning of the underlined word in the sentence based on the context clues.**

   When visiting the desert, the temperature tends to fluctuate, so you need to bring a variety of clothing.

   A. Rise
   B. Drop
   C. Change
   D. Stabilize

4. **The use of the suffix -*ous* in the word parsimonious indicates what about a person?**

   A. He/she is full of stinginess.
   B. He/she is against stinginess.
   C. He/she is supportive of stinginess.
   D. He/she is a person who studies stinginess.

5. **Which of the following prefixes means incorrect?**

   A. un-
   B. non-
   C. mis-
   D. over-

6. **What is the best definition of the word pugnacious?**

   A. Rude
   B. Harmful
   C. Deceiving
   D. Combative

7. **The following words have the same denotation. Which word has a negative connotation?**

   A. Poised
   B. Assured
   C. Arrogant
   D. Confident

8. **Whisk : Mix :: Flashlight : ____________**

   A. Hike
   B. Light
   C. Camp
   D. Travel

9. **Which word in the list of synonyms shows the strongest degree of the word?**

   A. Amusing
   B. Comical
   C. Uproarious
   D. Entertaining

Chapter 4 Vocabulary Acquisition Practice Quiz – Answer Key

1. C. The word "pitch" has more than one meaning. **See Lesson: Context Clues and Multiple Meaning Words.**

2. B. The meaning of bolt in the context of this sentence is "a quick movement in a particular direction." **See Lesson: Context Clues and Multiple Meaning Words.**

3. C. The meaning of fluctuate in the context of this sentence is "change." **See Lesson: Context Clues and Multiple Meaning Words.**

4. A. The suffix *-ous* means "full of or possessing," so a parsimonious person is one who is full of stinginess. **See Lesson: Root Words, Prefixes, and Suffixes.**

5. C. The prefix that means "incorrect" is *mis*. **See Lesson: Root Words, Prefixes, and Suffixes.**

6. D. The root *pug* means "war" or "fight," so pugnacious means combative. **See Lesson: Root Words, Prefixes, and Suffixes.**

7. C. Arrogant has a negative connotation. **See Lesson: Synonyms, Antonyms, and Analogies.**

8. B. A whisk is a tool used to mix in the same way that a flashlight is a tool used to light. **See Lesson: Synonyms, Antonyms, and Analogies.**

9. C. Uproarious is the word that shows the strongest degree in the list of synonyms. **See Lesson: Synonyms, Antonyms, and Analogies.**

Section II. Mathematics

CHAPTER 5 NUMBER AND QUANTITY

BASIC ADDITION AND SUBTRACTION

This lesson introduces the concept of numbers and their symbolic and graphical representations. It also describes how to add and subtract whole numbers.

Numbers

A **number** is a way to quantify a set of entities that share some characteristic. For example, a fruit basket might contain nine pieces of fruit. More specifically, it might contain three apples, two oranges, and four bananas. Note that a number is a quantity, but a **numeral** is the symbol that represents the number: 8 means the number eight, for instance.

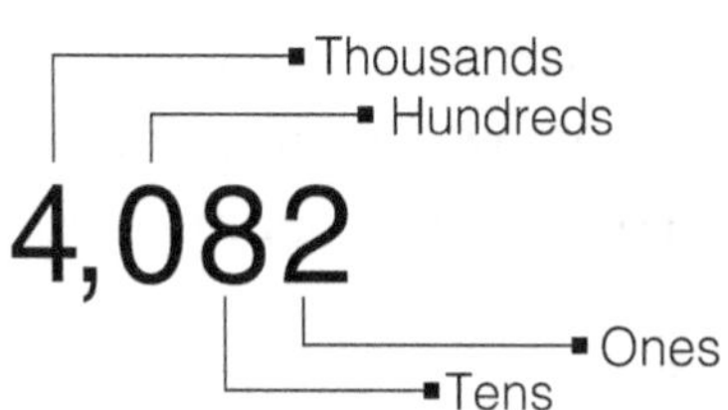

Although number representations vary, the most common is **base 10.** In base-10 format, each **digit** (or individual numeral) in a number is a quantity based on a multiple of 10. The base-10 system designates 0 through 9 as the numerals for zero through nine, respectively, and combines them to represent larger numbers. Thus, after counting from 1 to 9, the next number uses an additional digit: 10. That number means 1 group of 10 ones plus 0 additional ones. After 99, another digit is necessary, this time representing a hundred (10 sets of 10). This process of adding digits can go on indefinitely to express increasingly large numbers. For whole numbers, the rightmost digit is the ones place, the next digit to its left is the tens place, the next is the hundreds place, then the thousands place, and so on.

Classifying numbers can be convenient. The chart below lists a few common number sets.

Sets of Numbers	Members	Remarks
Natural numbers	1, 2, 3, 4, 5,...	The "counting" numbers
Whole numbers	0, 1, 2, 3, 4,...	The natural numbers plus 0
Integers	..., −3, −2, −1, 0, 1, 2, 3,...	The whole numbers plus all negative whole numbers
Real numbers	All numbers	The integers plus all fraction/decimal numbers in between
Rational numbers	All real numbers that can be expressed as p/q, where p and q are integers and q is nonzero	The natural numbers, whole numbers, and integers are all rational numbers
Irrational numbers	All real numbers that are not rational	The rational and irrational numbers together constitute the entire set of real numbers

Example

Jane has 4 pennies, 3 dimes, and 7 dollars. How many cents does she have?

A. 347 B. 437 C. 734 D. 743

The correct answer is **C.** The correct solution is 734. A penny is 1 cent. A dime (10 pennies) is 10 cents, and a dollar (100 pennies) is 100 cents. Place the digits in base-10 format: 7 hundreds, 3 tens, 4 ones, or 734.

The Number Line

The **number line** is a model that illustrates the relationships among numbers. The complete number line is infinite and includes every real number—both positive and negative. A ruler, for example, is a portion of a number line that assigns a **unit** (such as inches or centimeters) to each number. Typically, number lines depict smaller numbers to the left and larger numbers to the right. For example, a portion of the number line centered on 0 might look like the following:

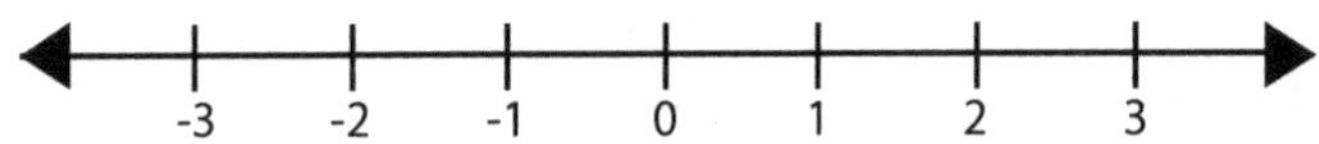

Because people learn about numbers in part through counting, they have a basic sense of how to order them. The number line builds on this sense by placing all the numbers (at least conceptually) from least to greatest. Whether a particular number is greater than or less than another is determined by comparing their relative positions. One number is greater than another if it is farther right on the number line. Likewise, a number is less than another if it is farther left on the number line. Symbolically, $<$ means "is less than" and $>$ means "is greater than." For example, $5 > 1$ and $9 < 25$.

Example

Place the following numbers in order from greatest to least: 5, –12, 0.

A. 0, 5, –12

B. –12, 5, 0

C. 5, 0, –12

D. –12, 0, 5

The correct answer is **C.** The correct solution is 5, 0, –12. Use the number line to order the numbers. Note that the question says *from greatest to least.*

> **BE CAREFUL!**
> When ordering negative numbers, think of the number line. Although $-10 > -2$ may seem correct, it is incorrect. Because −10 is to the left of −2 on the number line, $-10 < -2$.

Addition

Addition is the process of combining two or more numbers. For example, one set has 4 members and another set has 5 members. To combine the sets and find out how many members are in the new set, add 4 and 5 to get the **sum**. Symbolically, the expression is 4 + 5, where + is the **plus sign.** Pictorially, it might look like the following:

$$\begin{matrix}\circ\circ \\ \circ\circ\end{matrix} + \begin{matrix}\circ\circ \\ \circ\circ\circ\end{matrix} = \begin{matrix}\circ\circ\circ\circ \\ \circ\circ\circ\circ\circ\end{matrix}$$

To get the sum, combine the two sets of circles and then count them. The result is 9.

KEY POINT

The order of the numbers is irrelevant when adding.

Another way to look at addition involves the number line. When adding 4 + 5, for example, start at 4 on the number line and take 5 steps to the right. The stopping point will be 9, which is the sum.

Counting little pictures or using the number line works for small numbers, but it becomes unwieldy for large ones—even numbers such as 24 and 37 would be difficult to add quickly and accurately. A simple algorithm enables much faster addition of large numbers. It works with two or more numbers.

STEP BY STEP

Step 1. Stack the numbers, vertically aligning the digits for each place.

Step 2. Draw a plus sign (+) to the left of the bottom number and draw a horizontal line below the last number.

Step 3. Add the digits in the ones place.

Step 4. If the sum from Step 3 is less than 10, write it in the same column below the horizontal line. Otherwise, write the first (ones) digit below the line, then **carry** the second (tens) digit to the top of the next column.

Step 5. Going from right to left, repeat Steps 3–4 for the other places.

Step 6. If applicable, write the remaining carry digit as the leftmost digit in the sum.

Example

Evaluate the expression 154 + 98.

A. 250 B. 252 C. 352 D. 15,498

The correct answer is **B.** The correct solution is 252. Carefully follow the addition algorithm (see below). The process involves carrying a digit twice.

$$\begin{array}{r} 154 \\ +\ 98 \\ \hline \end{array} \rightarrow \begin{array}{r} {}^{1} \\ 154 \\ +\ 98 \\ \hline 2 \end{array} \rightarrow \begin{array}{r} {}^{11} \\ 154 \\ +\ 98 \\ \hline 52 \end{array} \rightarrow \begin{array}{r} {}^{11} \\ 154 \\ +\ 98 \\ \hline 252 \end{array}$$

Subtraction

Subtraction is the inverse (opposite) of addition. Instead of representing the sum of numbers, it represents the difference between them. For example, given a set containing 15 members, subtracting 3 of those members yields a **difference** of 12. Using the **minus sign**, the expression for this operation is $15 - 3 = 12$. As with addition, two approaches are counting pictures and using the number line. The first case might involve drawing 15 circles and then crossing off 3 of them; the difference is the number of remaining circles (12). To use the number line, begin at 15 and move left 3 steps to reach 12.

Again, these approaches are unwieldy for large numbers, but the subtraction algorithm eases evaluation by hand. This algorithm is only practical for two numbers at a time.

STEP BY STEP

Step 1. Stack the numbers, vertically aligning the digits in each place. Put the number you are subtracting *from* on top.

Step 2. Draw a minus sign (–) to the left of the bottom number and draw a horizontal line below the stack of numbers.

Step 3. Start at the ones place. If the digit at the top is larger than the digit below it, write the difference under the line. Otherwise, **borrow** from the top digit in the next-higher place by crossing it off, subtracting 1 from it, and writing the difference above it. Then add 10 to the digit in the ones place and perform the subtraction as normal.

Step 4. Going from right to left, repeat Step 3 for the rest of the places. If borrowing was necessary, make sure to use the new digit in each place, not the original one.

When adding or subtracting with negative numbers, the following rules are helpful. Note that x and y are used as placeholders for any real number.

$$x + (-y) = x - y$$

$$-x - y = -(x + y)$$

$$(-x) + (-y) = -(x + y)$$

$$x - y = -(y - x)$$

BE CAREFUL!

When dealing with numbers that have units (such as weights, currencies, or volumes), addition and subtraction are only possible when the numbers have the same unit. If necessary, convert one or more of them to equivalent numbers with the same unit.

Example

Kevin has 120 minutes to complete an exam. If he has already used 43, how many minutes does he have left?

A. 43 B. 77 C. 87 D. 163

The correct answer is **B.** The correct solution is 77. The first step is to convert this problem to a math expression. The goal is to find the difference between how many minutes Kevin has for the exam and how many he has left after 43 minutes have elapsed. The expression would be 120 – 43. Carefully follow the subtraction algorithm (see below). The process will involve borrowing a digit twice.

$$\begin{array}{r} \\ 120 \\ -\ 43 \\ \hline \\ \end{array} \longrightarrow \begin{array}{r} {\scriptstyle 1\ 10} \\ 1\not{2}0 \\ -\ 43 \\ \hline 7 \end{array} \longrightarrow \begin{array}{r} {\scriptstyle 0\ 11\ 10} \\ \not{1}\not{2}0 \\ -\ 43 \\ \hline 77 \end{array}$$

Let's Review!

- Numbers are positive and negative quantities and often appear in base-10 format.
- The number line illustrates the ordering of numbers.
- Addition is the combination of numbers. It can be performed by counting objects or pictures, moving on the number line, or using the addition algorithm.
- Subtraction is finding the difference between numbers. Like addition, it can be performed by counting, moving on the number line, or using the subtraction algorithm.

BASIC MULTIPLICATION AND DIVISION

This lesson describes the process of multiplying and dividing numbers and introduces the order of operations, which governs how to evaluate expressions containing multiple arithmetic operations.

Multiplication

Addition can be tedious if it involves multiple instances of the same numbers. For example, evaluating 29 + 29 is easy, but evaluating 29 + 29 + 29 + 29 + 29 is laborious. Note that this example contains five instances—or multiples—of 29. **Multiplication** replaces the repeated addition of the same number with a single, more concise operation. Using the **multiplication (or times) symbol** (×), the expression is

$$29 + 29 + 29 + 29 + 29 = 5 \times 29$$

The expression contains 5 multiples of 29. These numbers are the **factors** of multiplication. The result is called the **product.** In this case, addition shows that the product is 145. As with the other arithmetic operations, multiplication is easy for small numbers. Below is the multiplication table for whole numbers up to 12.

	1	2	3	4	5	6	7	8	9	10	11	12
1	1	2	3	4	5	6	7	8	9	10	11	12
2	2	4	6	8	10	12	14	16	18	20	22	24
3	3	6	9	12	15	18	21	24	27	30	33	36
4	4	8	12	16	20	24	28	32	36	40	44	48
5	5	10	15	20	25	30	35	40	45	50	55	60
6	6	12	18	24	30	36	42	48	54	60	66	72
7	7	14	21	28	35	42	49	56	63	70	77	84
8	8	16	24	32	40	48	56	64	72	80	88	96
9	9	18	27	36	45	54	63	72	81	90	99	108
10	10	20	30	40	50	60	70	80	90	100	110	120
11	11	22	33	44	55	66	77	88	99	110	121	132
12	12	24	36	48	60	72	84	96	108	120	132	144

When dealing with large numbers, the multiplication algorithm is more practical than memorization. The ability to quickly recall the products in the multiplication table is nevertheless crucial to using this algorithm.

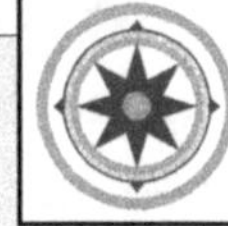

STEP BY STEP

Step 1. Stack the two factors, vertically aligning the digits in each place.

Step 2. Draw a multiplication symbol (×) to the left of the bottom number and draw a horizontal line below the stack.

Step 3. Begin with the ones digit in the lower factor. Multiply it with the ones digit from the top factor.

Step 4. If the product from Step 3 is less than 10, write it in the same column below the horizontal line. Otherwise, write the first (ones) digit below the line and carry the second (tens) digit to the top of the next column.

Step 5. Perform Step 4 for each digit in the top factor, adding any carry digit to the result. If an extra carry digit appears at the end, write it as the leftmost digit in the product.

Step 6. Going right to left, repeat Steps 3–4 for the other places in the bottom factor, starting a new line in each case.

Step 7. Add the numbers below the line to get the product.

Example

A certain type of screw comes in packs of 35. If a contractor orders 52 packs, how many screws does he receive?

A. 2　　B. 57　　C. 245　　D. 1,820

The correct answer is **D.** The first step is to convert this problem to a math expression. The goal is to find how many screws the contractor receives if he orders 52 packs of 35 each. The expression would be 52×35 (or 35×52). Carefully follow the multiplication algorithm (see below).

	→	→	→	→	→	→
	1	1	1	1 1	1 1	1 1
52	52	52	52	52	52	52
x 35	x 35	x 35	x 35	x 35	x 35	x 35
	0	260	260	260	260	260
			6	56	156	+ 156
						1,820

KEY POINT

As with addition, the order of numbers in a multiplication expression is irrelevant to the product. For example, $6 \times 9 = 9 \times 6$.

Division

Division is the inverse of multiplication, like subtraction is the inverse of addition. Whereas multiplication asks how many individuals are in 8 groups of 9 ($8 \times 9 = 72$), for example, division asks how many groups of 8 (or 9) are in 72. Division expressions use either the / or ÷ symbol. Therefore, $72 \div 9$ means: How many groups of 9 are in 72, or how many times does 9 go into 72? Thinking about the meaning of multiplication shows that $72 \div 9 = 8$ and $72 \div 8 = 9$. In the expression $72 \div 8 = 9$, 72 is the **dividend**, 8 is the **divisor**, and 9 is the **quotient**.

When the dividend is unevenly divisible by the divisor (e.g., $5 \div 2$), calculating the quotient with a **remainder** can be convenient. The quotient in this case is the maximum number of times the divisor goes into the dividend plus how much of the dividend is left over. To express the remainder, use an R. For example, the quotient of $5 \div 2$ is 2R1 because 2 goes into 5 twice with 1 left over.

Knowing the multiplication table allows quick evaluation of simple whole-number division. For larger numbers, the division algorithm enables evaluation by hand.

Unlike multiplication—but like subtraction—the order of the numbers in a division expression is important. Generally, changing the order changes the quotient.

STEP BY STEP

Step 1. Write the divisor and then the dividend on a single line.

Step 2. Draw a vertical line between them, connecting to a horizontal line over the dividend.

Step 3. If the divisor is smaller than the leftmost digit of the dividend, perform the remainder division and write the quotient (without the remainder) above that digit. If the divisor is larger than the leftmost digit, use the first two digits (or however many are necessary) until the number is greater than the divisor. Write the quotient over the rightmost digit in that number.

Step 4. Multiply the quotient digit by the divisor and write it under the dividend, vertically aligning the ones digit of the product with the quotient digit.

Step 5. Subtract the product from the digits above it.

Step 6. Bring down the next digit from the quotient.

Step 7. Perform Steps 3–6, using the most recent difference as the quotient.

Step 8. Write the remainder next to the quotient.

Example

Evaluate the expression 468 ÷ 26.

A. 18 B. 18R2 C. 494 D. 12,168

The correct answer is **A.** Carefully follow the division algorithm. In this case, the answer has no remainder.

$$26\overline{)468} \longrightarrow \begin{array}{r} 1 \\ 26\overline{)468} \\ 26 \end{array} \longrightarrow \begin{array}{r} 1 \\ 26\overline{)468} \\ \underline{-26} \\ 20 \end{array} \longrightarrow \begin{array}{r} 1 \\ 26\overline{)468} \\ \underline{-26\downarrow} \\ 208 \end{array} \longrightarrow \begin{array}{r} 18 \\ 26\overline{)468} \\ \underline{-26\downarrow} \\ 208 \\ \underline{-208} \\ 0 \end{array}$$

KEY POINT

Division by 0 is undefined. If it appears in an expression, something is wrong.

Signed Multiplication and Division

Multiplying and dividing signed numbers is simpler than adding and subtracting them because it only requires remembering two simple rules. First, if the two numbers have the same sign, their product or quotient is positive. Second, if they have different signs, their product or quotient is negative.

As a result, negative numbers can be multiplied or divided as if they are positive. Just keep track of the sign separately for the product or quotient. Note that negative numbers are sometimes written in parentheses to avoid the appearance of subtraction.

For Example:

$5 \times (-3) = -15$

$(-8) \times (-8) = 64$

$(-12) \div 3 = -4$

$(-100) \div (-25) = 4$

Example

Evaluate the expression (–7) × (–9).

A. −63 B. −16 C. 16 D. 63

The correct answer is **D.** Because both factors are negative, the product will be positive. Because the product of 7 and 9 is 63, the product of –7 and –9 is also 63.

Order of Operations

By default, math expressions work like most Western languages: they should be read and evaluated from left to right. However, some operations take precedence over others, which can change this default evaluation. Following this **order of operations** is critical. The mnemonic **PEMDAS** (**P**lease **E**xcuse **M**y **D**ear **A**unt **S**ally) helps in remembering how to evaluate an expression with multiple operations.

STEP BY STEP

P. Evaluate operations in parentheses (or braces/brackets). If the expression has parentheses within parentheses, begin with the innermost ones.

E. Evaluate exponential operations. (For expressions without exponents, ignore this step.)

MD. Perform all multiplication and division operations, going through the expression from left to right.

AS. Perform all addition and subtraction operations, going through the expression from left to right.

Because the order of numbers in multiplication and addition does not affect the result, the PEMDAS procedure only requires going from left to right when dividing or subtracting. At those points, going in the correct direction is critical to getting the right answer.

Calculators that can handle a series of numbers at once automatically evaluate an expression according to the order of operations. When available, calculators are a good way to check the results.

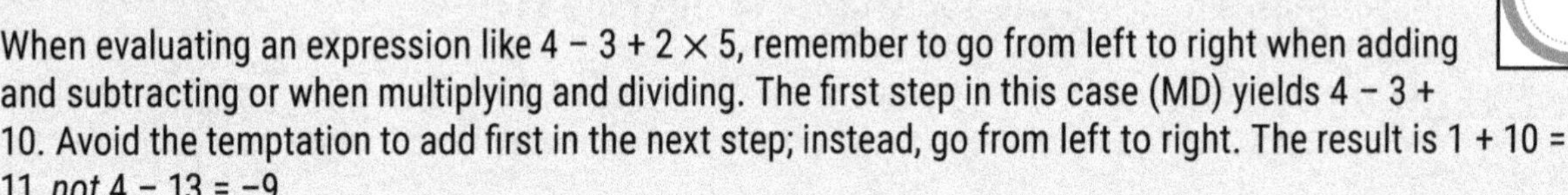

BE CAREFUL!

When evaluating an expression like $4 - 3 + 2 \times 5$, remember to go from left to right when adding and subtracting or when multiplying and dividing. The first step in this case (MD) yields $4 - 3 + 10$. Avoid the temptation to add first in the next step; instead, go from left to right. The result is $1 + 10 = 11$, *not* $4 - 13 = -9$.

Example

Evaluate the expression $8 \times (3 + 6) \div 3 - 2 + 5$.

A. 13 B. 17 C. 27 D. 77

The correct answer is **C**. Use the PEMDAS mnemonic. Start with parentheses. Then, do multiplication/division from left to right. Finally, do addition/subtraction from left to right.

$8 \times (3 + 6) \div 3 - 2 + 5$

$8 \times 9 \div 3 - 2 + 5$

$72 \div 3 - 2 + 5$

$24 - 2 + 5$

$22 + 5$

27

Let's Review!

- The multiplication table is important to memorize for both multiplying and dividing small whole numbers (up to about 12).
- Multiplication and division of large numbers by hand typically requires the multiplication and division algorithms.
- Multiplying and dividing signed numbers follows two simple rules: If the numbers have the same sign, the product or quotient is positive. If they have different signs, the product or quotient is negative.
- When evaluating expressions with several operations, carefully follow the order of operations; PEMDAS is a helpful mnemonic.

FACTORS AND MULTIPLES

This lesson shows the relationship between factors and multiples of a number. In addition, it introduces prime and composite numbers and demonstrates how to use prime factorization to determine all the factors of a number.

Factors of a Number

BE CAREFUL!

The term *factor* can mean any number being multiplied by another number, or it can mean a number by which another number is divisible. The two uses are related but slightly different. The context will generally clarify which meaning applies.

Multiplication converts two or more factors into a product. A given number, however, may be the product of more than one combination of factors; for example, 12 is the product of 3 and 4 and the product of 2 and 6. Limiting consideration to the set of whole numbers, a **factor of a number** (call it x) is a whole number whose product with any other whole number is equal to x. For instance, 2 is a factor of 12 because $12 \div 2$ is a whole number (6). Another way of expressing it is that 2 is a factor of 12 because 12 is **divisible** by 2.

A whole number always has at least two factors: 1 and itself. That is, for any whole number y, $1 \times y = y$. To test whether one number is a factor of a second number, divide the second by the first. If the quotient is whole, it is a factor. If the quotient is not whole (or it has a remainder), it is not a factor.

Example

Which number is not a factor of 54?

A. 1 B. 2 C. 4 D. 6

The correct answer is **C**. A number is a factor of another number if the latter is divisible by the former. The number 54 is divisible by 1 because $54 \times 1 = 54$, and it is divisible by 2 because $27 \times 2 = 54$. Also, $6 \times 9 = 54$. But $54 \div 4 = 13.5$ (or 13R2). Therefore, 4 is not a factor.

Multiples of a Number

Multiples of a number are related to factors of a number. A **multiple of a number** is that number's product with some integer. For example, if a hardware store sells a type of screw that only comes in packs of 20, customers must buy these screws in *multiples* of 20: that is, 20, 40, 60, 80, and so on. (Technically, 0 is also a multiple.) These numbers are equal to 20×1, 20×2, 20×3, 20×4, and so on. Similarly, measurements in feet represent multiples of 12 inches. A (whole-number) measurement in feet would be equivalent to 12 inches, 24 inches, 36 inches, and so on.

When counting by twos or threes, multiples are used. But because the multiples of a number are the product of that number with the integers, multiples can also be negative. For the number 2, the multiples are the set {..., −6, −4, −2, 0, 2, 4, 6,...}, where the ellipsis dots indicate that the set continues the pattern indefinitely in both directions. Also, the number can be any real number: the multiples of π (approximately 3.14) are {..., −3π, −2π, −1π, 0, 1π, 2π, 3π,...}. Note that the notation 2π, for example, means 2 × π.

The positive multiples (along with 0) of a whole number are all numbers for which that whole number is a factor. For instance, the positive multiples of 5 are 0, 5, 10, 15, 20, 25, 30, and so on. That full set contains all (whole) numbers for which 5 is a factor. Thus, one number is a multiple of a second number if the second number is a factor of the first.

Example

If a landowner subdivides a parcel of property into multiples of 7 acres, how many acres can a buyer purchase?

A. 1 B. 15 C. 29 D. 42

The correct answer is **D.** Because the landowner subdivides the property into multiples of 7 acres, a buyer must choose an acreage from the list 7 acres, 14 acres, 21 acres, and so on. That list includes 42 acres. Another way to solve the problem is to find which answer is divisible by 7 (that is, which number has 7 as a factor).

Prime and Composite Numbers

For some real-world applications, such as cryptography, factors and multiples play an important role. One important way to classify whole numbers is by whether they are prime or composite. A **prime** number is any whole (or natural) number greater than 1 that has only itself and 1 as factors. The smallest example is 2: because 2 only has 1 and 2 as factors, it is prime. **Composite** numbers have at least one factor other than 1 and themselves. The smallest composite number is 4: in addition to 1 and 4, it has 2 as a factor.

BE CAREFUL!

Avoid the temptation to call 1 a prime number. Although it only has itself and 1 as factors, those factors are the same number. Hence, 1 is fundamentally different from the prime numbers, which start at 2.

Determining whether a number is prime can be extremely difficult—hence its value in cryptography. One simple test that works for some numbers is to check whether the number is even or odd. An **even number** is divisible by 2; an **odd number** is not. To determine whether a number is even or odd, look at the last (rightmost) digit. If that digit is even (0, 2, 4, 6, or 8), the number is even. Otherwise, it is odd. Another simple test works for multiples of 3. Add all the digits in the number. If the sum is divisible by 3, the original number is also divisible by 3. This rule can be successively applied multiple times until the sum of digits is manageable. That number is then composite.

Example

Which number is prime?

A. 6 B. 16 C. 61 D. 116

The correct answer is **C.** When applicable, the easiest way to identify a number greater than 2 as composite rather than prime is to check whether it is even. All even numbers greater than 2 are composite. By elimination, 61 is prime.

Prime Factorization

Determining whether a number is prime, even for relatively small numbers (less than 100), can be difficult. One tool that can help both solve this problem and identify all factors of a number is **prime factorization.** One way to do prime factorization is to make a **factor tree.**

The procedure below demonstrates the process.

STEP BY STEP

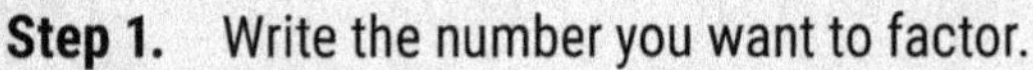

Step 1. Write the number you want to factor.

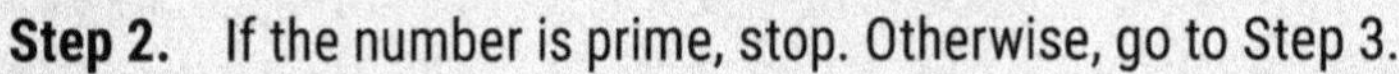

Step 2. If the number is prime, stop. Otherwise, go to Step 3.

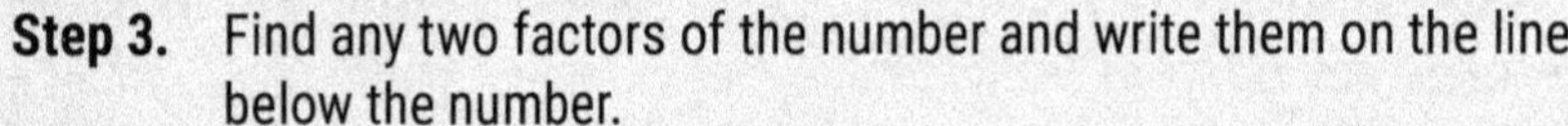

Step 3. Find any two factors of the number and write them on the line below the number.

Step 4. "Connect" the factors and the number using line segments. The result will look somewhat like an inverted tree, particularly as the process continues.

Step 5. Repeat Steps 2–4 for all composite factors in the tree.

The numbers in the factor tree are either "branches" (if they are connected downward to other numbers) or "leaves" (if they have no further downward connections). The leaves constitute all the prime factors of the original number: when multiplied together, their product is that number. Moreover, any product of two or more of the leaves is a factor of the original number. Thus, using prime factorization helps find any and all factors of a number, although the process can be tedious when performed by hand (particularly for large numbers). Below is a factor tree for the number 96. All the leaves are circled for emphasis.

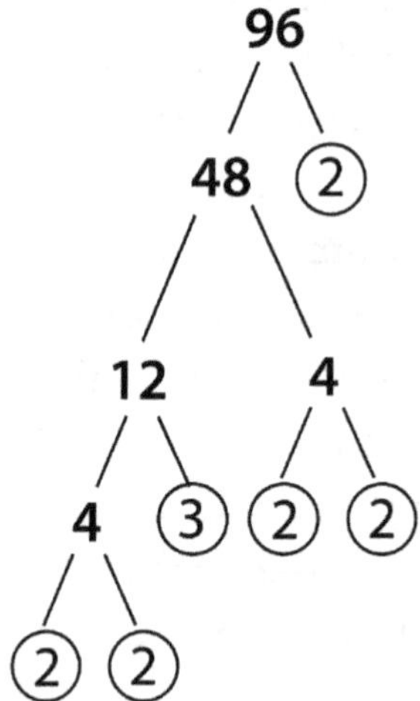

2x2x3x2x2x2=96

Example

Which list includes all the unique prime factors of 84?

A. 2, 3, 7 B. 3, 4, 7 C. 3, 5, 7 D. 1, 2, 3, 7

The correct answer is **A.** One approach is to find the prime factorization of 84. The factor tree shows that $84 = 2 \times 2 \times 3 \times 7$. Alternatively, note that answer D includes 1, which is not prime. Answer B includes 4, which is a composite number. Since answer C includes 5, which is not a factor of 84, the only possible answer is A.

Let's Review!

- A whole number is divisible by all of its factors, which are also whole numbers by definition.
- Multiples of a number are all possible products of that number and the integers.
- A prime number is a whole number greater than 1 that has no factors other than itself and 1.
- A composite number is a whole number greater than 1 that is not prime (that is, it has factors other than itself and 1).
- Even numbers are divisible by 2; odd numbers are not.
- Prime factorization yields all the prime factors of a number. The factor-tree method is one way to determine prime factorization.

STANDARDS OF MEASURE

This lesson discusses the conversion within and between the standard system and the metric system and between 12-hour clock time and military time.

Length Conversions

The basic units of measure of length in the standard measurement system are inches, feet, yards, and miles. There are 12 inches (in.) in 1 foot (ft.), 3 feet (ft.) in 1 yard (yd.), and 5,280 feet (ft.) in 1 mile (mi.).

The basic unit of measure of metric length is meters. There are 1,000 millimeters (mm), 100 centimeters (cm), and 10 decimeters (dm) in 1 meter (m). There are 10 meters (m) in 1 dekameter (dam), 100 meters (m) in 1 hectometer (hm), and 1,000 meters (m) in 1 kilometer (km).

BE CAREFUL!
There are some cases where multiple conversions must be performed to determine the correct units.

To convert from one unit to the other, multiply by the appropriate factor.

Examples

1. **Convert 27 inches to feet.**

   A. 2 feet B. 2.25 feet C. 3 feet D. 3.25 feet

   The correct answer is **B**. The correct solution is 2.25 feet. 27 in $\times \frac{1\text{ ft}}{12\text{ in}} = \frac{27}{12} = 2.25$ ft.

2. **Convert 67 millimeters to centimeters.**

   A. 0.0067 centimeters
   B. 0.067 centimeters
   C. 0.67 centimeters
   D. 6.7 centimeters

   The correct answer is **D**. The correct solution is 6.7 centimeters. 67 mm $\times \frac{1\text{ cm}}{10\text{ mm}} = \frac{67}{10} = 6.7$ cm.

Volume and Weight Conversions

There are volume conversion factors for standard and metric volumes.

The volume conversions for standard volume are shown in the table.

Measurement	Conversion
Pints (pt.) and fluid ounces (fl. oz.)	1 pint equals 16 fluid ounces
Quarts (qt.) and pints (pt.)	1 quart equals 2 pints
Quarts (qt.) and gallons (gal.)	1 gallon equals 4 quarts

The basic unit of volume for the metric system is liters. There are 1,000 milliliters (mL) in 1 liter (L) and 1,000 liters (L) in 1 kiloliter (kL).

There are weight conversion factors for standard and metric weights.

The basic unit of weight for the standard measurement system is pounds. There are

16 ounces (oz.) in 1 pound (lb.) and

2,000 pounds (lb.) in 1 ton (T).

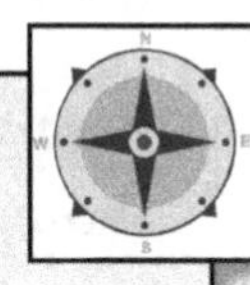

KEEP IN MIND

The conversions within the metric system are multiples of 10.

The basic unit of weight for the metric system is grams.

Measurement	Conversion
Milligrams (mg) and grams (g)	1,000 milligrams equals 1 gram
Centigrams (cg) and grams (g)	100 centigrams equals 1 gram
Kilograms (kg) and grams (g)	1 kilogram equals 1,000 grams
Metric tons (t) and kilograms (kg)	1 metric ton equals 1,000 kilograms

Examples

1. **Convert 8 gallons to pints.**

   A. 1 pint B. 4 pints C. 16 pints D. 64 pints

   The correct answer is **D.** The correct solution is 64 pints. $8 \text{ gal} \times \frac{4 \text{ qt}}{1 \text{ gal}} \times \frac{2 \text{ pt}}{1 \text{ qt}} = 64 \text{ pt.}$

2. **Convert 7.5 liters to milliliters.**

   A. 75 milliliters B. 750 milliliters C. 7,500 milliliters D. 75,000 milliliters

   The correct answer is **C.** The correct solution is 7,500 milliliters. $7.5 \text{ L} \times \frac{1{,}000 \text{ mL}}{1 \text{ L}} = 7{,}500 \text{ mL.}$

3. **Convert 12.5 pounds to ounces.**

   A. 142 ounces B. 150 ounces C. 192 ounces D. 200 ounces

   The correct answer is **D.** The correct solution is 200 ounces. $12.5 \text{ lb} \times \frac{16 \text{ oz}}{1 \text{ lb}} = 200 \text{ oz.}$

4. **Convert 84 grams to centigrams.**

   A. 0.84 centigrams B. 8.4 centigrams C. 840 centigrams D. 8,400 centigrams

   The correct answer is **D.** The correct solution is 8,400 centigrams. $84 \text{ g} \times \frac{100 \text{ cg}}{1 \text{ g}} = 8{,}400 \text{ cg.}$

Conversions between Standard and Metric Systems

The table shows the common conversions of length, volume, and weight between the standard and metric systems.

Measurement	Conversion
Centimeters (cm) and inches (in.)	2.54 centimeters equals 1 inch
Meters (m) and feet (ft.)	1 meter equals 3.28 feet
Kilometers (km) and miles (mi.)	1.61 kilometers equals 1 mile
Quarts (qt.) and liters (L)	1.06 quarts equals 1 liter
Liters (L) and gallons (gal.)	3.79 liters equals 1 gallon
Grams (g) and ounces (oz.)	28.3 grams equals 1 ounce
Kilograms (kg) and pounds (lb.)	1 kilogram equals 2.2 pounds

There are many additional conversion factors, but this lesson uses only the common ones. Most factors have been rounded to the nearest hundredth for accuracy.

STEP BY STEP

Step 1. Choose the appropriate conversion factor within each system, if necessary.

Step 2. Choose the appropriate conversion factor from the standard and metric conversion.

Step 3. Multiply and simplify to the nearest hundredth.

Examples

1. **Convert 12 inches to centimeters.**

   A. 4.72 centimeters B. 14.54 centimeters C. 28.36 centimeters D. 30.48 centimeters

   The correct answer is **D**. The correct solution is 30.48 centimeters. $12 \text{ in} \times \frac{2.54 \text{ cm}}{1 \text{ in}} = 30.48 \text{ cm}$.

2. **Convert 8 kilometers to feet.**

   A. 13,118.01 feet B. 26,236.02 feet C. 34,003.20 feet D. 68,006.40 feet

   The correct answer is **B**. The correct solution is 26,236.02 feet. $8 \text{ km} \times \frac{1 \text{ mi}}{1.61 \text{ km}} \times \frac{5{,}280 \text{ ft}}{1 \text{ mi}} = \frac{42{,}240}{1.61} = 26{,}236.02 \text{ ft}$.

3. **Convert 2 gallons to milliliters.**

   A. 527 milliliters B. 758 milliliters C. 5,270 milliliters D. 7,580 milliliters

   The correct answer is **D**. The correct solution is 7,580 milliliters.
   $2 \text{ gal} \times \frac{3.79 \text{ L}}{1 \text{ gal}} \times \frac{1{,}000 \text{ mL}}{1 \text{ L}} = 7{,}580 \text{ mL}$.

4. **Convert 16 kilograms to pounds.**

A. 7.27 pounds B. 18.2 pounds C. 19.27 pounds D. 35.2 pounds

The correct answer is **D**. The correct solution is 35.2 pounds. $16 \text{ kg} \times \frac{2.2 \text{ lb}}{1 \text{ kg}} = 35.2 \text{ lb}$.

Time Conversions

Two ways to keep time are 12-hour clock time using a.m. and p.m. and military time based on a 24-hour clock. Keep these three key points in mind:

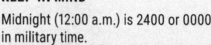

KEEP IN MIND

Midnight (12:00 a.m.) is 2400 or 0000 in military time.

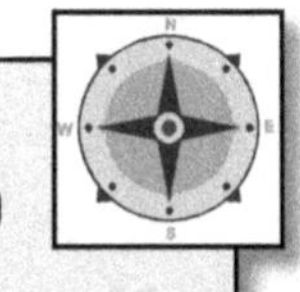

- The hours from 1:00 a.m. to 12:59 p.m. are the same in both methods. For example, 9:15 a.m. in 12-hour clock time is 0915 in military time.
- From 1:00 p.m. to 11:59 p.m., add 12 hours to obtain military time. For example, 4:07 p.m. in 12-hour clock time is 1607 in military time.
- From 12:01 a.m. to 12:59 a.m. in 12-hour clock time, military time is from 0001 to 0059.

Example

Identify 9:27 p.m. in military time.

A. 0927 B. 1927 C. 2127 D. 2427

The correct answer is **C**. The correct solution is 2127. Add 1200 to the time, 1200 + 927 = 2127.

Let's Review!

- To convert from one unit to another, choose the appropriate conversion factors.
- In many cases, it is necessary to use multiple conversion factors.

Chapter 5 Number and Quantity Practice Quiz

1. **Evaluate the expression 8 – 27.**
   A. –35
   B. –19
   C. 0
   D. 19

2. **Evaluate the expression 102 + 3 + 84 + 27.**
   A. 105
   B. 216
   C. 250
   D. 513

3. **How much change should a customer expect if she is buying a $53 item and hands the cashier two $50 bills?**
   A. $3
   B. $47
   C. $57
   D. $100

4. **When dealing with a series of multiplication and division operations, which is the correct approach to evaluating them?**
   A. Evaluate all division operations first.
   B. Evaluate the expression from left to right.
   C. Evaluate all multiplication operations first.
   D. None of the above.

5. **Evaluate the expression 28 × 43.**
   A. 71
   B. 196
   C. 1,204
   D. 1,960

6. **Evaluate the expression 3 + 1 – 5 + 2 – 6.**
   A. –9
   B. –5
   C. 0
   D. 17

7. **Which number is a factor of 128?**
   A. 3
   B. 6
   C. 12
   D. 16

8. **How many prime factors does 42 have?**
   A. 1
   B. 2
   C. 3
   D. 4

9. **If a factor tree for a prime factorization has four leaves—3, 2, 5, and 7—what is the number being factored?**
   A. 7
   B. 5
   C. 210
   D. Not enough information

10. **Convert 16,000 ounces to tons.**
    A. 0.5 ton
    B. 1 ton
    C. 1.5 tons
    D. 2 tons

11. **Convert 99 meters to kilometers.**
    A. 0.0099 kilometers
    B. 0.099 kilometers
    C. 0.9 centimeters
    D. 9.9 centimeters

12. **Identify 12:45 a.m. in military time.**
    A. 0045
    B. 0145
    C. 1245
    D. 1345

Chapter 5 Number and Quantity Practice Quiz — Answer Key

1. B. The correct solution is −19. Because the subtraction algorithm does not apply directly in this case (the first number is smaller than the second), first use the rule that $x - y = -(y - x)$. So, $8 - 27 = -(27 - 8)$. Applying the algorithm to $27 - 8$ yields 19, then $-(27 - 8) = -19$. **See Lesson: Basic Addition and Subtraction.**

2. B. The correct solution is 216. Use the addition algorithm. Add the numbers two at a time or all at once. The latter approach will involve two carry digits. **See Lesson: Basic Addition and Subtraction.**

3. B. The correct solution is $47. The customer gives the cashier $100, which is the sum of $50 and $50. To find out how much change she receives, calculate the difference between $100 and $53, which is $47. **See Lesson: Basic Addition and Subtraction.**

4. B. Multiplication and division have equivalent priority in the order of operations. In this case, the expression must be evaluated from left to right. **See Lesson: Basic Multiplication and Division.**

5. C. Use the multiplication algorithm. It involves adding 84 and 1,120 to get the product of 1,204. **See Lesson: Basic Multiplication and Division.**

6. B. This expression only involves addition and subtraction, but its evaluation must go from left to right. **See Lesson: Basic Multiplication and Division.**

$3 + 1 - 5 + 2 - 6$

$4 - 5 + 2 - 6$

$(-1) + 2 - 6$

$1 - 6$

-5

7. D. To determine whether a number is a factor of another number, divide the second number by the first number. If the quotient is whole, the first number is a factor. In this case, 128 is only divisible by 16. **See Lesson: Factors and Multiples.**

8. C. The prime factorization—for example, using a factor tree—shows that 42 has the prime factors 2, 3, and 7 because $2 \times 3 \times 7 = 42$. **See Lesson: Factors and Multiples.**

9. C. The number being factored in a prime factorization is the product of all its prime factors. The leaves in a factor tree are these prime factors. Therefore, the number is their product. In this case, it is $3 \times 2 \times 5 \times 7 = 210$. **See Lesson: Factors and Multiples.**

10. A. The correct solution is 0.5 ton.
$16{,}000 \text{ oz} \times \frac{1 \text{ lb}}{16 \text{ oz}} \times \frac{1\text{T}}{2{,}000 \text{ lb}} = \frac{16{,}000}{32{,}000} = 0.5 \text{ T}$. **See Lesson: Standards of Measure.**

11. B. The correct solution is 0.099 kilometers. $99 \text{ m} \times \frac{1 \text{ km}}{1{,}000 \text{ m}} = \frac{99}{1{,}000} = 0.099 \text{ km}$. **See Lesson: Standards of Measure.**

12. A. The correct solution is 0045. Subtract 1200 from the time, 1245 – 1200 = 0045. **See Lesson: Standards of Measure.**

CHAPTER 6 ALGEBRA

DECIMALS AND FRACTIONS

This lesson introduces the basics of decimals and fractions. It also demonstrates changing decimals to fractions, changing fractions to decimals, and converting between fractions, decimals, and percentages.

Introduction to Fractions

A fraction represents part of a whole number. The top number of a fraction is the **numerator,** and the bottom number of a fraction is the **denominator.** The numerator is smaller than the denominator for a **proper fraction.** The numerator is larger than the denominator for an **improper fraction.**

Proper Fractions	Improper Fractions
$\frac{2}{5}$	$\frac{5}{2}$
$\frac{7}{12}$	$\frac{12}{7}$
$\frac{19}{20}$	$\frac{20}{19}$

KEEP IN MIND

When comparing fractions, the denominators of the fractions must be the same.

An improper fraction can be changed to a **mixed number**. A mixed number is a whole number and a proper fraction. To write an improper fraction as a mixed number, divide the denominator into the numerator. The result is the whole number. The remainder is the numerator of the proper fraction, and the value of the denominator does not change. For example, $\frac{5}{2}$ is $2\frac{1}{2}$ because 2 goes into 5 twice with a remainder of 1. To write an improper fraction as a mixed number, multiply the whole number by the denominator and add the result to the numerator. The results become the new numerator. For example, $2\frac{1}{2}$ is $\frac{5}{2}$ because 2 times 2 plus 1 is 5 for the new numerator.

When comparing fractions, the denominators must be the same. Then, look at the numerator to determine which fraction is larger. If the fractions have different denominators, then a **least common denominator** must be found. This number is the smallest number that can be divided evenly into the denominators of all fractions being compared.

To determine the largest fraction from the group $\frac{1}{3}, \frac{3}{5}, \frac{2}{3}, \frac{2}{5}$, the first step is to find a common denominator. In this case, the least common denominator is 15 because 3 times 5 and 5 times 3 is 15. The second step is to convert the fractions to a denominator of 15.

The fractions with a denominator of 3 have the numerator and denominator multiplied by 5, and the fractions with a denominator of 5 have the numerator and denominator multiplied by 3, as shown below:

$$\frac{1}{3} \times \frac{5}{5} = \frac{5}{15}, \frac{3}{5} \times \frac{3}{3} = \frac{9}{15}, \frac{2}{3} \times \frac{5}{5} = \frac{10}{15}, \frac{2}{5} \times \frac{3}{3} = \frac{6}{15}$$

Now, the numerators can be compared. The largest fraction is $\frac{2}{3}$ because it has a numerator of 10 after finding the common denominator.

Examples

1. **Which fraction is the least?**

   A. $\frac{3}{5}$ B. $\frac{3}{4}$ C. $\frac{1}{5}$ D. $\frac{1}{4}$

   The correct answer is **C**. The correct solution is $\frac{1}{5}$ because it has the smallest numerator compared to the other fractions with the same denominator. The fractions with a common denominator of 20 are $\frac{3}{5} = \frac{12}{20}, \frac{3}{4} = \frac{15}{20}, \frac{1}{5} = \frac{4}{20}, \frac{1}{4} = \frac{5}{20}$.

2. **Which fraction is the greatest?**

   A. $\frac{5}{6}$ B. $\frac{1}{2}$ C. $\frac{2}{3}$ D. $\frac{1}{6}$

   The correct answer is **A**. The correct solution is $\frac{5}{6}$ because it has the largest numerator compared to the other fractions with the same denominator. The fractions with a common denominator of 6 are $\frac{5}{6} = \frac{5}{6}, \frac{1}{2} = \frac{3}{6}, \frac{2}{3} = \frac{4}{6}, \frac{1}{6} = \frac{1}{6}$.

Introduction to Decimals

A **decimal** is a number that expresses part of a whole. Decimals show a portion of a number after a decimal point. Each number to the left and right of the decimal point has a specific place value. Identify the place values for 645.3207.

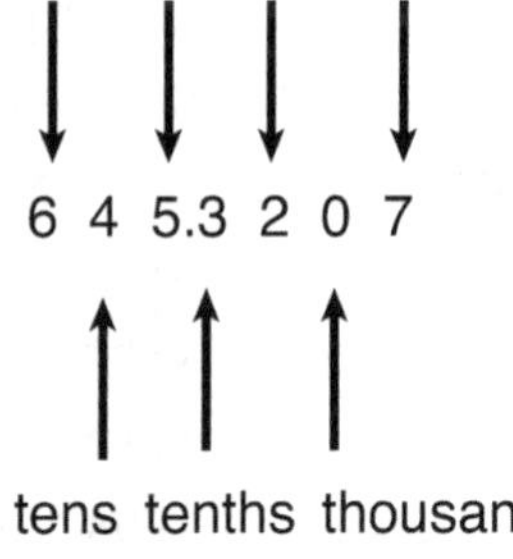

When comparing decimals, compare the numbers in the same place value. For example, determine the greatest decimal from the group 0.4, 0.41, 0.39, and 0.37. In these numbers, there is a value to the right of the decimal point. Comparing the tenths places, the numbers with 4 tenths (0.4 and 0.41) are greater than the numbers with three tenths (0.39 and 0.37).

0.4

0.41

0.39

0.37

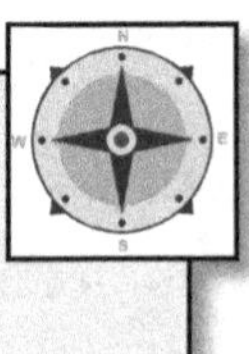

KEEP IN MIND

When comparing decimals, compare the place value where the numbers are different.

Then, compare the hundredths in the 4 tenths numbers. The value of 0.41 is greater because there is a 1 in the hundredths place versus a 0 in the hundredths place.

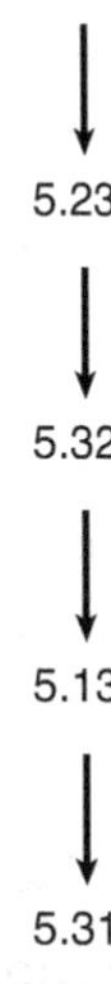

Here is another example: determine the least decimal of the group 5.23, 5.32, 5.13, and 5.31. In this group, the ones value is 5 for all numbers. Then, comparing the tenths values, 5.13 is the smallest number because it is the only value with 1 tenth.

Examples

1. **Which decimal is the greatest?**

   A. 0.07 B. 0.007 C. 0.7 D. 0.0007

   The correct answer is **C.** The solution is 0.7 because it has the largest place value in the tenths.

2. **Which decimal is the least?**

   A. 0.0413 B. 0.0713 C. 0.0513 D. 0.0613

   The correct answer is **A.** The correct solution is 0.0413 because it has the smallest place value in the hundredths place.

Changing Decimals and Fractions

Three steps change a decimal to a fraction.

STEP BY STEP

Step 1. Write the decimal divided by 1 with the decimal as the numerator and 1 as the denominator.

Step 2. Multiply the numerator and denominator by 10 for every number after the decimal point. (For example, if there is 1 decimal place, multiply by 10. If there are 2 decimal places, multiply by 100).

Step 3. Reduce the fraction completely.

To change the decimal 0.37 to a fraction, start by writing the decimal as a fraction with a denominator of one, $\frac{0.37}{1}$. Because there are two decimal places, multiply the numerator and denominator by 100, $\frac{0.37 \times 100}{1 \times 100} = \frac{37}{100}$. The fraction does not reduce, so $\frac{37}{100}$ is 0.37 in fraction form.

Similarly, to change the decimal 2.4 to a fraction start by writing the decimal as a fraction with a denominator of one, $\frac{0.4}{1}$, and ignore the whole number. Because there is one decimal place, multiply the numerator and denominator by 10, $\frac{0.4 \times 10}{1 \times 10} = \frac{4}{10}$. The fraction does reduce: $2\frac{4}{10} = 2\frac{2}{5}$ is 2.4 in fraction form.

The decimal $0.\overline{3}$ as a fraction is $\frac{0.\overline{3}}{1}$. In the case of a repeating decimal, let $n = 0.\overline{3}$ *and* $10n = 3.\overline{3}$. Then, $10n–n = 3.\overline{3}–0.\overline{3}$, resulting in $9n = 3$ and solution of $n = \frac{3}{9} = \frac{1}{3}$. The decimal $0.\overline{3}$ is $\frac{1}{3}$ as a fraction.

Examples

1. **Change 0.38 to a fraction. Simplify completely.**

   A. $\frac{3}{10}$ B. $\frac{9}{25}$ C. $\frac{19}{50}$ D. $\frac{2}{5}$

   The correct answer is **C.** The correct solution is $\frac{19}{50}$ because $\frac{0.38}{1} = \frac{38}{100} = \frac{19}{50}$.

2. **Change $1.\overline{1}$ to a fraction. Simplify completely.**

   A. $1\frac{1}{11}$ B. $1\frac{1}{9}$ C. $1\frac{1}{6}$ D. $1\frac{1}{3}$

   The correct answer is **B.** The correct solution is $1\frac{1}{9}$. Let $n = 1.\overline{1}$ and $10n = 11.\overline{1}$. Then, $10n–n = 11.\overline{1}–1.\overline{1}$, resulting in $9n = 10$ and solution of $n = \frac{10}{9} = 1\frac{1}{9}$.

Two steps change a fraction to a decimal.

STEP BY STEP

Step 1. Divide the denominator by the numerator. Add zeros after the decimal point as needed.

Step 2. Complete the process when there is no remainder or the decimal is repeating.

To convert $\frac{1}{5}$ to a decimal, rewrite $\frac{1}{5}$ as a long division problem and add zeros after the decimal point, $1.0 \div 5$. Complete the long division and $\frac{1}{5}$ as a decimal is 0.2. The division is complete because there is no remainder.

To convert $\frac{8}{9}$ to a decimal, rewrite $\frac{8}{9}$ as a long division problem and add zeros after the decimal point, $8.00 \div 9$. Complete the long division, and $\frac{8}{9}$ as a decimal is $0.\overline{8}$. The process is complete because the decimal is complete.

To rewrite the mixed number $2\frac{3}{4}$ as a decimal, the fraction needs changed to a decimal. Rewrite $\frac{3}{4}$ as a long division problem and add zeros after the decimal point, $3.00 \div 4$. The whole number is needed for the answer and is not included in the long division. Complete the long division, and $2\frac{3}{4}$ as a decimal is 2.75.

Examples

1. **Change $\frac{9}{10}$ to a decimal. Simplify completely.**

   A. 0.75 B. 0.8 C. 0.85 D. 0.9

   The correct answer is **D**. The correct answer is 0.9 because $\frac{9}{10} = 9.0 \div 10 = 0.9$.

2. **Change $\frac{5}{6}$ to a decimal. Simplify completely.**

   A. 0.73 B. $0.7\overline{6}$ C. $0.8\overline{3}$ D. 0.86

   The correct answer is **C**. The correct answer is $0.8\overline{3}$ because $\frac{5}{6} = 5.000 \div 6 = 0.8\overline{3}$.

Convert among Fractions, Decimals, and Percentages

Fractions, decimals, and percentages can change forms, but they are equivalent values.

There are two ways to change a decimal to a percent. One way is to multiply the decimal by 100 and add a percent sign. 0.24 as a percent is 24%.

Another way is to move the decimal point two places to the right. The decimal 0.635 is 63.5% as a percent when moving the decimal point two places to the right.

Any decimal, including repeating decimals, can change to a percent. $0.\overline{3}$ as a percent is $0.\overline{3} \times 100 = 33.\overline{3}\%$.

Example

Write 0.345 as a percent.

A. 3.45%   B. 34.5%   C. 345%   D. 3450%

The correct answer is **B.** The correct answer is 34.5% because 0.345 as a percent is 34.5%.

There are two ways to change a percent to a decimal. One way is to remove the percent sign and divide the decimal by 100. For example, 73% as a decimal is 0.73.

Another way is to move the decimal point two places to the left. For example, 27.8% is 0.278 as a decimal when moving the decimal point two places to the left.

Any percent, including repeating percents, can change to a decimal. For example, $44.\overline{4}\%$ as a decimal is $44.\overline{4} \div 100 = 0.\overline{4}$.

Example

Write 131% as a decimal.

A. 0.131   B. 1.31   C. 13.1   D. 131

The correct answer is **B.** The correct answer is 1.31 because 131% as a decimal is 131 ÷ 100 = 1.31.

Two steps change a fraction to a percent.

STEP BY STEP

Step 1. Divide the numerator and denominator.

Step 2. Multiply by 100 and add a percent sign.

To change the fraction $\frac{3}{5}$ to a decimal, perform long division to get 0.6. Then, multiply 0.6 by 100 and $\frac{3}{5}$ is the same as 60%.

To change the fraction $\frac{7}{8}$ to a decimal, perform long division to get 0.875. Then, multiply 0.875 by 100 and $\frac{7}{8}$ is the same as 87.5%.

Fractions that are repeating decimals can also be converted to a percent. To change the fraction $\frac{2}{3}$ to a decimal, perform long division to get $0.\overline{6}$. Then, multiply $0.\overline{6}$ by 100 and the percent is $66.\overline{6}\%$.

Example

Write $2\frac{1}{8}$ as a percent.

A. 21.2%   B. 21.25%   C. 212%   D. 212.5%

The correct answer is **D.** The correct answer is 212.5% because $2\frac{1}{8}$ as a percent is 2.125 x 100 = 212.5%.

Two steps change a percent to a fraction.

STEP BY STEP

Step 1. Remove the percent sign and write the value as the numerator with a denominator of 100.

Step 2. Simplify the fraction.

Remove the percent sign from 45% and write as a fraction with a denominator of 100, $\frac{45}{100}$. The fraction reduces to $\frac{9}{20}$.

Remove the percent sign from 22.8% and write as a fraction with a denominator of 100, $\frac{22.8}{100}$. The fraction reduces to $\frac{228}{1000} = \frac{57}{250}$.

Repeating percentages can change to a fraction. Remove the percent sign from $16.\overline{6}\%$ and write as a fraction with a denominator of 100, $\frac{16.\overline{6}}{100}$. The fraction simplifies to $\frac{0.1\overline{6}}{1} = \frac{1}{6}$.

Example

Write 72% as a fraction.

A. $\frac{27}{50}$ B. $\frac{7}{10}$ C. $\frac{18}{25}$ D. $\frac{3}{4}$

The correct answer is **C**. The correct answer is $\frac{18}{25}$ because 72% as a fraction is $\frac{72}{100} = \frac{18}{25}$.

Let's Review!

- A fraction is a number with a numerator and a denominator. A fraction can be written as a proper fraction, an improper fraction, or a mixed number. Changing fractions to a common denominator enables you to determine the least or greatest fraction in a group of fractions.
- A decimal is a number that expresses part of a whole. By comparing the same place values, you can find the least or greatest decimal in a group of decimals.
- A number can be written as a fraction, a decimal, and a percent. These are equivalent values. Numbers can be converted between fractions, decimals, and percents by following a series of steps.

MULTIPLICATION AND DIVISION OF FRACTIONS

This lesson introduces how to multiply and divide fractions.

Multiplying a Fraction by a Fraction

The multiplication of fractions does not require changing any denominators like adding and subtracting fractions do. To multiply a fraction by a fraction, multiply the numerators together and multiply the denominators together. For example, $\frac{2}{3} \times \frac{4}{5}$ is $\frac{2 \times 4}{3 \times 5}$, which is $\frac{8}{15}$.

Sometimes, the final solution reduces. For example, $\frac{3}{5} \times \frac{1}{9} = \frac{3 \times 1}{5 \times 9} = \frac{3}{45}$. The fraction $\frac{3}{45}$ reduces to $\frac{1}{15}$.

Simplifying fractions can occur before completing the multiplication. In the previous problem, the numerator of 3 can be simplified with the denominator of 9: $\frac{\cancel{3}^{1}}{5} \times \frac{1}{\cancel{9}_{3}} = \frac{1}{15}$. This method of simplifying only occurs with the multiplication of fractions.

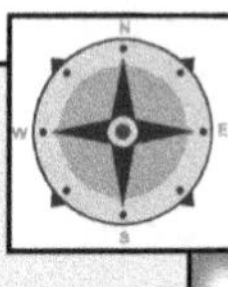

KEEP IN MIND

The product of multiplying a fraction by a fraction is always less than 1.

Examples

1. **Multiply $\frac{1}{2} \times \frac{3}{4}$.**

   A. $\frac{1}{4}$ B. $\frac{1}{2}$ C. $\frac{3}{8}$ D. $\frac{2}{3}$

   The correct answer is **C**. The correct solution is $\frac{3}{8}$ because $\frac{1}{2} \times \frac{3}{4} = \frac{3}{8}$.

2. **Multiply $\frac{2}{3} \times \frac{5}{6}$.**

   A. $\frac{1}{9}$ B. $\frac{5}{18}$ C. $\frac{5}{9}$ D. $\frac{7}{18}$

   The correct answer is **C**. The correct solution is $\frac{5}{9}$ because $\frac{2}{3} \times \frac{5}{6} = \frac{10}{18} = \frac{5}{9}$.

Multiply a Fraction by a Whole or Mixed Number

Multiplying a fraction by a whole or mixed number is similar to multiplying two fractions. When multiplying by a whole number, change the whole number to a fraction with a denominator of 1. Next, multiply the numerators together and the denominators together. Rewrite the final answer as a mixed number. For example: $\frac{9}{10} \times 3 = \frac{9}{10} \times \frac{3}{1} = \frac{27}{10} = 2\frac{7}{10}$.

When multiplying a fraction by a mixed number or multiplying two mixed numbers, the process is similar.

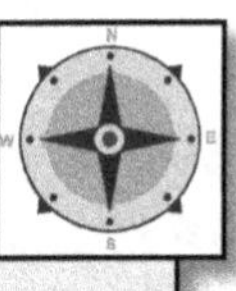

KEEP IN MIND

Always change a mixed number to an improper fraction when multiplying by a mixed number.

For example, multiply $\frac{10}{11} \times 3\frac{1}{2}$. Change the mixed number to an improper fraction, $\frac{10}{11} \times \frac{7}{2}$. Multiply the numerators together and multiply the denominators together, $\frac{70}{22}$. Write the improper fraction as a mixed number, $3\frac{4}{22}$. Reduce if necessary, $3\frac{2}{11}$.

This process can also be used when multiplying a whole number by a mixed number or multiplying two mixed numbers.

Examples

1. **Multiply $4 \times \frac{5}{6}$.**

   A. $\frac{5}{24}$ B. $2\frac{3}{4}$ C. $3\frac{1}{3}$ D. $4\frac{5}{6}$

   The correct answer is **C**. The correct solution is $3\frac{1}{3}$ because $\frac{4}{1} \times \frac{5}{6} = \frac{20}{6} = 3\frac{2}{6} = 3\frac{1}{3}$.

2. **Multiply $1\frac{1}{2} \times 1\frac{1}{6}$.**

   A. $1\frac{1}{12}$ B. $1\frac{1}{4}$ C. $1\frac{3}{8}$ D. $1\frac{3}{4}$

   The correct answer is **D**. The correct solution is $1\frac{3}{4}$ because $\frac{3}{2} \times \frac{7}{6} = \frac{21}{12} = 1\frac{9}{12} = 1\frac{3}{4}$.

Dividing a Fraction by a Fraction

Some basic steps apply when dividing a fraction by a fraction. The information from the previous two sections is applicable to dividing fractions.

STEP BY STEP

Step 1. Leave the first fraction alone.

Step 2. Find the reciprocal of the second fraction.

Step 3. Multiply the first fraction by the reciprocal of the second fraction.

Step 4. Rewrite the fraction as a mixed number and reduce the fraction completely.

Divide, $\frac{3}{10} \div \frac{1}{2}$. Find the reciprocal of the second fraction, which is $\frac{2}{1}$.

Now, multiply the fractions, $\frac{3}{10} \times \frac{2}{1} = \frac{6}{10}$. Reduce $\frac{6}{10}$ to $\frac{3}{5}$.

Divide, $\frac{4}{5} \div \frac{3}{8}$. Find the reciprocal of the second fraction, which is $\frac{8}{3}$.

Now, multiply the fractions, $\frac{4}{5} \times \frac{8}{3} = \frac{32}{15}$. Rewrite the fraction as a mixed number, $\frac{32}{15} = 2\frac{2}{15}$.

Examples

1. **Divide $\frac{1}{2} \div \frac{5}{6}$.**

   A. $\frac{5}{12}$ B. $\frac{3}{5}$ C. $\frac{5}{6}$ D. $1\frac{2}{3}$

   The correct answer is **B**. The correct solution is $\frac{3}{5}$ because $\frac{1}{2} \times \frac{6}{5} = \frac{6}{10} = \frac{3}{5}$.

2. **Divide $\frac{2}{3} \div \frac{3}{5}$.**

A. $\frac{2}{15}$ B. $\frac{2}{5}$ C. $1\frac{1}{15}$ D. $1\frac{1}{9}$

The correct answer is **D**. The correct solution is $1\frac{1}{9}$ because $\frac{2}{3} \times \frac{5}{3} = \frac{10}{9} = 1\frac{1}{9}$.

Dividing a Fraction and a Whole or Mixed Number

Some basic steps apply when dividing a fraction by a whole number or a mixed number.

STEP BY STEP

Step 1. Write any whole number as a fraction with a denominator of 1. Write any mixed numbers as improper fractions.

Step 2. Leave the first fraction (improper fraction) alone.

Step 3. Find the reciprocal of the second fraction.

Step 4. Multiply the first fraction by the reciprocal of the second fraction.

Step 5. Rewrite the fraction as a mixed number and reduce the fraction completely.

Divide, $\frac{3}{10} \div 3$. Rewrite the expression as $\frac{3}{10} \div \frac{3}{1}$. Find the reciprocal of the second fraction, which is $\frac{1}{3}$. Multiply the fractions, $\frac{3}{10} \times \frac{1}{3} = \frac{3}{30} = \frac{1}{10}$. Reduce $\frac{3}{30}$ to $\frac{1}{10}$.

Divide, $2\frac{4}{5} \div 1\frac{3}{8}$. Rewrite the expression as $\frac{14}{5} \div \frac{11}{8}$. Find the reciprocal of the second fraction, which is $\frac{8}{11}$.

Multiply the fractions, $\frac{14}{5} \times \frac{8}{11} = \frac{112}{55} = 2\frac{2}{55}$. Reduce $\frac{112}{55}$ to $2\frac{2}{55}$.

Examples

1. **Divide $\frac{2}{3} \div 4$.**

A. $\frac{1}{12}$ B. $\frac{1}{10}$ C. $\frac{1}{8}$ D. $\frac{1}{6}$

The correct answer is **D**. The correct answer is $\frac{1}{6}$ because $\frac{2}{3} \times \frac{1}{4} = \frac{2}{12} = \frac{1}{6}$.

2. **Divide $1\frac{5}{12} \div 1\frac{1}{2}$.**

A. $\frac{17}{18}$ B. $1\frac{5}{24}$ C. $1\frac{5}{6}$ D. $2\frac{1}{8}$

The correct answer is **A**. The correct answer is $\frac{17}{18}$ because $\frac{17}{12} \div \frac{3}{2} = \frac{17}{12} \times \frac{2}{3} = \frac{34}{36} = \frac{17}{18}$.

Let's Review!

- The process to multiply fractions is to multiply the numerators together and multiply the denominators together. When there is a mixed number, change the mixed number to an improper fraction before multiplying.
- The process to divide fractions is to find the reciprocal of the second fraction and multiply the fractions. As with multiplying, change any mixed numbers to improper fractions before dividing.

EQUATIONS WITH ONE VARIABLE

This lesson introduces how to solve linear equations and linear inequalities.

One-Step Linear Equations

A **linear equation** is an equation where two expressions are set equal to each other. The equation is in the form $ax + b = c$, where a is a non-zero constant and b and c are constants. The exponent on a linear equation is always 1, and there is no more than one solution to a linear equation.

There are four properties to help solve a linear equation.

Property	Definition	Example with Numbers	Example with Variables
Addition Property of Equality	Add the same number to both sides of the equation.	$x–3 = 9$ $x–3 + 3 = 9 + 3$ $x = 12$	$x–a = b$ $x–a + a = b + a$ $x = a + b$
Subtraction Property of Equality	Subtract the same number from both sides of the equation.	$x + 3 = 9$ $x + 3–3 = 9–3$ $x = 6$	$x + a = b$ $x + a–a = b–a$ $x = b–a$
Multiplication Property of Equality	Multiply both sides of the equation by the same number.	$\frac{x}{3} = 9$ $\frac{x}{3} \times 3 = 9 \times 3$ $x = 27$	$\frac{x}{a} = b$ $\frac{x}{a} \times a = b \times a$ $x = ab$
Division Property of Equality	Divide both sides of the equation by the same number.	$3x = 9$ $\frac{3x}{3} = \frac{9}{3}$ $x = 3$	$ax = b$ $\frac{ax}{a} = \frac{b}{a}$ $x = \frac{b}{a}$

Example

Solve the equation for the unknown, $\frac{w}{2} = –6$.

A. –12 B. –8 C. –4 D. –3

The correct answer is **A**. The correct solution is –12 because both sides of the equation are multiplied by 2.

Two-Step Linear Equations

A two-step linear equation is in the form $ax + b = c$, where a is a non-zero constant and b and c are constants. There are two basic steps in solving this equation.

STEP BY STEP

Step 1. Use addition and subtraction properties of an equation to move the variable to one side of the equation and all number terms to the other side of the equation.

Step 2. Use multiplication and division properties of an equation to remove the value in front of the variable.

Examples

1. **Solve the equation for the unknown, $\frac{x}{-2} - 3 = 5$.**

A. −16 B. −8 C. 8 D. 16

The correct answer is **A**. The correct solution is −16.

$\frac{x}{-2} = 8$	Add 3 to both sides of the equation.
$x = -16$	Multiply both sides of the equation by −2.

2. **Solve the equation for the unknown, $4x + 3 = 8$.**

A. −2 B. $-\frac{5}{4}$ C. $\frac{5}{4}$ D. 2

The correct answer is **C**. The correct solution is $\frac{5}{4}$.

$4x = 5$	Subtract 3 from both sides of the equation.
$x = \frac{5}{4}$	Divide both sides of the equation by 4.

3. **Solve the equation for the unknown w, $P = 21 + 2w$.**

A. $2P - 21 = w$ B. $\frac{P-21}{2} = w$ C. $2P + 21 = w$ D. $\frac{P+21}{2} = w$

The correct answer is **B**. The correct solution is $\frac{P-21}{2} = w$.

$P - 21 = 2w$	Subtract 21 from both sides of the equation.
$\frac{P-21}{2} = w$	Divide both sides of the equation by 2.

Multi-Step Linear Equations

In these basic examples of linear equations, the solution may be evident, but these properties demonstrate how to use an opposite operation to solve for a variable. Using these properties, there are three steps in solving a complex linear equation.

STEP BY STEP

Step 1. Simplify each side of the equation. This includes removing parentheses, removing fractions, and adding like terms.

Step 2. Use addition and subtraction properties of an equation to move the variable to one side of the equation and all number terms to the other side of the equation.

Step 3. Use multiplication and division properties of an equation to remove the value in front of the variable.

In Step 2, all of the variables may be placed on the left side or the right side of the equation. The examples in this lesson will place all of the variables on the left side of the equation.

When solving for a variable, apply the same steps as above. In this case, the equation is not being solved for a value, but for a specific variable.

Examples

1. **Solve the equation for the unknown, $2(4x + 1)–5 = 3–(4x–3)$.**

   A. $\frac{1}{4}$ B. $\frac{3}{4}$ C. $\frac{4}{3}$ D. 4

   The correct answer is **B**. The correct solution is $\frac{3}{4}$.

$8x + 2–5 = 3–4x + 3$	Apply the distributive property.
$8x–3 = –4x + 6$	Combine like terms on both sides of the equation.
$12x–3 = 6$	Add $4x$ to both sides of the equation.
$12x = 9$	Add 3 to both sides of the equation.
$x = \frac{3}{4}$	Divide both sides of the equation by 12.

2. **Solve the equation for the unknown, $\frac{2}{3}x + 2 = -\frac{1}{2}x + 2(x + 1)$.**

   A. 0 B. 1 C. 2 D. 3

   The correct answer is **A**. The correct solution is 0.

$\frac{2}{3}x + 2 = -\frac{1}{2}x + 2x + 2$	Apply the distributive property.
$4x + 12 = –3x + 12x + 12$	Multiply all terms by the least common denominator of 6 to eliminate the fractions.
$4x + 12 = 9x + 12$	Combine like terms on the right side of the equation.
$–5x = 12$	Subtract $9x$ from both sides of the equation.
$–5x = 0$	Subtract 12 from both sides of the equation.
$x = 0$	Divide both sides of the equation by –5.

3. **Solve the equation for the unknown for x, $y-y_1 = m(x-x_1)$.**

A. $y-y_1 + mx_1$ B. $my - my_1 + mx_1$ C. $\frac{y-y_1+x_1}{m}$ D. $\frac{y-y_1+mx_1}{m}$

The correct answer is **D**. The correct solution is $\frac{y-y_1+mx_1}{m}$

$y-y_1 = mx-mx_1$ Apply the distributive property.

$y-y_1 + mx_1 = mx$ Add mx_1 to both sides of the equation.

$\frac{y-y_1+mx_1}{m} = x$ Divide both sides of the equation by m.

Solving Linear Inequalities

A **linear inequality** is similar to a linear equation, but it contains an inequality sign (<, >, ≤, ≥). Many of the steps for solving linear inequalities are the same as for solving linear equations. The major difference is that the solution is an infinite number of values. There are four properties to help solve a linear inequality.

Property	Definition	Example
Addition Property of Inequality	Add the same number to both sides of the inequality.	$x-3 < 9$ $x-3+3 < 9+3$ $x < 12$
Subtraction Property of Inequality	Subtract the same number from both sides of the inequality.	$x+3 > 9$ $x+3-3 > 9-3$ $x > 6$
Multiplication Property of Inequality (when multiplying by a positive number)	Multiply both sides of the inequality by the same number.	$\frac{x}{3} \geq 9$ $\frac{x}{3} \times 3 \geq 9 \times 3$ $x \geq 27$
Division Property of Inequality (when multiplying by a positive number)	Divide both sides of the inequality by the same number.	$3x \leq 9$ $\frac{3x}{3} \leq \frac{9}{3}$ $x \leq 3$
Multiplication Property of Inequality (when multiplying by a negative number)	Multiply both sides of the inequality by the same number.	$\frac{x}{-3} \geq 9$ $\frac{x}{-3} \times -3 \geq 9 \times -3$ $x \leq -27$
Division Property of Inequality (when multiplying by a negative number)	Divide both sides of the inequality by the same number.	$-3x \leq 9$ $\frac{-3x}{-3} \leq \frac{9}{-3}$ $x \geq -3$

Multiplying or dividing both sides of the inequality by a negative number reverses the sign of the inequality.

In these basic examples, the solution may be evident, but these properties demonstrate how to use an opposite operation to solve for a variable. Using these properties, there are three steps in solving a complex linear inequality.

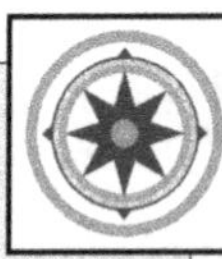

STEP BY STEP

Step 1. Simplify each side of the inequality. This includes removing parentheses, removing fractions, and adding like terms.

Step 2. Use addition and subtraction properties of an inequality to move the variable to one side of the equation and all number terms to the other side of the equation.

Step 3. Use multiplication and division properties of an inequality to remove the value in front of the variable. Reverse the inequality sign if multiplying or dividing by a negative number.

In Step 2, all of the variables may be placed on the left side or the right side of the inequality. The examples in this lesson will place all of the variables on the left side of the inequality.

Examples

1. **Solve the inequality for the unknown, $3(2+x) < 2(3x-1)$.**

A. $x < -\frac{8}{3}$ B. $x > -\frac{8}{3}$ C. $x < \frac{8}{3}$ D. $x > \frac{8}{3}$

The correct answer is **D**. The correct solution is $x > \frac{8}{3}$.

$6+3x < 6x-2$	Apply the distributive property.
$6-3x < -2$	Subtract $6x$ from both sides of the inequality.
$-3x < -8$	Subtract 6 from both sides of the inequality.
$x > \frac{8}{3}$	Divide both sides of the inequality by -3.

2. **Solve the inequality for the unknown, $\frac{1}{2}(2x-3) \geq \frac{1}{4}(2x+1)-2$.**

A. $x > -7$ B. $x > -3$ C. $x \geq -\frac{3}{2}$ D. $x \geq -\frac{1}{2}$

The correct answer is **D**. The correct solution is $x \geq -\frac{1}{2}$.

$2(2x-3) \geq 2x+1-8$	Multiply all terms by the least common denominator of 4 to eliminate the fractions.
$4x-6 \geq 2x+1-8$	Apply the distributive property.
$4x-6 \geq 2x-7$	Combine like terms on the right side of the inequality.
$2x-6 \geq -7$	Subtract $2x$ from both sides of the inequality.
$2x \geq -1$	Add 6 to both sides of the inequality.
$x \geq -\frac{1}{2}$	Divide both sides of the inequality by 2.

Let's Review!

- A linear equation is an equation with one solution. Using opposite operations solves a linear equation.
- The process to solve a linear equation or inequality is to eliminate fractions and parentheses and combine like terms on the same side of the sign. Then, solve the equation or inequality by using inverse operations.

EQUATIONS WITH TWO VARIABLES

This lesson discusses solving a system of linear equations by substitution, elimination, and graphing, as well as solving a simple system of a linear and a quadratic equation.

Solving a System of Equations by Substitution

A **system of linear equations** is a set of two or more linear equations in the same variables. A solution to the system is an ordered pair that is a solution in all the equations in the system. The ordered pair (1, -2) is a solution for the system of equations $\begin{matrix} 2x + y = 0 \\ -x + 2y = -5 \end{matrix}$ because $\begin{matrix} 2(1) + (-2) = 0 \\ -1 + 2(-2) = -5 \end{matrix}$ makes both equations true.

One way to solve a system of linear equations is by substitution.

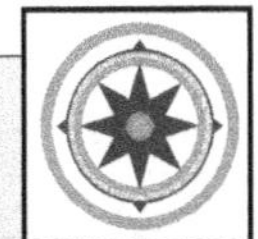

STEP BY STEP

Step 1. Solve one equation for one of the variables.

Step 2. Substitute the expression from Step 1 into the other equation and solve for the other variable.

Step 3. Substitute the value from Step 2 into one of the original equations and solve.

All systems of equations can be solved by substitution for any one of the four variables in the problem. The most efficient way of solving is locating the $1x$ or $1y$ in the equations because this eliminates the possibility of having fractions in the equations.

Examples

1. **Solve the system of equations, $\begin{matrix} x = y + 6 \\ 4x + 5y = 60 \end{matrix}$.**

A. (10, 12) B. (6, 12) C. (6, 4) D. (10, 4)

The correct answer is **D**. The correct solution is (10, 4).

The first equation is already solved for x.

$4(y + 6) + 5y = 60$	Substitute $y + 6$ in for x in the first equation.
$4y + 24 + 5y = 60$	Apply the distributive property.
$9y + 24 = 60$	Combine like terms on the left side of the equation.
$9y = 36$	Subtract 24 from both sides of the equation.
$y = 4$	Divide both sides of the equation by 9.
$x = 4 + 6$	Substitute 4 in the first equation for y.
$x = 10$	Simplify using order of operations.

2. **Solve the system of equations,** $\begin{matrix} 3x + 2y = 41 \\ -4x + y = -18 \end{matrix}$.

A. (5, 13) B. (6, 6) C. (7, 10) D. (10, 7)

The correct answer is **C**. The correct solution is (7, 10).

$y = 4x - 18$	Solve the second equation for y by adding $4x$ to both sides of the equation.
$3x + 2(4x - 18) = 41$	Substitute $4x - 18$ in for y in the first equation.
$3x + 8x - 36 = 41$	Apply the distributive property.
$11x - 36 = 41$	Combine like terms on the left side of the equation.
$11x = 77$	Add 36 to both sides of the equation.
$x = 7$	Divide both sides of the equation by 11.
$-4(7) + y = -18$	Substitute 7 in the second equation for x.
$-28 + y = -18$	Simplify using order of operations.
$y = 10$	Add 28 to both sides of the equation.

Solving a System of Equations by Elimination

Another way to solve a system of linear equations is by elimination.

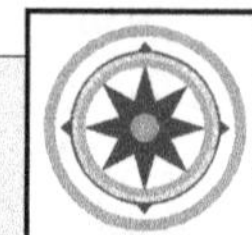

STEP BY STEP

Step 1. Multiply, if necessary, one or both equations by a constant so at least one pair of like terms has opposite coefficients.

Step 2. Add the equations to eliminate one of the variables.

Step 3. Solve the resulting equation.

Step 4. Substitute the value from Step 3 into one of the original equations and solve for the other variable.

All system of equations can be solved by the elimination method for any one of the four variables in the problem. One way of solving is locating the variables with opposite coefficients and adding the equations. Another approach is multiplying one equation to obtain opposite coefficients for the variables.

Examples

1. **Solve the system of equations,** $\begin{matrix} \mathbf{3x + 5y = 28} \\ \mathbf{-4x - 5y = -34} \end{matrix}$.

   A. (12, 6) B. (6, 12) C. (6, 2) D. (2, 6)

   The correct answer is **C**. The correct solution is (6, 2).

$-x = -6$	Add the equations.
$x = 6$	Divide both sides of the equation by -1.
$3(6) + 5y = 28$	Substitute 6 in the first equation for x.
$18 + 5y = 28$	Simplify using order of operations.
$5y = 10$	Subtract 18 from both sides of the equation.
$y = 2$	Divide both sides of the equation by 5.

2. **Solve the system of equations,** $\begin{matrix} \mathbf{-5x + 5y = 0} \\ \mathbf{2x - 3y = -3} \end{matrix}$.

   A. (2, 2) B. (3, 3) C. (6, 6) D. (9, 9)

   The correct answer is **B**. The correct solution is (3, 3).

$-10x + 10y = 0$	Multiply all terms in the first equation by 2.
$10x - 15y = -15$	Multiply all terms in the second equation by 5.
$-5y = -15$	Add the equations.
$y = 3$	Divide both sides of the equation by -5.
$2x - 3(3) = -3$	Substitute 3 in the second equation for y.
$2x - 9 = -3$	Simplify using order of operations.
$2x = 6$	Add 9 to both sides of the equation.
$x = 3$	Divide both sides of the equation by 2.

Solving a System of Equations by Graphing

Graphing is a third method of a solving system of equations. The point of intersection is the solution for the graph. This method is a great way to visualize each graph on a coordinate plane.

STEP BY STEP

Step 1. Graph each equation in the coordinate plane.

Step 2. Estimate the point of intersection.

Step 3. Check the point by substituting for x and y in each equation of the original system.

The best approach to graphing is to obtain each line in slope-intercept form. Then, graph the y-intercept and use the slope to find additional points on the line.

Example

Solve the system of equations by graphing, $\begin{matrix} y = 3x-2 \\ y = x-4 \end{matrix}$.

A.

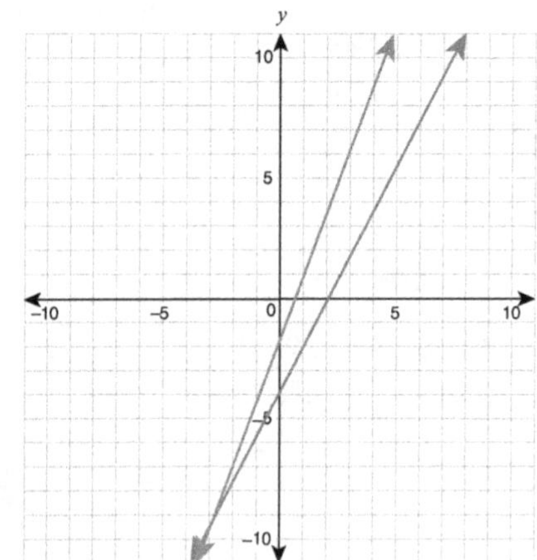

C.

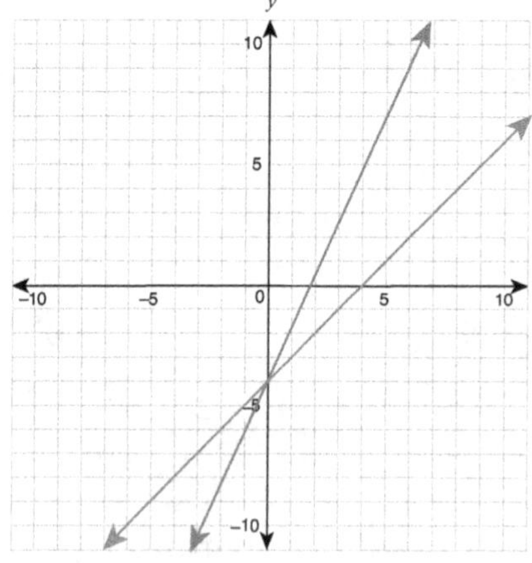

B.

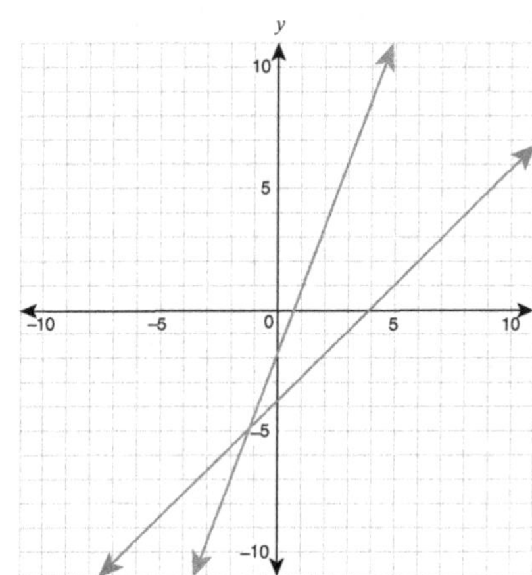

D.

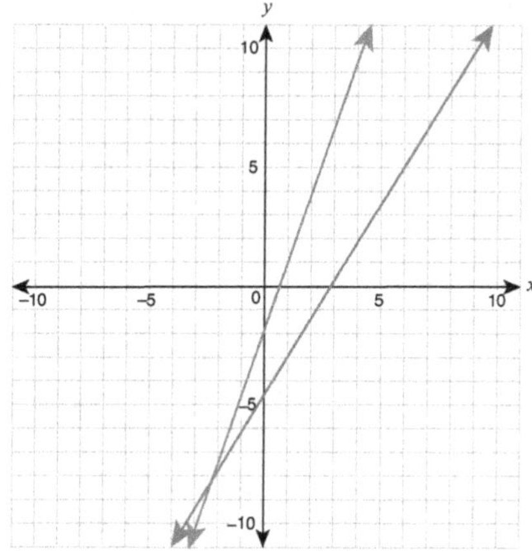

The correct answer is **B.** The correct graph has the two lines intersect at (-1, -5).

Solving a System of a Linear Equation and an Equation of a Circle

There are many other types of systems of equations. One example is the equation of a line $y = mx$ and the equation of a circle $x^2 + y^2 = r^2$ where r is the radius. With this system of equations, there can be two ordered pairs that intersect between the line and the circle. If there is one ordered pair, the line is tangent to the circle.

This system of equations is solved by substituting the expression mx in for y in the equation of a circle. Then, solve the equation for x. The values for x are substituted into the linear equation to find the value for y.

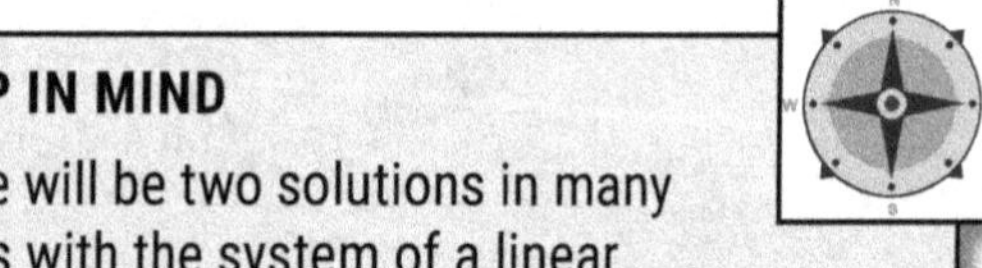

KEEP IN MIND

There will be two solutions in many cases with the system of a linear equation and an equation of a circle.

Example

Solve the system of equations, $\begin{matrix} y = -3x \\ x^2 + y^2 = 10 \end{matrix}$.

A. (1, 3) and (−1, −3)

B. (1, −3) and (−1, 3)

C. (−3, 10) and (3, −10)

D. (3, 10) and (−3, −10)

The correct answer is **B.** The correct solutions are (1, −3) and (−1, 3).

$x^2 + (-3x)^2 = 10$	Substitute $-3x$ in for y in the second equation.
$x^2 + 9x^2 = 10$	Apply the exponent.
$10x^2 = 10$	Combine like terms on the left side of the equation.
$x^2 = 1$	Divide both sides of the equation by 10.
$x = \pm 1$	Apply the square root to both sides of the equation.
$y = -3(1) = -3$	Substitute 1 in the first equation and multiply.
$y = -3(-1) = 3$	Substitute −1 in the first equation and multiply.

Let's Review!

- There are three ways to solve a system of equations: graphing, substitution, and elimination. Using any method will result in the same solution for the system of equations.
- Solving a system of a linear equation and an equation of a circle uses substitution and usually results in two solutions.

Solving Real-World Mathematical Problems

This lesson introduces solving real-world mathematical problems by using estimation and mental computation. This lesson also includes real-world applications involving integers, fractions, and decimals.

Estimating

Estimations are rough calculations of a solution to a problem. The most common use for estimation is completing calculations without a calculator or other tool. There are many estimation techniques, but this lesson focuses on integers, decimals, and fractions.

KEEP IN MIND

An estimation is an educated guess at the solution to a problem.

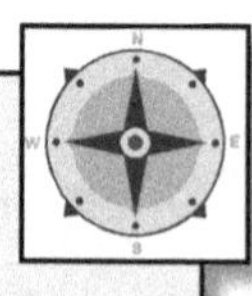

To round a whole number, round the value to the nearest ten or hundred. The number 142 rounds to 140 for the nearest ten and to 100 for the nearest hundred. The context of the problem determines the place value to which to round.

In most problems with fractions and decimals, the context of the problem requires rounding to the nearest whole number. Rounding these values makes calculation easier and provides an accurate estimation to the solution of the problem.

Other estimation strategies include the following:

- Using friendly or compatible numbers
- Using numbers that are easy to compute
- Adjusting numbers after rounding

Example

There are 168 hours in a week. Carson does the following:

- Sleeps 7.5 hours each day of the week
- Goes to school 6.75 hours five days a week
- Practices martial arts and basketball 1.5 hours each three times a week
- Reads and studies 1.75 hours every day
- Eats 1.5 hours every day

Estimate the remaining number of hours.

A. 30 B. 35 C. 40 D. 45

The correct answer is **C**. The correct solution is 40. He sleeps about 56 hours, goes to school for 35 hours, practices for 9 hours, reads and studies for about 14 hours, and eats for about 14 hours. This is 128 hours. Therefore, Carson has about 40 hours remaining.

Real-World Integer Problems

The following five steps can make solving word problems easier:

1. Read the problem for understanding.
2. Visualize the problem by drawing a picture or diagram.
3. Make a plan by writing an expression to represent the problem.
4. Solve the problem by applying mathematical techniques.
5. Check the answer to make sure it answers the question asked.

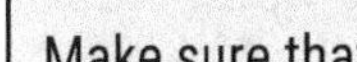

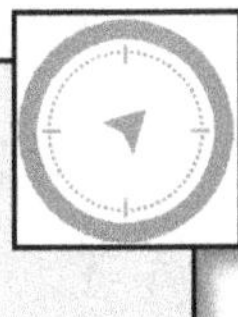

BE CAREFUL!

Make sure that you read the problem fully before visualizing and making a plan.

In basic problems, the solution may be evident, but make sure to demonstrate knowledge of writing the expression. In multi-step problems, first make a plan with the correct expression. Then, apply the correct calculation.

Examples

1. **The temperature on Monday was –9°F, and on Tuesday it was 8°F. What is the difference in temperature, in °F?**

   A. –17° B. –1° C. 1° D. 17°

   The correct answer is **D**. The correct solution is 17° because 8–(–9) = 17°F.

2. **A golfer's last 12 rounds were –2, +4, –3, –1, +5, +3, –4, –5, –2, –6, –1, and 0. What is the average of these rounds?**

   A. –12 B. –1 C. 1 D. 12

   The correct answer is **B**. The correct solution is –1. The total of the scores is –12. The average is –12 divided by 12, which is –1.

Real-World Fraction and Decimal Problems

The five steps in the previous section are applicable to solving real-world fraction and decimal problems. The expressions with one step require only one calculation: addition, subtraction, multiplication, or division. The problems with multiple steps require writing out the expressions and performing the correct calculations.

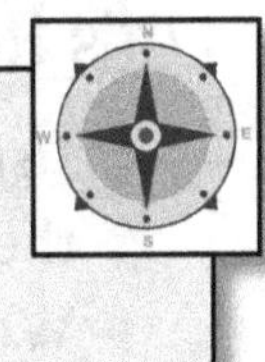

KEEP IN MIND

Estimating the solution first can help determine if a calculation is completed correctly.

Examples

1. **The length of a room is $7\frac{2}{3}$ feet. When the length of the room is doubled, what is the new length in feet?**

   A. $14\frac{2}{3}$ B. $15\frac{1}{3}$ C. $15\frac{2}{3}$ D. $16\frac{1}{3}$

   The correct answer is **B**. The correct solution is $15\frac{1}{3}$. The length is multiplied by 2, $7\frac{2}{3} \times 2 = \frac{23}{3} \times \frac{2}{1} = \frac{46}{3} = 15\frac{1}{3}$ feet.

2. **A fruit salad is a mixture of $1\frac{3}{4}$ pounds of apples, $2\frac{1}{4}$ pounds of grapes, and $1\frac{1}{4}$ pounds of bananas. After the fruit is mixed, $1\frac{1}{2}$ pounds are set aside, and the rest is divided into three containers. What is the weight in pounds of one container?**

   A. $1\frac{1}{5}$ B. $1\frac{1}{4}$ C. $1\frac{1}{3}$ D. $1\frac{1}{2}$

   The correct answer is **B**. The correct solution is $1\frac{1}{4}$. The amount available for the containers is $1\frac{3}{4} + 2\frac{1}{4} + 1\frac{1}{4} - 1\frac{1}{2} = 5\frac{1}{4} - 1\frac{1}{2} = 5\frac{1}{4} - 1\frac{2}{4} = 4\frac{5}{4} - 1\frac{2}{4} = 3\frac{3}{4}$. This amount is divided into three containers, $3\frac{3}{4} \div 3 = \frac{15}{4} \times \frac{15}{12} = 1\frac{3}{12} = 1\frac{1}{4}$ pounds.

3. **In 2016, a town had 17.4 inches of snowfall. In 2017, it had 45.2 inches of snowfall. What is the difference in inches?**

   A. 27.2 B. 27.8 C. 28.2 D. 28.8

   The correct answer is **B**. The correct solution is 27.8 because $45.2 - 17.4 = 27.8$ inches.

4. **Mike bought items that cost \$4.78, \$3.49, \$6.79, \$9.78, and \$14.05. He had a coupon worth \$5.00. If he paid with a \$50.00 bill, then how much change does he receive?**

   A. \$16.11 B. \$18.11 C. \$21.11 D. \$23.11

   The correct answer is **A**. The correct solution is \$16.11. The total bill is \$38.89, less the coupon is \$33.89. The amount of change is \$50.00–\$33.89 = \$16.11.

Let's Review!

- Using estimation is beneficial to determine an approximate solution to the problem when the numbers are complex.
- When solving a word problem with integers, fractions, or decimals, first read and visualize the problem. Then, make a plan, solve, and check the answer.

CHAPTER 6 ALGEBRA PRACTICE QUIZ

1. **Which decimal is the greatest?**

   A. 1.7805 C. 1.7085
   B. 1.5807 D. 1.8057

2. **Change $0.\overline{63}$ to a fraction. Simplify completely.**

   A. $\frac{5}{9}$ C. $\frac{2}{3}$
   B. $\frac{7}{11}$ D. $\frac{5}{6}$

3. **Write $0.\overline{1}$ as a percent.**

   A. $0.\overline{1}\%$ C. $11.\overline{1}\%$
   B. $1.\overline{1}\%$ D. $111.\overline{1}\%$

4. **Solve the equation for the unknown, $4x + 3 = 8$.**

   A. -2 C. $\frac{5}{4}$
   B. $-\frac{5}{4}$ D. 2

5. **Solve the inequality for the unknown, $3x + 5 - 2(x + 3) > 4(1 - x) + 5$.**

   A. $x > 2$ C. $x > 10$
   B. $x > 9$ D. $x > 17$

6. **Solve the equation for h, $SA = 2\pi rh + 2\pi r^2$.**

   A. $2\pi rSA - 2\pi r^2 = h$
   B. $2\pi rSA + 2\pi r^2 = h$
   C. $\frac{SA - 2\pi r^2}{2\pi r} = h$
   D. $\frac{SA + 2\pi r^2}{2\pi r} = h$

7. **Solve the system of equations, $\begin{matrix} y = -2x + 3 \\ y + x = 5 \end{matrix}$.**

   A. (-2, 7) C. (2, -7)
   B. (-2, -7) D. (2, 7)

8. **Solve the system of equations, $\begin{matrix} 2x - 3y = -1 \\ x + 2y = 24 \end{matrix}$.**

   A. (7, 10) C. (6, 8)
   B. (10, 7) D. (8, 6)

9. **Divide $1\frac{5}{6} \div 1\frac{1}{3}$.**

   A. $1\frac{5}{18}$ C. $2\frac{4}{9}$
   B. $1\frac{3}{8}$ D. $3\frac{1}{6}$

10. **Multiply $1\frac{1}{4} \times 1\frac{1}{2}$.**

    A. $1\frac{1}{8}$ C. $1\frac{2}{3}$
    B. $1\frac{1}{3}$ D. $1\frac{7}{8}$

11. **Divide $\frac{1}{10} \div \frac{2}{3}$.**

    A. $\frac{1}{15}$ C. $\frac{3}{20}$
    B. $\frac{1}{10}$ D. $\frac{3}{5}$

12. **A store has 75 pounds of bananas. Eight customers buy 3.3 pounds, five customers buy 4.25 pounds, and one customer buys 6.8 pounds. How many pounds are left in stock?**

    A. 19.45 C. 20.45
    B. 19.55 D. 20.55

13. Solve the system of equations by graphing, $\begin{matrix} 3x + y = -1 \\ 2x - y = -4 \end{matrix}$.

A.

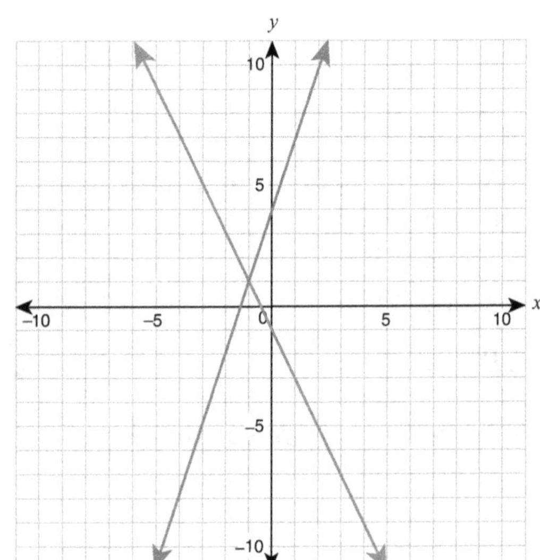

C.

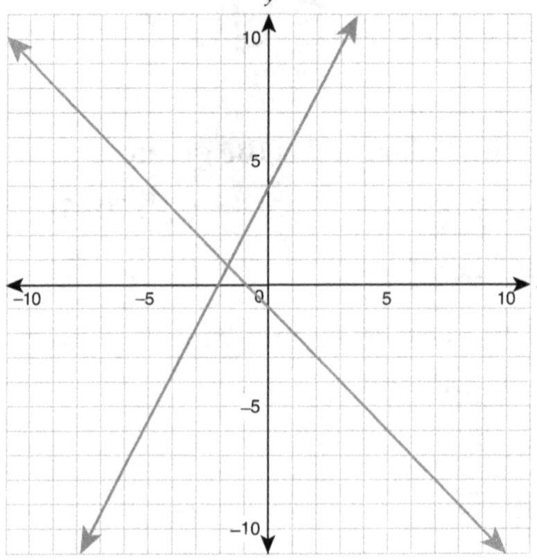

B.

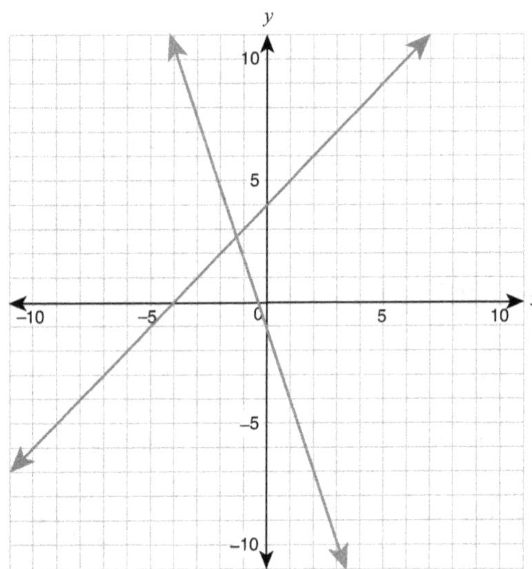

D.

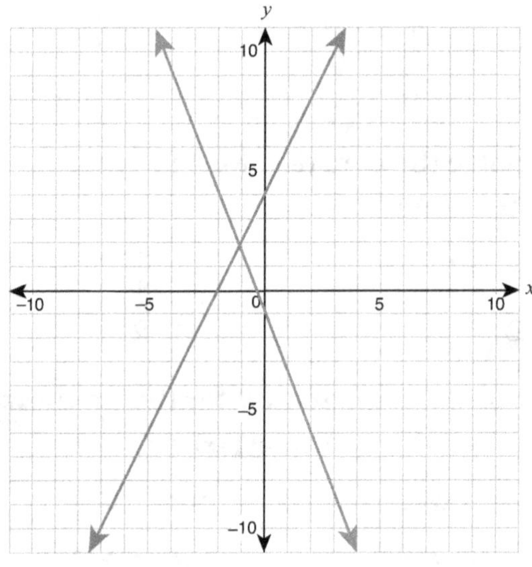

14. A rectangular garden needs a border. The length is $15\frac{3}{5}$ feet, and the width is $3\frac{2}{3}$ feet. What is the perimeter in feet?

A. $18\frac{5}{8}$

B. $19\frac{4}{15}$

C. $37\frac{1}{4}$

D. $38\frac{8}{15}$

15. A historical society has 8 tours daily 5 days a week, with 32 people on each tour. Estimate the number of people who can be on the tour in 50 weeks.

A. 25,000

B. 50,000

C. 75,000

D. 100,000

Chapter 6 Algebra Practice Quiz – Answer Key

1. D. The correct solution is 1.8057 because 1.8057 contains the largest value in the tenths place. **See Lesson: Decimals and Fractions.**

2. B. The correct solution is $\frac{7}{11}$. Let $n = 0.\overline{63}$ and $100n = 63.\overline{63}$. Then, $100n - n = 63.\overline{63} - 0.\overline{63}$ resulting in $99n = 63$ and solution of $n = \frac{63}{99} = \frac{7}{11}$. **See Lesson: Decimals and Fractions.**

3. C. The correct answer is $11.\overline{1}\%$ because $0.\overline{1}$ as a percent is $0.\overline{1} \times 100 = 11.\overline{1}\%$. **See Lesson: Decimals and Fractions.**

4. C. The correct solution is $\frac{5}{4}$.

$4x = 5$	Subtract 3 from both sides of the equation.
$x = \frac{5}{4}$	Divide both sides of the equation by 4.

See Lesson: Equations with One Variable.

5. A. The correct solution is $x > 2$.

$3x + 5 - 2x - 6 > 4 - 4x + 5$	Apply the distributive property.
$x - 1 > -4x + 9$	Combine like terms on both sides of the inequality.
$5x - 1 > 9$	Add $4x$ to both sides of the inequality.
$5x > 10$	Add 1 to both sides of the inequality.
$x > 2$	Divide both sides of the inequality by 5.

See Lesson: Equations with One Variable.

6. C. The correct solution is $\frac{SA - 2\pi r^2}{2\pi r} = h$.

$SA - 2\pi r^2 = 2\pi rh$	Subtract $2\pi r^2$ from both sides of the equation.
$\frac{SA - 2\pi r^2}{2\pi r} = h$	Divide both sides of the equation by $2\pi r$.

See Lesson: Equations with One Variable.

7. A. The correct solution is (-2, 7).

	The first equation is already solved for y.
$-2x + 3 + x = 5$	Substitute $-2x + 3$ in for y in the second equation.
$-x + 3 = 5$	Combine like terms on the left side of the equation.
$-x = 2$	Subtract 3 from both sides of the equation.
$x = -2$	Divide both sides of the equation by -1.
$y = -2(-2) + 3$	Substitute -2 in the first equation for x.
$y = 4 + 3 = 7$	Simplify using order of operations.

See Lesson: Equations with Two Variables.

8. B. The correct solution is (10, 7).

$-2x - 4y = -48$	Multiply all terms in the second equation by -2.
$-7y = -49$	Add the equations.
$y = 7$	Divide both sides of the equation by -7.
$x + 2(7) = 24$	Substitute 7 in the second equation for y.
$x + 14 = 24$	Simplify using order of operations.
$x = 10$	Subtract 14 from both sides of the equation.

See Lesson: Equations with Two Variables.

9. B. The correct answer is $1\frac{3}{8}$ because $\frac{11}{6} \div \frac{4}{3} = \frac{11}{6} \times \frac{3}{4} = \frac{33}{24} = 1\frac{9}{24} = 1\frac{3}{8}$. **See Lesson: Multiplication and Division of Fractions.**

10. D. The correct solution is $1\frac{7}{8}$ because $\frac{5}{4} \times \frac{3}{2} = \frac{15}{8} = 1\frac{7}{8}$. **See Lesson: Multiplication and Division of Fractions.**

11. C. The correct solution is $\frac{3}{20}$ because $\frac{1}{10} \times \frac{3}{2} = \frac{3}{20}$. **See Lesson: Multiplication and Division of Fractions.**

12. D. The correct solution is 20.55 because the number of pounds purchased is $8(3.3) + 5(4.25) + 6.8 = 26.4 + 21.25 + 6.8 = 54.45$ pounds. The number of pounds remaining is $75 - 54.45 = 20.55$ pounds. **See Lesson: Solving Real-World Mathematical Problems.**

13. D. The correct graph has the two lines intersect at (-1, 2). **See Lesson: Equations with Two Variables.**

14. D. The correct solution is $38\frac{8}{15}$ because $15\frac{3}{5} + 3\frac{2}{3} = 15\frac{9}{15} + 3\frac{10}{15} = 18\frac{19}{15}(2) = \frac{289}{15} \times \frac{2}{1} = \frac{578}{15} = 38\frac{8}{15}$ feet. **See Lesson: Solving Real-World Mathematical Problems.**

15. C. The correct solution is 75,000 because by estimation $10(5)(30)(50) = 75{,}000$ people can be on the tour in 50 weeks. **See Lesson: Solving Real-World Mathematical Problems.**

CHAPTER 7 FUNCTIONS

SOLVING QUADRATIC EQUATIONS

This lesson introduces solving quadratic equations by the square root method, completing the square, factoring, and using the quadratic formula.

Solving Quadratic Equations by the Square Root Method

A **quadratic equation** is an equation where the highest variable is squared. The equation is in the form $ax^2 + bx + c = 0$, where a is a non-zero constant and b and c are constants. There are at most two solutions to the equation because the highest variable is squared. There are many methods to solve a quadratic equation.

This section will explore solving a quadratic equation by the square root method. The equation must be in the form of $ax^2 = c$, or there is no x term.

STEP BY STEP

Step 1. Use multiplication and division properties of an equation to remove the value in front of the variable.

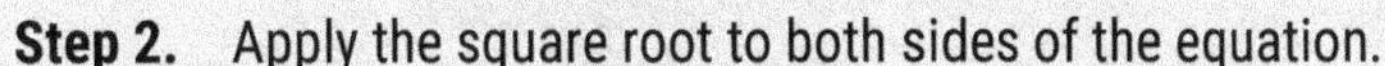

Step 2. Apply the square root to both sides of the equation.

Note: The positive and negative square root make the solution true. For the equation $x^2 = 9$, the solutions are -3 and 3 because $3^2 = 9$ and $(-3)^2 = 9$.

Example

Solve the equation by the square root method, $4x^2 = 64$.

A. 4 B. 8 C. ±4 D. ±8

The correct answer is **C**. The correct solution is ±4.

$x^2 = 16$	Divide both sides of the equation by 4.
$x = \pm 4$	Apply the square root to both sides of the equation.

Solving Quadratic Equations by Completing the Square

A quadratic equation in the form $x^2 + bx$ can be solved by a process known as completing the square. The best time to solve by completing the square is when the b term is even.

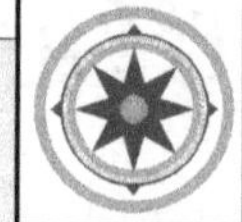

STEP BY STEP

Step 1. Divide all terms by the coefficient of x^2.

Step 2. Move the number term to the right side of the equation.

Step 3. Complete the square $\left(\frac{b}{2}\right)^2$ and add this value to both sides of the equation.

Step 4. Factor the left side of the equation.

Step 5. Apply the square root to both sides of the equation.

Step 6. Use addition and subtraction properties to move all number terms to the right side of the equation.

Examples

1. **Solve the equation by completing the square, $x^2 - 8x + 12 = 0$.**

A. –2 and –6 B. 2 and –6 C. –2 and 6 D. 2 and 6

The correct answer is **D**. The correct solutions are 2 and 6.

$x^2 - 8x = -12$	Subtract 12 from both sides of the equation.
$x^2 - 8x + 16 = -12 + 16$	Complete the square, $\left(-\frac{8}{2}\right)^2 = (-4)^2 = 16$.
	Add 16 to both sides of the equation.
$x^2 - 8x + 16 = 4$	Simplify the right side of the equation.
$(x-4)^2 = 4$	Factor the left side of the equation.
$x - 4 = \pm 2$	Apply the square root to both sides of the equation.
$x = 4 \pm 2$	Add 4 to both sides of the equation.
$x = 4 - 2 = 2,\ x = 4 + 2 = 6$	Simplify the right side of the equation.

2. **Solve the equation by completing the square, $x^2 + 6x - 8 = 0$.**

A. $-3 \pm \sqrt{17}$ B. $3 \pm \sqrt{17}$ C. $-3 \pm \sqrt{8}$ D. $3 \pm \sqrt{8}$

The correct answer is **A**. The correct solutions are $-3 \pm \sqrt{17}$.

$x^2 + 6x = 8$	Add 8 to both sides of the equation.
$x^2 + 6x + 9 = 8 + 9$	Complete the square, $\left(\frac{6}{2}\right)^2 = 3^2 = 9$. Add 9 to both sides of the equation.
$x^2 + 6x + 9 = 17$	Simplify the right side of the equation.
$(x + 3)^2 = 17$	Factor the left side of the equation.
$x + 3 = \pm\sqrt{17}$	Apply the square root to both sides of the equation.
$x = -3 \pm \sqrt{17}$	Subtract 3 from both sides of the equation.

Solving Quadratic Equations by Factoring

Factoring can only be used when a quadratic equation is factorable; other methods are needed to solve quadratic equations that are not factorable.

STEP BY STEP

Step 1. Simplify if needed by clearing any fractions and parentheses.

Step 2. Write the equation in standard form, $ax^2 + bx + c = 0$.

Step 3. Factor the quadratic equation.

Step 4. Set each factor equal to zero.

Step 5. Solve the linear equations using inverse operations.

The quadratic equation will have two solutions if the factors are different or one solution if the factors are the same.

Examples

1. **Solve the equation by factoring, $x^2 – 13x + 42 = 0$.**

A. –6, –7 B. –6, 7 C. 6, –7 D. 6, 7

The correct answer is **D**. The correct solutions are 6 and 7.

$(x–6)(x–7) = 0$	Factor the equation.
$(x–6) = 0$ or $(x–7) = 0$	Set each factor equal to 0.
$x–6 = 0$	Add 6 to both sides of the equation to solve for the first factor.
$x = 6$	
$x–7 = 0$	Add 7 to both sides of the equation to solve for the second factor.
$x = 7$	

2. **Solve the equation by factoring, $9x^2 + 30x + 25 = 0$.**

A. $-\frac{5}{3}$ B. $-\frac{3}{5}$ C. $\frac{3}{5}$ D. $\frac{5}{3}$

The correct answer is **A**. The correct solution is $-\frac{5}{3}$.

$(3x + 5)(3x + 5) = 0$	Factor the equation.
$(3x + 5) = 0$ or $(3x + 5) = 0$	Set each factor equal to 0.
$(3x + 5) = 0$	Set one factor equal to zero since both factors are the same.
$3x + 5 = 0$	Subtract 5 from both sides of the equation and divide both sides of the equation by 3 to solve.
$3x = –5$	
$x = -\frac{5}{3}$	

Solving Quadratic Equations by the Quadratic Formula

Many quadratic equations are not factorable. Another method of solving a quadratic equation is by using the quadratic formula. This method can be used to solve any quadratic equation in the form . Using the coefficients *a*, *b*, and *c*, the quadratic formula is $x = \frac{-b \pm \sqrt{b^2-4ac}}{2a}$. The values are substituted into the formula, and applying the order of operations finds the solution(s) to the equation.

The solution of the quadratic formula in these examples will be exact or estimated to three decimal places. There may be cases where the exact solutions to the quadratic formula are used.

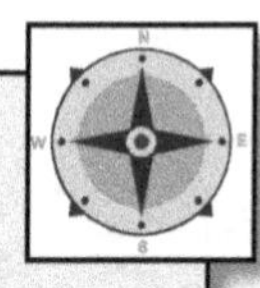

KEEP IN MIND

Watch the negative sign in the formula. Remember that a number squared is always positive.

Examples

1. **Solve the equation by the quadratic formula, $x^2-5x-6=0$.**

   A. –6 and –1 B. 6 and –1 C. –6 and 1 D. 6 and 1

   The correct answer is **B.** The correct solutions are 6 and –1.

   $x = \frac{-(-5) \pm \sqrt{(-5)^2-4(1)(-6)}}{2(1)}$ Substitute 1 for *a*, –5 for *b*, and –6 for *c*.

   $x = \frac{5 \pm \sqrt{25-(-24)}}{2}$ Apply the exponent and perform the multiplication.

   $x = \frac{5 \pm \sqrt{49}}{2}$ Perform the subtraction.

   $x = \frac{5 \pm 7}{2}$ Apply the square root.

   $x = \frac{5+7}{2}$, $x = \frac{5-7}{2}$ Separate the problem into two expressions.

   $x = \frac{12}{2} = 6$, $x = \frac{-2}{2} = -1$ Simplify the numerator and divide.

2. **Solve the equation by the quadratic formula, $2x^2 + 4x-5 = 0$.**

   A. –0.87 and –2.87 B. 0.87 and –2.87 C. –0.87 and 2.87 D. 0.87 and 2.87

   The correct answer is **B.** The correct solutions are –0.87 and –2.87.

   $x = \frac{-4 \pm \sqrt{4^2-4(2)(-5)}}{2(2)}$ Substitute 2 for *a*, 4 for *b*, and –5 for *c*.

   $x = \frac{-4 \pm \sqrt{16-(-40)}}{4}$ Apply the exponent and perform the multiplication.

   $x = \frac{-4 \pm \sqrt{56}}{4}$ Perform the subtraction.

   $x = \frac{-4 \pm 7.48}{4}$ Apply the square root.

   $x = \frac{-4+7.48}{4}$, $x = \frac{-4-7.48}{4}$ Separate the problem into two expressions.

   $x = \frac{3.48}{4} = 0.87$, $x = \frac{-11.48}{4} = -2.87$ Simplify the numerator and divide.

Let's Review!

There are four methods to solve a quadratic equation algebraically:

- The square root method is used when there is a squared variable term and a constant term.
- Completing the square is used when there is a squared variable term and an even variable term.
- Factoring is used when the equation can be factored.
- The quadratic formula can be used for any quadratic equation.

POLYNOMIALS

This lesson introduces adding, subtracting, and multiplying polynomials. It also explains polynomial identities that describe numerical expressions.

Adding and Subtracting Polynomials

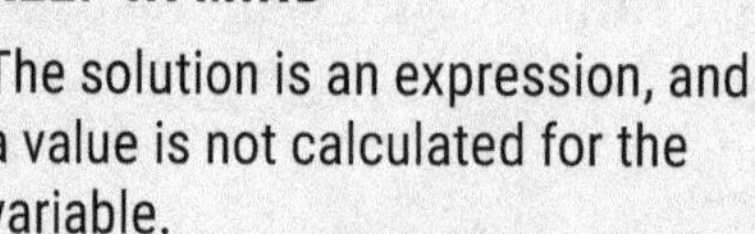
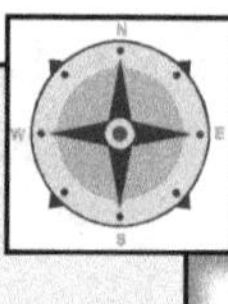

KEEP IN MIND

The solution is an expression, and a value is not calculated for the variable.

A **polynomial** is an expression that contains exponents, variables, constants, and operations. The exponents of the variables are only whole numbers, and there is no division by a variable. The operations are addition, subtraction, multiplication, and division. Constants are terms without a variable. A polynomial of one term is a **monomial**; a polynomial of two terms is a **binomial**; and a polynomial of three terms is a **trinomial.**

To add polynomials, combine like terms and write the solution from the term with the highest exponent to the term with the lowest exponent. To simplify, first rearrange and group like terms. Next, combine like terms.

$(3x^2 + 5x - 6) + (4x^3 - 3x + 4) = 4x^3 + 3x^2 + (5x - 3x) + (-6 + 4) = 4x^3 + 3x^2 + 2x - 2$

To subtract polynomials, rewrite the second polynomial using an additive inverse. Change the minus sign to a plus sign, and change the sign of every term inside the parentheses. Then, add the polynomials.

$(3x^2 + 5x - 6) - (4x^3 - 3x + 4) = (3x^2 + 5x - 6) + (-4x^3 + 3x - 4) = -4x^3 + 3x^2 + (5x + 3x) + (-6 - 4)$
$= -4x^3 + 3x^2 + 8x - 10$

Examples

1. **Perform the operation, $(2y^2 - 5y + 1) + (-3y^2 + 6y + 2)$.**

   A. $y^2 + y + 3$ B. $-y^2 - y + 3$ C. $y^2 - y + 3$ D. $-y^2 + y + 3$

   The correct answer is **D**. The correct solution is $-y^2 + y + 3$.

   $(2y^2 - 5y + 1) + (-3y^2 + 6y + 2) = (2y^2 - 3y^2) + (-5y + 6y) + (1 + 2) = -y^2 + y + 3$

2. **Perform the operation, $(3x^2y + 4xy - 5xy^2) - (x^2y - 3xy - 2xy^2)$.**

   A. $2x^2y - 7xy + 3xy^2$
   C. $2x^2y + 7xy - 3xy^2$
   B. $2x^2y + 7xy + 3xy^2$
   D. $2x^2y - 7xy - 3xy^2$

   The correct answer is **C**. The correct solution is $2x^2y + 7xy - 3xy^2$.

   $(3x^2y + 4xy - 5xy^2) - (x^2y - 3xy - 2xy^2) = (3x^2y + 4xy - 5xy^2) + (-x^2y + 3xy + 2xy^2)$
   $= (3x^2y - x^2y) + (4xy + 3xy) + (-5xy^2 + 2xy^2) = 2x^2y + 7xy - 3xy^2$

Multiplying Polynomials

BE CAREFUL!

Make sure that you apply the distributive property to all terms in the polynomials.

Multiplying polynomials comes in many forms. When multiplying a monomial by a monomial, multiply the coefficients and apply the multiplication rule for the power of an exponent.

$4xy(3x^2y) = 12x^3y^2$.

When multiplying a monomial by a polynomial, multiply each term of the polynomial by the monomial.

$4xy(3x^2y-2xy^2) = 4xy(3x^2y) + 4xy(-2xy^2) = 12x^3y^2-8x^2y^3$.

When multiplying a binomial by a binomial, apply the distributive property and combine like terms.

$(3x-4)(2x+5) = 3x(2x+5)-4(2x+5) = 6x^2 + 15x-8x-20 = 6x^2 + 7x-20$

When multiplying a binomial by a trinomial, apply the distributive property and combine like terms.

$(x+2)(3x^2-2x+3) = (x+2)(3x^2) + (x+2)(-2x) + (x+2)(3) = 3x^3 + 6x^2-2x^2-4x + 3x + 6 = 3x^3 +$

$4x^2-x+6$

Examples

1. **Multiply, $3xy^2(2x^2y)$.**

   A. $6x^2y^2$ B. $6x^3y^2$ C. $6x^3y^3$ D. $6x^2y^3$

   The correct answer is **C**. The correct solution is $6x^3y^3$. $3xy^2(2x^2y) = 6x^3y^3$.

2. **Multiply, $-2xy(3xy-4x^2y^2)$.**

   A. $-6x^2y^2 + 8x^3y^3$ B. $-6x^2y^2-8x^3y^3$ C. $-6xy + 8x^3y^3$ D. $-6xy-8x^3y^3$

   The correct answer is **A**. The correct solution is $-6x^2y^2 + 8x^3y^3$.

   $-2xy(3xy-4x^2y^2) = -2xy(3xy)-2xy(-4x^2y^2) = -6x^2y^2 + 8x^3y^3$

Polynomial Identities

BE CAREFUL!

Pay attention to the details of each polynomial identity and apply them appropriately.

There are many polynomial identities that show relationships between expressions.

- Difference of two squares: $a^2-b^2 = (a-b)(a+b)$
- Square of a binomial: $(a+b)^2 = a^2 + 2ab + b^2$
- Square of a binomial: $(a-b)^2 = a^2-2ab + b^2$
- Sum of cubes: $a^3 + b^3 = (a+b)(a^2-ab+b^2)$
- Difference of two cubes: $a^3-b^3 = (a-b)(a^2+ab+b^2)$

Examples

1. **Apply the polynomial identity to rewrite $x^2 + 6x + 9$.**

   A. $x^2 + 9$ B. $(x^2 + 3)^2$ C. $(x + 3)^2$ D. $(3x)^2$

   The correct answer is **C**. The correct solution is $(x + 3)^2$. The expression $x^2 + 6x + 9$ is rewritten as $(x + 3)^2$ because the value of a is x and the value of b is 3.

2. **Apply the polynomial identity to rewrite $x^3 – 1$.**

   A. $(x + 1)(x^2 + x + 1)$
   B. $(x – 1)(x^2 + x – 1)$
   C. $(x + 1)(x^2 + x – 1)$
   D. $(x – 1)(x^2 + x + 1)$

   The correct answer is **D**. The correct solution is $(x – 1)(x^2 + x + 1)$ because the value of a and the value of b is 1. Refer to the polynomial identity for the difference of two cubes equation.

Let's Review!

- Adding, subtracting, and multiplying are commonly applied to polynomials. The key step in applying these operations is combining like terms.
- Polynomial identities require rewriting polynomials into different forms.

RATIOS, PROPORTIONS, AND PERCENTAGES

This lesson reviews percentages and ratios and their application to real-world problems. It also examines proportions and rates of change.

Percentages

A **percent** or **percentage** represents a fraction of some quantity. It is an integer or decimal number followed by the symbol %. The word *percent* means "per hundred." For example, 50% means 50 per 100. This is equivalent to half, or 1 out of 2.

Converting between numbers and percents is easy. Given a number, multiply by 100 and add the % symbol to get the equivalent percent. For instance, 0.67 is equal to $0.67 \times 100 = 67\%$, meaning 67 out of 100. Given a percent, eliminate the % symbol and divide by 100. For instance, 23.5% is equal to $23.5 \div 100 = 0.235$.

Although percentages between 0% and 100% are the most obvious, a percent can be any real number, including a negative number. For example, $1.35 = 135\%$ and $-0.872 = -87.2\%$. An example is a gasoline tank that is one-quarter full: one-quarter is $\frac{1}{4}$ or 0.25, so the tank is 25% full. Another example is a medical diagnostic test that has a certain maximum normal result. If a patient's test exceeds that value, its representation can be a percent greater than 100%. For instance, a reading that is 1.22 times the maximum normal value is 122% of the maximum normal value. Likewise, when measuring increases in a company's profits as a percent from one year to the next, a negative percent can represent a decline. That is, if the company's profits fell by one-tenth, the change was –10%.

Example

If 15 out of every 250 contest entries are winners, what percentage of entries are winners?

A. 0.06% B. 6% C. 15% D. 17%

The correct answer is **B.** First, convert the fraction $\frac{15}{250}$ to a decimal: 0.06. To get the percent, multiply by 100% (that is, multiply by 100 and add the % symbol). Of all entries, 6% are winners.

Ratios

A **ratio** expresses the relationship between two numbers and is expressed using a colon or fraction notation. For instance, if 135 runners finish a marathon but 22 drop out, the ratio of finishers to non-finishers is 135:22 or $\frac{135}{22}$. These expressions are equal.

BE CAREFUL!

Avoid confusing standard ratios with odds (such as "3:1 odds"). Both may use a colon, but their meanings differ. In general, a ratio is the same as a fraction containing the same numbers.

Ratios also follow the rules of fractions. Performing arithmetic operations on ratios follows the same procedures as on fractions. Ratios should also generally appear in lowest terms. Therefore, the constituent numbers in a ratio represent the relative quantities of each side, not absolute quantities. For example, because the ratio 1:2 is equal to 2:4, 5:10, and 600:1,200, ratios are insufficient to determine the absolute number of entities in a problem.

Example

If the ratio of women to men in a certain industry is 5:4, how many people are in that industry?

A. 9
B. 20
C. 900
D. Not enough information

The correct answer is **D**. The ratio 5:4 is the industry's relative number of women to men. But the industry could have 10 women and 8 men, 100 women and 80 men, or any other breakdown whose ratio is 5:4. Therefore, the question provides too little information to answer. Had it provided the total number of people in the industry, it would have been possible to determine how many women and how many men are in the industry.

KEY POINT

Mathematically, ratios act just like fractions. For example, the ratio 8:13 is mathematically the same as the fraction $\frac{8}{13}$.

Proportions

A **proportion** is an equation of two ratios. An illustrative case is two equivalent fractions:

$$\frac{21}{28} = \frac{3}{4}$$

This example of a proportion should be familiar: going left to right, it is the conversion of one fraction to an equivalent fraction in lowest terms by dividing the numerator and denominator by the same number (7, in this case).

Equating fractions in this way is correct, but it provides little information. Proportions are more informative when one of the numbers is unknown. Using a question mark (?) to represent an unknown number, setting up a proportion can aid in solving problems involving different scales. For instance, if the ratio of maple saplings to oak saplings in an acre of young forest is 7:5 and that acre contains 65 oaks, the number of maples in that acre can be determined using a proportion: $\frac{7}{5} = \frac{?}{65}$

Note that to equate two ratios in this manner, the numerators must contain numbers that represent the same entity or type, and so must the denominators. In this example, the numerators represent maples and the denominators represent oaks.

$$\frac{7 \text{ maples}}{5 \text{ oaks}} = \frac{? \text{ maples}}{65 \text{ oaks}}$$

Recall from the properties of fractions that if you multiply the numerator and denominator by the same number, the result is an equivalent fraction. Therefore, to find the unknown in this proportion, first divide the denominator on the right by the denominator on the left. Then, multiply the quotient by the numerator on the left.

$65 \div 5 = 13$

$\frac{7 \times 13}{5 \times 13} = \frac{?}{65}$

The unknown (?) is $7 \times 13 = 91$. In the example, the acre of forest has 91 maple saplings.

DID YOU KNOW?

When taking the reciprocal of both sides of a proportion, the proportion still holds. When setting up a proportion, ensure that the numerators represent the same type and the denominators represent the same type.

Example

If a recipe calls for 3 parts flour to 2 parts sugar, how much sugar does a baker need if she uses 12 cups of flour?

A. 2 cups B. 3 cups C. 6 cups D. 8 cups

The correct answer is **D.** The baker needs 8 cups of sugar. First, note that "3 parts flour to 2 parts sugar" is the ratio 3:2. Set up the proportion using the given amount of flour (12 cups), putting the flour numbers in either the denominators or the numerators (either will yield the same answer): $\frac{3}{2} = \frac{12}{?}$

Since $12 \div 3 = 4$, multiply 2×4 to get 8 cups of sugar.

Rates of Change

Numbers that describe current quantities can be informative, but how they change over time can provide even greater insight into a problem. The rate of change for some quantity is the ratio of the quantity's difference over a specific time period to the length of that period. For example, if an automobile increases its speed from 50 mph to 100 mph in 10 seconds, the rate of change of its speed (its acceleration) is

$$\frac{100 \text{ mph} - 50 \text{ mph}}{10 \text{ s}} = \frac{50 \text{ mph}}{10 \text{ s}} = 5 \text{ mph per second} = 5 \text{ mph/s}$$

The basic formula for the rate of change of some quantity is $\frac{x_f - x_i}{t_f - t_i}$, where t_f is the "final" (or ending) time and t_i is the "initial" (or starting) time. Also, x_f is the (final) quantity at (final) time t_f, and x_i is the (initial) quantity at (initial) time t_i. In the example above, the final time is 10 seconds and the initial time is 0 seconds—hence the omission of the initial time from the calculation.

According to the rules of fractions, multiplying the numerator and denominator by the same number yields an equivalent fraction, so you can reverse the order of the terms in the formula:

$$\frac{x_f-x_i}{t_f-t_i}=\frac{-1}{-1}\times\frac{x_f-x_i}{t_f-t_i}=\frac{x_i-x_f}{t_i-t_f}$$

The key to getting the correct rate of change is to ensure that the first number in the numerator and the first number in the denominator correspond to each other (that is, the quantity from the numerator corresponds to the time from the denominator). This must also be true for the second number.

TEST TIP

To convert a quantity's rate of change to a percent, divide it by the quantity at the *initial* time and multiply by 100%. To convert to a ratio, just skip the multiplication step.

Example

If the population of an endangered frog species fell from 2,250 individuals to 2,115 individuals in a year, what is that population's annual rate of increase?

A. –135% B. –6% C. 6% D. 135%

The correct answer is **B.** The population's rate of increase was –6%. The solution in this case involves two steps. First, calculate the population's annual rate of change using the formula. It will yield the change in the number of individuals.

$$\frac{2{,}115-2{,}250}{1\text{ year}-0\text{ year}}=-135\text{ per year}$$

Second, divide the result by the initial population. Finally, convert to a percent.

$$\frac{-135\text{ per year}}{2{,}250}=-0.06\text{ per year}$$

$$(-0.06\text{ per year})\times 100\%=-6\%\text{ per year}$$

Since the question asks for the *annual* rate of increase, the "per year" can be dropped. Also, note that the answer must be negative to represent the decreasing population.

Let's Review!

- A percent—meaning "per hundred"—represents a relative quantity as a fraction or decimal. It is the absolute number multiplied by 100 and followed by the % symbol.
- A ratio is a relationship between two numbers expressed using fraction or colon notation (for example, $\frac{3}{2}$ or 3:2). Ratios behave mathematically just like fractions.
- An equation of two ratios is called a proportion. Proportions are used to solve problems involving scale
- Rates of change are the speeds at which quantities increase or decrease. The formula $\frac{x_f-x_i}{t_f-t_i}$ provides the rate of change of quantity x over the period between some initial (i) time and final (f) time.

POWERS, EXPONENTS, ROOTS, AND RADICALS

This lesson introduces how to apply the properties of exponents and examines square roots and cube roots. It also discusses how to estimate quantities using integer powers of 10.

Properties of Exponents

An expression that is a repeated multiplication of the same factor is a **power**. The **exponent** is the number of times the **base** is multiplied. For example, 6^2 is the same as 6 times 6, or 36. There are many rules associated with exponents.

Property	Definition	Examples
Product Rule (Same Base)	$a^m \times a^n = a^{m+n}$	$4^1 \times 4^4 = 4^{1+4} = 4^5 = 1024$ $x^1 \times x^4 = x^{1+4} = x^5$
Product Rule (Different Base)	$a^m \times b^m = (a \times b)^m$	$2^2 \times 3^2 = (2 \times 3)^2 = 6^2 = 36$ $3^3 \times x^3 = (3 \times x)^3 = (3x)^3 = 27x^3$
Quotient Rule (Same Base)	$\frac{a^m}{a^n} = a^{m-n}$	$\frac{4^4}{4^2} = 4^{4-2} = 4^2 = 16$ $\frac{x^6}{x^3} = x^{6-3} = x^3$
Quotient Rule (Different Base)	$\frac{a^m}{b^m} = \left(\frac{a}{b}\right)^m$	$\frac{4^4}{3^4} = \left(\frac{4}{3}\right)^4$ $\frac{x^6}{y^6} = \left(\frac{x}{y}\right)^6$
Power of a Power Rule	$(a^m)^n = a^{mn}$	$(2^2)^3 = 2^{2\times3} = 2^6 = 64$ $(x^5)^8 = x^{5\times8} = x^{40}$
Zero Exponent Rule	$a^0 = 1$	$64^0 = 1$ $y^0 = 1$
Negative Exponent Rule	$a^{-m} = \frac{1}{a^m}$	$3^{-3} = \frac{1}{3^3} = \frac{1}{27}$ $\frac{1}{x^{-3}} = x^3$

For many exponent expressions, it is necessary to use multiplication rules to simplify the expression completely.

KEEP IN MIND

The expressions $(-2)^2 = (-2) \times (-2) = 4$ and $-2^2 = -(2 \times 2) = -4$ have different results because of the location of the negative signs and parentheses. For each problem, focus on each detail to simplify completely and correctly.

Examples

1. **Simplify $(3^2)^3$.**

   A. 18

   B. 216

   C. 243

   D. 729

   The correct answer is **D**. The correct solution is 729 because $(3^2)^3 = 3^{2\times3} = 3^6 = 729$.

2. **Simplify $(2x^2)^4$.**

   A. $2x^8$ B. $4x^4$ C. $8x^6$ D. $16x^8$

   The correct answer is **D.** The correct solution is $16x^8$ because $(2x^2)^4 = 2^4(x^2)^4 = 2^4x^{2\times4} = 16x^8$.

3. **Simplify $\left(\frac{x^{-2}}{y^2}\right)^3$.**

   A. $\frac{1}{x^6y^6}$ B. $\frac{x^6}{y^6}$ C. $\frac{y^6}{x^6}$ D. x^6y^6

   The correct answer is **A.** The correct solution is $\frac{1}{x^6y^6}$ because $\left(\frac{x^{-2}}{y^2}\right)^3 = \left(\frac{1}{x^2y^2}\right)^3 = \frac{1}{x^{2\times3}y^{2\times3}} = \frac{1}{x^6y^6}$.

Square Root and Cube Roots

The **square** of a number is the number raised to the power of 2. The **square root** of a number, when the number is squared, gives that number. $10^2 = 100$, so the square of 100 is 10, or $\sqrt{100} = 10$. **Perfect squares** are numbers with whole number square roots, such as 1, 4, 9, 16, and 25.

Squaring a number and taking a square root are opposite operations, meaning that the operations undo each other. This means that $\sqrt{x^2} = x$ and $(\sqrt{x})^2 = x$. When solving the equation $x^2 = p$, the solutions are $x = \pm\sqrt{p}$ because a negative value squared is a positive solution.

The **cube** of a number is the number raised to the power of 3. The **cube root** of a number, when the number is cubed, gives that number. $10^3 = 1000$, so the cube of 1,000 is 10, or $\sqrt[3]{1000} = 10$. **Perfect cubes** are numbers with whole number cube roots, such as 1, 8, 27, 64, and 125.

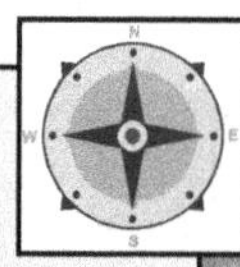

KEEP IN MIND

Most square roots and cube roots are not perfect roots.

Cubing a number and taking a cube root are opposite operations, meaning that the operations undo each other. This means that $\sqrt[3]{x^3} = x$ and $(\sqrt[3]{x})^3 = x$. When solving the equation $x^3 = p$, the solution is $x = \sqrt[3]{p}$.

If a number is not a perfect square root or cube root, the solution is an approximation. When this occurs, the solution is an irrational number. For example, $\sqrt{2}$ is the irrational solution to $x^2 = 2$.

Examples

1. **Solve $x^2 = 121$.**

   A. –10, 10 B. –11, 11 C. –12, 12 D. –13, 13

   The correct answer is **B.** The correct solution is –11, 11 because the square root of 121 is 11. The values of –11 and 11 make the equation true.

2. **Solve $x^3 = 125$.**

   A. 1 B. 5 C. 10 D. 25

   The correct answer is **B.** The correct solution is 5 because the cube root of 125 is 5.

Express Large or Small Quantities as Multiples of 10

KEEP IN MIND

A positive exponent in scientific notation represents a large number, while a negative exponent represents a small number.

Scientific notation is a large or small number written in two parts. The first part is a number between 1 and 10. In these problems, the first digit will be a single digit. The number is followed by a multiple to a power of 10. A positive integer exponent means the number is greater than 1, while a negative integer exponent means the number is smaller than 1.

The number 3×10^4 is the same as $3 \times 10{,}000 = 30{,}000$.

The number 3×10^{-4} is the same as $3 \times 0.0001 = 0.0003$.

For example, the population of the United States is about 3×10^8, and the population of the world is about 7×10^9. The population of the United States is 300,000,000, and the population of the world is 7,000,000,000. The world population is about 20 times larger than the population of the United States.

Examples

1. **The population of China is about 1×10^9, and the population of the United States is about 3×10^8. How many times larger is the population of China than the population of the United States?**

   A. 2 B. 3 C. 4 D. 5

   The correct answer is **B**. The correct solution is 3 because the population of China is about 1,000,000,000 and the population of the United States is about 300,000,000. So the population is about 3 times larger.

2. **A red blood cell has a length of 8×10^{-6} meter, and a skin cell has a length of 3×10^{-5} meter. How many times larger is the skin cell?**

   A. 1 B. 2 C. 3 D. 4

   The correct answer is **D**. The correct solution is 4 because 3×10^{-5} is 0.00003 and 8×10^{-6} is 0.000008. So, the skin cell is about 4 times larger.

Let's Review!

- The properties and rules of exponents are applicable to generate equivalent expressions.
- Only a few whole numbers out of the set of whole numbers are perfect squares. Perfect cubes can be positive or negative.
- Numbers expressed in scientific notation are useful to compare large or small numbers.

Chapter 7 Functions Practice Quiz

1. **Multiply, $(x-1)(x^2 + 2x + 3)$.**

   A. $x^3 + x^2 + x-3$
   B. x^3-x^2-x-3
   C. $x^3 + x^2-x-3$
   D. $x^3-x^2 + x-3$

2. **Apply the polynomial identity to rewrite $9x^2-30x + 25$.**

   A. $(3x + 5)(3x-5)$
   B. $(3x-5)^2$
   C. $(3x-5)(3x-1)$
   D. $(3x-5)(3x + 1)$

3. **Perform the operation, $(3y^2 + 4y)-(5y^3-2y^2 + 3)$.**

   A. $-5y^3 + y^2 + 4y-3$
   B. $-5y^3 + 5y^2 + 4y + 3$
   C. $-5y^3 + y^2 + 4y + 3$
   D. $-5y^3 + 5y^2 + 4y-3$

4. **Solve $x^3 = 343$.**

   A. 6
   B. 7
   C. 8
   D. 9

5. **One online seller has about 6×10^8 online orders, and another online seller has about 5×10^7 online orders. How many times more orders does the first company have?**

   A. 12
   B. 15
   C. 20
   D. 32

6. **Simplify $\frac{x^2y^{-2}}{x^{-3}y^3}$.**

   A. $\frac{x^5}{y^5}$
   B. $\frac{y^5}{x^5}$
   C. $\frac{1}{x^5y^5}$
   D. x^5y^5

7. **What is 15% of 64?**

   A. 5:48
   B. 15:64
   C. 48:5
   D. 64:15

8. **Which number satisfies the proportion $\frac{378}{?} = \frac{18}{7}$?**

   A. 18
   B. 147
   C. 972
   D. 2,646

9. **If a tree grows an average of 4.2 inches in a day, what is the rate of change in its height per month? Assume a month is 30 days.**

   A. 0.14 inches per month
   B. 4.2 inches per month
   C. 34.2 inches per month
   D. 126 inches per month

10. **Solve the equation by the quadratic formula, $11x^2-14x + 4 = 0$.**

    A. -0.84 and -0.43
    B. 0.84 and -0.43
    C. -0.84 and 0.43
    D. 0.84 and 0.43

11. **Solve the equation by any method, $3x^2-5 = 22$.**

    A. 0
    B. ±1
    C. ±2
    D. ±3

12. **Solve the equation by the square root method, $5x^2 + 10 = 10$.**

    A. 0
    B. 1
    C. 2
    D. 3

CHAPTER 7 FUNCTIONS PRACTICE QUIZ – ANSWER KEY

1. A. The correct solution is $x^3 + x^2 + x - 3$.

$$(x-1)(x^2 + 2x + 3) = (x-1)(x^2) + (x-1)(2x) + (x-1)(3) = x^3 - x^2 + 2x^2 - 2x + 3x - 3 = x^3 + x^2 + x - 3$$

See Lesson: Polynomials.

2. B. The correct solution is $(3x-5)^2$. The expression $9x^2 - 30x + 25$ is rewritten as $(3x-5)^2$ because the value of a is $3x$ and the value of b is 5. **See Lesson: Polynomials.**

3. D. The correct solution is $-5y^3 + 5y^2 + 4y - 3$.

$$(3y^2 + 4y) - (5y^3 - 2y^2 + 3) = (3y^2 + 4y) + (-5y^3 + 2y^2 - 3) = -5y^3 + (3y^2 + 2y^2) + 4y - 3 = -5y^3 + 5y^2 + 4y - 3$$

See Lesson: Polynomials.

4. B. The correct solution is 7 because the cube root of 343 is 7. **See Lesson: Powers, Exponents, Roots, and Radicals.**

5. A. The correct solution is 12 because the first company has about 600,000,000 orders and the second company has about 50,000,000 orders. So, the first company is about 12 times larger. **See Lesson: Powers, Exponents, Roots, and Radicals.**

6. A. The correct solution is $\frac{x^5}{y^5}$ because $\frac{x^2y^{-2}}{x^{-3}y^3} = x^{2-(-3)}y^{-2-3} = x^5y^{-5} = \frac{x^5}{y^5}$. **See Lesson: Powers, Exponents, Roots, and Radicals.**

7. C. Either set up a proportion or just note that this question is asking for a fraction of a specific number: 15% (or $\frac{3}{20}$) of 64. Multiply $\frac{3}{20}$ by 64 to get $\frac{48}{5}$, or 48:5. **See Lesson: Ratios, Proportions, and Percentages.**

8. B. The number 147 satisfies the proportion. First, divide 378 by 18 to get 21. Then, multiply 21 by 7 to get 147. Check your answer by dividing 147 by 7: the quotient is also 21, so 147 satisfies the proportion. **See Lesson: Ratios, Proportions, and Percentages.**

9. D. The rate of change is 126 inches per month. One approach is to set up a proportion.

$$\frac{1 \text{ day}}{4.2 \text{ inches}} = \frac{30 \text{ days}}{?}$$

Since 1 month is equivalent to 30 days, multiply the rate of change per day by 30 to get the rate of change per month. 4.2 inches multiplied by 30 is 126 inches. Thus, the growth rate is 126 inches per month. **See Lesson: Ratios, Proportions, and Percentages.**

10. D. The correct solutions are 0.84 and 0.43.

$x = \frac{-(-14) \pm \sqrt{(-14)^2-4(11)(4)}}{2(11)}$	Substitute 11 for *a*, –14 for *b*, and 4 for *c*.
$x = \frac{14 \pm \sqrt{196-176}}{22}$	Apply the exponent and perform the multiplication.
$x = \frac{14 \pm \sqrt{20}}{22}$	Perform the subtraction.
$x = \frac{14 \pm 4.47}{22}$	Apply the square root.
$x = \frac{14 + 4.47}{22}, x = \frac{14-4.47}{22}$	Separate the problem into two expressions.
$x = \frac{18.47}{22} = 0.84, x = \frac{9.53}{22} = 0.43$	Simplify the numerator and divide.

See Lesson: Solving Quadratic Equations.

11. D. The correct solutions are ±3. Solve this equation by the square root method.

$3x^2 = 27$	Add 5 to both sides of the equation.
$x^2 = \pm 9$	Divide both sides of the equation by 3.
$x = \pm 3$	Apply the square root to both sides of the equation.

See Lesson: Solving Quadratic Equations.

12. A. The correct solution is 0.

$5x^2 = 0$	Subtract 10 from both sides of the equation.
$x^2 = 0$	Divide both sides of the equation by 5.
$x = 0$	Apply the square root to both sides of the equation.

See Lesson: Solving Quadratic Equations.

CHAPTER 8 GEOMETRY

CONGRUENCE

This lesson discusses basic terms for geometry. Many polygons have the property of lines of symmetry, or rotational symmetry. Rotations, reflections, and translations are ways to create congruent polygons.

Geometry Terms

The terms *point*, *line*, and *plane* help define other terms in geometry. A point is an exact location in space with no size and has a label with a capital letter. A line has location and direction, is always straight, and has infinitely many points that extend in both directions. A plane has infinitely many intersecting lines that extend forever in all directions.

The diagram shows point W, point X, point Y, and point Z. The line is labeled as $\overleftrightarrow{WX}$, and the plane is Plane A or Plane WYZ (or any three points in the plane).

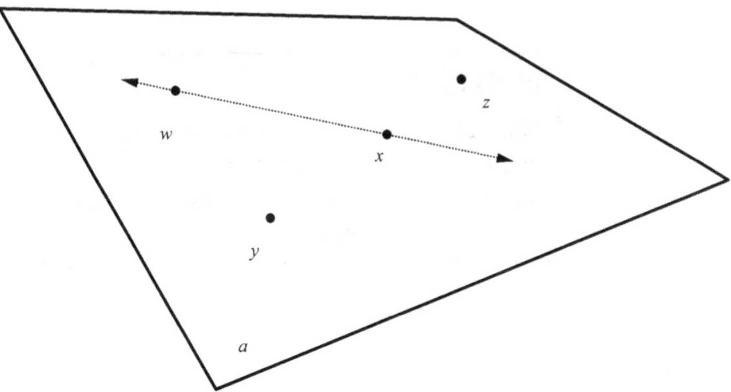

With these definitions, many other geometry terms can be defined. *Collinear* is a term for points that lie on the same line, and *coplanar* is a term for points and/or lines within the same plane. A line segment is a part of a line with two endpoints. For example, $\overline{WX}$ has endpoints W and X. A ray has an endpoint and extends forever in one direction. For example, $\longrightarrow AB$ has an endpoint of A, and $\longrightarrow BA$ has an endpoint of B. The intersection of lines, planes, segment, or rays is a point or a set of points.

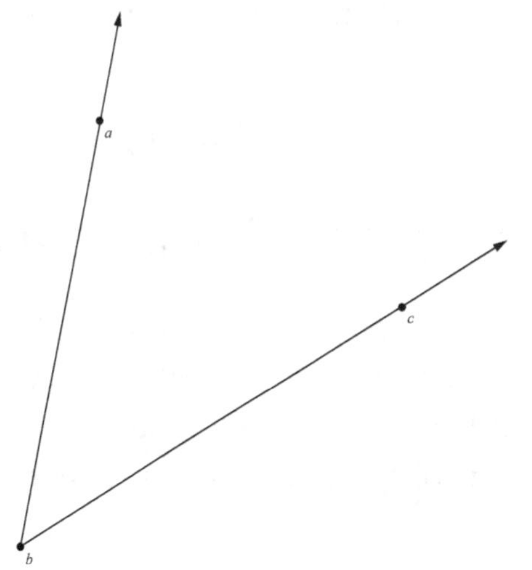

Some key statements that are evident in geometry are

- There is exactly one straight line through any two points.
- There is exactly one plane that contains any three non-collinear points.
- A line with points in the plane lies in the plane.
- Two lines intersect at a point.
- Two planes intersect at a line.

Two rays that share an endpoint form an angle. The vertex is the common endpoint of the two rays that form an angle. When naming an angle, the vertex is the center point. The angle below is named $\angle ABC$ or $\angle CBA$.

An acute angle has a measure between 0° and 90°, and a 90° angle is a right angle. An obtuse angle has a measure between 90° and 180°, and a 180° angle is a straight angle.

There are two special sets of lines. Parallel lines are at least two lines that never intersect within the same plane. Perpendicular lines intersect at one point and form four angles.

Example

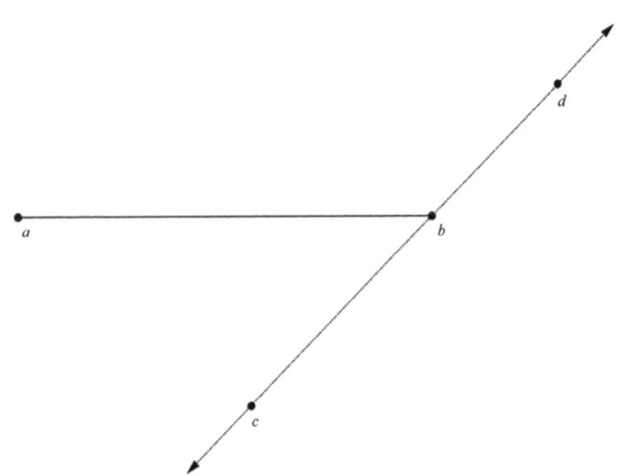

> **BE CAREFUL!**
> Lines are always named with two points, a plane can be named with three points, and an angle is named with the vertex as the center point.

Describe the diagram.

A. Points *A*, *B*, *C*, and *D* are collinear.

B. Points *A*, *C*, and *D* are collinear.

C. $\overline{CD}$ intersects $\overleftrightarrow{AB}$ at point *B*.

D. $\overline{AB}$ intersects $\overleftrightarrow{CD}$ at point *B*.

The correct answer is **D.** The correct solution is $\overline{AB}$ intersects $\overleftrightarrow{CD}$ at point *B*. The segment intersects the line at point *B*.

Line and Rotational Symmetry

Symmetry is a reflection or rotation of a shape that allows that shape to be carried onto itself. Line symmetry, or reflection symmetry, is when two halves of a shape are reflected onto each other across a line. A shape may have none, one, or several lines of symmetry. A kite has one line of symmetry, and a scalene triangle has no lines of symmetry.

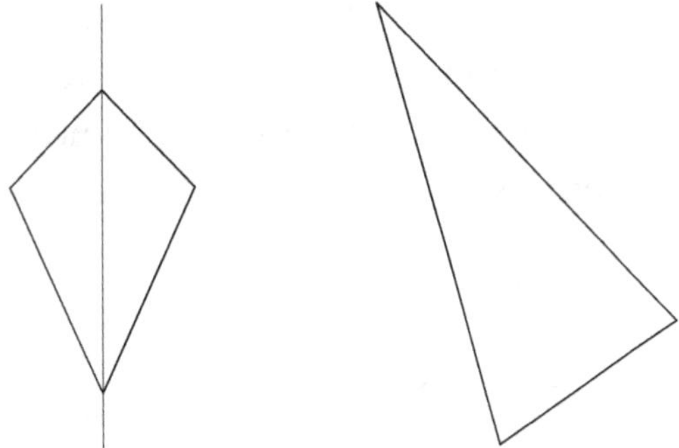

Rotational symmetry is when a figure can be mapped onto itself by a rotation about a point through any angle between 0° and 360°. The order of rotational symmetry is the number of times the object can be rotated. If there is no rotational symmetry, the order is 1 because the object can only be rotated 360° to map the figure onto itself. A square has 90° rotational symmetry and is order 4 because it can be rotated 90°, 180°, 270°, and 360°. A trapezoid has no rotational symmetry and is order 1 because it can only be rotated 360° to map onto itself.

KEEP IN MIND

A polygon can have both, neither, or either reflection and rotational symmetry.

Example

What is the rotational symmetry for a regular octagon?

A. 30° B. 45° C. 60° D. 75°

The correct answer is **B**. The correct solution is 45°. For a regular polygon, divide 360° by the eight sides of the octagon to obtain 45°.

Rotations, Reflections, and Translations

There are three types of transformations: rotations, reflections, and translations. A rotation is a turn of a figure about a point in a given direction. A reflection is a flip over a line of symmetry, and a translation is a slide horizontally, vertically, or both. Each of these transformations produces a congruent image.

A rotation changes ordered pairs (x, y) in the coordinate plane. A 90° rotation counterclockwise about the point becomes $(-y, x)$, a 180° rotation counterclockwise about the point becomes $(-x, -y)$, and a 270° rotation the point becomes $(y, -x)$. Using the point (6, −8),

- 90° rotation counterclockwise about the origin (8, 6)
- 180° rotation counterclockwise about the origin (−6, 8)
- 270° rotation counterclockwise about the origin (−8, −6)

A reflection also changes ordered pairs (x, y) in the coordinate plane. A reflection across the x-axis changes the sign of the y-coordinate, and a reflection across the y-axis changes the sign of the x-coordinate. A reflection over the line $y = x$ changes the points to (y, x), and a reflection over the line $y = -x$ changes the points to $(-y, -x)$. Using the point $(6, -8)$,

- A reflection across the x-axis $(6, 8)$
- A reflection across the y-axis $(-6, -8)$
- A reflection over the line $y = x$ $(-8, 6)$
- A reflection over the line $y = -x$ $(8, -6)$

KEEP IN MIND

A rotation is a turn, a reflection is a flip, and a translation is a slide.

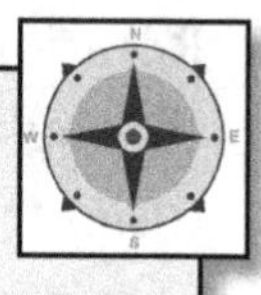

A translation changes ordered pairs (x, y) left or right and/or up or down. Adding a positive value to an x-coordinate is a translation to the right, and adding a negative value to an x-coordinate is a translation to the left. Adding a positive value to a y-coordinate is a translation up, and adding a negative value to a y-coordinate is a translation down. Using the point $(6, -8)$,

- A translation of $(x + 3)$ is a translation right 3 units $(9, -8)$
- A translation of $(x - 3)$ is a translation left 3 units $(3, -8)$
- A translation of $(y + 3)$ is a translation up 3 units $(6, -5)$
- A translation of $(y - 3)$ is a translation down 3 units $(6, -11)$

Example

ΔABC has points A (3, –2), B (2, –1), and C (–1, 4), which after a transformation become A' (2, 3), B' (1, 2), and C' (–4, –1). What is the transformation between the points?

A. Reflection across the x-axis

B. Reflection across the y-axis

C. Rotation of 90° counterclockwise

D. Rotation of 270° counterclockwise

The correct answer is **C**. The correct solution is a rotation of 90° counterclockwise because the points (x, y) become $(y, -x)$.

Let's Review!

- The terms *point, line*, and *plane* help define many terms in geometry.
- Symmetry allows a figure to carry its shape onto itself. This can be reflectional or rotational symmetry.
- Three transformations are rotation (turn), reflection (flip), and translation (slide).

Similarity, Right Triangles, and Trigonometry

This lesson defines and applies terminology associated with coordinate planes. It also demonstrates how to find the area of two-dimensional shapes and the surface area and volume of three-dimensional cubes and right prisms.

Coordinate Plane

The **coordinate plane** is a two-dimensional number line with the horizontal axis called the **x-axis** and the vertical axis called the **y-axis**. Each **ordered pair** or **coordinate** is listed as (x, y). The center point is the origin and has an ordered pair of (0, 0). A coordinate plane has four quadrants.

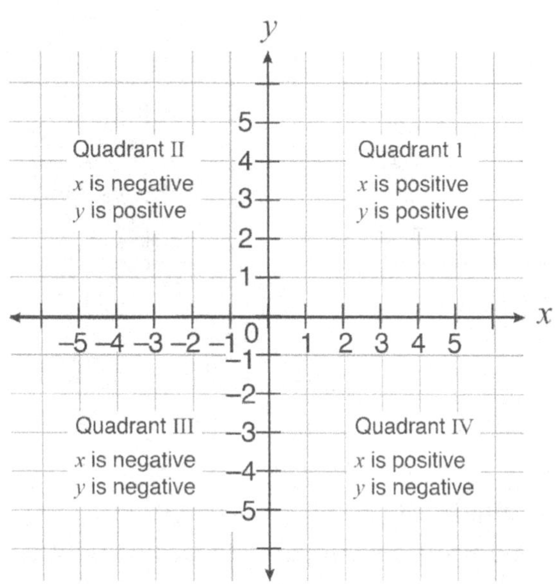

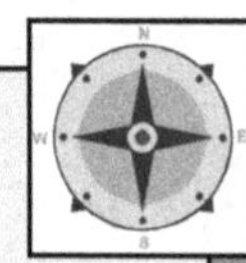

KEEP IN MIND

The *x*-coordinates are positive to the right of the *y*-axis. The *y*-coordinates are positive above the *x*-axis.

To graph a point in the coordinate plane, start with the x-coordinate. This point states the number of steps to the left (negative) or to the right (positive) from the origin. Then, the y-coordinate states the number of steps up (positive) or down (negative) from the x-coordinate.

Given a set of ordered pairs, points can be drawn in the coordinate plane to create polygons. The length of a segment can be found if the segment has the same first coordinate or the same second coordinate.

Examples

1. **Draw a triangle with the coordinates (–2, –1), (–3, 5), (–4, 2).**

A.

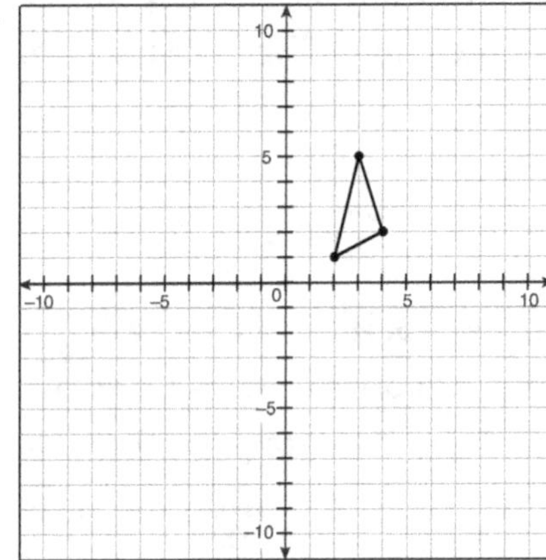

C.

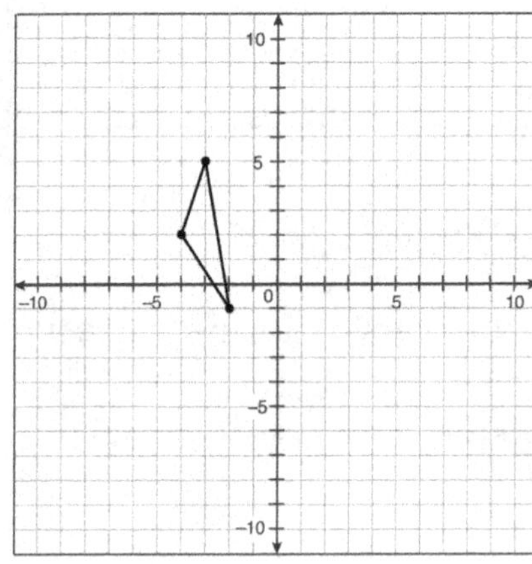

B.

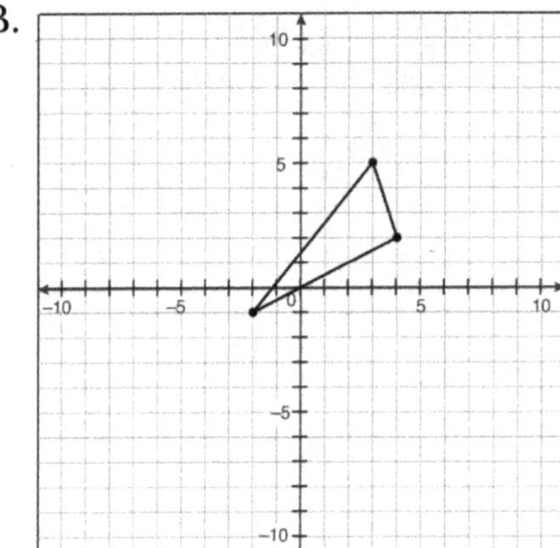

D.

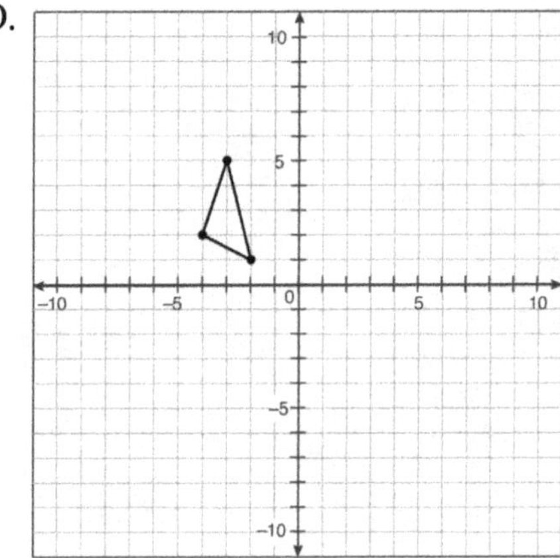

The correct answer is **C.** The first point is in the third quadrant because x is negative and y is negative, and the last two points are in the second quadrant because x is negative and y is positive.

2. **Given the coordinates for a rectangle (4, 8), (4, –2), (–1, –2), (–1, 8), find the length of each side of the rectangle.**

A. 3 units and 6 units

B. 3 units and 10 units

C. 5 units and 6 units

D. 5 units and 10 units

The correct answer is **D.** The correct solution is 5 units and 10 units. The difference between the x-coordinates is $4-(-1) = 5$ units, and the difference between the y-coordinates is $8-(-2) = 10$ units.

3. **The dimensions for a soccer field are 45 meters by 90 meters. One corner of a soccer field on the coordinate plane is (–45, –30). What could a second coordinate be?**

A. (–45, 30)

B. (–45, 45)

C. (–45, 60)

D. (–45, 75)

The correct answer is **C.** The correct solution is (–45, 60) because 90 can be added to the y-coordinate, $-30 + 90 = 60$.

Area of Two-Dimensional Objects

The **area** is the number of unit squares that fit inside a two-dimensional object. A unit square is one unit long by one unit wide, which includes 1 foot by 1 foot and 1 meter by 1 meter. The unit of measurement for area is units squared (or feet squared, meters squared, and so on). The following are formulas for calculating the area of various shapes.

BE CAREFUL!

Make sure that you apply the correct formula for area of each two-dimensional object.

- Rectangle: The product of the length and the width, $A = lw$.
- Parallelogram: The product of the base and the height, $A = bh$.
- Square: The side length squared, $A = s^2$.
- Triangle: The product of one-half the base and the height, $A = \frac{1}{2}bh$.
- Trapezoid: The product of one-half the height and the sum of the bases, $A = \frac{1}{2}h(b_1 + b_2)$.
- Regular polygon: The product of one-half the **apothem** (a line from the center of the regular polygon that is perpendicular to a side) and the sum of the perimeter, $A = \frac{1}{2}ap$.

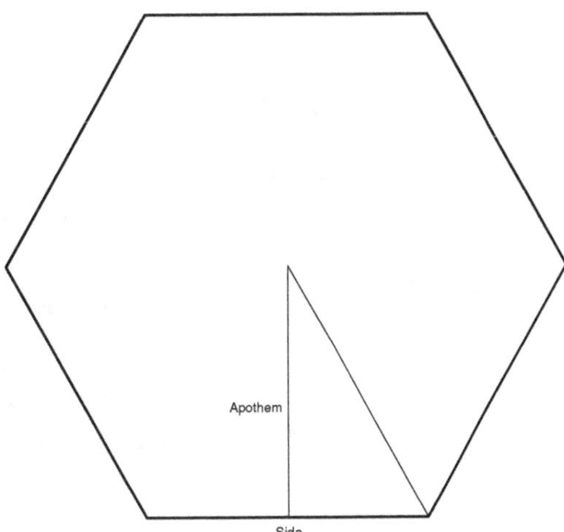

Examples

1. **A trapezoid has a height of 3 centimeters and bases of 8 centimeters and 10 centimeters. Find the area in square centimeters.**

   A. 18 B. 27 C. 52 D. 55

   The correct answer is **B.** The correct solution is 27. Substitute the values into the formula and simplify using the order of operations, $A = \frac{1}{2}h(b_1 + b_2) = \frac{1}{2}(3)(8 + 10) = \frac{1}{2}(3)(18) = 27$ square centimeters.

2. **A regular decagon has a side length of 12 inches and an apothem of 6 inches. Find the area in square inches.**

   A. 120 B. 360 C. 720 D. 960

   The correct answer is **B**. The correct solution is 360. Simplify using the order of operations, $A = \frac{1}{2}ap = \frac{1}{2}(6)(12(10)) = 360$ square inches.

3. **Two rectangular rooms need to be carpeted. The dimensions of the first room are 18 feet by 19 feet, and the dimensions of the second room are 12 feet by 10 feet. What is the total area to be carpeted in square feet?**

   A. 118 B. 236 C. 342 D. 462

   The correct answer is **D**. The correct solution is 462. Substitute the values into the formula and simplify using the order of operations, $A = lw + lw = 18(19) + 12(10) = 342 + 120 = 462$ square feet.

4. **A picture frame is in the shape of a right triangle with legs 9 centimeters and 12 centimeters and hypotenuse of 15 centimeters. What is the area in square centimeters?**

   A. 54 B. 90 C. 108 D. 180

   The correct answer is **A**. The correct solution is 54. Substitute the values into the formula and simplify using the order of operations, $A = \frac{1}{2}bh = \frac{1}{2}(9)(12) = 54$ square centimeters.

Surface Area and Volume of Cubes and Right Prisms

A three-dimensional object has length, width, and height. **Cubes** are made up of six congruent square faces. A **right prism** is made of three sets of congruent faces, with at least two sets of congruent rectangles.

BE CAREFUL!

Surface area is a two-dimensional calculation, and volume is a three-dimensional calculation.

The **surface area** of any three-dimensional object is the sum of the area of all faces. The formula for the surface area of a cube is $SA = 6s^2$ because there are six congruent faces. For a right rectangular prism, the surface area formula is $SA = 2lw + 2lh + 2hw$ because there are three sets of congruent rectangles. For a triangular prism, the surface area formula is twice the area of the base plus the area of the other three rectangles that make up the prism.

The **volume** of any three-dimensional object is the amount of space inside the object. The volume formula for a cube is $V = s^3$. The volume formula for a rectangular prism is the area of the base times the height, or $V = Bh$.

Examples

1. **A cube has a side length of 5 centimeters. What is the surface area in square centimeters?**

   A. 20 B. 25 C. 125 D. 150

   The correct answer is **D**. The correct solution is 150. Substitute the values into the formula and simplify using the order of operations, $SA = 6s^2 = 6(5^2) = 6(25) = 150$ square centimeters.

2. **A cube has a side length of 5 centimeters. What is the volume in cubic centimeters?**

   A. 20 B. 25 C. 125 D. 180

   The correct answer is **C**. The correct solution is 125. Substitute the values into the formula and simplify using the order of operations, $V = s^3 = 5^3 = 125$ cubic centimeters.

3. **A right rectangular prism has dimensions of 4 inches by 5 inches by 6 inches. What is the surface area in square inches?**

   A. 60 B. 74 C. 120 D. 148

   The correct answer is **D**. The correct solution is 148. Substitute the values into the formula and simplify using the order of operations, $SA = 2lw + 2lh + 2hw = 2(4)(5) + 2(4)(6) + 2(6)(5) = 40 + 48 + 60 = 148$ square inches.

4. **A right rectangular prism has dimensions of 4 inches by 5 inches by 6 inches. What is the volume in cubic inches?**

   A. 60 B. 62 C. 120 D. 124

   The correct answer is **C**. The correct solution is 120. Substitute the values into the formula and simplify using the order of operations, $V = lwh = 4(5)(6) = 120$ cubic inches.

Let's Review!

- The coordinate plane is a two-dimensional number line that is used to display ordered pairs. Two-dimensional shapes can be drawn on the plane, and the length of the objects can be determined based on the given coordinates.
- The area of a two-dimensional object is the amount of space inside the shape. There are area formulas to use to calculate the area of various shapes.
- For a three-dimensional object, the surface area is the sum of the area of the faces and the volume is the amount of space inside the object. Cubes and right rectangular prisms are common three-dimensional solids.

CIRCLES

This lesson introduces concepts of circles, including finding the circumference and the area of the circle.

Circle Terminology

A **circle** is a figure composed of points that are equidistant from a given point. The **center** is the point from which all points are equidistant. A **chord** is a segment whose endpoints are on the circle, and the **diameter** is a chord that goes through the center of the circle. The **radius** is a segment with one endpoint at the center of the circle and one endpoint on the circle. **Arcs** have two endpoints on the circle and all points on a circle between those endpoints.

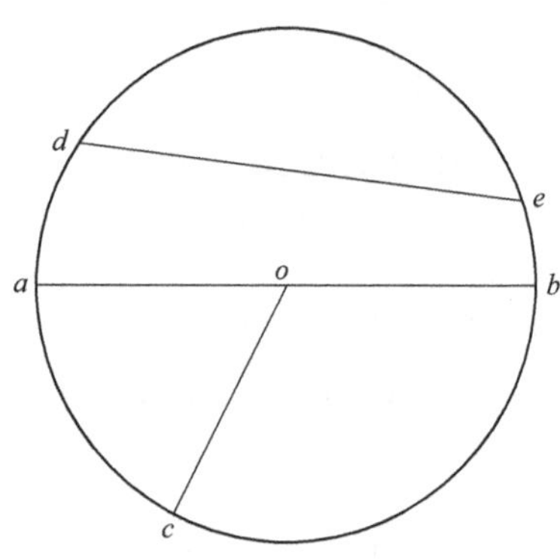

In the circle at the right, O is the center, $\overline{OC}$ is the radius, $\overline{AB}$ is the diameter, $\overline{DE}$ is a chord, and $\widehat{AD}$ is an arc.

Example

Identify a diameter of the circle.

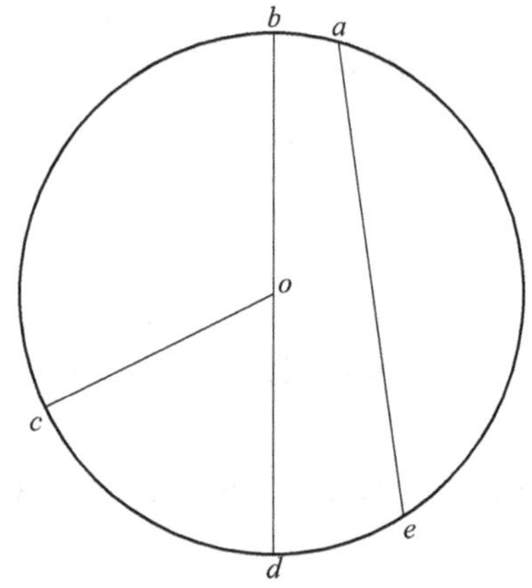

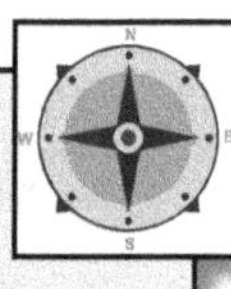

KEEP IN MIND

The radius is one-half the length of the diameter of the circle.

A. $\overline{BD}$ B. $\overline{OC}$ C. $\overline{DO}$ D. $\overline{AE}$

The correct answer is **A.** The correct solution is $\overline{BD}$ because points B and D are on the circle and the segment goes through the center O.

Circumference and Area of a Circle

The **circumference** of a circle is the perimeter, or the distance, around the circle. There are two ways to find the circumference. The formulas are the product of the diameter and pi or the product of twice the radius and pi. In symbol form, the formulas are $C = \pi d$ or $C = 2\pi r$.

BE CAREFUL!

Make sure that you apply the correct formula for circumference and area of a circle.

The **area** of a circle is the amount of space inside a circle. The formula is the product of pi and the radius squared. In symbol form, the formula is $A = \pi r^2$. The area is always expressed in square units.

Given the circumference or the area of a circle, the radius and the diameter can be determined. The given measurement is substituted into the appropriate formula. Then, the equation is solved for the radius or the diameter.

Examples

1. **Find the circumference in centimeters of a circle with a diameter of 8 centimeters. Use 3.14 for π.**

   A. 12.56 B. 25.12 C. 50.24 D. 100.48

   The correct answer is **B**. The correct solution is 25.12 because $C = \pi d \approx 3.14(8) \approx 25.12$ centimeters.

2. **Find the area in square inches of a circle with a radius of 15 inches. Use 3.14 for π.**

   A. 94.2 B. 176.63 C. 706.5 D. 828.96

   The correct answer is **C**. The correct solution is 706.5 because $A = \pi r^2 \approx 3.14(15)^2 \approx 3.14(225) \approx 706.5$ square inches.

3. **A circle has a circumference of 70 centimeters. Find the diameter to the nearest tenth of a centimeter. Use 3.14 for π.**

   A. 11.1 B. 22.3 C. 33.5 D. 44.7

   The correct answer is **B**. The correct solution is 22.3 because $C = \pi d; 70 = 3.14d; d \approx 22.3$ centimeters.

4. **A circle has an area of 95 square centimeters. Find the radius to the nearest tenth of a centimeter. Use 3.14 for π.**

   A. 2.7 B. 5.5 C. 8.2 D. 10.9

   The correct answer is **B**. The correct solution is 5.5 because $A = \pi r^2; 95 = 3.14r^2; 30.25 = r^2;\ r \approx 5.5$ centimeters.

Finding Circumference or Area Given the Other Value

Given the circumference of a circle, the area of the circle can be found. First, substitute the circumference into the formula and find the radius. Substitute the radius into the area formula and simplify.

Reverse the process to find the circumference given the area. First, substitute the area into the area formula and find the radius. Substitute the radius into the circumference formula and simplify.

BE CAREFUL!

Pay attention to the details with each formula and apply them in the correct order.

Examples

1. **The circumference of a circle is 45 inches. Find the area of the circle in square inches. Round to the nearest tenth. Use 3.14 for π.**

   A. 51.8 B. 65.1 C. 162.8 D. 204.5

   The correct answer is **C**. The correct solution is 162.8.

   $C = 2\pi r; 45 = 2(3.14)r; 45 = 6.28r; r \approx 7.2$ inches. $A = \pi r^2 \approx 3.14(7.2)^2 \approx 3.14(51.84) \approx 162.8$ square inches.

2. **The area of a circle is 60 square centimeters. Find the circumference of the circle in centimeters. Round to the nearest tenth. Use 3.14 for π.**

   A. 4.4 B. 13.8 C. 19.1 D. 27.6

   The correct answer is **D**. The correct solution is 27.6.

   $A = \pi r^2; 60 = 3.14r^2; 19.11 = r^2; r \approx 4.4$ centimeters. $C = 2\pi r; C = 2(3.14)4.4 \approx 27.6$ centimeters.

Let's Review!

- Key terms related to circles are *radius, diameter, chord,* and *arc*. Note that the diameter is twice the radius.
- The circumference or the perimeter of a circle is the product of pi and the diameter or twice the radius and pi.
- The area of the circle is the product of pi and the radius squared.

MEASUREMENT AND DIMENSION

This lesson applies the formulas of volume for cylinders, pyramids, cones, and spheres to solve problems.

Volume of a Cylinder

A **cylinder** is a three-dimensional figure with two identical circular bases and a rectangular lateral face.

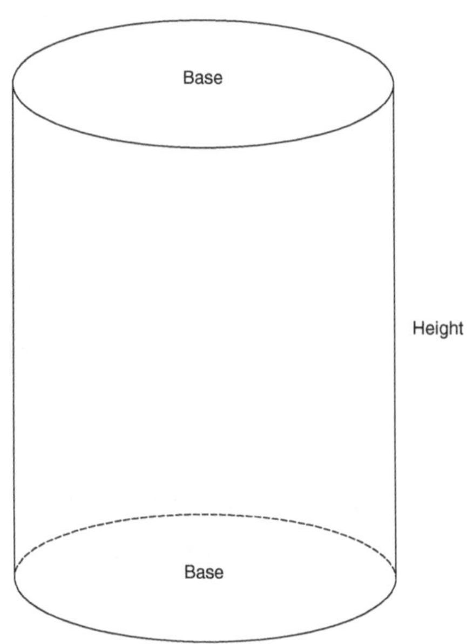

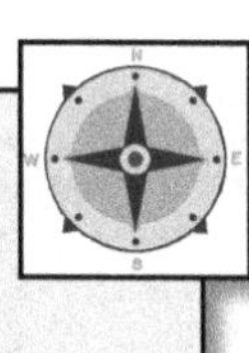

KEEP IN MIND

The volume of a cylinder can be expressed in terms of π, and the volume is measured in cubic units.

The volume of a cylinder equals the product of the area of the base and the height of the cylinder. This is the same formula used to calculate the volume of a right prism. In this case, the area of a base is a circle, so the formula is $V = Bh = \pi r^2 h$. The height is the perpendicular distance between the two circular bases.

Example

Find the volume of a cylinder in cubic centimeters with a radius of 13 centimeters and a height of 12 centimeters.

A. 156π B. 312π C. $1{,}872\pi$ D. $2{,}028\pi$

The correct answer is **D**. The correct solution is $2{,}028\pi$. Substitute the values into the formula and simplify using the order of operations, $V = \pi r^2 h = \pi 13^2(12) = \pi(169)(12) = 2{,}028\pi$ cubic centimeters.

Volume of a Pyramid and a Cone

A **pyramid** is a three-dimensional solid with one base and all edges from the base meeting at the top, or apex. Pyramids can have any two-dimensional shape as the base. A **cone** is similar to a pyramid, but it has a circle instead of a polygon for the base.

BE CAREFUL!

Make sure that you apply the correct formula for area of the base for a pyramid.

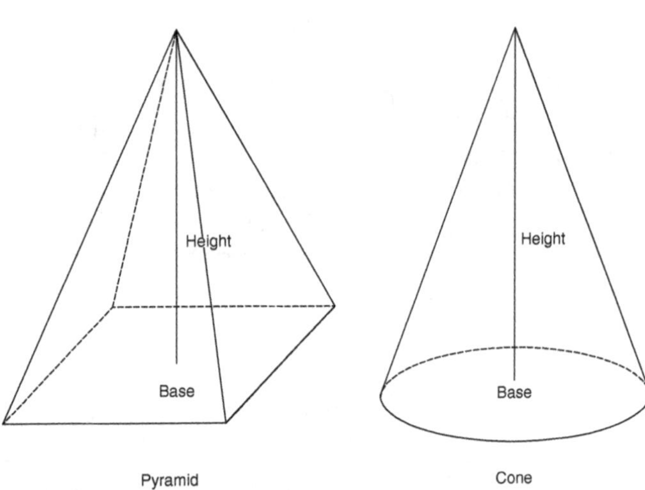

The formula for the volume of a pyramid is similar to a prism, $V = \frac{1}{3}Bh$ where B is the area of the base. The base is a circle for a cone, and the formula for the volume is $V = \frac{1}{3}Bh = \frac{1}{3}\pi r^2 h$.

Examples

1. **A regular hexagonal pyramid has base with side lengths of 5 centimeters and an apothem of 3 centimeters. If the height is 6 centimeters, find the volume in cubic centimeters.**

   A. 90 B. 180 C. 270 D. 360

   The correct answer is **A**. The correct solution is 90. Substitute the values into the formula and simplify using the order of operations, $V = \frac{1}{3}Bh = \frac{1}{3}(\frac{1}{2}ap)h = \frac{1}{3}(\frac{1}{2}(3)(30))6 = 90$ cubic centimeters.

2. **A cone has a radius of 10 centimeters and a height of 9 centimeters. Find the volume in cubic centimeters.**

   A. 270π B. 300π C. 810π D. 900π

   The correct answer is **B**. The correct solution is 300π. Substitute the values into the formula and simplify using the order of operations, $V = \frac{1}{3}\pi r^2 h = \frac{1}{3}\pi 10^2(9) = \frac{1}{3}\pi(100)(9) = 300\pi$ cubic centimeters.

Volume of a Sphere

A **sphere** is a round, three-dimensional solid, with every point on its surface equidistant to the center. The formula for the volume of a sphere is represented by just the radius of the sphere. The volume of a sphere is $V = \frac{4}{3}\pi r^3$. The volume of a hemi (half) of a sphere is $V = \left(\frac{1}{2}\right)\frac{4}{3}\pi r^3 = \frac{2}{3}\pi r^3$.

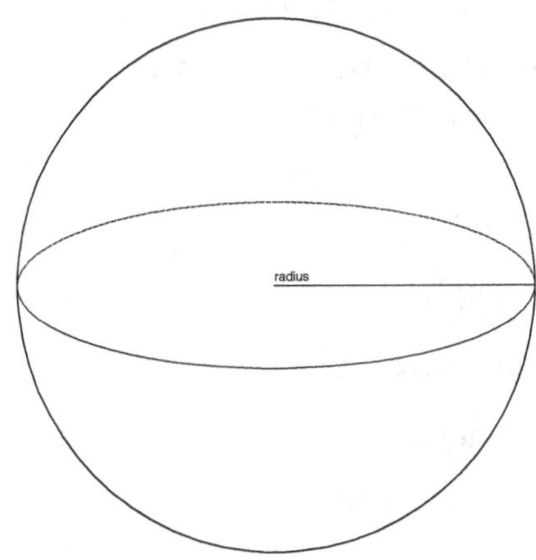

BE CAREFUL!

The radius is cubed, not squared, for the volume of a sphere.

Example

A sphere has a radius of 3 centimeters. Find the volume of a sphere in cubic centimeters.

A. 18π B. 27π C. 36π D. 45π

The correct answer is **C**. The correct solution is 36π. Substitute the values into the formula and simplify using the order of operations, $V = \frac{4}{3}\pi r^3 = \frac{4}{3}\pi 3^3 = \frac{4}{3}\pi(27) = 36\pi$ cubic centimeters.

Let's Review!

- The volume is the capacity of a three-dimensional object and is expressed in cubic units.
- The volume formula for a cylinder is the product of the area of the base (which is a circle) and the height of the cylinder.
- The volume formula for a pyramid or cone is one-third of the product of the area of the base (a circle in the case of the cone) and the height of the pyramid or cone.
- The volume formula for a sphere is $V = \frac{4}{3}\pi r^3$.

Chapter 8 Geometry Practice Quiz

1. **The bottom of a plastic pool has an area of 64 square feet. What is the radius to the nearest tenth of a foot? Use 3.14 for π.**

   A. 2.3 C. 6.9

   B. 4.5 D. 10.2

2. **The area of a circular hand mirror is 200 square centimeters. Find the circumference of the mirror to the nearest tenth of a centimeter. Use 3.14 for π.**

   A. 25.1 C. 75.3

   B. 50.2 D. 100.4

3. **The circumference of a pie is 300 centimeters. Find the area of one-fourth of the pie to the nearest tenth of a square centimeter. Use 3.14 for π.**

   A. 1,793.6 C. 7,174.4

   B. 2,284.8 D. 14,348.8

4. **A regular hexagon has a rotational order of 6. What is the smallest number of degrees for the figure to be rotated onto itself?**

   A. 30° C. 90°

   B. 60° D. 120°

5. **ΔGHI has points $G(2, 7)$, $H(-3, -8)$, and $I(-6, 0)$. After a transformation, the points are $G'(7, 2)$, $H'(-8, -3)$, and $I'(0, -6)$. What is the transformation between the points?**

   A. Reflection across the x-axis

   B. Reflection across the y-axis

   C. Reflection across the line of $y = x$

   D. Reflection across the line of $y = -x$

6. **Name the right angle in the diagram.**

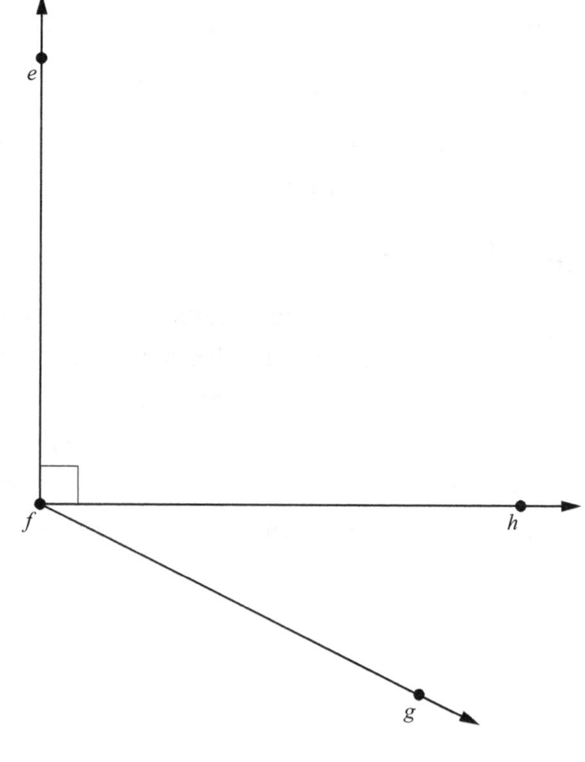

   A. $\angle EHF$ C. $\angle EFH$

   B. $\angle EFG$ D. $\angle EGF$

7. The volume of a cone is 28π cubic inches, and its diameter is 2 inches. What is the height of the cone?

A. 2 inches
B. 4 inches
C. 6 inches
D. 8 inches

8. A hemi-sphere has a radius of 6 centimeters. Find the volume in cubic centimeters.

A. 72π
B. 144π
C. 288π
D. 576π

9. A rectangular pyramid has a height of 7 meters and a volume of 112 cubic meters. Find the area of the base in square meters.

A. 16
B. 28
C. 42
D. 48

10. A right rectangular prism has dimensions of 3 inches by 6 inches by 9 inches. What is the surface area in square inches?

A. 162
B. 198
C. 232
D. 286

11. A right triangle has a base of 6 inches and a hypotenuse of 10 inches. Find the height in inches of the triangle if the area is 24 square inches.

A. 4
B. 6
C. 8
D. 10

12. Draw a rectangle with the coordinates (5,7), (5,1), (1,1), (1,7).

A.

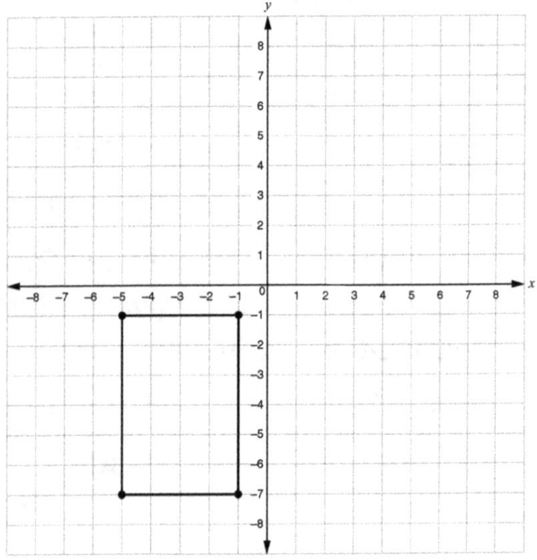

B.

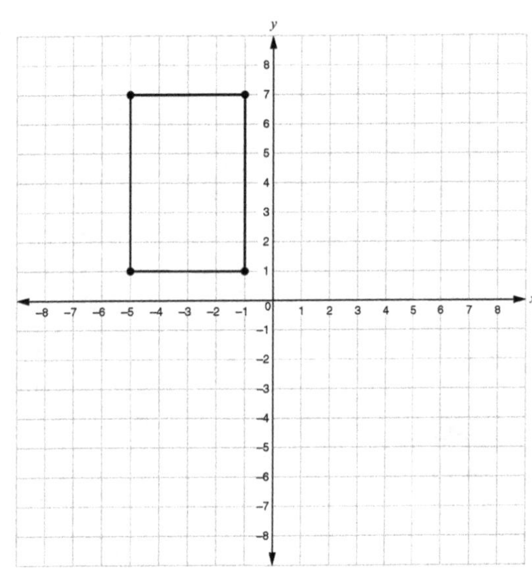

C.

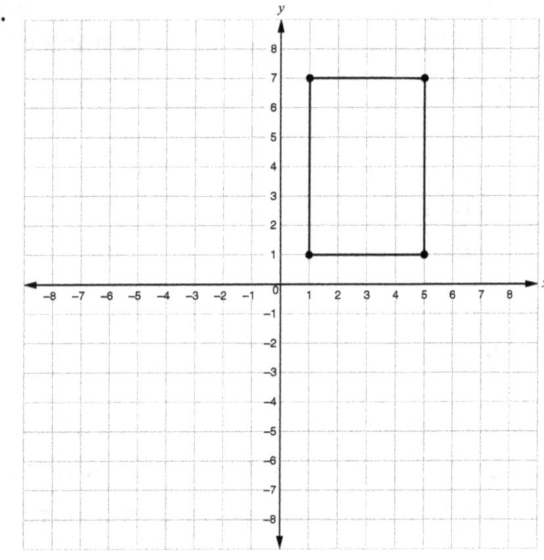

D.

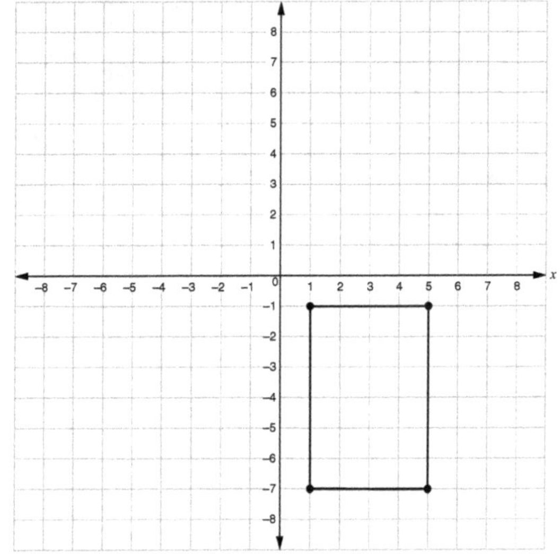

Chapter 8 Geometry Practice Quiz – Answer Key

1. B. The correct solution is 4.5 because $A = \pi r^2; 64 = 3.14 r^2; 20.38 = r^2;\ r \approx 4.5$ feet. **See Lesson: Circles.**

2. B. The correct solution is 50.2. $A = \pi r^2; 200 = 3.14 r^2; 63.69 = r^2; r \approx 8.0$ centimeters. $C = 2\pi r; C = 2(3.14)8.0 \approx 50.2$ centimeters. **See Lesson: Circles.**

3. A. The correct solution is 1,793.6. $C = 2\pi r; 300 = 2(3.14)r; 300 = 6.28r; r \approx 47.8$ centimeters. $A = \frac{1}{4}\pi r^2 \approx \frac{1}{4}(3.14)(47.8)^2 \approx \frac{1}{4}3.14(2{,}284.84) \approx 1793.6$ square centimeters. **See Lesson: Circles.**

4. B. The correct solution is 60°. For a regular hexagon, divide 360° by the six sides to obtain 60°. **See Lesson: Congruence.**

5. C. The correct solution is a reflection across the line of $y = x$ because the points (x, y) become (y, x). **See Lesson: Congruence.**

6. C. The correct solution is $\angle EFH$ because the vertex of the right angle is F and the other two points are E and H. **See Lesson: Congruence.**

7. C. The correct solution is 6 inches. Substitute the values into the formula, $2\pi = \frac{1}{3}\pi(1)^2 h$ and simplify using the right side of the equation by applying the exponent and multiplying, $2\pi = \frac{1}{3}\pi(1)h,\ 2\pi = \frac{1}{3}\pi h$. Multiply both sides of the equation by 3 to get a solution of 6 inches. **See Lesson: Measurement and Dimension.**

8. B. The correct solution is 144π. Substitute the values into the formula and simplify using the order of operations, $V = \frac{2}{3}\pi r^3 = \frac{2}{3}\pi(6^3) = \frac{2}{3}\pi(216) = 144\pi$ cubic centimeters. **See Lesson: Measurement and Dimension.**

9. D. The correct solution is 48. Substitute the values into the formula, $112 = \frac{1}{3}B(7)$ and simplify the right side of the equation, $112 = \frac{7}{3}B$. Multiply both sides of the equation by the reciprocal, $B = 48$ square meters. **See Lesson: Measurement and Dimension.**

10. B. The correct solution is 198. Substitute the values into the formula and simplify using the order of operations, $SA = 2lw + 2lh + 2hw = 2(3)(6) + 2(6)(9) + 2(9)(3) = 36 + 108 + 54 = 198$ square inches. **See Lesson: Similarity, Right Triangles, and Trigonometry.**

11. C. The correct solution is 8. Substitute the values into the formula, $24 = \frac{1}{2}(6)h$ and simplify the right side of the equation, $24 = 3h$. Divide both sides of the equation by 3, $h = 8$ inches. **See Lesson: Similarity, Right Triangles, and Trigonometry.**

12. C. All points are in the first quadrant. **See Lesson: Similarity, Right Triangles, and Trigonometry.**

CHAPTER 9 STATISTICS AND PROBABILITY

INTERPRETING GRAPHICS

This lesson discusses how to create a bar, line, and circle graph and how to interpret data from these graphs. It also explores how to calculate and interpret the measures of central tendency.

Creating a Line, Bar, and Circle Graph

A line graph is a graph with points connected by segments that examines changes over time. The horizontal axis contains the independent variable (the input value), which is usually time. The vertical axis contains the dependent variable (the output value), which is an item that measures a quantity. A line graph will have a title and an appropriate scale to display the data. The graph can include more than one line.

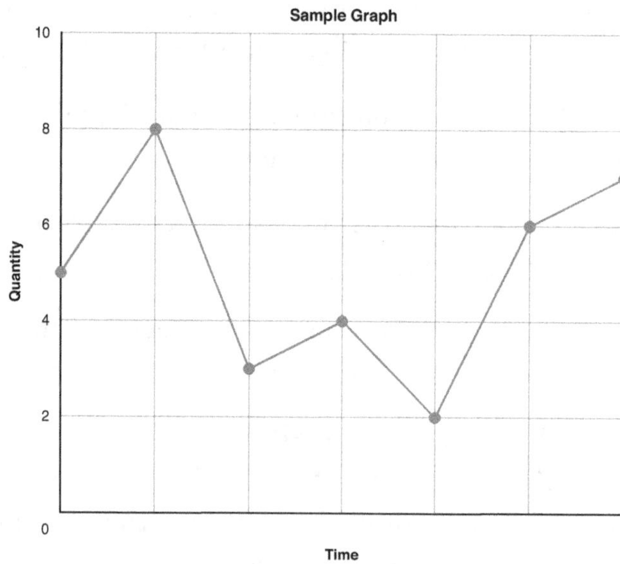

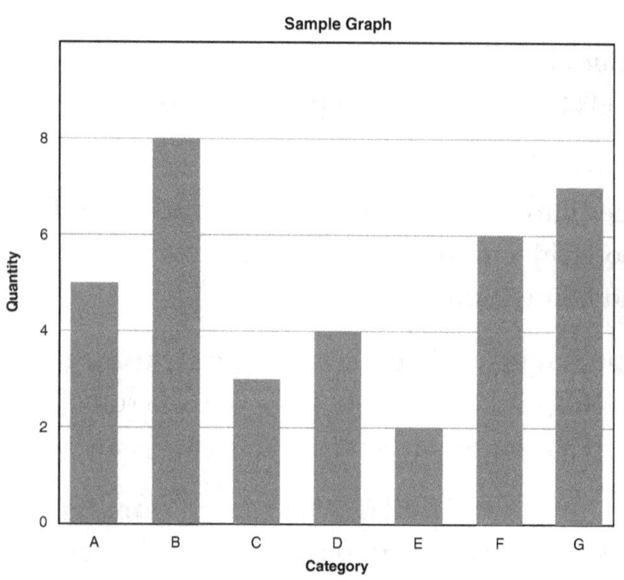

A bar graph uses rectangular horizontal or vertical bars to display information. A bar graph has categories on the horizontal axis and the quantity on the vertical axis. Bar graphs need a title and an appropriate scale for the frequency. The graph can include more than one bar.

BE CAREFUL

Make sure to use the appropriate scale for each type of graph.

A circle graph is a circular chart that is divided into parts, and each part shows the relative size of the value. To create a circle graph, find the total number and divide each part by the total to find the percentage. Then, to find the part of the circle, multiply each percent by 360°. Draw each part of the circle and create a title.

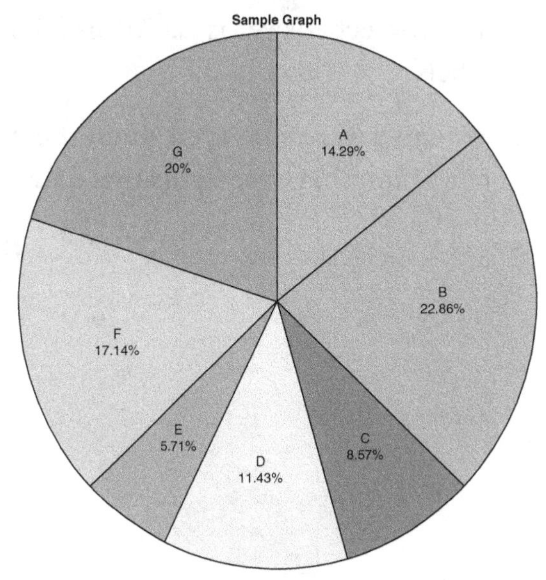

Examples

1. **The table shows the amount of rainfall in inches. Select the line graph that represents this data.**

Day	1	2	3	4	5	6	7	8	9	10	11	12
Rainfall Amount	0.5	0.2	0.4	1.1	1.6	0.9	0.7	1.3	1.5	0.8	0.5	0.1

A.
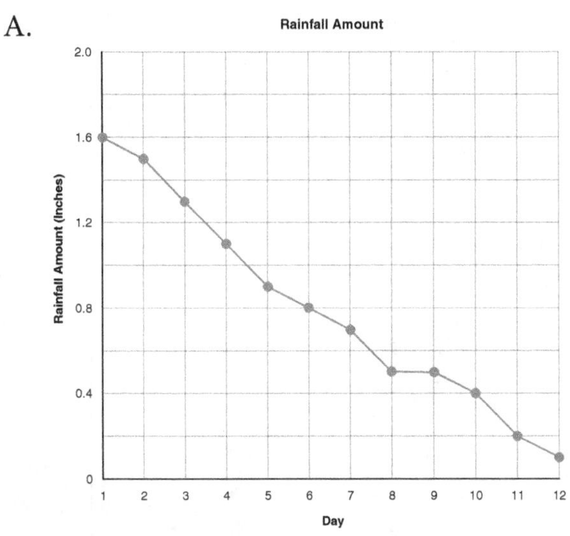

C.
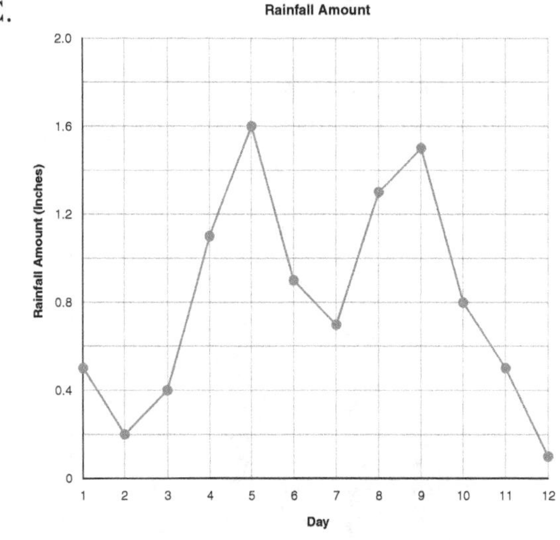

B.
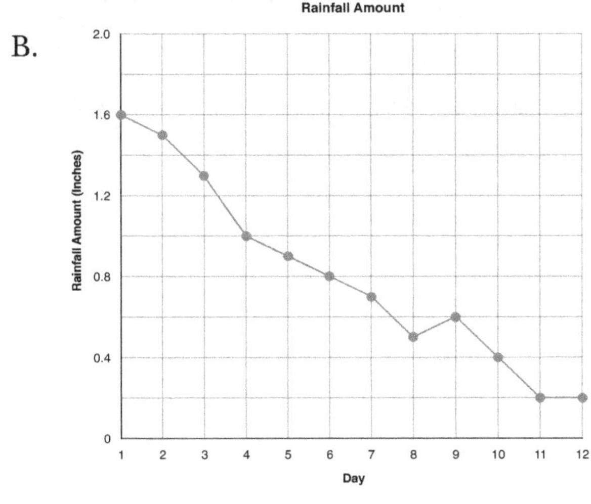

D.
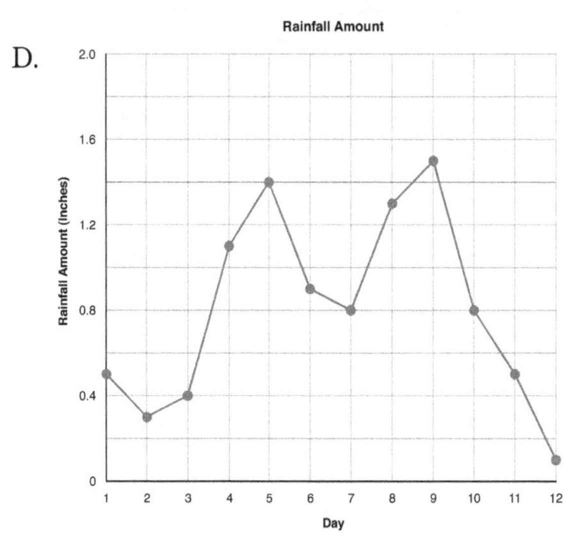

The correct answer is **C**. The graph is displayed correctly for the days with the appropriate labels.

2. **Students were surveyed about their favorite pet, and the table shows the results. Select the bar graph that represents this data.**

Pet	Quantity
Dog	14
Cat	16
Fish	4
Bird	8
Gerbil	7
Pig	3

A.
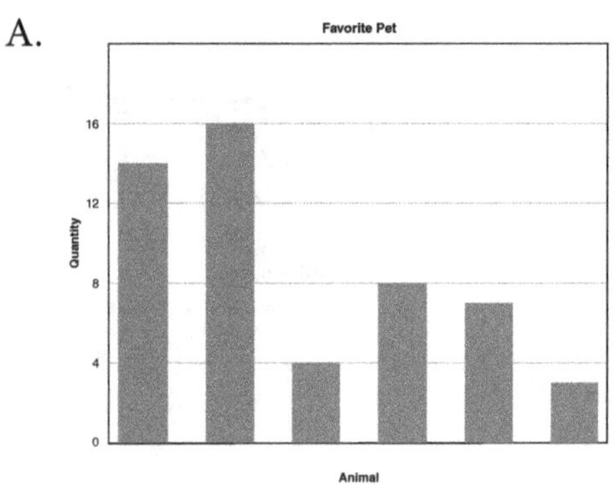

C.
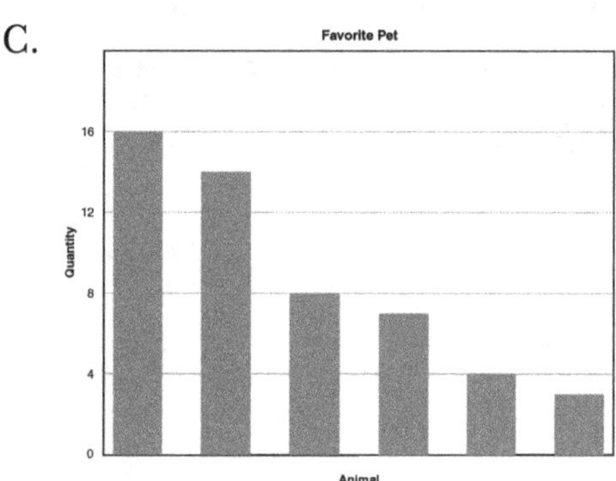

B.
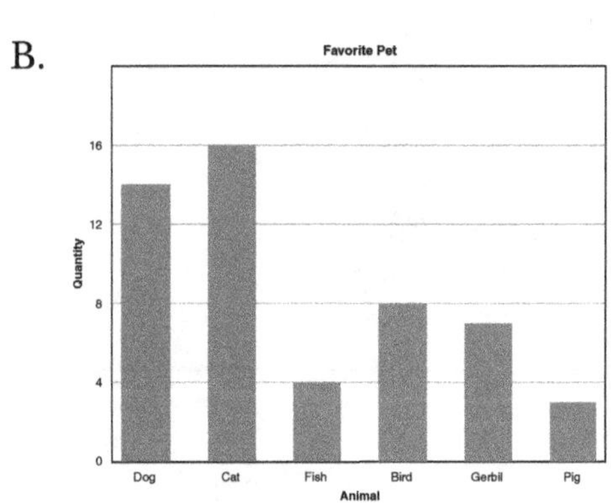

D.
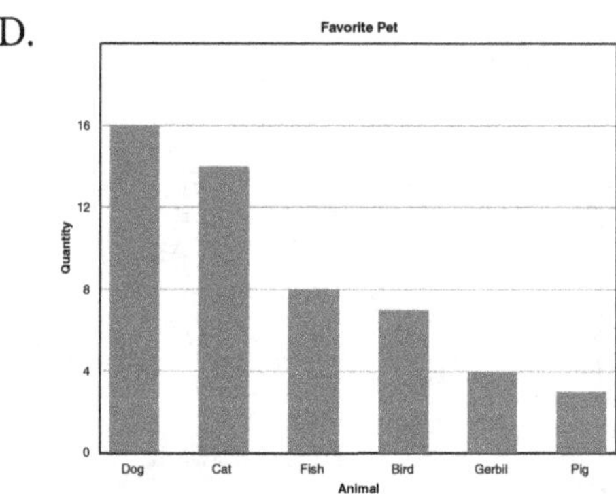

The correct answer is **B**. The bar graph represents each pet correctly and is labeled correctly.

3. **The table shows the amount a family spends each month. Select the circle graph that represents the data.**

Item	Food/Household Items	Bills	Mortgage	Savings	Miscellaneous
Amount	$700	$600	$400	$200	$100

A.

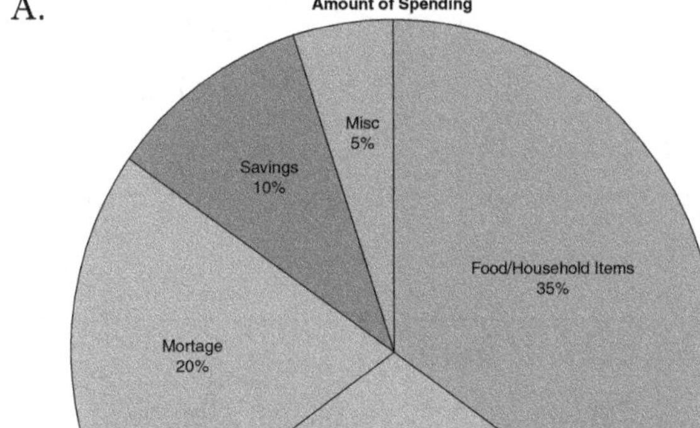

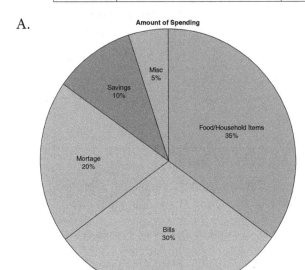

C.

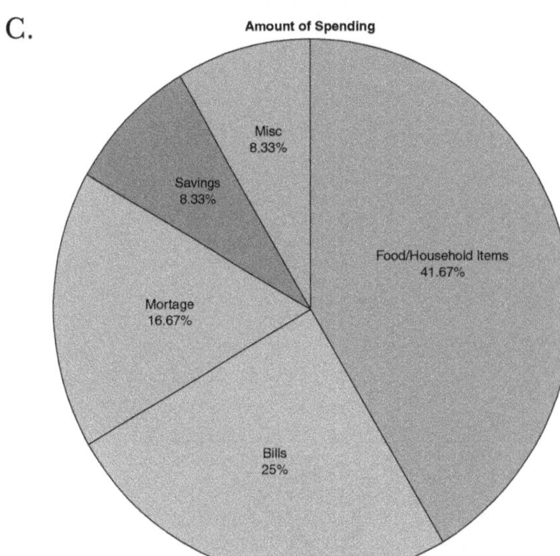

B.

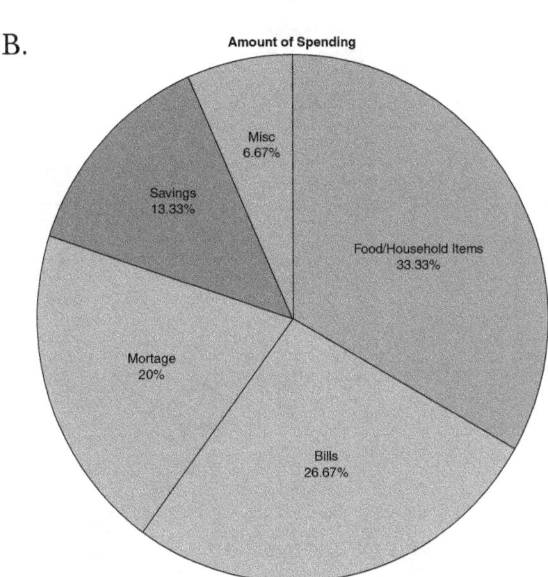

D.

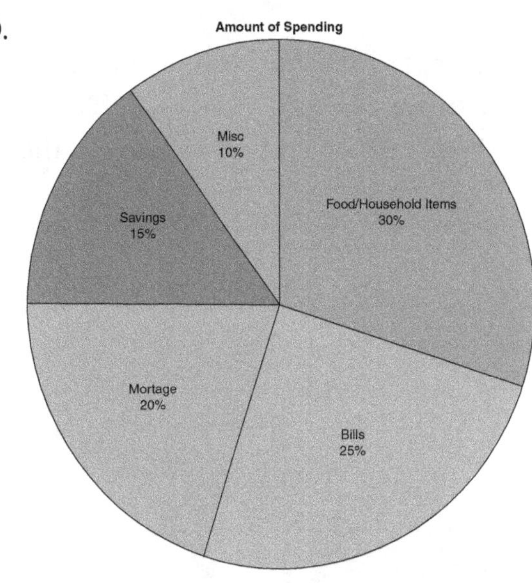

The correct answer is **A.** The total amount spent each month is $2,000. The section of the circle for food and household items is $\frac{700}{2,000} = 0.35 = 35\%$. The section of the circle for bills is $\frac{600}{2,000} = 0.30 = 30\%$. The section of the circle for mortgage is $\frac{400}{2,000} = 0.20 = 20\%$. The section of the circle for savings is $\frac{200}{2,000} = 0.10 = 10\%$. The section of the circle for miscellaneous is $\frac{100}{2,000} = 0.05 = 5\%$.

Interpreting and Evaluating Line, Bar, and Circle Graphs

Graph and charts are used to create visual examples of information, and it is important to be able to interpret them. The examples from Section 1 can show a variety of conclusions.

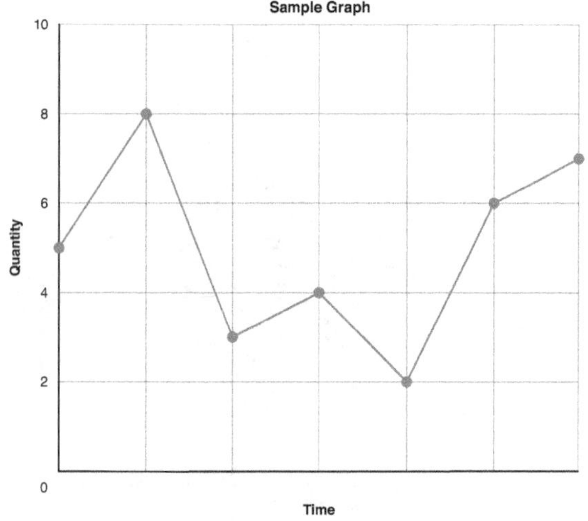

- The minimum value is 2, and the maximum value is 8.
- The largest decrease is between the second and third points.
- The largest increase is between the fifth and sixth points.

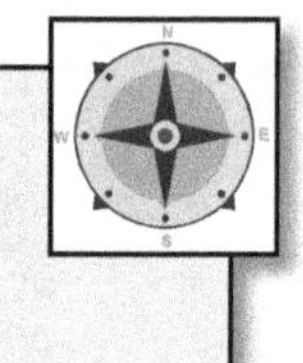

KEEP IN MIND

Read and determine the parts of the graph before answering questions related to the graph.

- Category B is the highest with 8.
- Category E is the lowest with 2.
- There are no categories that are the same.

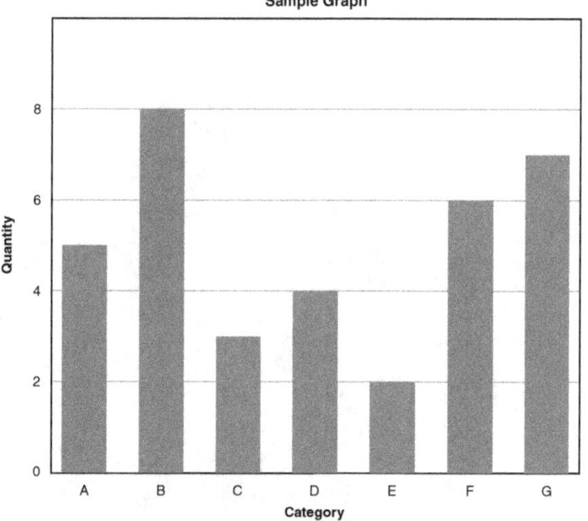

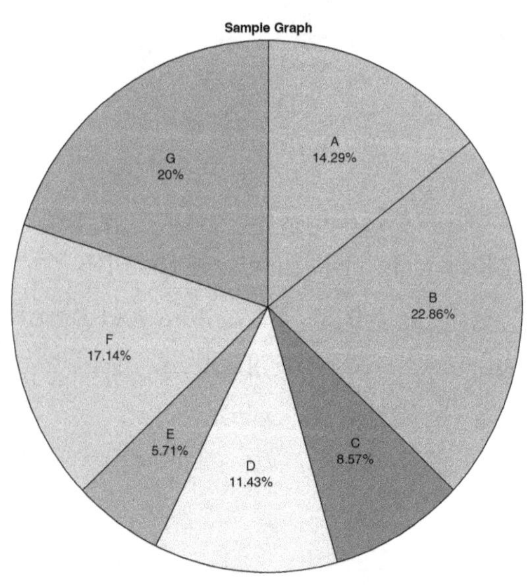

- Category B is the largest with 22.86%.
- Category E is the smallest with 5.71%.
- All of the categories are less than one-fourth of the graph.

Examples

1. **The line chart shows the number of minutes a commuter drove to work during a month. Which statement is true for the line chart?**

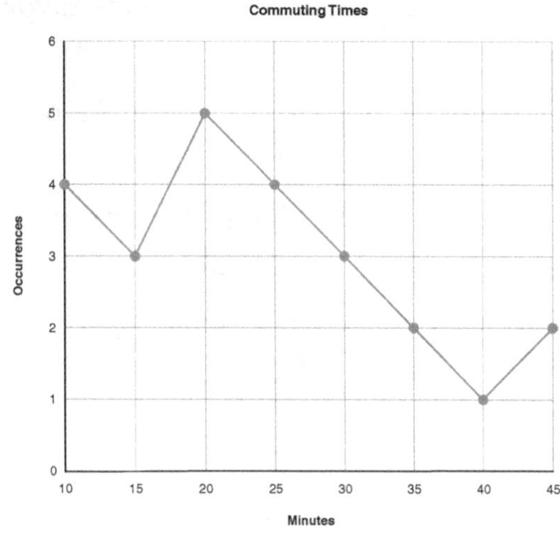

A. The commuter drove 25 minutes to work the most times

B. The commuter drove 25 minutes to work the fewest times.

C. The commuter took 10 minutes and 25 minutes twice during the month.

D. The commuter took 35 minutes and 45 minutes twice during the month.

The correct answer is **D.** The commuter took 35 minutes and 45 minutes twice during the month.

2. **The bar chart shows the distance different families traveled for summer vacation. Which statement is true for the bar chart?**

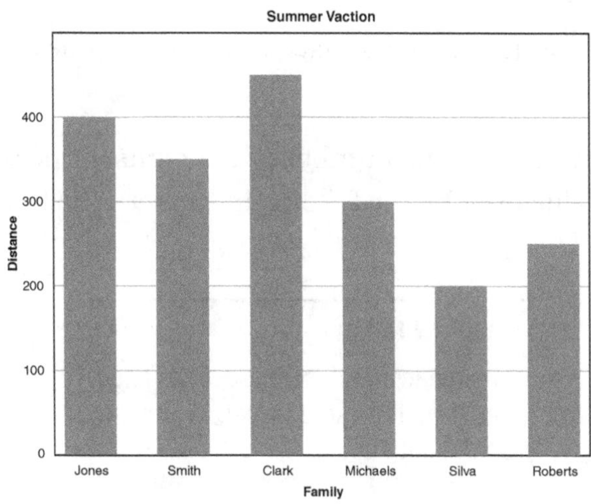

A. All families drove more than 200 miles.

B. The Clark family traveled 250 miles more than the Silva family.

C. The Roberts family traveled more miles than the Michaels family.

D. The Jones family is the only family that traveled 400 miles or more.

The correct answer is **B.** The correct solution is the Clark family traveled 250 miles more than the Silva family. The Clark family traveled 450 miles, and the Silva family traveled 200 miles, making the difference 250 miles.

3. Students were interviewed about their favorite subject in school. The circle graph shows the results. Which statement is true for the circle graph?

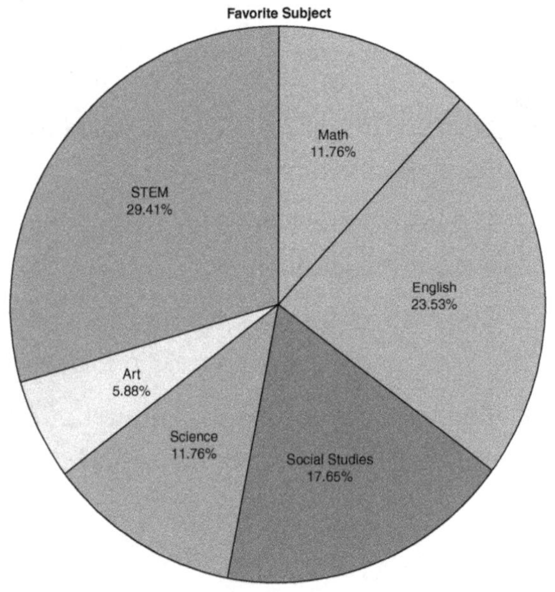

A. Math is the smallest percent for favorite subject.

B. The same number of students favor science and social studies.

C. English and STEM together are more than half of the respondents.

D. English and social students together are more than half of the respondents.

The correct answer is **C**. The correct solution is English and STEM together are more than half of the respondents because these values are more than 50% combined.

Mean, Median, Mode, and Range

The mean, median, mode, and range are common values related to data sets. These values can be calculated using the data set 2, 4, 7, 6, 8, 5, 6, and 3.

The mean is the sum of all numbers in a data set divided by the number of elements in the set. The sum of items in the data set is 41. Divide the value of 41 by the 8 items in the set. The mean is 5.125.

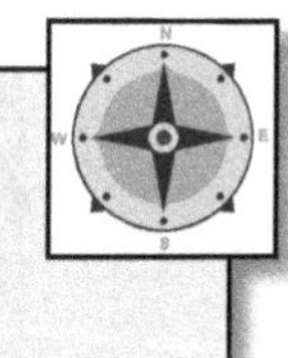

KEEP IN MIND

The mean, median, mode, and range can have the same values, depending on the data set.

The median is the middle number of a data set when written in order. If there are an odd number of items, the median is the middle number. If there are an even number of items, the median is the mean of the middle two numbers. The numbers in order are 2, 3, 4, 5, 6, 6, 7, 8. The middle two numbers are 5 and 6. The mean of the two middle numbers is 5.5, which is the median.

The mode is the number or numbers that occur most often. There can be no modes, one mode, or many modes. In the data set, the number 6 appears twice, making 6 the mode.

The range is the difference between the highest and lowest values in a data set. The highest value is 8 and the lowest value is 2, for a range of 6.

Examples

1. **Find the mean and the median for the data set 10, 20, 40, 20, 30, 50, 40, 60, 30, 10, 40, 20, 50, 70, and 80.**

   A. The mean is 40, and the median is 38.

   B. The mean is 38, and the median is 40.

   C. The mean is 36, and the median is 50.

   D. The mean is 50, and the median is 36.

   The correct answer is **B.** The correct solution is the mean is 38 and the median is 40. The sum of all items is 570 divided by 15, which is 38. The data set in order is 10, 10, 20, 20, 20, 30, 30, 40, 40, 40, 50, 50, 60, 70, 80. The median number is 40.

2. **Find the mode and the range for the data set 10, 20, 40, 20, 30, 50, 40, 60, 30, 10, 40, 20, 50, 70, and 80.**

   A. The mode is 20, and the range is 70.

   B. The mode is 40, and the range is 70.

   C. The modes are 20 and 40, and the range is 70.

   D. The modes are 20, 40, and 70, and the range is 70.

   The correct answer is **C.** The correct solution is the modes are 20 and 40 and the range is 70. The modes are 20 and 40 because each of these numbers appears three times. The range is the difference between 80 and 10, which is 70.

Let's Review!

- A bar graph, line graph, and circle graph are different ways to summarize and represent data.
- The mean, median, mode, and range are values that can be used to interpret the meaning of a set of numbers.

STATISTICAL MEASURES

This lesson explores the different sampling techniques using random and non-random sampling. The lesson also distinguishes among different study techniques. In addition, it provides simulations that compare results with expected outcomes.

Probability and Non-Probability Sampling

A population includes all items within a set of data, while a sample consists of one or more observations from a population.

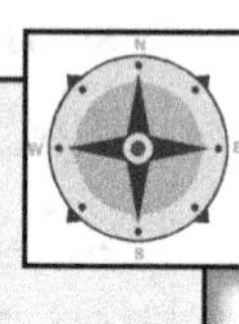

KEEP IN MIND

Probability sampling is random, and non-probability sampling is not random.

The collection of data samples from a population is an important part of research and helps researcher draw conclusions related to populations. Probability sampling creates a sample from a population by using random sampling techniques. Every person within a population has an equal chance of being selected for a sample. Non-probability sampling creates a sample from a population without using random sampling techniques.

There are four types of probability sampling. Simple random sampling is assigning a number to each member of a population and randomly selecting numbers. Stratified sampling uses simple random sampling after the population is split into equal groups. Systematic sampling chooses every n^{th} member from a list or a group. Cluster random sampling uses natural groups in a population: the population is divided into groups, and random samples are collected from groups.

Each type of probability sampling has an advantage and a disadvantage when finding an appropriate sample.

Probability Sampling	Advantage	Disadvantage
Simple random sampling	Most cases have a sample representative of a population	Not efficient for large samples
Stratified random sampling	Creates layers of random samples from different groups representative of a population	Not efficient for large samples
Systematic sampling	Creates a sample representative of population without a random number selection	Not as random as simple random sampling
Cluster random sampling	Relatively easy and convenient to implement	Might not work if clusters are different from one another

There are four types of non-probability sampling. Convenience sampling produces samples that are easy to access. Volunteer sampling asks for volunteers or recommendations for a sample. Purposive sampling bases samples on specific characteristics by selecting samples from a group that meets the qualifications of the study. Quota sampling is choosing samples of groups of the subpopulation.

Examples

1. **A factory is studying the quality of beverage samples. There are 50 bottles randomly chosen from one shipment every 60 minutes. What type of sampling is used?**

   A. Systematic sampling
   B. Simple random sampling
   C. Cluster random sampling
   D. Stratified random sampling

   The correct answer is **C**. The correct solution is cluster random sampling because bottles of beverage are selected within specific boundaries.

2. **A group conducting a survey asks a person for his or her opinion. Then, the group asks the person being surveyed for the names of 10 friends to obtain additional options. What type of sampling is used?**

   A. Quota sampling
   B. Volunteer sampling
   C. Purposive sampling
   D. Convenience sampling

   The correct answer is **B**. The correct solution is volunteer sampling because the group is looking for recommendations.

Census, Surveys, Experiments, Observational Studies

Various sampling techniques are used to collect data from a population. These are in the form of a census, a survey, observational studies, or experiments.

KEEP IN MIND

A census includes everyone within a population, and a survey includes every subject of a sample. An observational study involves watching groups randomly, and an experiment involves assigning groups.

A census collects data by asking everyone in a population the same question. Asking everyone at school or everyone at work are examples of a census. A survey collects data on every subject within a sample. The subjects can be determined by convenience sampling or by simple random sampling. Examples of surveys are asking sophomores at school or first shift workers at work.

In an observational study, data collection occurs by watching or observing an event. Watching children who play outside and observing if they drink water or sports drinks is an example. An experiment is way of finding information by assigning people to groups and collecting data on observations. Assigning one group of children to drink water and another group to drink sports drinks after playing and making comparisons is an example of an experiment.

Examples

1. **A school wants to create a census to identify students' favorite subject in school. Which group should the school ask?**

   A. All staff
   B. All students
   C. All sophomores
   D. All male students

   The correct answer is **B.** The correct solution is all students because this gathers information on the entire population.

2. **A researcher records the arrival time of employees at a job based on their actual start time. What type of study is this?**

   A. Census
   B. Survey
   C. Experiment
   D. Observational study

   The correct answer is **D.** The correct solution is observational study because the researcher is observing the time the employees arrive at work.

3. **The local county wants to test the water quality of a stream by collecting samples. What should the county collect?**

   A. The water quality at one spot
   B. The water quality under trees
   C. The water quality under bridges
   D. The water quality at different spots

   The correct answer is **D.** The correct solution is the water quality at different spots because this survey allows for the collection of different samples.

Simulations

A simulation enables researchers to study real-world events by modeling events. Advantages of simulations are that they are quick, easy, and inexpensive; the disadvantage is that the results are approximations. The steps to complete a simulation are as follows:

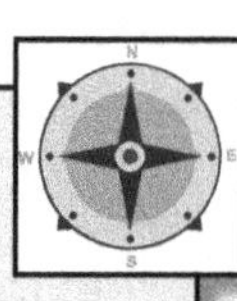

KEEP IN MIND

A simulation is only useful if the results closely mirror real-world outcomes.

- Describe the outcomes.
- Assign a random value to the outcomes.
- Choose a source to generate the outcomes.
- Generate values for the outcomes until a consistent pattern emerges.
- Analyze the results.

Examples

1. **A family has two children and wants to simulate the gender of the children. Which object would be beneficial to use for the simulation?**

   A. Coin

   B. Four-section spinner

   C. Six-sided number cube

   D. Random number generator

   The correct answer is **B.** The correct solution is a four-section spinner because there are four possible outcomes of the event (boy/boy, boy/girl, girl/boy, and girl/girl).

2. **There are six options from which to choose a meal at a festival. A model using a six-sided number cube is used to represent the simulation.**

Hamburger	Chicken	Hot Dog	Bratwurst	Pork Chop	Fish	Total
1	2	3	4	5	6	
83	82	85	89	86	75	500

   Choose the statement that correctly answers whether the simulation of using a six-sided number cube is consistent with the actual number of dinners sold and then explains why or why not.

   A. The simulation is consistent because it has six equally likely outcomes.

   B. The simulation is consistent because it has two equally likely outcomes.

   C. The simulation is not consistent because of the limited number of outcomes.

   D. The simulation is not consistent because of the unlimited number of outcomes.

   The correct answer is **A.** The correct solution is the simulation is consistent because it has six equally likely outcomes. The six-sided number cube provides consistent outcomes because there is an equal opportunity to select any dinner.

Let's Review!

- Probability (random) sampling and non-probability (not random) sampling are ways to collect data.
- Censuses, surveys, experiments, and observational studies are ways to collect data from a population.
- A simulation is way to model random events and compare the results to real-world outcomes.

Statistics & Probability: The Rules of Probability

This lesson explores a sample space and its outcomes and provides an introduction to probability, including how to calculate expected values and analyze decisions based on probability.

Sample Space

A **sample space** is the set of all possible outcomes. Using a deck of cards labeled 1–10, the sample space is 1, 2, 3, 4, 5, 6, 7, 8, 9, and 10. An **event** is a subset of the sample space. For example, if a card is drawn and the outcome of the event is an even number, possible results are 2, 4, 6, 8, 10.

The **union** of two events is everything in both events, and the notation is $A \bigcup B$. The union of events is associated with the word *or.* For example, a card is drawn that is either a multiple of 3 or a multiple of 4. The set containing the multiples of 3 is 3, 6, and 9. The set containing the multiples of 4 is 4 and 8. The union of the set is 3, 4, 6, 8, and 9.

KEEP IN MIND

The intersection of an event can have no values. The intersection of drawing a card that is even and odd is a set with no values because a card cannot be both even and odd. The complement of an event is the "not," or the opposite of, the event.

The **intersection** of two events is all of the events in both sets, and the notation is $A \bigcap B$. The intersection of events is associated with the word *and.* For example, a card is drawn that is even and a multiple of 4. The set containing even numbers is 2, 4, 6, 8, and 10. The set containing the multiples of 4 is 4 and 8. The intersection is 4 and 8 because these numbers are in both sets.

The **complement** of an event is an outcome that is not part of the set. The complement of an event is associated with the word *not.* A card is drawn and is not a multiple of 5. The set not containing multiples of 5 is 1, 2, 3, 4, 6, 7, 8, and 9. The complement of not a multiple of 5 is 1, 2, 3, 4, 6, 7, 8, and 9.

Examples

Use the following table of the results when rolling two six-sided number cubes.

1, 1	1, 2	1, 3	1, 4	1, 5	1, 6
2, 1	2, 2	2, 3	2, 4	2, 5	2, 6
3, 1	3, 2	3, 3	3, 4	3, 5	3, 6
4, 1	4, 2	4, 3	4, 4	4, 5	4, 6
5, 1	5, 2	5, 3	5, 4	5, 5	5, 6
6, 1	6, 2	6, 3	6, 4	6, 5	6, 6

1. **How many possible outcomes are there for the union of rolling a sum of 3 or a sum of 5?**

   A. 2 B. 4 C. 6 D. 8

   The correct answer is **C**. The correct solution is 6 possible outcomes. There are two options for the first event (2, 1) and (1, 2). There are 4 options for the second event (4, 1), (3, 2), (2, 3), and (1, 4). The union of two events is six possible outcomes.

2. **How many possible outcomes are there for the intersection of rolling a double and a multiple of 3?**

   A. 0 B. 2 C. 4 D. 6

   The correct answer is **B**. The correct solution is 2 possible outcomes. There are six options for the first event (1, 1), (2, 2), (3, 3), (4, 4), (5, 5), and (6, 6). There are 12 options for the second event of the multiple of three. The intersection is (3, 3) and (6, 6) because these numbers meet both requirements.

3. **How many possible outcomes are there for the complement of rolling a 3 and a 5?**

   A. 16 B. 18 C. 27 D. 36

   The correct answer is **A**. The correct solution is 16 possible outcomes. There are 16 options of not rolling a 3 or a 5.

Probability

The **probability** of an event is the number of favorable outcomes divided by the total number of possible outcomes.

BE CAREFUL!
Make sure that you apply the correct formula for the probability of an event.

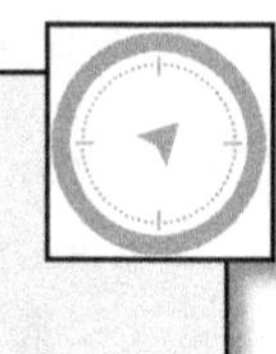

$$Probability = \frac{\text{number of favorable outcomes}}{\text{number of possible outcomes}}$$

Probability is a value between 0 (event does not happen) and 1 (event will happen). For example, the probability of getting heads when a coin is flipped is $\frac{1}{2}$ because heads is 1 option out of 2 possibilities. The probability of rolling an odd number on a six-sided number cube is $\frac{3}{6} = \frac{1}{2}$ because there are three odd numbers, 1, 3, and 5, out of 6 possible numbers.

The probability of an "or" event happening is the sum of the events happening. For example, the probability of rolling an odd number or a 4 on a six-sided number cube is $\frac{4}{6}$. The probability of rolling an odd number is $\frac{3}{6}$, and the probability of rolling a 4 is $\frac{1}{6}$. Therefore, the probability is $\frac{3}{6} + \frac{1}{6} = \frac{4}{6} = \frac{2}{3}$.

The probability of an "and" event happening is the product of the probability of two or more events. The probability of rolling 6 three times in a row is $\frac{1}{216}$. The probability of a single event is $\frac{1}{6}$, and this fraction is multiplied three times to find the probability, $\frac{1}{6} \times \frac{1}{6} \times \frac{1}{6}$. There are cases of "with replacement" when the item is returned to the pile and "without replacement" when the item is not returned to the pile.

The probability of a "not" event happening is 1 minus the probability of the event occurring. For example, the probability of not rolling 6 three times in a row is $1 - \frac{1}{216} = \frac{215}{216}$.

Examples

1. **A deck of cards contains 40 cards divided into 4 colors: red, blue, green, and yellow. Each group has cards numbered 0–9. What is the probability of selecting an 8?**

   A. $\frac{1}{10}$ B. $\frac{1}{8}$ C. $\frac{1}{4}$ D. $\frac{1}{2}$

   The correct answer is **A.** The correct solution is $\frac{1}{10}$. There are 4 cards out of 40 that contain the number 8, making the probability $\frac{4}{40} = \frac{1}{10}$.

2. **A deck of cards contains 40 cards divided into 4 colors: red, blue, green, and yellow. Each group has cards numbered 0–9. What is the probability of selecting an even or a red card?**

   A. $\frac{1}{4}$ B. $\frac{3}{8}$ C. $\frac{5}{8}$ D. $\frac{3}{4}$

   The correct answer is **C.** The correct solution is $\frac{5}{8}$. There are 20 even cards and 10 red cards. The overlap of 5 red even cards is subtracted from the probability, $\frac{20}{40} + \frac{10}{40} - \frac{5}{40} = \frac{25}{40} = \frac{5}{8}$.

3. **A deck of cards contains 40 cards divided into 4 colors: red, blue, green, and yellow. Each group has cards numbered 0–9. What is the probability of selecting a blue card first, replacing the card, and selecting a 9?**

   A. $\frac{1}{100}$ B. $\frac{1}{80}$ C. $\frac{1}{40}$ D. $\frac{1}{20}$

   The correct answer is **C.** The correct solution is $\frac{1}{40}$. There are 10 blue cards and 4 cards that contain the number 9. The probability of the event is $\frac{10}{40} \times \frac{4}{40} = \frac{40}{1600} = \frac{1}{40}$.

4. **A deck of cards contains 40 cards divided into 4 colors: red, blue, green, and yellow. Each group has cards numbered 0–9. What is the probability of NOT selecting a green card?**

   A. $\frac{1}{4}$ B. $\frac{3}{8}$ C. $\frac{1}{2}$ D. $\frac{3}{4}$

   The correct answer is **D.** The correct solution is $\frac{3}{4}$. There are 10 cards that are green, making the probability of NOT selecting a green card $1 - \frac{10}{40} = \frac{30}{40} = \frac{3}{4}$.

Calculating Expected Values and Analyzing Decisions Based on Probability

The **expected value** of an event is the sum of the products of the probability of an event times the payoff of an event. A good example is calculating the expected value for buying a lottery ticket. There is a one in a hundred million chance that a person would win \$50 million. Each ticket costs \$2. The expected value is

$$\frac{1}{100{,}000{,}000}(50{,}000{,}000-2) + \frac{99{,}999{,}999}{100{,}000{,}000}(-2) = \frac{49{,}999{,}998}{100{,}000{,}000} - \frac{199{,}999{,}998}{100{,}000{,}000} = -\frac{150{,}000{,}000}{100{,}000{,}000} = -\$1.50$$

On average, one should expect to lose \$1.50 each time the game is played. Analyzing the information, the meaning of the data shows that playing the lottery would result in losing money every time.

BE CAREFUL!

The expected value will not be the same as the actual value unless the probability of winning is 100%.

Examples

1. **What is the expected value of an investment if the probability is $\frac{1}{5}$ of losing \$1,000, $\frac{1}{4}$ of no gain, $\frac{2}{5}$ of making \$1,000, and $\frac{3}{20}$ of making \$2,000?**

   A. \$0 B. \$200 C. \$500 D. \$700

   The correct answer is **C**. The correct solution is \$500. The expected value is $\frac{1}{5}(-1{,}000) + \frac{1}{4}(0) + \frac{2}{5}(1{,}000) + \frac{3}{20}(2{,}000) = -200 + 0 + 400 + 300 = \$500$.

2. **The table below shows the value of the prizes and the probability of winning a prize in a contest.**

Prize	\$10	\$100	\$5,000	\$50,000
Probability	1 in 50	1 in 1,000	1 in 50,000	1 in 250,000

   Calculate the expected value.

   A. \$0.10 B. \$0.20 C. \$0.50 D. \$0.60

   The correct answer is **D**. The correct solution is \$0.60. The probability for each event is

Prize	\$10	\$100	\$5,000	\$50,000	Not Winning
Probability	1 in 50 = 0.02	1 in 1,000 = 0.001	1 in 50,000 = 0.00002	1 in 250,000 = 0.000004	0.978976

   The expected value is $0.02(10) + 0.001(100) + 0.00002(5{,}000) + 0.000004(50{,}000) + 0.978976(0) =$

   $0.2 + 0.1 + 0.1 + 0.2 + 0 = \$0.60$.

3. **Which option results in the largest loss on a product?**

   A. 40% of gaining \$100,000 and 60% of losing \$100,000

   B. 60% of gaining \$250,000 and 40% of losing \$500,000

   C. 30% of gaining \$400,000 and 70% of losing \$250,000

   D. 60% of gaining \$250,000 and 40% of losing \$450,000

   The correct answer is **C**. The correct solution is 30% of gaining \$400,000 and 70% of losing \$250,000. The expected value is $0.30(400{,}000) + 0.7(-250{,}000) = 120{,}000 + (-175{,}000) = -55{,}000$.

Let's Review!

- The sample space is the number of outcomes of an event. The union, the intersection, and the complement are related to the sample space.
- The probability of an event is the number of possible events divided by the total number of outcomes. There can be "and," "or," and "not" probabilities.
- The expected value of an event is based on the payout and probability of an event occurring.

INTERPRETING CATEGORICAL AND QUANTITATIVE DATA

This lesson discusses how to represent and interpret data for a dot plot, a histogram, and a box plot. It compares multiple sets of data by using the measures of center and spread and examines the impact of outliers.

Representing Data on a Number Line

There are two types of data: quantitative and categorical. Quantitative variables are numerical, such as number of people in a household, bank account balance, and number of cars sold. Categorical variables are not numerical, and there is no inherent way to order them. Example are classes in college, types of pets, and party affiliations. The information for these data sets can be arranged on a number line using dot plots, histograms, and box plots.

A dot plot is a display of data using dots. The dots represent the number of times an item appears. Below is a sample of a dot plot.

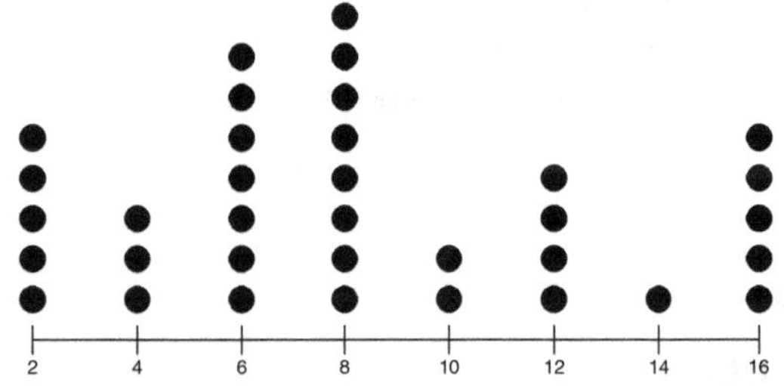

The mean and median can be determined by looking at a dot plot. The mean is the sum of all items divided by the number of dots. The median is the middle dot or the average of the middle two dots.

A histogram is a graphical display that has bars of various heights. It is similar to a bar chart, but the numbers are grouped into ranges. The bins, or ranges of values, of a histogram have equal lengths, such as 10 or 50 units. Continuous data such as weight, height, and amount of time are examples of data shown in a histogram. In the histogram to the right, the bin length is 8 units.

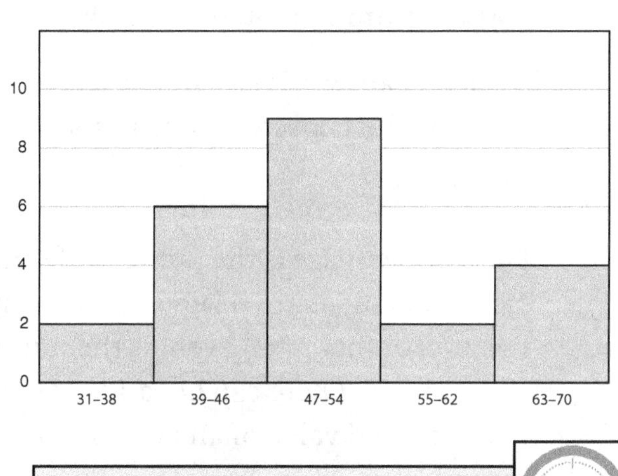

It is not possible to calculate the mean and median by looking at a histogram because there is a bin size rather than a single value on the horizontal axis. Histograms are beneficial when working with a large set of data.

BE CAREFUL!

Make sure to carefully interpret the data for any graphical display.

A box plot (or box-and-whisker plot) is a graphical display of the minimum, first quartile, median, third quartile, and maximum of a set of data. Recall the minimum is the smallest value and the maximum is the largest value in a set of data. The median is the middle number when the data set is written in order. The first quartile is the middle number between the minimum and the median. The third quartile is the middle number between the median and the maximum.

In the data display below, the minimum is 45, the first quartile is 50, the median is 57, the third quartile is 63, and the maximum is 75. With most box-and-whisker plots, the data is not symmetrical.

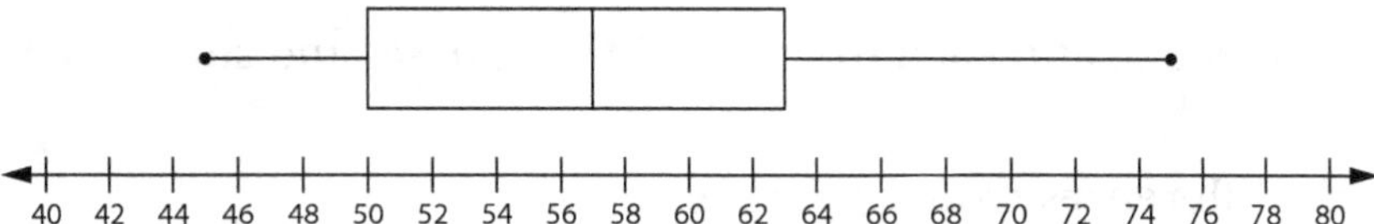

Example

The histogram below shows a basketball team's winning margin during the season. Which statement is true for the histogram?

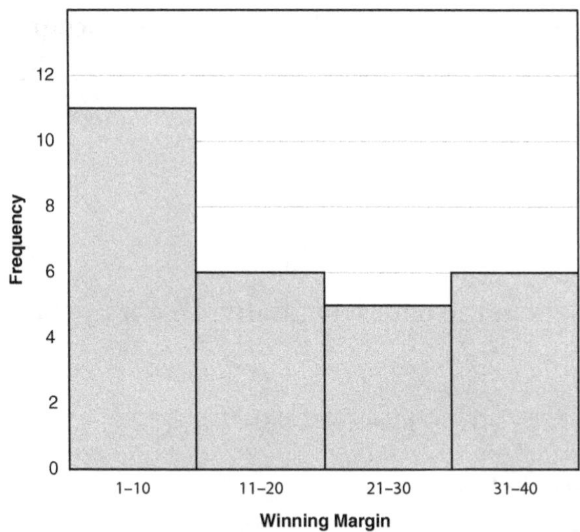

A. The team played a total of 30 games.

B. The frequency for 20–30 points is the same as for 30–40 points.

C. The sum of the frequency for the last two bins is the same as the first bin.

D. The frequency for 0–10 is twice the frequency for any other winning margin.

The correct answer is **C**. The correct solution is the sum of the frequency for the last two bins is the same as the first bin. The frequency of the first bin is 11, the frequency of the third bin is 5, and the frequency of the fourth bin is 6. The sum of the frequency of the last two bins is the same as the first bin.

Comparing Center and Spread of Multiple Data Sets

The measures of center are the mean (average) and median (middle number when written in order). These values describe the expected value of a data set. Very large or very small numbers affect the mean, but they do not affect the median.

The measures of spread are standard deviation (how far the numbers of a data set are from the mean) and interquartile range (the difference between the third and first quartile values).

To find the standard deviation:

- Find the mean.
- Find the difference between the mean and each member of the date set and square that result.
- Find the mean of the squared differences from the previous step.
- Apply the square root.

The larger the value for the standard deviation, the greater the spread of values from the mean. The larger the value for the interquartile range, the greater the spread of the middle 50% of values from the median.

Symmetric data has values that are close together, and the mean, median, and mode occur near the same value. The mean and standard deviation are used to explain multiple data sets and are evident in dot plots.

For example, consider this data set.

10, 10, 11, 11, 11, 12, 12, 12, 12, 12, 13, 13, 13, 14, 14

The mean is found by finding the sum of the numbers in the data set and dividing it by the number of items in the set, as follows:

$10 + 10 + 11 + 11 + 11 + 12 + 12 + 12 + 12 + 12 + 13 + 13 + 13 + 14 + 14 = 180 \div 15 = 12.$

The standard deviation calculation is shown in the table below.

Data	Data – Mean	(Data – Mean)^2
10	–2	4
10	–2	4
11	–1	1
11	–1	1
11	–1	1
12	0	0
12	0	0
12	0	0
12	0	0

Data	Data – Mean	(Data – Mean)^2
12	0	0
13	1	1
13	1	1
13	1	1
14	2	4
14	2	4

The sum of the last column is 22. The standard deviation is $\sqrt{\frac{22}{15}} \approx 1.211$.

Next, consider this data set.

8, 8, 9, 10, 11, 12, 12, 12, 12, 12, 13, 14, 15, 16, 16

The mean is $8 + 8 + 9 + 10 + 11 + 12 + 12 + 12 + 12 + 12 + 13 + 14 + 15 + 16 + 16 = 180 \div 15 = 12$.

The standard deviation calculation is shown in the table below.

Data	Data – Mean	(Data – Mean)^2
8	−4	16
8	−4	16
9	−3	9
10	−2	4
11	−1	1
12	0	0
12	0	0
12	0	0
12	0	0
12	0	0
13	1	1
14	2	4
15	3	9
16	4	16
16	4	16

The sum of the last column is 92. The standard deviation is $\sqrt{\frac{92}{15}} \approx 2.476$.

Therefore, the second set of data has values that are farther from the mean than the first data set.

When data is skewed, a group of its values are close and the remaining values are evenly spread. The median and interquartile range are used to explain multiple data sets and are evident in dot plots and box plots.

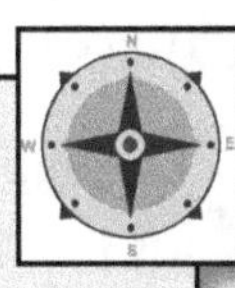

KEEP IN MIND

Compare the same measure of center or variation to draw accurate conclusions when comparing data sets.

The data set 10, 10, 11, 11, 11, 11, 11, 11, 12, 12, 12, 13, 13, 14, 15 has a median of 11 and an interquartile range of 2. The data set 10, 11, 12, 12, 13, 13, 14, 14, 14, 14, 14, 14, 14, 15, 15 has a median of 14 and an interquartile range of 2. The median is greater in the second data set, but the spread of data is the same for both sets of data.

Example

The box plots below show the heights of students in inches for two classes. Choose the statement that is true for the median and the interquartile range.

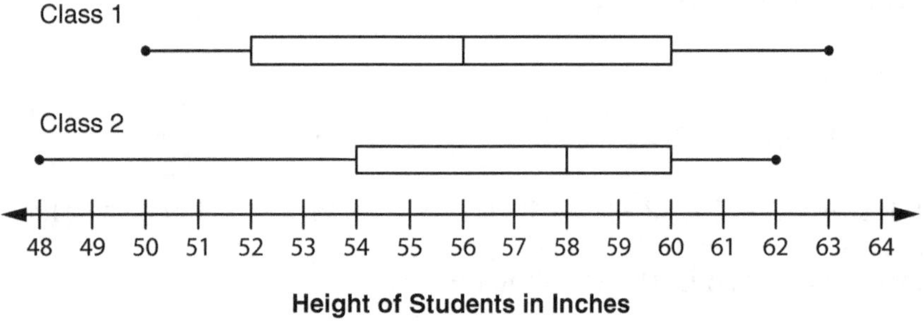

A. The median and interquartile range are greater for class 1.

B. The median and interquartile range are greater for class 2.

C. The median is greater for class 1, and the interquartile range is greater for class 2.

D. The median is greater for class 2, and the interquartile range is greater for class 1.

The correct answer is **D**. The correct solution is the median is greater for class 2, and the interquartile range is greater for class 1. The median is 58 inches for class 2 and 56 inches for class 1. The interquartile range is 8 inches for class 1 and 6 inches for class 2.

Determining the Effect of Extreme Data Points

An outlier is a value that is much smaller or much larger than rest of the values in a data set. This value has an impact on the mean and standard deviation values and occasionally has an impact on the median and interquartile range values.

The data set of 10, 10, 11, 11, 11, 12, 12, 12, 12, 12, 13, 13, 13, 14, 14 has a mean of 12 and a standard deviation of 1.211. If an outlier of 50 is added, the data set has a mean of has a mean of 14.38 and a standard deviation of 9.273. The outlier has increased the mean by more than 2, and the spread of the data has increased significantly.

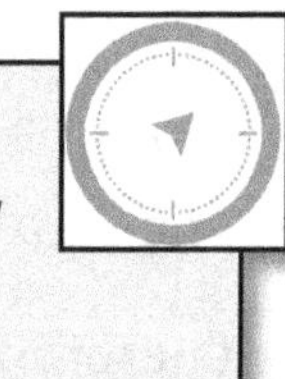

BE CAREFUL!

There may be a high outlier and a low outlier that may not have an impact on data.

The data set 10, 10, 11, 11, 11, 11, 11, 11, 12, 12, 12, 13, 13, 14, 15 has a median of 11 and an interquartile range of 2. If an outlier of 50 is added, the median slightly increases to 11.5 and the interquartile range remains 2.

Example

A little league basketball team scores 35, 38, 40, 36, 41, 42, 39, 35, 29, 32, 37, 33 in its first 12 games. In its next game, the team scores 12 points. Which statement describes the mean and standard deviation?

A. The mean increases, and the standard deviation increases.

B. The mean decreases, and the standard deviation increases.

C. The mean increases, and the standard deviation decreases.

D. The mean decreases, and the standard deviation decreases.

The correct answer is **B**. The correct solution is the mean decreases, and the standard deviation increases. The outlier value is lower than all other values, which results in a decrease for the mean. The standard deviation increases because the outlier of 12 is a value far away from the mean.

Let's Review!

- Dot plots, histograms, and box plots summarize and represent data on a number line.
- The mean and standard deviation are used to compare symmetric data sets.
- The median and interquartile range are used to compare skewed data sets.
- Outliers can impact measures of center and spread, particularly mean and standard deviation.

Chapter 9 Statistics and Probability Practice Quiz

1. **Two companies have made a chart of paid time off. Which statement describes the mean and standard deviation?**

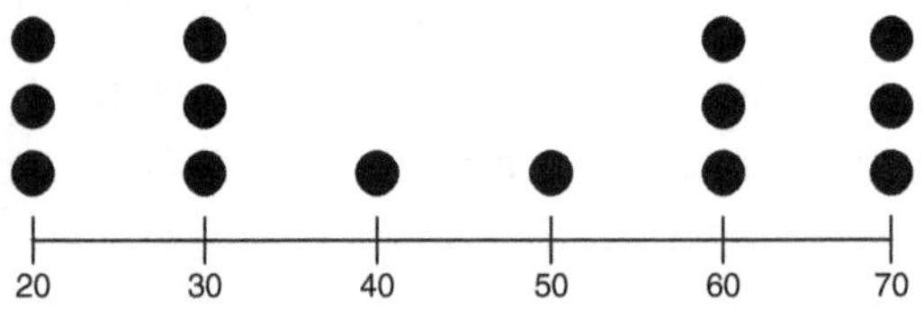

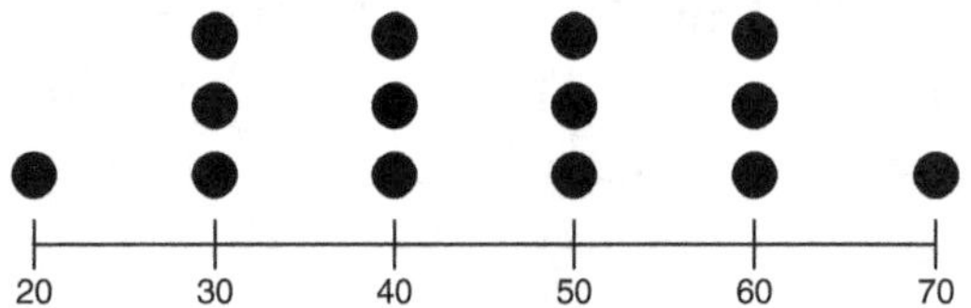

A. The means are the same, but the standard deviation is smaller for Company B.

B. The means are the same, but the standard deviation is smaller for Company A.

C. The mean is greater for Company A, and the standard deviation is smaller for Company A.

D. The mean is greater for Company B, and the standard deviation is smaller for Company B.

2. **A basketball player scores 18, 17, 20, 23, 15, 24, 22, 28, 5. What is the effect of removing the outlier on the mean and standard deviation?**

A. The mean and the standard deviation increase.

B. The mean and the standard deviation decrease.

C. The standard deviation increases, but the mean decreases.

D. The standard deviation decreases, but the mean increases.

3. **Find the median from the dot plot.**

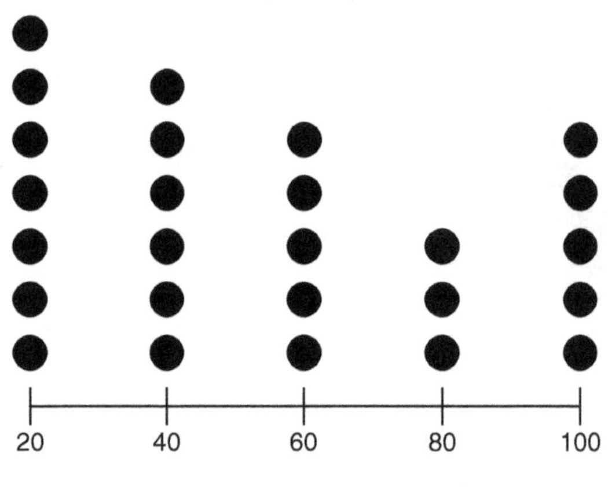

A. 40

B. 50

C. 60

D. 70

4. **The table shows the number of students in grades kindergarten through sixth grade. Select the correct bar graph for this data.**

Grade	Kindergarten	1st	2nd	3rd	4th	5th	6th
Number of Students	135	150	140	155	145	165	170

A.

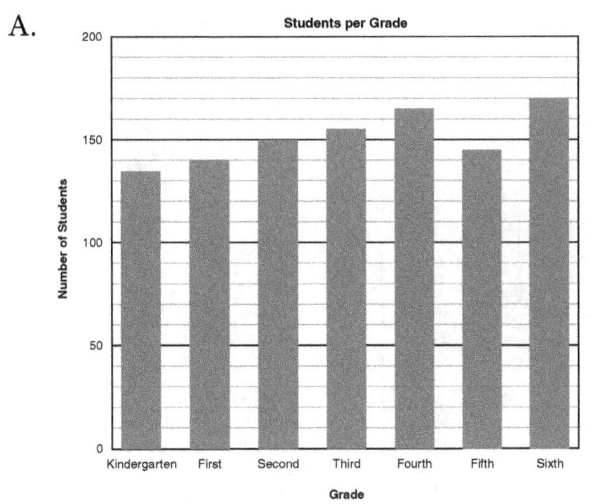

C.

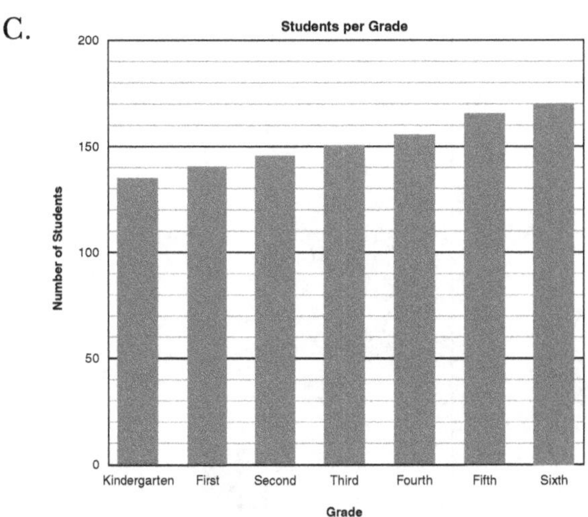

B.

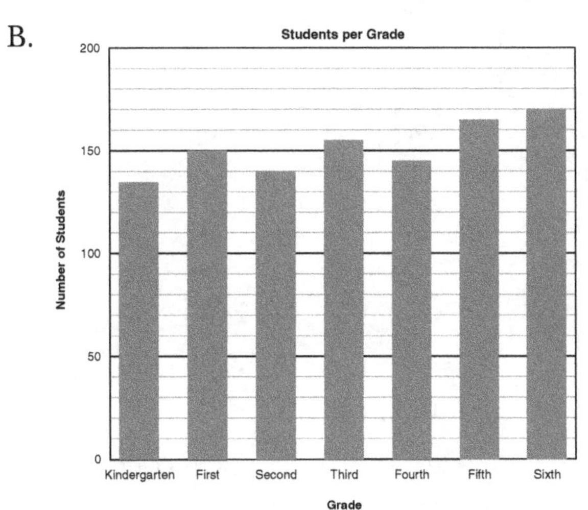

D.

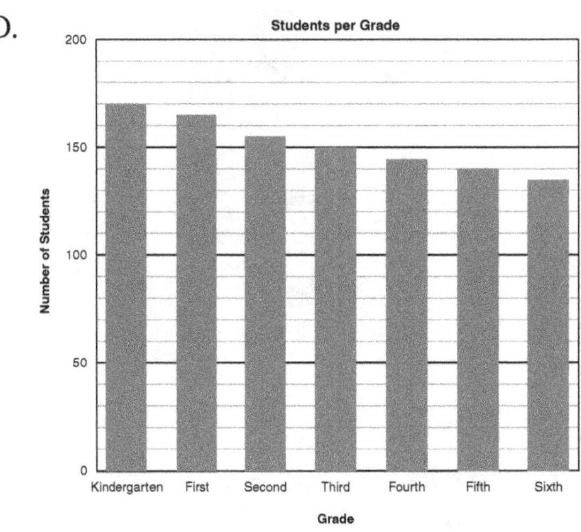

5. **The bar chart shows the number of items collected for a charity drive. Which statement is true for the bar chart?**

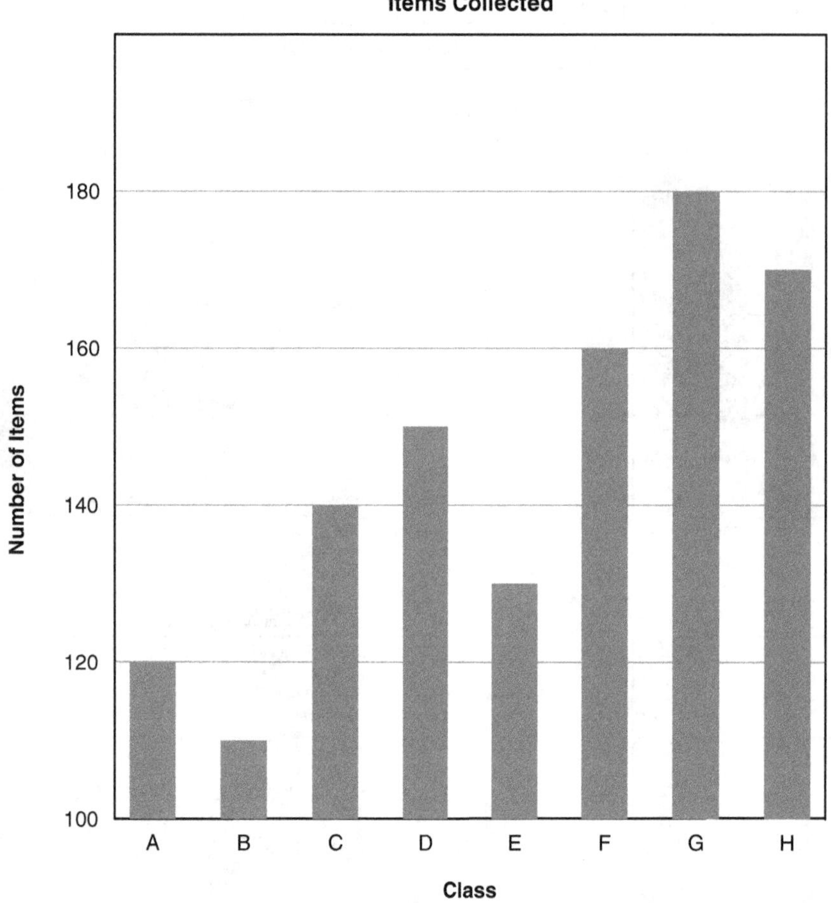

A. Classes F, G, and H each collected more than 150 items.

B. Classes D, F, and G each collected more than 150 items.

C. Classes C, D, and E each collected more than 140 items.

D. Classes A, B, and C each collected more than 140 items.

6. The circle graph shows the number of votes for each candidate. How many votes were cast for candidate D if there were 25,000 voters?

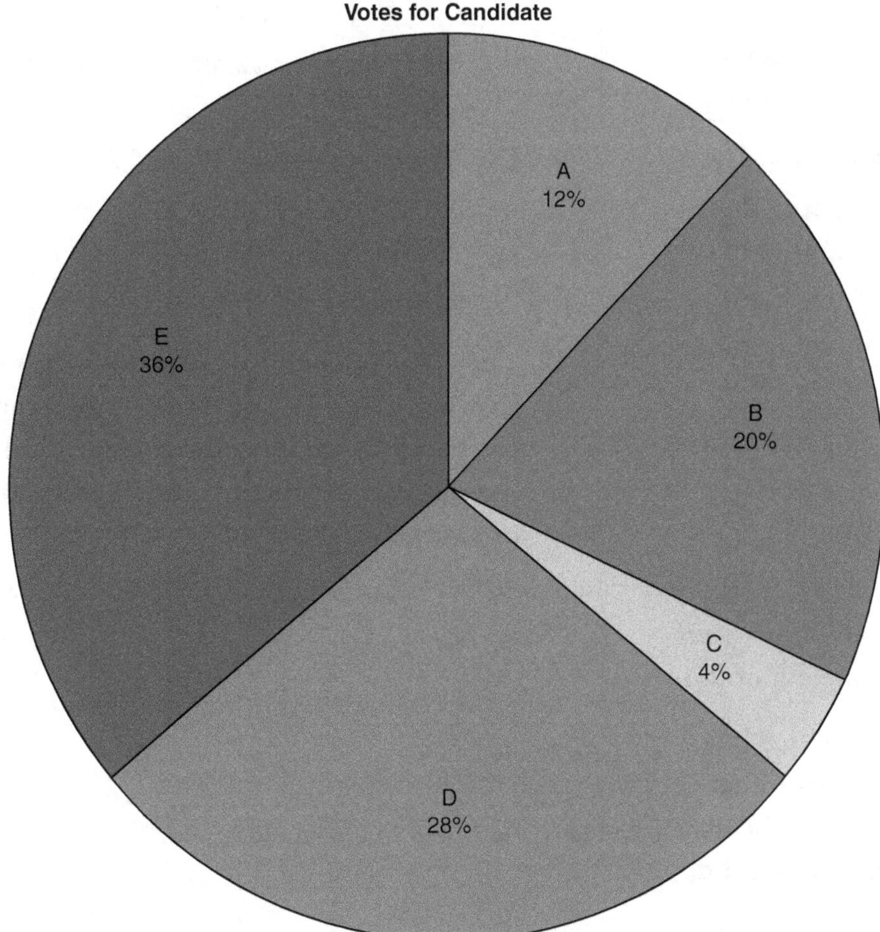

A. 3,000 votes
B. 5,000 votes
C. 7,000 votes
D. 9,000 votes

7. A factory is investigating defects in screwdrivers that have been placed in containers to be shipped to stores. Random containers are selected for the team leader to review. What type of sampling is used?

A. Systematic sampling
B. Simple random sampling
C. Cluster random sampling
D. Stratified random sampling

8. A study looked at a random sample of people and watched their use of social media on mobile devices. The researcher looked at which group of users were happier. What type of study is this?

A. Census
B. Survey
C. Experiment
D. Observational study

9. There are four available pen colors to choose. A simulation is used to represent the number of times each pen is used.

Red	Blue	Black	Green	Total
1,248	1,260	1,247	1,245	5,000

Choose the statement that correctly explains why or why not seeing these results questions the probability of one out of four for each color.

A. Yes, because of the limited number of outcomes

B. Yes, because not enough simulations were completed

C. No, because the probability of each color is not exactly one out of four

D. No, because the probability of each color is very close to one out of four

10. A bag contains 10 red marbles, 8 black marbles, and 7 white marbles. What is the probability of selecting a black marble first and a red marble second with no replacement?

A. $\frac{8}{25}$

B. $\frac{16}{125}$

C. $\frac{2}{15}$

D. $\frac{7}{75}$

11. Which option results in the greatest gain on an investment?

A. 100% of gaining $1,000

B. 60% of gaining $2,500 and 40% of gaining $0

C. 75% of gaining $1,000 and 25% of gaining $1,500

D. 70% of gaining $1,500 and 30% of gaining $1,000

12. There are 60 students attending classes in town. There are 40 students in dance class and 30 students in art class. Find the number of students in either dance or art class.

A. 30

B. 40

C. 50

D. 60

Chapter 9 Statistics and Probability Practice Quiz – Answer Key

1. A. The correct solution is the means are the same, but the standard deviation is smaller for Company B. The standard deviation is smaller for Company B because more values are closer to the mean. **See Lesson: Interpreting Categorical and Quantitative Data.**

2. D. The correct solution is the standard deviation decreases, but the mean increases. The standard deviation from 6.226 and 3.951 when the low outlier is removed. The mean increases from 19.11 to 20.88 because the outlier, 5, is the lowest value. **See Lesson: Interpreting Categorical and Quantitative Data.**

3. B. The correct solution is 50. The middle two values are 40 and 60, and the average of these values is 50. **See Lesson: Interpreting Categorical and Quantitative Data.**

4. B. The correct solution is B because the number of students for each grade is correct. **See Lesson: Interpreting Graphics.**

5. A. The correct solution is classes F, G, and H collected more than 150 items. Class F collected 160 items, class G collected 180 items, and class H collected 170 items. **See Lesson: Interpreting Graphics.**

6. C. The correct solution is 7,000 votes because 28% of 25,000 is 7,000 voters. **See Lesson: Interpreting Graphics.**

7. D. The correct solution is stratified random sampling because the screwdrivers are placed into containers and the containers are randomly selected. **See Lesson: Statistical Measures.**

8. D. The correct solution is observational study because people were not randomly assigned to group and their behaviors were observed. **See Lesson: Statistical Measures.**

9. D. The correct solution is no, because the probability of each color is very close to one out of four. The more simulations, the closer the results will be to the actual probability of one out of four for each color. **See Lesson: Statistical Measures.**

10. C. The correct solution is $\frac{2}{15}$. There are 8 marbles out of 25 for the first event and 10 marbles out of 24 for the second event. The probability of the event is $\frac{8}{25} \times \frac{10}{24} = \frac{80}{600} = \frac{2}{15}$. **See Lesson: Statistics & Probability: The Rules of Probability.**

11. B. The correct solution is 60% of gaining \$2,500 and 40% of gaining \$0. The expected value is $0.60(2{,}500) + 0.40(0) = \$1{,}500$. **See Lesson: Statistics & Probability: The Rules of Probability.**

12. C. The correct solution 50 because there are 70 students in both classes less the total students is 10 students. Then, subtract 10 students from the total, which is 50 students. **See Lesson: Statistics & Probability: The Rules of Probability.**

SECTION III. READING

CHAPTER 10 KEY IDEAS AND DETAILS

MAIN IDEAS, TOPIC SENTENCES, AND SUPPORTING DETAILS

To read effectively, you need to know how to identify the most important information in a text. You must also understand how ideas within a text relate to one other.

Main Ideas

The central or most important idea in a text is the **main idea**. As a reader, you need to avoid confusing the main idea with less important details that may be interesting but not central to the author's point.

The **topic** of a text is slightly different than the main idea. The topic is a word or phrase that describes roughly what a text is about. A main idea, in contrast, is a complete sentence that states the topic and explains what an author wants to say about it.

All types of texts can contain main ideas. Read the following informational paragraph and try to identify the main idea:

> The immune system is the body's defense mechanism. It fights off harmful bacteria, viruses, and substances that attack the body. To do this, it uses cells, tissues, and organs that work together to resist invasion.

The topic of this paragraph is the immune system. The main idea can be expressed in a sentence like this: "This paragraph defines and describes the immune system." Ideas about organisms and substances that invade the body are not the central focus. The topic and main idea must always be directly related to every sentence in the text, as the immune system is here.

Read the persuasive paragraph below and consider the topic and main idea:

> Football is not a healthy activity for kids. It causes head injuries that harm the ability to learn and achieve. It causes painful bodily injuries that can linger into adulthood. It teaches aggressive behavioral habits that make life harder for players after they have left the field.

The topic of this paragraph is youth football, and the main idea is that kids should not play the game. Note that if you are asked to state the main idea of a persuasive text, it is your job to be objective. This means you should describe the author's opinion, not make an argument of your own in response.

Both of the example paragraphs above state their main idea explicitly. Some texts have an implicit, or suggested, main idea. In this case, you need to figure out the main idea using the details as clues.

FOR EXAMPLE

The following fictional paragraph has an implicit main idea:

Daisy parked her car and sat gripping the wheel, not getting out. A few steps to the door. A couple of knocks. She could give him the news in two words. She'd already decided what she was going to do, so it didn't matter what he said, not really. Still, she couldn't make her feet carry her to the door.

The main idea here is that Daisy feels reluctant to speak to someone. This point is not stated outright, but it is clear from the details of Daisy's thoughts and actions.

Topic Sentences

Many paragraphs identify the topic and main idea in a single sentence. This is called a **topic sentence,** and it often appears at the beginning of a paragraph. However, a writer may choose to place a topic sentence anywhere in the text.

Some paragraphs contain an introductory sentence to grab the reader's attention before clearly stating the topic. A paragraph may begin by asking a rhetorical question, presenting a striking idea, or showing why the topic is important. When authors use this strategy, the topic sentence usually comes second:

> Have you ever wondered how your body fights off a nasty cold? **It uses a complex defense mechanism called the immune system.** The immune system fights off harmful bacteria, viruses, and substances that attack the body. To do this, it uses cells, tissues, and organs that work together to resist invasion.

Here, the first sentence grabs the attention, and the second, **boldfaced** topic sentence states the main idea. The remaining sentences provide further information, explaining what the immune system does and identifying its basic components.

COMPARE!

The informational paragraph above contains a question that grabs the attention at the beginning. The writer could convey the same information with a little less flair by omitting this device. The version you read in Section 1 does exactly this. (The topic sentence below is **boldfaced.**)

> **The immune system is the body's defense mechanism.** It fights off harmful bacteria, viruses, and substances that attack the body. To do this, it uses cells, tissues, and organs that work together to resist invasion.

Look back at the football paragraph from Section 1. Which sentence is the topic sentence?

Sometimes writers wait until the end of a paragraph to reveal the main idea in a topic sentence. When you're reading a paragraph that is organized this way, you may feel like you're reading a bit of a puzzle. It's not fully clear what the piece is about until you get to the end:

> It causes head injuries that harm the ability to learn and achieve. It causes painful bodily injuries that can linger through the passage of years. It teaches aggressive behavioral habits that make life harder for players after they have left the field. **Football is not a healthy activity for kids.**

Note that the topic—football—is not actually named until the final, **boldfaced** topic sentence. This is a strong hint that this final sentence is the topic sentence. Other paragraphs with this structure may contain several examples or related ideas and then tie them together with a summary statement near the end.

Supporting Details

The **supporting details** of a text develop the main idea, contribute further information, or provide examples.

All of the supporting details in a text must relate back to the main idea. In a text that sets out to define and describe the immune system, the supporting details could explain how the immune system works, define parts of the immune system, and so on.

> **Main Idea:** The immune system is the body's defense mechanism.
>
> **Supporting Detail:** It fights off harmful bacteria, viruses, and substances that attack the body.
>
> **Supporting Detail:** To do this, it uses cells, tissues, and organs that work together to resist invasion.

The above text could go on to describe white blood cells, which are a vital part of the body's defense system against disease. However, the supporting details in such a text should *not* drift off into descriptions of parts of the body that make no contribution to immune response.

Supporting details may be facts or opinions. A single text can combine both facts and opinions to develop a single main idea.

> **Main Idea:** Football is not a healthy activity for kids.
>
> **Supporting Detail:** It teaches aggressive behavioral habits that make life harder for players after they have left the field.
>
> **Supporting Detail:** In a study of teenage football players by Dr. Sophia Ortega at Harvard University, 28% reported involvement in fights or other violent incidents, compared with 19% of teenage boys who were not involved in sports.

The first supporting detail above states an opinion. The second is still related to the main idea, but it provides factual information to back up the opinion. Further development of this paragraph could contain other types of facts, including information about football injuries and anecdotes about real players who got hurt playing the game.

Let's Review!

- The main idea is the most important piece of information in a text.
- The main idea is often expressed in a topic sentence.
- Supporting details develop the main idea, contribute further information, or provide examples.

Summarizing Text and Using Text Features

Effective readers need to know how to identify and restate the main idea of a text through summary. They must also follow complex instructions, figure out the sequence of events in a text that is not presented in order, and understand information presented in graphics.

Summary Basics

A **summary** is a text that restates the ideas from a different text in a new way. Every summary needs to include the main idea of the original. Some summaries may include information about the supporting details as well.

The content and level of detail in a summary vary depending on the purpose. For example, a journalist may summarize a recent scientific study in a newspaper profile of its authors. A graduate student might briefly summarize the same study in a paper questioning its conclusions. The journalist's version would likely use fairly simple language and restate only the main points. The student's version would likely use specialized scientific vocabulary and include certain supporting details, especially the ones most applicable to the argument the student intends to make later.

The language of a summary must be substantially different from the original. It should not retain the structure and word choice of the source text. Rather, it should provide a completely new way of stating the ideas.

Read the passage below and the short summary that follows:

> **Original:** There is no need for government regulations to maintain a minimum wage because free market forces naturally adjust wages on their own. Workers are in short supply in our thriving economy, and businesses must offer fair wages and working conditions to attract labor. Business owners pay employees well because common sense dictates that they cannot succeed any other way.
>
> **Effective Summary:** The author argues against minimum wage laws. He claims free market forces naturally keep wages high in a healthy economy with a limited labor supply.

KEY POINT!

Many ineffective summaries attempt to imitate the structure of the original text and change only individual words. This makes the writing process difficult, and it can lead to unintentional plagiarism.

Ineffective Summary (Plagiarism): It is unnecessary for government regulations to create a minimum wage because capitalism adjusts wages without help. Good labor is rare in our excellent economy, and businesses need to offer fair wages and working conditions in order to attract workers.

The above text is an example of structural plagiarism. Summary writing does not just involve rewriting the original words one by one. An effective summary restates the main ideas of the text in a wholly original way.

The effective summary above restates the main ideas in a new but objective way. Objectivity is a key quality of an effective summary. A summary does not exaggerate, judge, or distort the author's original ideas.

> **Not a Summary:** The author makes a wild and unsupportable claim that minimum wage laws are unnecessary because market forces keep wages high without government intervention.

Although the above text might be appropriate in persuasive writing, it makes its own claims and judgments rather than simply restating the original author's ideas. It would not be an effective sentence in a summary.

In some cases, particularly dealing with creative works like fiction and poetry, summaries may mention ideas that are clearly implied but not stated outright in the original text. For example, a mobster in a thriller novel might turn to another character and say menacingly, "I wouldn't want anything to happen to your sweet little kids." A summary of this passage could objectively say the mobster had threatened the other character. But everything in the summary needs to be clearly supportable in the text. The summary could not go on to say how the other character feels about the threat unless the author describes it.

Attending to Sequence and Instructions

Events happen in a sequence. However, many written texts present events out of order to create an effect on the reader. Nonfiction writers such as journalists and history writers may use this strategy to create surprise or bring particular ideas to the forefront. Fiction writers may interrupt the flow of a plot to interweave bits of a character's history or to provide flashes of insight into future events. Readers need to know how to untangle this presentation of events and figure out what actually happened first, second, and third. Consider the following passage:

> The man in dark glasses was looking for something. He checked his pockets. He checked his backpack. He walked back to his car, unlocked the doors, and inspected the area around the seats. Shaking his head, he re-locked the doors and rubbed his forehead in frustration. When his hand bumped his sunglasses, he finally realized where he had put them.

This passage does not mention putting the sunglasses on until the end, but it is clear from context that the man put them on first, before beginning his search. You can keep track of sequence by paying attention to time words like *when* and *before,* noticing grammatical constructions *he had* that indicate when events happened, and making common sense observations like the fact that the man is wearing his dark glasses in the first sentence.

Sequence is also an important aspect of reading technical and functional documents such as recipes and other instructions. If such documents present many steps in a large text block without illustrations or visual breaks, you may need to break them down and categorize them yourself. Always read all the steps first and think about how to follow them before jumping in.

To see why, read the pancake recipe below:

> Combine flour, baking powder, sugar, and salt. Break the eggs into a separate bowl. Add milk and oil to the beaten eggs. Combine dry and liquid ingredients and stir. While you are doing the above, put a small amount of oil into a pan and heat it on medium heat. When it is hot, spoon batter onto the pan.

To follow directions like these effectively, a reader must break them down into categories, perhaps even rewriting them in a numbered list and noting when to start steps like heating the pan, which may be worth doing in a different order than it appears above.

Interpreting Graphics

Information is often presented in pictures, graphs, or diagrams. These **graphic elements** may provide information to back up an argument, illustrate factual information or instructions, or present key facts and statistics.

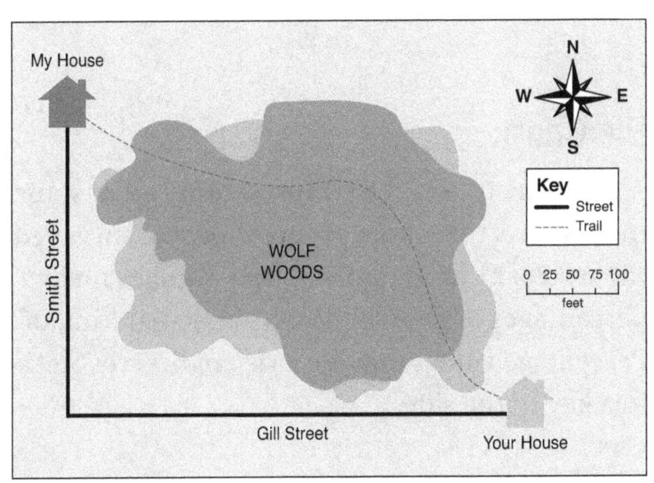

When you read charts and graphs, it is important to look carefully at all the information presented, including titles and labels, to be sure that you are interpreting the visuals correctly.

Diagram

A diagram presents a picture with labels that shows the parts of an object or functions of a mechanism. The diagram of a knee joint below shows the parts of the knee. Like many diagrams, it is placed in relation to a larger object—in this case, a leg—to clarify how the labeled parts fit into a larger context.

Flowchart

A flowchart shows a sequence of actions or decisions involved in a complex process. A flowchart usually begins with an oval-shaped box that asks a yes-no question or gives an instruction. Readers follow arrows indicating possible responses. This helps readers figure out how to solve a problem, or it illustrates how a complex system works.

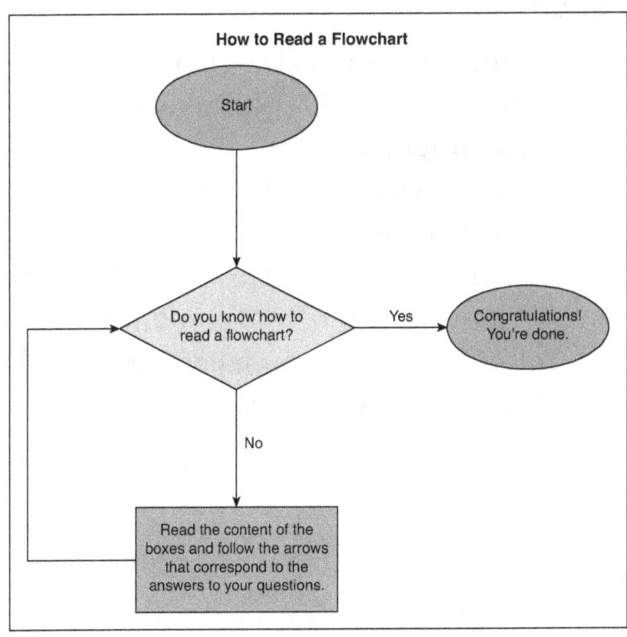

Bar Graph

A bar graph uses bars of different sizes to represent numbers. Larger bars show larger numbers to convey the magnitude of differences between two numeric values at a glance. In this case, each rectangle shows the number of candy bars of different types that a particular group of people ate.

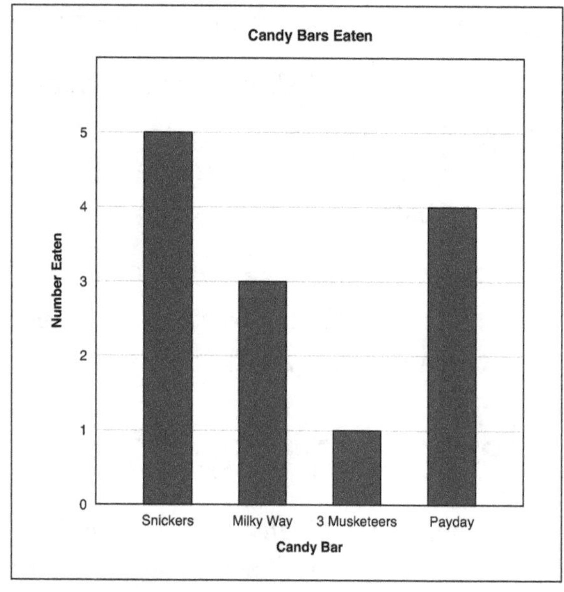

Pie Chart

A pie chart is useful for representing all of something—in this case, the whole group of people surveyed about their favorite kind of pie. Larger wedges mean larger percentages of people liked a particular kind of pie. Percentage values may be written directly on the chart or in a key to the side.

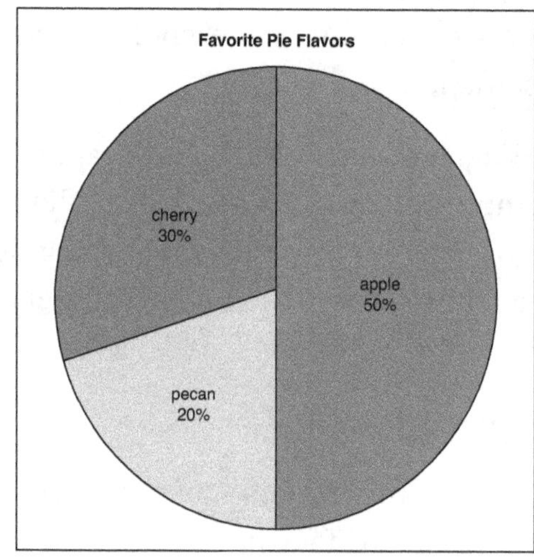

Let's Review!

- A summary restates the main ideas of a text in different words.
- A summary should objectively restate ideas in the present tense and give credit to the original author.
- Effective readers need to mentally reconstruct the basic sequence of events authors present out of order.
- Effective readers need to approach complex instructions by grouping steps into categories or considering how best to approach the steps.
- Information may be presented graphically in the form of diagrams, flowcharts, graphs, or charts.

Understanding Primary Sources, Making Inferences, and Drawing Conclusions

Effective readers must understand the difference between types of sources and choose credible sources of information to support research. Readers must also consider the content of their reading materials and draw their own conclusions.

Primary Sources

When we read and research information, we must differentiate between different types of sources. Sources are often classified depending on how close they are to the original creation or discovery of the information they present.

Primary sources include firsthand witness accounts of events, research described by the people who conducted it, and any other original information. Contemporary researchers can often access mixed media versions of primary sources such as video and audio recordings, photographs of original work, and so on. Note that original content is still considered primary even if it is reproduced online or in a book.

> **Examples:** Diaries, scientific journal articles, witness testimony, academic conference presentations, business memos, speeches, letters, interviews, and original literature and artwork.

Secondary sources respond to, analyze, summarize, or comment on primary sources. They add value to a discussion of the topic by giving readers new ways to think about the content. However, they may also introduce errors or layers of bias. Secondary sources may be very good sources of information, but readers must evaluate them carefully.

> **Examples:** Biographies, books and articles that summarize research for wider audiences, analyses of original literature and artwork, histories, political commentary.

Tertiary sources compile information in a general, highly summarized, and sometimes simplified way. Their purpose is not to add anything to the information, but rather to present the information in an accessible manner, often for audiences who are only beginning to familiarize themselves with a topic.

> **Examples:** Encyclopedias, guidebooks, literature study guides.

Source Materials in Action

Primary sources are often considered most trustworthy because they are closest to the original material and least likely to contain errors. However, readers must take a common sense approach to evaluating trustworthiness. For example, a single letter written by one biased witness of a historical event may not provide as much insight into what really happened as a secondary account by a historian who has considered the points of view of a dozen firsthand witnesses.

Tertiary sources are useful for readers attempting to gain a quick overview of understanding about a subject. They are also a good starting point for readers looking for keywords and subtopics to use for further research of a subject. However, they are not sufficiently detailed or credible to support an article, academic paper, or other document intended to add valuable analysis and commentary on a subject.

Evaluating Credibility

Not everything you read is equally trustworthy. Many sources contain mistakes, faulty reasoning, or deliberate misinformation designed to manipulate you. Effective readers seek out information from **credible**, or trustworthy, sources.

There is no single formula for determining credibility. Readers must make judgment calls based on individual texts and their purpose.

FOR EXAMPLE

Most sources should attempt to be objective. But if you're reading an article that makes an argument, you do not need to demand perfect objectivity from the source. The purpose of a persuasive article is to defend a point of view. As long as the author does this openly and defends the point of view with facts, logic, and other good argumentative techniques, you may trust the source.

Other sources may seem highly objective but not be credible. For example, some scientific studies meet all the criteria for credibility below except the one about trustworthy publishers. If a study is funded or conducted by a company that stands to profit from it, you should treat the results with skepticism no matter how good the information looks otherwise.

Sources and References

Credible texts are primary sources or secondary sources that refer to other trustworthy sources. If the author consults experts, they should be named, and their credentials should be explained. Authors should not attempt to hide where they got their information. Vague statements like "studies show" are not as trustworthy as statements that identify who completed a study.

Objectivity

Credible texts usually make an effort to be objective. They use clear, logical reasoning. They back arguments up with facts, expert opinions, or clear explanations. The assumptions behind the arguments do not contain obvious stereotypes.

Emotional arguments are acceptable in some argumentative writing, but they should not be manipulative. For example, photos of starving children may be acceptable for raising awareness of a famine, but they need to be respectful of both the victims and the audience—not just there for shock value.

Date of Publication

Information changes quickly in some fields, especially the sciences and technology. When researching a fast-changing topic, look for sources published in the last ten years.

Author Information

If an author and/or a respected organization take public credit for information, it is more likely to be reliable. Information published anonymously on the Internet may be suspicious because nobody is clearly responsible for mistakes. Authors with strong credentials such as university professors in a given field are more trustworthy than authors with no clear resume.

Publisher Information

Information published by the government, a university, a major national news organization, or another respected organization is often more credible. On the Internet, addresses ending in .edu or .gov may be more trustworthy than .com addresses. Publishers who stand to profit or otherwise benefit from the content of a text are always questionable.

BE CAREFUL!

Strong credentials only make a source more trustworthy if the credentials are related to the topic. A Columbia University Professor of Archeology is a credible source on ancient history. But if she writes a parenting article, it's not necessarily more credible than a parenting article by someone without a flashy university title.

Professionalism

Credible sources usually look professional and present information free of grammatical errors or major factual errors.

Making Inferences and Drawing Conclusions

In reading—and in life—people regularly make educated guesses based on limited information. When we use the information we have to figure out something nobody has told us directly, we are making an **inference**. People make inferences every day.

> **Example:** You hear a loud thump. Then a pained voice says, "Honey, can you bring the first aid kit?"

From the information above, it is reasonable to infer that the speaker is hurt. The thumping noise, the pain in the speaker's voice, and the request for a first aid kit all suggest this conclusion.

When you make inferences from reading, you use clues presented in the text to help you draw logical conclusions about what the author means. Before you can make an inference, you must read the text carefully and understand the explicit, or overt, meaning. Next, you must look for clues to any implied, or suggested, meanings behind the text. Finally, consider the clues in light of your prior knowledge and the author's purpose, and draw a conclusion about the meaning.

> As soon as Raizel entered the party, someone handed her a plate. She stared down at the hot dog unhappily.
>
> "What?" asked an unfamiliar woman nearby with an edge to her voice. "You don't eat dead animal?"

From the passage above, it would be reasonable to infer that the unfamiliar woman has a poor opinion of vegetarians. Several pieces of information suggest this: her combative tone, the edge in her voice, and the mocking question at the end.

When you draw inferences from a text, make sure your conclusion is truly indicated by the clues provided.

> Author Glenda Davis had high hopes for her children's book *Basketball Days*. But when the novel was released with a picture of a girl on the cover, boys refused to pick it up. The author reported this to her publisher, and the paperback edition was released with a new cover—this time featuring a dog and a basketball hoop. After that, many boys read the book. And Davis never heard anyone complain that the main character was a girl.

The text above implies that boys are reluctant to read books with a girl on the cover. A hasty reader might stop reading early and conclude that boys are reluctant to read about girls—but this inference is not suggested by the full text.

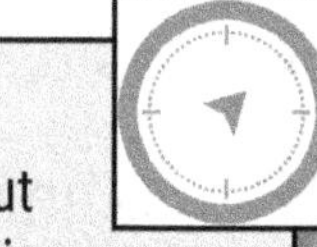

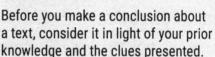

BE CAREFUL!

Before you make a conclusion about a text, consider it in light of your prior knowledge and the clues presented.

After reading the paragraph above, you might suspect that Raizel is a vegetarian. But the text does not fully support that conclusion. There are many reasons why Raizel might not want to eat a hot dog.

Perhaps she is keeping kosher, or she has social anxiety that makes it difficult to eat at parties, or she simply isn't hungry. The above inference about the unfamiliar woman's dislike for vegetarians is strongly supported. But you'd need further evidence before you could safely conclude that Raizel is actually a vegetarian.

Let's Review!

- Effective readers must consider the credibility of their sources.
- Primary sources are usually considered the most trustworthy.
- Readers must often make inferences about ideas that are implied but not explicitly stated in a text.

Chapter 10 Key Ideas and Details Practice Quiz

1. **Which type of graphic element would be most helpful for teaching the names of the parts of a bicycle?**

   A. Diagram
   B. Pie chart
   C. Bar graph
   D. Flowchart

Read the following sentence and answer questions 2-4.

Numerous robotic missions to Mars have revealed tantalizing evidence of a planet that may once have been capable of supporting life.

2. **Imagine this sentence is a *supporting detail* in a well-developed paragraph. Which of the following sentences would best function as a *topic sentence*?**

   A. Venus is an intensely hot planet surrounded by clouds full of drops of sulfuric acid.

   B. Of all the destinations within human reach, Mars is the planet most similar to Earth.

   C. Liquid water—a necessary ingredient of life—may once have flowed on the planet's surface.

   D. Space research is a costly, frivolous exercise that brings no clear benefit to people on Earth.

3. **Imagine this sentence is the *topic sentence* of a well-developed paragraph. Which of the following sentences would best function as a *supporting detail*?**

   A. Of all the destinations within human reach, Mars is the planet most similar to Earth.

   B. Venus is an intensely hot planet surrounded by clouds full of drops of sulfuric acid.

   C. Space research is a costly, frivolous exercise that brings no clear benefit to people on Earth.

   D. Liquid water—a necessary ingredient of life—may once have flowed on the planet's surface.

4. **How could this sentence function as a *supporting detail* in a persuasive text arguing that space research is worth the expense and effort because it teaches us more about Earth and ourselves?**

   A. By using statistics to back up an argument that needs support to be believed

   B. By showing how a space discovery could earn money for investors here on Earth

   C. By providing an example of a space discovery that enhances our understanding of life

   D. By developing the main idea that no space discovery can reveal information about Earth

The bar graph below provides information about book sales for a book called *The Comings,* which is the first book in a trilogy. Study the image and answer questions 5-6.

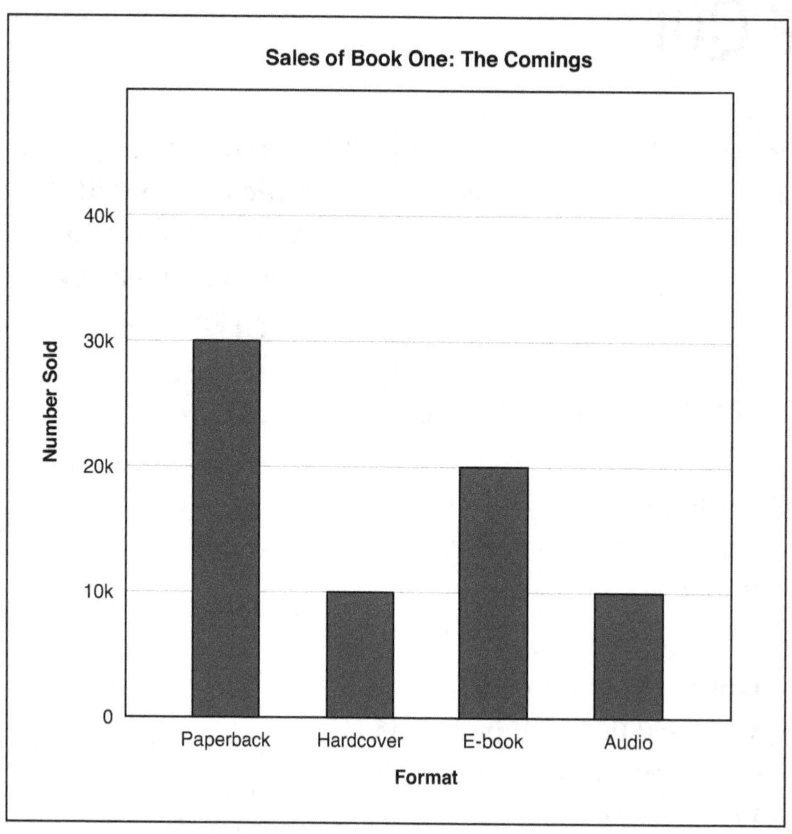

5. **Which type of book has sold the most copies?**

   A. E-book
   B. Hardcover
   C. Paperback
   D. Audio book

6. **The marketing director for *The Comings* wants to use a different strategy for publishing book two in the series. Which argument does the bar graph *best* support?**

   A. The first book in the trilogy has only sold 10,000 copies.
   B. The second book in the trilogy should not be released in hardcover.
   C. The second book in the trilogy should only be released as an e-book.
   D. The second and third books in the trilogy should be combined into one.

Study the infographic below and answer questions 7-9.

https://www.cdc.gov/nccdphp/dch/images/infographics/getmoving_15-18.png

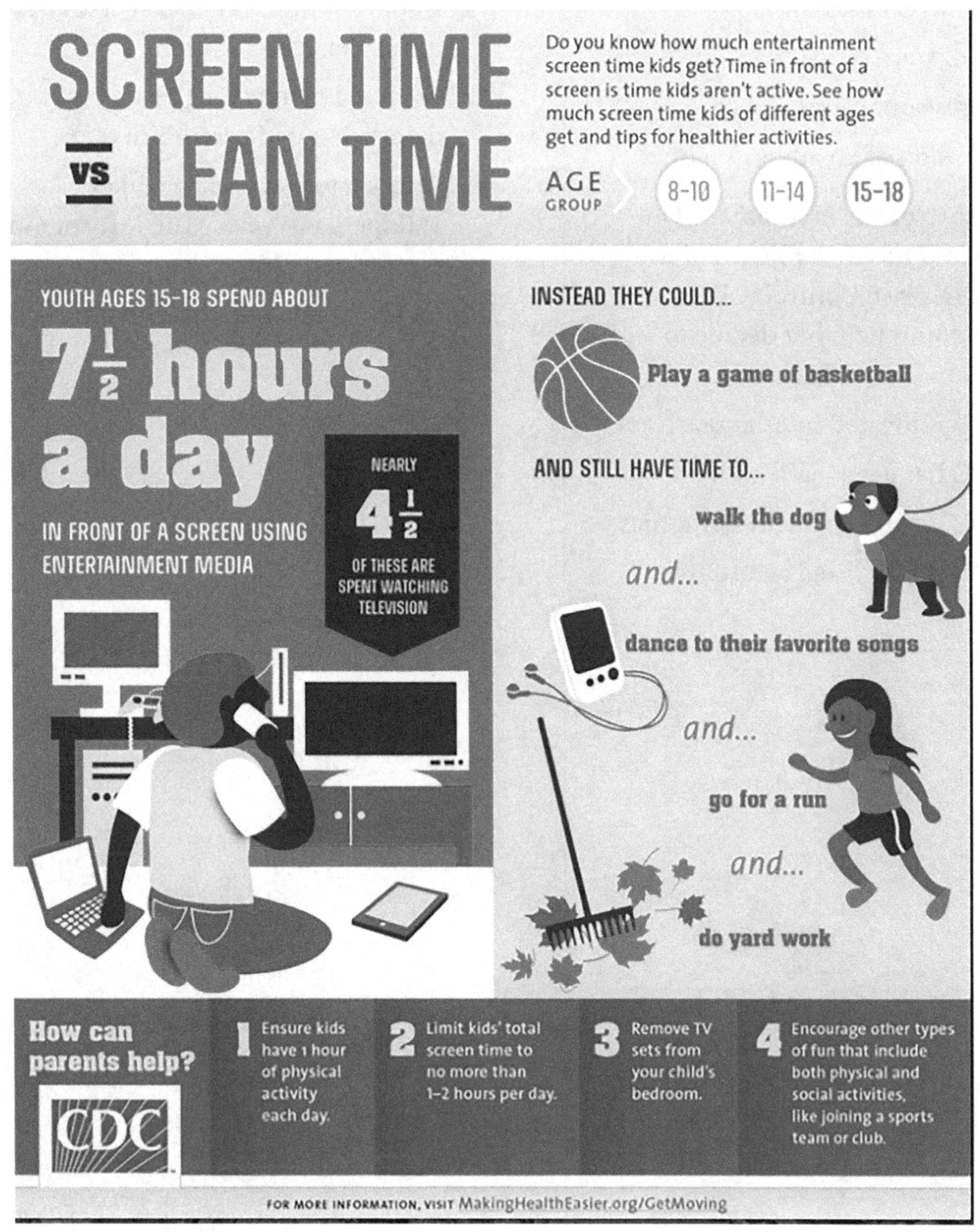

Credit: Center for Disease Control and Prevention. https://www.cdc.gov/nccdphp/dnpao/multimedia/infographics/getmoving.html

7. **Which of the following is not a sign that the infographic is credible?**
   A. The use of verifiable facts
   B. The list of source materials
   C. The professional appearance
   D. The inclusion of an author's name

8. **Zetta is unsure of the credibility of this source and has never heard of the Centers for Disease Control (CDC). Which fact could help her decide to trust it?**
   A. The CDC is located in Atlanta.
   B. The CDC has a .gov web address.
   C. The CDC creates many infographics.
   D. The CDC is also listed as a source consulted.

9. **What could a skeptical reader do to verify the facts on the infographic?**
   A. Interview one teenager to ask about his or her screen time.
   B. Follow the links for the sources and determine their credibility.
   C. Check a tertiary source like Wikipedia to verify the information.
   D. Find different values for screen time on someone's personal blog.

Chapter 10 Key Ideas and Details Practice Quiz – Answer Key

1. A. A diagram illustrates complex visual ideas, so it could show which part of a bicycle is which and how they fit together. **See Lesson: Summarizing Text and Using Text Features.**

2. B. The sentence above conveys factual information about Mars in an excited tone that suggests a positive interest in the subject. This makes it most likely to fit into an informational paragraph sharing facts about Mars. **See Lesson: Main Ideas, Topic Sentences, and Supporting Details.**

3. D. If the above sentence were a topic sentence, its supporting details would likely share information to develop the idea that Mars may have supported life in the past. **See Lesson: Main Ideas, Topic Sentences, and Supporting Details.**

4. C. The sentence above could act as an example to show how space discoveries teach us about Earth and ourselves. **See Lesson: Main Ideas, Topic Sentences, and Supporting Details.**

5. C. Larger bars in a bar graph indicate higher numbers. This book has sold more paperback copies than any other. **See Lesson: Summarizing Text and Using Text Features.**

6. B. The bar graph shows fewer hardcover sales than any other kind. This could help support an argument that later books should only be released in electronic and paperback forms. **See Lesson: Summarizing Text and Using Text Features.**

7. D. It is usually a good sign if an author is clearly named in a source. Although this source is authored by an organization, the CDC, instead of a single author, there are many other signs it is credible. **See Lesson: Understanding Primary Sources, Making Inferences, and Drawing Conclusions.**

8. B. When presenting this type of information, a government organization with a .gov web address is typically considered a reputable source. **See Lesson: Understanding Primary Sources, Making Inferences, and Drawing Conclusions.**

9. B. One way to verify facts is to check the sources an author used. Verifying facts elsewhere may also be a good idea, but it is important to use reputable primary or secondary sources. **See Lesson: Understanding Primary Sources, Making Inferences, and Drawing Conclusions.**

CHAPTER 11 CRAFT AND STRUCTURE

FORMAL AND INFORMAL LANGUAGE

In English, there is formal language that is used most often in writing, and informal language that is most often used in speaking, but there are situations where one is more appropriate than the other. This lesson will cover differentiating contexts for (1) formal language and (2) informal language.

Formal Language

Formal language is often associated with writing for professional and academic purposes, but it is also used when giving a speech or a lecture. An essay written for a class will always use **formal language. Formal language** is used in situations where people are not extremely close and when one needs to show respect to another person. Certain qualities and contexts differentiate **formal language** from informal language.

Formal language does not use contractions.

- It doesn't have that - It does not have that.
- He's been offered a new job - He has been offered a new job.

Formal language also uses complete sentences.

- So much to tell you - I have so much to tell you.
- Left for the weekend - We left for the weekend.

Formal language includes more formal and polite vocabulary.

- The class starts at two - The class commences at two.
- I try to be the best person I can be - I endeavor to be the best person I can be.

Formal language is not personal and normally does not use the pronouns "I" and "We" as the subject of a sentence.

- I argue that the sky is blue - This essay argues that the sky is blue.
- We often associate green with grass - Green is often associated with grass.

Formal language also does not use slang.

- It's raining cats and dogs - It is raining heavily.
- Patients count on doctors to help them - Patients expect doctors to help them.

Informal Language

Informal language is associated with speaking, but is also used in text messages, emails, letters, and postcards. It is the language a person would use with their friends and family.

Informal language uses contractions.

- I can't go to the movie tomorrow.
- He doesn't have any manners.

Informal language can include sentence fragments.

- See you
- Talk to you later

Informal language uses less formal vocabulary such as slang.

- The dog drove me up the wall.
- I was so hungry I could eat a horse.
- I can always count on you.

Informal language is personal and uses pronouns such as "I" and "We" as the subject of a sentence.

- I am in high school.
- We enjoy going to the beach in the summer.

Let's Review!

- **Formal language** is used in professional and academic writing and talks. It does not have contractions, uses complete sentences, uses polite and formal vocabulary, not slang, and is not personal and generally does not use the pronouns "I" and "We" as the subject of a sentence.
- **Informal language** is used in daily life when communicating with friends and family through conversations, text messages, emails, letters, and postcards. It uses contractions, can be sentence fragments, uses less formal vocabulary and slang, and is personal and uses pronouns such as "I" and "We" as the subject of a sentence.

Tone, Mood, and Transition Words

Authors use language to show their emotions and to make readers feel something too. They also use transition words to help guide the reader from one idea to the next.

Tone and Mood

The **tone** of a text is the author's or speaker's attitude toward the subject. The tone may reflect any feeling or attitude a person can express: happiness, excitement, anger, boredom, or arrogance.

Readers can identify tone primarily by analyzing word choice. The reader should be able to point to specific words and details that help to establish the tone.

> **Example:** The train rolled past miles and miles of cornfields. The fields all looked the same. They swayed the same. They produced the same dull nausea in the pit of my stomach. I'd been sent out to see the world, and so I looked, obediently. What I saw was sameness.

Here, the author is expressing boredom and dissatisfaction. This is clear from the repetition of words like "same" and "sameness." There's also a sense of unpleasantness from phrases like "dull nausea" and passivity from words like "obediently."

Sometimes an author uses an ironic tone. Ironic texts often mean the opposite of what they actually say. To identify irony, you need to rely on your prior experience and common sense to help you identify texts with words and ideas that do not quite match.

> **Example:** With that, the senator dismissed the petty little problem of mass shootings and returned to the really important issue: his approval ratings.

Here the author flips around the words most people would usually use to discuss mass murder and popularity. By calling a horrific issue "petty" and a trivial issue "important," the author highlights what she sees as a politician's backwards priorities. Except for the phrase "mass shootings," the words here are light and airy—but the tone is ironic and angry.

BE CAREFUL!

When you're asked to identify the tone of a text, be sure to keep track of *whose* tone you're supposed to identify, and which part of the text the question is referencing. The author's tone can be different from that of the characters in fiction or the people quoted in nonfiction.

Example: The reporter walked quickly, panting to catch up to the senator's entourage. "Senator Biltong," she said. "Are you going to take action on mass shootings?"

"Sure, sure. Soon," the senator said vaguely. Then he turned to greet a newcomer. "Ah ha! Here's the man who can fix my approval ratings!" And with that, he returned to the really important issue: his popularity.

*

In the example above, the author's tone is ironic and angry. But the tone of the senator's dialogue is different. The line beginning with the words "Sure, sure" has a distracted tone. The line beginning with "Ah ha!" has a pleased tone.

A concept related to tone is **mood**, or the feelings an author produces in the reader. To determine the mood of a text, a reader can consider setting and theme as well as word choice and tone. For example, a story set in a haunted house may produce an unsettled or frightened feeling in a reader.

Tone and mood are often confused. This is because they are sometimes the same. For instance, in an op-ed article that describes children starving while food aid lies rotting, the author may use an outraged tone and simultaneously arouse an outraged mood in the reader.

However, tone and mood can be different. When they are, it's useful to have different words to distinguish between the author's attitude and the reader's emotional reaction.

> **Example:** I had to fly out of town at 4 a.m. for my trip to the Bahamas, and my wife didn't even get out of bed to make me a cup of coffee. I told her to, but she refused just because she'd been up five times with our newborn. I'm only going on vacation for one week, and she's been off work for a month! She should show me a little consideration.

Here, the tone is indignant. The mood will vary depending on the reader, but it is likely to be unsympathetic.

Transitions

Authors use connecting words and phrases, or **transitions**, to link ideas and help readers follow the flow of their thoughts. The number of possible ways to transition between ideas is almost limitless.

Below are a few common transition words, categorized by the way they link ideas.

Transitions	Examples
Time and sequence transitions orient the reader within a text. They can also help show when events happened in time.	*First, second, next, now, then, at this point, after, afterward, before this, previously, formerly, thereafter, finally, in conclusion*
Addition or emphasis transitions let readers know the author is building on an established line of thought. Many place extra stress on an important idea.	*Moreover, also, likewise, furthermore, above all, indeed, in fact*
Example transitions introduce ideas that illustrate a point.	*For example, for instance, to illustrate, to demonstrate*
Causation transitions indicate a cause-and-effect relationship.	*As a result, consequently, thus*
Contrast transitions indicate a difference between ideas.	*Nevertheless, despite, in contrast, however*

Transitions may look different depending on their function within the text. Within a paragraph, writers often choose short words or expressions to provide transitions and smooth the flow. Between paragraphs or larger sections of text, transitions are usually longer. They may use some of the key words or ideas above, but the author often goes into detail restating larger concepts and explaining their relationships more thoroughly.

Between Sentences: Students who cheat do not learn what they need to know. *As a result,* they get farther behind and face greater temptation to cheat in the future.

Between Paragraphs: *As a result of the cheating behaviors described above,* students find themselves in a vicious cycle.

Longer transitions like the latter example may be useful for keeping the reader clued in to the author's focus in an extended text. But long transitions should have clear content and function. Some long transitions, such as the very wordy "due to the fact that" take up space without adding more meaning and are considered poor style.

Let's Review!

- Tone is the author's or speaker's attitude toward the subject.
- Mood is the feeling a text creates in the reader.
- Transitions are connecting words and phrases that help readers follow the flow of a writer's thoughts.

THE AUTHOR'S PURPOSE AND POINT OF VIEW

In order to understand, analyze, and evaluate a text, readers must know how to identify the author's purpose and point of view. Readers also need to attend to an author's language and rhetorical strategies.

Author's Purpose

When writers put words on paper, they do it for a reason. This reason is the author's **purpose**. Most writing exists for one of three purposes: to inform, to persuade, or to entertain.

TEST TIP

You may have learned about a fourth purpose for writing: conveying an emotional experience. Many poems as well as some works of fiction, personal essays, and memoirs are written to give the reader a sense of how an event or moment might feel. This type of text is rarely included on placement tests, and if it is, it tends to be lumped in with literature meant to entertain.

If a text is designed to share knowledge, its purpose is to **inform**. Informational texts include technical documents, cookbooks, expository essays, journalistic newspaper articles, and many nonfiction books. Informational texts are based on facts and logic, and they usually attempt an objective tone. The style may otherwise vary; some informational texts are quite dry, whereas others have an engaging style.

If a text argues a point, its purpose is to **persuade**. A persuasive text attempts to convince a reader to believe a certain point of view or take a certain action. Persuasive texts include op-ed newspaper articles, book and movie reviews, project proposals, and argumentative essays. Key signs of persuasive texts include judgments, words like *should*, and other signs that the author is sharing opinions.

If a text is primarily for fun, its purpose is to **entertain**. Entertaining texts usually tell stories or present descriptions. Entertaining texts include novels, short stories, memoirs, and some poems. Virtually all stories are lumped into this category, even if they describe unpleasant experiences.

CONNECTIONS

You may have read elsewhere that readers can break writing down into the following basic categories. These categories are often linked to the author's purpose.

Narrative writing tells a story and is usually meant to entertain.
Expository writing explains an idea and is usually meant to inform.
Technical writing explains a mechanism or process and is usually meant to inform.
Persuasive writing argues a point and, as the label suggests, is meant to persuade.

A text can have more than one purpose. For example, many traditional children's stories come with morals or lessons. These are meant both to entertain children and persuade them to behave in ways society considers appropriate. Also, commercial nonfiction texts like popular science books are often written in an engaging or humorous style. The purpose of such a text is to inform while also entertaining the reader.

Point of View

Every author has a general outlook or set of opinions about the subject. These make up the author's **point of view.**

To determine point of view, a reader must recognize implicit clues in the text and use them to develop educated guesses about the author's worldview. In persuasive texts, the biggest clue is the author's explicit argument. From considering this argument, a reader can usually make some inferences about point of view. For instance, if an author argues that parents should offer kids opportunities to exercise throughout the day, it would be reasonable to infer that the author has an overall interest in children's health, and that he or she is troubled by the idea of kids pursuing sedentary behaviors like TV watching.

It is more challenging to determine point of view in a text meant to inform. Because the writer does not present an explicit argument, readers must examine assumptions and word choice to determine the writer's point of view.

> **Example:** Models suggest that at the current rate of global warming, hurricanes in 2100 will move 9 percent slower and drop 24 percent more rain. Longer storm durations and rainfall rates will likely translate to increased economic damage and human suffering.

It is reasonable to infer that the writer of this passage has a general trust for science and scientists. This writer assumes that global warming is happening, so it is clear he or she is not a global warming denier. Although the writer does not suggest a plan to prevent future storm damage, the emphasis on negative effects and the use of negative words like "damage" and "suffering" suggest that the author is worried about global warming.

Texts meant to entertain also contain clues about the author's point of view. That point of view is usually evident from the themes and deeper meanings. For instance, a memoirist who writes an upbeat story about a troubled but loving family is likely to believe strongly in the power of love. Note, however, that in this type of work, it is not possible to determine point of view merely from one character's words or actions. For instance, if a character says, "Your mother's love doesn't matter much if she can't take care of you," the reader should *not* automatically assume the writer agrees with that statement. Narrative writers often present a wide range of characters with varying outlooks on life. A reader can only determine the author's point of view by considering the work as a whole. The attitudes that are most emphasized and the ones that win out in the end are likely to reflect the author's point of view.

Rhetorical Strategies

Rhetorical strategies are the techniques an author uses to support an argument or develop a main idea. Effective readers need to study the language of a text and determine how the author is supporting his or her points.

One strategy is to appeal to the reader's reason. This is the foundation of effective writing, and it simply means that the writer relies on factual information and the logical conclusions that follow from it. Even persuasive writing uses this strategy by presenting facts and reasons to back up the author's opinions.

> **Ineffective:** Everyone knows *Sandra and the Lumps* is the best band of the new millennium.
>
> **Effective:** The three most recent albums by *Sandra and the Lumps* are the first, second, and third most popular records released since the turn of the millennium.

Another strategy is to establish trust. A writer can do this by choosing credible sources and by presenting ideas in a clear and professional way. In persuasive writing, writers may show they are trustworthy by openly acknowledging that some people hold contradicting opinions and by responding fairly to those positions. Writers should never attack or misrepresent their opponents' position.

> **Ineffective:** People who refuse to recycle are too lazy to protect their children's future.
>
> **Effective:** According to the annual Throw It Out Questionnaire, many people dislike the onerous task of sorting garbage, and some doubt that their effort brings any real gain.

A final strategy is to appeal to the reader's emotions. For instance, a journalist reporting on the opioid epidemic could include a personal story about an addict's attempts to overcome substance abuse. Emotional content can add a human dimension to a story that would be missing if the writer only included statistics and expert opinions. But emotions are easily manipulated, so writers who use this strategy need to be careful. Emotions should never be used to distort the truth or scare readers into agreeing with the writer.

> **Ineffective:** If you don't take action on gun control, you're basically killing children.
>
> **Effective:** Julie was puzzling over the Pythagorean Theorem when she heard the first gunshot.

Let's Review!

- Every text has a purpose.
- Most texts are meant to inform, persuade, or entertain.
- Texts contain clues that imply an author's outlook or set of opinions about the subject.
- Authors use rhetorical strategies to appeal to reason, establish trust, or invoke emotions.

Chapter 11 Craft and Structure Practice Quiz

1. **Which of the following sentences uses the MOST informal language?**
   A. The house creaked at night.
   B. I ate dinner with my friend.
   C. It's sort of a bad time.
   D. The water trickled slowly.

2. **In which of the following situations would it be best to use informal language?**
   A. In a seminar
   B. Writing a postcard
   C. Talking to your boss
   D. Participating in a professional conference

3. **Which of the following sentences uses the MOST formal language?**
   A. Thanks for letting me know.
   B. I want to thank you for telling me.
   C. I appreciate you telling me about this issue.
   D. Thank you for bringing this issue to my attention.

Read the passage below and answer questions 4-6.

The train was the most amazing thing ever even though it didn't go "choo choo." The toddler pounded on the railing of the bridge and supplied the sound herself. "Choo choo! Choo choooooo!" she shouted as the train cars whizzed along below.

In the excitement, she dropped her favorite binky.

Later, when she noticed the binky missing, all the joy went out of the world. The wailing could be heard three houses down. The toddler's usual favorite activities were garbage—even waving to Hank the garbage man, which she refused to do, so that Hank went away looking mildly hurt. It was clear the little girl would never, ever, ever recover from her loss.

Afterward, she played at the park.

4. **Which adjectives best describe the tone of the passage?**
   A. Ironic, angry
   B. Earnest, angry
   C. Ironic, humorous
   D. Earnest, humorous

5. **Which sentence from the passage is clearly ironic?**
   A. "Choo choo! Choo choooooo!" she shouted as the train cars whizzed along below.
   B. Later, when she noticed the binky missing, all the joy went out of the world.
   C. The wailing could be heard three houses down.
   D. Afterward, she played at the park.

6. **The author of the passage first establishes the ironic tone by:**
   A. describing the child's trip to play at the park.
   B. calling the train "the most amazing thing ever."
   C. pretending that the child can make the sounds "choo chooooo!"
   D. claiming inaccurately that the lost binky was the child's "favorite."

7. **What is the most likely purpose of a popular science book describing recent advances in genetics?**
   A. To decide
   B. To inform
   C. To persuade
   D. To entertain

8. **Which phrase describes the set of techniques an author uses to support an argument or develop a main idea?**
   A. Points of view
   B. Logical fallacies
   C. Statistical analyses
   D. Rhetorical strategies

9. **What is the most likely purpose of an article that claims some genetic research is immoral?**
   A. To decide
   B. To inform
   C. To persuade
   D. To entertain

Chapter 11 Craft and Structure Practice Quiz – Answer Key

1. C. *It's sort of a bad time.* The sentence has contractions and uses informal and slang words. **See Lesson: Formal and Informal Language.**

2. B. *Writing a postcard.* It is an informal mode of communication between close friends and relatives. **See Lesson: Formal and Informal Language.**

3. D. *Thank you for bringing this issue to my attention.* The sentence uses the most formal and polite vocabulary. **See Lesson: Formal and Informal Language.**

4. C. This passage ironically is a humorous description of a toddler's emotions, written by an adult who has enough experience to know that a toddler's huge emotions will pass. **See Lesson: Tone, Mood, and Transition Words.**

5. B. Authors use irony when their words do not literally mean what they say. The joy does not really go out of the world when a toddler loses her binky—but it may seem that way to the child. **See Lesson: Tone, Mood, and Transition Words.**

6. B. This passage establishes irony in the opening sentence by applying the superlative phrase "the most amazing thing ever" to an ordinary occurrence. **See Lesson: Tone, Mood, and Transition Words.**

7. B. If a book is describing information, its purpose is to inform. **See Lesson: The Author's Purpose and Point of View.**

8. D. The techniques an author uses to support an argument or develop a main idea are called rhetorical strategies. **See Lesson: The Author's Purpose and Point of View.**

9. C. An article that takes a moral position is meant to persuade. **See Lesson: The Author's Purpose and Point of View.**

Chapter 12 Integration of Knowledge and Ideas

Facts, Opinions, and Evaluating an Argument

Nonfiction writing is based on facts and real events, but most nonfiction nevertheless expresses a point of view. Effective readers must evaluate the author's point of view and form their own conclusions about the points in the text.

Fact and Opinion

Many texts make an **argument.** In this context, the word *argument* has nothing to do with anger or fighting. It simply means the author is trying to convince readers of something.

Arguments are present in a wide variety of texts. Some relate to controversial issues, for instance by advocating support for a political candidate or change in laws. Others may defend a certain interpretation of facts or ideas. For example, a literature paper may argue that an author's story suggests a certain theme, or a science paper may argue for a certain interpretation of data. An argument may also present a plan of action such as a business strategy.

To evaluate an argument, readers must distinguish between **fact** and **opinion**. A fact is verifiably true. An opinion is someone's belief.

> **Fact:** Seattle gets an average of 37 inches of rain per year.
>
> **Opinion:** The dark, rainy, cloudy weather makes Seattle an unpleasant place to live in winter.

Meteorologists measure rainfall directly, so the above fact is verifiably true. The statement "it is unpleasant" clearly reflects a feeling, so the second sentence is an opinion.

The difference between fact and opinion is not always straightforward. For instance, a text may present a fact that contains an opinion within it:

> **Fact:** Nutritionist Fatima Antar questions the wisdom of extreme carbohydrate avoidance.

Assuming the writer can prove that this sentence genuinely reflects Fatima Antar's beliefs, it is a factual statement of her point of view. The reader may trust that Fatima Antar really holds this opinion, whether or not the reader is convinced by it.

If a text makes a judgment, it is not a fact:

Opinion: The patient's seizure drug regimen caused horrendous side effects.

This sentence uses language that different people would interpret in different ways. Because people have varying ideas about what they consider "horrendous," this sentence is an opinion as it is written, even though the actual side effects and the patient's opinion of them could both be verified.

COMPARE!

Small changes to the statement about seizure drugs could turn it into a factual statement:

Fact: The patient's seizure drug regiment caused side effects such as migraines, confusion, and dangerously high blood pressure.

The above statement can be verified because the patient and other witnesses could confirm the exact nature of her symptoms. This makes it a fact.

Fact: The patient reported that her seizure drug regimen caused horrendous side effects.

This statement can also be verified because the patient can verify that she considers the side effects horrendous. By framing the statement in this way, the writer leaves nothing up to interpretation and is clearly in the realm of fact.

The majority of all arguments contain both facts and opinions, and strong arguments may contain both fact and opinion elements. It is rare for an argument to be composed entirely of facts, but it can happen if the writer is attempting to convince readers to accept factual information that is little-known or widely questioned. Most arguments present an author's opinion and use facts, reasoning, and expert testimony to convince readers.

Evaluating an Argument

Effective readers must evaluate an argument and decide whether or not it is valid. To do this, readers must consider every claim the author presents, including both the main argument and any supporting statements. If an argument is based on poor reasoning or insufficient evidence, it is not valid—even if you agree with the main idea.

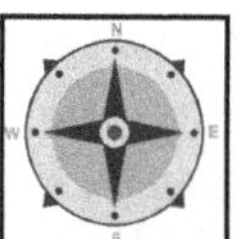

KEY POINT!

Most of us want to agree with arguments that reflect our own beliefs. But it is inadvisable to accept an argument that is not properly rooted in good reasoning. Consider the following statements about global climate change:

Poor Argument: It just snowed fifteen inches! How can anyone say the world is getting warmer?

Poor Argument: It's seventy degrees in the middle of February! How can anyone deny global warming?

Both of these arguments are based on insufficient evidence. Each relies on *one* weather event in *one* location to support an argument that the entire world's climate is or is not changing. There is not nearly enough information here to support an argument on either side.

Beware of any argument that presents opinion information as fact.

> **False Claim of Fact**: I know vaccines cause autism because my niece began displaying autism symptoms after receiving her measles vaccine.

The statement above states a controversial idea as fact without adequate evidence to back it up. Specifically, it makes a false claim of cause and effect about an incident that has no clear causal relationship.

Any claim that is not supported by sufficient evidence is an example of **faulty reasoning**.

Type of Faulty Reasoning	Definition	Example	Explanation
Circular Reasoning	Restating the argument in different words instead of providing evidence	Baseball is the best game in the world because it is more fun than any other game.	Here, everything after the word *because* says approximately the same thing as everything before it. It looks like the author is providing a reason, but no evidence has actually been offered.
Either/Or Fallacy	Presenting an issue as if it involves only two choices when in fact it is not so simple	Women should focus on motherhood, not careers.	This statement assumes that women cannot do both. It also assumes that no woman needs a career in order to provide for her children.
Overgeneralizations	Making a broad claim based on too little evidence	All elderly people have negative stereotypes of teenagers.	This statement lumps a whole category of people into a group and claims the whole group shares the same belief—always an unlikely prospect.

Most texts about evaluating arguments focus on faulty reasoning and false statements of fact. But arguments that attempt to misrepresent facts as opinions are equally suspicious. A careful reader should be skeptical of any text that denies clear physical evidence or questions the truth of events that have been widely verified.

Assumptions and Biases

A well-reasoned argument should be supported by facts, logic, and clearly explained opinions. But most arguments are also based on **assumptions**, or unstated and unproven ideas about what is true. Consider the following argument:

> **Argument:** To improve equality of opportunity for all children, schools in underprivileged areas should receive as much taxpayer funding as schools in wealthy districts.

This argument is based on several assumptions. First is the assumption that all children should have equal opportunities. Another is that taxpayer-funded public schools are the best way to provide these opportunities. Whether or not you disagree with either of these points, it is worth noting that the second idea in particular is not the only way to proceed. Readers who examine the assumptions behind an argument can sometimes find points of disagreement even if an author's claims and logic are otherwise sound.

Examining an author's assumptions can also reveal a writer's biases. A **bias** is a preconceived idea that makes a person more likely to show unfair favor for certain thoughts, people, or groups. Because every person has a different experience of the world, every person has a different set of biases. For example, a person who has traveled widely may feel differently about world political events than someone who has always lived in one place.

Virtually all writing is biased to some degree. However, effective writing attempts to avoid bias as much as possible. Writing that is highly biased may be based on poor assumptions that render the entire argument invalid.

Highly biased writing often includes overgeneralizations. Words like *all, always, never,* and so on may indicate that the writer is overstating a point. While these words can exist in true statements, unbiased writing is more likely to qualify ideas using words like *usually, often,* and *rarely.*

Another quality of biased writing is excessively emotional word choice. When writers insult people who disagree with them or engage the emotions in a way that feels manipulative, they are being biased.

> **Biased:** Power-hungry politicians don't care that their standardized testing requirements are producing a generation of overanxious, incurious, impractical kids.
>
> **Less biased:** Politicians need to recognize that current standardized testing requirements are causing severe anxiety and other negative effects in children.

Biased writing may also reflect stereotypical thinking. A **stereotype** is a particularly harmful type of bias that applies specifically to groups of people. Stereotypical thinking is behind racism, sexism, homophobia, and so on. Even people who do not consider themselves prejudiced can use language that reflects common stereotypes. For example, the negative use of the word *crazy* reflects a stereotype against people with mental illnesses.

Historically, writers in English have used male nouns and pronouns to indicate all people. Revising such language for more inclusivity is considered more effective in contemporary writing.

> **Biased:** The history of the human race proves that man is a violent creature.
>
> **Less biased:** The history of the human race proves that people are violent.

Let's Review!

- A text meant to convince someone of something is making an argument.
- Arguments may employ both facts and opinions.
- Effective arguments must use valid reasoning.
- Arguments are based on assumptions that may be reasonable or highly biased.
- Almost all writing is biased to some degree, but strong writing makes an effort to eliminate bias.

EVALUATING AND INTEGRATING DATA

Effective readers do more than absorb and analyze the content of sentences, paragraphs, and chapters. They recognize the importance of features that stand out in and around the text, and they understand and integrate knowledge from visual features like maps and charts.

Text Features

Elements that stand out from a text are called **text features**. Text features perform many vital functions.

- **Introducing the Topic and Organizing Information**

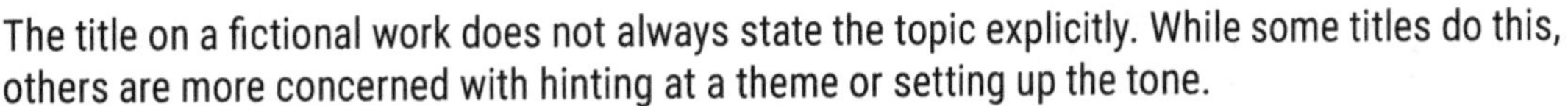

COMPARE!

The title on a fictional work does not always state the topic explicitly. While some titles do this, others are more concerned with hinting at a theme or setting up the tone.

- *Titles* – The title of a nonfiction text typically introduces the topic. Titles are guiding features of organization because they give clues about what is and is not covered. The title of this section, "Text Features," covers exactly that—not, for example, implicit ideas.
- *Headings and Subheadings* – Headings and subheadings provide subtopic information about supporting points and let readers scan to see how information is organized. The subheadings of this page organize text features according to the functions they perform.

- **Helping the Reader Find Information**

- *Table of Contents* – The table of contents of a long work lists chapter titles and other large-scale information so readers can predict the content. This helps readers to determine whether or not a text will be useful to them and to find sections relevant to their research.
- *Index* – In a book, the index is an alphabetical list of topics covered, complete with page numbers where the topics are discussed. Readers looking for information on one small subtopic can check the index to find out which pages to view.
- *Footnotes and Endnotes* – When footnotes and endnotes list sources, they allow the reader to find and evaluate the information an author is citing.

- **Emphasizing Concepts**

- *Formatting Features* – Authors may use formatting features such as *italics*, **boldfacing** or underlining to emphasize a word, phrase, or other important information in a text.
- *Bulleting and numbering* – Bullet points and numbered lists set off information and allow readers to scan for bits of information they do not know. It also helps to break down a list of steps.

- **Presenting Information and Illustrating Ideas**
    - *Graphic Elements* – Charts, graphs, diagrams, and other graphic elements present data succinctly, illustrate complex ideas, or otherwise convey information that would be difficult to glean from text alone.
- **Providing Peripheral Information**
    - *Sidebars* – Sidebars are text boxes that contain information related to the topic but not essential to the overall point.
    - *Footnotes and Endnotes* – Some footnotes and endnotes contain information that is not essential to the development of the main point but may nevertheless interest readers and researchers.[1]

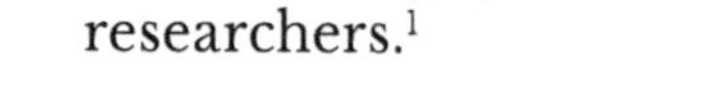

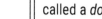

FUN FACT!

Online, a sidebar is sometimes called a *doobly doo.*

P.S. This is an example of a sidebar.

Maps and Charts

To read maps and charts, you need to understand what the labels, symbols, and pictures mean. You also need to know how to make decisions using the information they contain.

Maps

Maps are stylized pictures of places as seen from above. A map may have a box labeled "Key" or "Legend" that provides information about the meanings of colors, lines, or symbols. On the map below, the key shows that a solid line is a road and a dotted line is a trail.

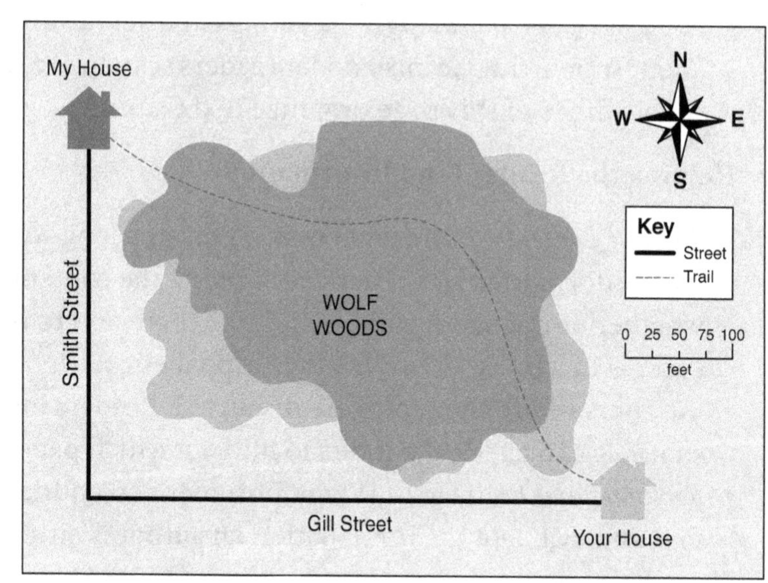

There may also be a line labeled "scale" that helps you figure out how far you need to travel to get from one point on the map to another. In the example below, an inch is only 100 feet, so a trip from one end to the other is not far.

Some maps, including the example above, have compasses that show directions. If no compass is pictured, assume the top of the map is north.

---

1 Anthony Grafton's book *The Footnote: A Curious History* is an in-depth history of the origins and development of the footnote. (Also, this is an example of a footnote.)

Charts

Nutrition Facts Labels

Nutrition facts labels are charts many people see daily, but not everyone knows how to read them. The top third of the label lists calorie counts, serving sizes, and amount of servings in a package. If a package contains more than one serving, a person who eats the entire contents of the package may be consuming many times the number of calories listed per serving.

The label below lists the content of nutrients such as fats and carbohydrates, and so on. According to the label, a person who eats one serving of the product in the package will ingest 30 mg of cholesterol, or 10% of the total cholesterol he or she should consume in a day.

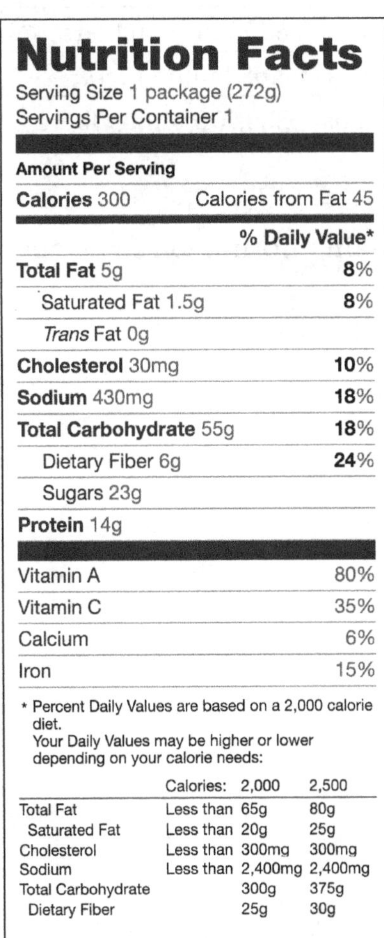

Nutrition Facts

Serving Size 1 package (272g)
Servings Per Container 1

Amount Per Serving

Calories 300	Calories from Fat 45
	% Daily Value*
Total Fat 5g	**8%**
Saturated Fat 1.5g	**8%**
Trans Fat 0g	
Cholesterol 30mg	**10%**
Sodium 430mg	**18%**
Total Carbohydrate 55g	**18%**
Dietary Fiber 6g	**24%**
Sugars 23g	
Protein 14g	
Vitamin A	80%
Vitamin C	35%
Calcium	6%
Iron	15%

* Percent Daily Values are based on a 2,000 calorie diet.
Your Daily Values may be higher or lower depending on your calorie needs:

	Calories:	2,000	2,500
Total Fat	Less than	65g	80g
Saturated Fat	Less than	20g	25g
Cholesterol	Less than	300mg	300mg
Sodium	Less than	2,400mg	2,400mg
Total Carbohydrate		300g	375g
Dietary Fiber		25g	30g

KEEP IN MIND . . .

The percentages on a Nutrition Facts label do not (and are not meant to) add up to 100. Instead, they show how much of a particular nutrient is contained in a serving of the product, as a proportion of a single person's Daily Value for that nutrient. The Daily Value is the total amount of a nutrient a person is supposed to eat in a day, based on a 2000-calorie diet.

In general, a percentage of 5% or less is considered low, whereas a percentage of 20% or more is considered high. A higher percentage can be good or bad, depending on whether or not a person should be trying to get more of a particular ingredient. People need to get plenty of vitamins, minerals, and fiber. In contrast, most people need to limit their intake of fat, cholesterol, and sodium.

Tables

Tables organize information into vertical columns and horizontal rows. Below is a table that shows how much water falls on areas of various sizes when it rains one inch. It shows, for instance, that a 40' x 70' roof receives 1,743 gallons of rain during a one-inch rainfall event.

Area	Area (square miles)	Area (square kilometers)	Amount of Water (gallons)	Amount of Water (liters)
My roof 40 x 70 feet	.0001	.000257	1,743 gallons	6,601 liters
1 acre (1 square mile = 640 acres)	.00156	.004	27,154 gallons	102,789 liters
1 square mile	1	2.6	17.38 million gallons	65.78 million liters
Atlanta, Georgia	132.4	342.9	2.293 billion gallons	8.68 billion liters
United States	3,537,438	9,161,922	61,474 billion gallons	232,700 billion liters

Let's Review!

- Readers must understand how and why text features make certain information stand out from the text.
- Readers must understand and interpret the content of maps and charts.

TYPES OF PASSAGES, TEXT STRUCTURES, GENRE AND THEME

To read effectively, you must understand what kind of text you are reading and how it is structured. You must also be able to look behind the text to find its deeper meanings.

Types of Passages

There are many ways of breaking texts down into categories. To do this, you need to consider the author's **purpose**, or what the text exists to do. Most texts exist to inform, persuade, or entertain. You also need to consider what the text does—whether it tells a story, describes facts, or develops a point of view.

Type of Passage	Examples
Narrative writing tells a story. The story can be fictional, or it can describe real events. The primary purpose of narrative writing is to entertain.	• An autobiography • A memoir • A short story • A novel
Expository writing provides an explanation or a description. Many academic essays and informational nonfiction books are expository writing. Stylistically, expository writing is highly varied. Although the explanations can be dry and methodical, many writers use an artful or entertaining style. Expository writing is nonfiction. Its primary purpose is to inform.	• A book about a historical event • An essay describing the social impacts of a new technology • A description of changing gender roles in marriages • A philosophical document exploring the nature of truth.
Technical writing explains a complex process or mechanism. Whereas expository writing is often academic, technical writing is used in practical settings such as businesses. The style of a technical document is almost always straightforward and impersonal. Technical writing is nonfiction, and its purpose is to inform.	• Recipes • Instructions • User manuals • Process descriptions
Persuasive writing makes an argument. It asks readers to believe something or do something. Texts that make judgments, such as movie reviews, are persuasive because they are attempting to convince readers to accept a point of view. Texts that suggest a plan are also persuasive because they are trying to convince readers to take an action. As the name "persuasive writing" indicates, the author's primary purpose is to persuade.	• Op-ed newspaper articles • Book reviews • Project proposals • Advertisements • Persuasive essays

BE CAREFUL!

Many texts have more than one purpose.

A text that tells a story is usually meant to entertain, but it can also be meant to persuade. For example, there is a well-known story called "Never Cry Wolf" about a boy who habitually lies. At the end, when he needs help, nobody believes him. This story is meant to entertain, but it is also trying to convince readers not to tell lies.

Similarly, many explanatory texts are meant to inform readers in an entertaining way. For example, a nonfiction author may describe a scientific topic using humor and wacky examples to make it fun for popular audiences to read.

Also, expository writing can look similar to persuasive writing, especially when it touches on topics that are controversial or emotional. For example, if an essay says social media is changing society, many readers assume it means social media is changing society *in a negative way.* If the writing makes this kind of value judgment or uses words like *should,* it is persuasive writing. But if the author is merely describing changes, the text is expository.

Text Structures

Authors rarely present ideas within a text in a random order. Instead, they organize their thoughts carefully. To read effectively, you must be able to recognize the **structure** of a text. That is, you need to identify the strategies authors use to organize their ideas. The five most common text structures are listed below.

Text Structure	Examples
In a **sequence** text, an author explains what happened first, second, third, and so on. In other words, a sequence text is arranged in **chronological order**, or time order. This type of text may describe events that have already happened or events that may happen in the future.	• A story about a birthday party. • A historical paper about World War II. • A list of instructions for baking a cake. • A series of proposed steps in a plan for business expansion.
A **compare/contrast** text explains the similarities and differences between two or more subjects. Authors may compare and contrast people, places, ideas, events, cultures, and so on.	• An essay describing the similarities and differences between women's experiences in medieval Europe and Asia. • A section in an op-ed newspaper article explaining the similarities and differences between two types of gun control.
A **cause/effect** text describes an event or action and its results. The causes and effects discussed can be actual or theoretical. That is, the author can describe the results of a historical event or predict the results of a possible future event.	• An explanation of ocean acidification and the coral bleaching that results. • A paper describing a proposed new law and its likely effects on the economy.
A **problem-solution** text presents a problem and outlines a solution. Sometimes it also predicts or analyzes the results of the solution. The solution can be something that already happened or a plan the author is proposing. Note that a problem can sometimes be expressed in terms of a wish or desire that the solution fulfills.	• An explanation of the problems smallpox caused and the strategies scientists used to eradicate it. • A business plan outlining a group of potential customers and the strategy a company should use to get their business.

Text Structure	Examples
A **description** text creates a mental picture for the reader by presenting concrete details in a coherent order. Description texts are usually arranged spatially. For instance, authors may describe the subject from top to bottom, or they may describe the inside first and then the outside, etc.	• An explanation of the appearance of a character in a story. • A paragraph in a field guide detailing the features of a bird. • A section on an instruction sheet describing how the final product should look.

CONNECTIONS

Different types of texts can use the same structures.

1. A story about a birthday party is a narrative, and its purpose is to entertain.
2. A historical paper about a war is an expository text meant to inform.
3. A list of instructions for baking a cake is a technical text meant to inform.
4. A series of proposed steps in a plan for business expansion is a persuasive text meant to persuade.

If all of these texts list ideas in chronological order, explaining what happened (or what may happen in the future) first, second, third, and so on, they are all using a sequence structure.

Genre and Theme

Literature can be organized into categories called **genres**. The two major genres of literature are fiction and nonfiction.

Fiction is made up. It can be broken down into many sub-genres, or sub-categories. The following are some of the common ones:

- Short story – Short work of fiction.
- Novel – Book-length work of fiction.
- Science fiction – A story set in the future
- Romance – A love story
- Mystery – A story that answers a concrete question, often about who committed a crime
- Mythology – A traditional story that reflects cultural traditions and beliefs but does not usually teach an explicit lesson
- Legends – Traditional stories that are presented as histories, even though they often contain fantastical or magical elements
- Fables – Traditional stories meant to teach an explicit lesson

COMPARE!

The differences between myths and fables are sometimes hard to discern.

Myths are often somewhat religious in nature. For instance, stories about Ancient Greek gods and goddesses are myths. These stories reflect cultural beliefs, for example by showing characters being punished for failing to please their gods. But the lesson is implicit. These stories do not usually end with a moral lesson that says to readers, "Do not displease the gods!"

Fables are often for children, and they usually end with a sentence stating an explicit moral. For example, there's a story called "The Tortoise and the Hare," in which a tortoise and a hare agree to have a race. The hare, being a fast animal, gets cocky and takes a lot of breaks while the tortoise plods slowly toward the finish line without stopping. Because the tortoise keeps going, it eventually wins. The story usually ends with the moral, "Slow and steady win the race."

Nonfiction is true. Like fiction, it can be broken down into many sub-genres. The following are some of the common ones:

- Autobiography and memoir – The author's own life story
- Biography – Someone else's life story (not the author's)
- Histories – True stories about real events from the past
- Criticism and reviews – A response or judgment on another piece of writing or art
- Essay – A short piece describing the author's outlook or point of view.

CONNECTIONS

Everything under "Fiction" and several items under "Nonfiction" above are examples of narrative writing. We use labels like "narrative" and "persuasive" largely when we discuss writing tasks or the author's purpose. We could use these labels here too, but at the moment we're more concerned with the words that are most commonly used in discussions about literature's deeper meanings.

Literature reflects the human experience. Texts from different genres often share similar **themes**, or deeper meanings. Texts from different cultures do too. For example, a biography of a famous civil rights activist may highlight the same qualities of heroism and interconnectedness that appear in a work of mythology from Ancient India. Other common themes in literature may relate to war, love, survival, justice, suffering, growing up, and other experiences that are accessible to virtually all human beings.

Many students confuse the term *theme* with the term *moral*. A **moral** is an explicit message contained in the text, like "Don't lie" or "Crime doesn't pay." Morals are a common feature of fables and other traditional stories meant to teach lessons to children. Themes, in contrast, are implicit. Readers must consider the clues in the story and figure out themes for themselves. Because of this, themes are debatable. For testing purposes, questions focus on themes that are clearly and consistently indicated by clues within the text.

Let's Review!

- Written texts can be organized into the following categories: narrative, expository, technical, and persuasive.
- Texts of all categories may use the following organizational schemes or structures: sequence, compare/contrast, cause/effect, problem-solution, description.
- Literature can be organized into genres including fiction, nonfiction, and many sub-genres.
- Literature across genres and cultures often reflects the same deeper meanings, or themes.

KEEP IN MIND . . .

The text structures above do not always work in isolation. Authors often combine two or more structures within one text. For example, a business plan could be arranged in a problem-solution structure as the author describes what the business wants to achieve and how she proposes to achieve it. The "how" portion could also use a sequence structure as the author lists the steps to follow first, second, third, and so on.

Chapter 12 Integration of Knowledge and Ideas Practice Quiz

1. **Which of the following is *not* a function of text features?**
   A. Introducing the topic
   B. Emphasizing a concept
   C. Making the theme explicit
   D. Providing peripheral information

2. **If a map does not have a compass, north is:**
   A. up.
   B. down.
   C. right.
   D. left.

3. **The purpose of an index is to tell readers:**
   A. how to find sources that back up key ideas in the text.
   B. who wrote the text and what his or her credentials are.
   C. where to find information on a given subject within a book.
   D. why the author believes the main idea of a text is important.

Read the following passage and answer questions 4-5.

Overworked public school teachers are required by law to spend extra time implementing Individual Educational Plans for students with learning and attention challenges. This shortchanges children who are actually engaged in their education by depriving them of an equal amount of individualized attention.

4. **What assumption behind this passage reflects negative stereotypical thinking?**
   A. Public school teachers are generally overworked and underpaid.
   B. Students with learning disabilities are not engaged in their education.
   C. Laws require teachers to provide accommodations to certain students.
   D. Teachers have a finite amount of attention to divide between students.

5. **The above argument is invalid because the author:**
   A. suggests that some students do not need as much attention because they learn the material more quickly.
   B. uses derogatory and disrespectful word choice to describe people who think, learn, and process information differently.
   C. describes public school teachers in a negative way that makes it seem as though they have no interest in helping students.
   D. professes an interest in equality for all students while simultaneously suggesting some students are more worthy than others.

6. **Which statement, if true, is a fact?**
   A. The 1918 flu pandemic killed more people than World War I.
   B. The 1918 flu pandemic was more devastating than World War I.
   C. The 1918 flu pandemic was a terrifying display of nature's power.
   D. The 1918 flu pandemic caused greater social instability than the plague.

Read the following passage and answer questions 7-9.

There is inherent risk associated with the use of Rip Gym facilities. Although all Rip Gym customers sign a Risk Acknowledgment and Consent Form before gaining access to our grounds and equipment, litigation remains a possibility if customers suffer injuries due to negligence. Negligence complaints may include either staff mistakes or avoidable problems with equipment and facilities. It is therefore imperative that all Rip Gym employees follow the Safety Protocol in the event of a customer complaint.

Reports of Unsafe Equipment and Environs

Rip Gym employees must always respond promptly and seriously to any customer report of a hazard in our equipment or facilities, even if the employee judges the complaint frivolous. **Customers may not use rooms or equipment that have been reported unsafe until the following steps have been taken, in order, to confirm and/or resolve the problem.**

1. Place "Warning," "Out of Order," or "Off Limits" signs in the affected area or on the affected equipment, as appropriate. **Always follow this step first, before handling paperwork or attempting to resolve the reported problem.**
2. Fill out a Hazard Complaint Form. Include the name of the customer making the complaint and the exact wording of the problems being reported.
3. Visually check the area or equipment in question to verify the problem.
   a) If the report appears to be **accurate** and a resolution is necessary, proceed to step 4.
   b) If the report appears to be **inaccurate**, consult the manager on duty.
4. Determine whether you are qualified to correct the problem. Problems **all** employees are qualified to correct are listed on page 12 of the Employee Handbook.
   a) Employees who have **not** undergone training for equipment repair and maintenance must....

7. **This passage is best described as a(n):**
   A. narrative text.
   B. technical text.
   C. expository text.
   D. persuasive text.

8. **Which term best describes the structure of the opening paragraph?**

    A. Sequence

    B. Description

    C. Problem-solution

    D. Compare/contrast

9. **Which term best describes the structure of the section under the subheading "Reports of Unsafe Equipment and Environs"?**

    A. Sequence

    B. Description

    C. Cause/effect

    D. Compare/contrast

Chapter 12 Integration of Knowledge and Ideas Practice Quiz – Answer Key

1. C. Although the title of a fictional work may hint at a theme, a theme is a message that is, by definition, not stated explicitly. **See Lesson: Evaluating and Integrating Data.**

2. A. By convention, north on a map is up. Mapmakers include a compass if they break this convention for some reason. **See Lesson: Evaluating and Integrating Data.**

3. C. An index lists subtopics of a book along with page numbers where those topics will be covered. **See Lesson: Evaluating and Integrating Data.**

4. B. The writer of this passage suggests implicitly that only students without learning and attention challenges are engaged in their education. This assumption reflects a negative stereotype that renders the entire argument faulty. **See Lesson: Facts, Opinions, and Evaluating an Argument.**

5. B. The author of the passage uses the phrase "students with learning and attention challenges" to refer to students who think and learn differently. This is not derogatory, but even so, the passage implies that people who experience these differences are less engaged in their education. **See Lesson: Facts, Opinions, and Evaluating an Argument.**

6. A. All of these statements contain beliefs or feelings that are subject to interpretation except the statement about the number of people killed in the 1918 flu pandemic compared to World War I. This is a verifiable piece of information, or a fact. **See Lesson: Facts, Opinions, and Evaluating an Argument.**

7. B. This is a technical text written to inform the reader about a complex process. **See Lesson: Types of Passages, Text Structures, Genre and Theme.**

8. C. The opening paragraph has a problem-solution structure. The problem it describes involves risks of injury and litigation, and the solution is that employees follow a process designed to minimize those risks. **See Lesson: Types of Passages, Text Structures, Genre and Theme.**

9. A. The step-by-step instructions under the subheading follow a sequential structure. Note key words and phrases such as "first" and "in order." **See Lesson: Types of Passages, Text Structures, Genre and Theme.**

Section IV. Science

Chapter 13 Scientific Reasoning

Designing an Experiment

This lesson introduces the idea of experimental design and the factors one must consider to build a successful experiment.

Scientific Reasoning

When conducting scientific research, two types of scientific reasoning can be used to address scientific problems: inductive reasoning and deductive reasoning. Both forms of reasoning are also used to generate a hypothesis. **Inductive reasoning** involves drawing a general conclusion from specific observations. This form of reasoning is referred to as the "from the bottom up" approach. Information gathered from specific observations can be used to make a general conclusion about the topic under investigation. In other words, conclusions are based on observed patterns in data.

FOR EXAMPLE

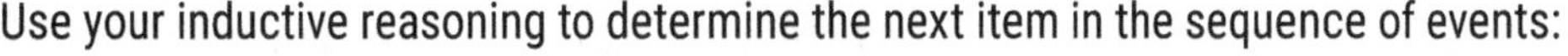

Use your inductive reasoning to determine the next item in the sequence of events:

1. fall, winter, spring . . .
2. 4, 8, 12 . . .

Deductive reasoning is the logical approach of making a prediction about a general principle to draw a specific conclusion. It is recognized as the "from the top down" approach. For example, deductive reasoning is used to test a theory by collecting data that challenges the theory.

DID YOU KNOW?

While Francis Bacon was developing the scientific method, he advocated for the use of inductive reasoning. This is why inductive reasoning is considered to be at the heart of the scientific method.

Example

Which is an example of deductive reasoning?

A. A scientist concludes that a plant species is drought resistant after watching it survive a hot summer.

B. After a boy observes where the sun rises, he tells his mom that the sun will rise in the east in the morning.

C. Since it is well established that noble gases are stable, scientists can safely say that the noble gas neon is stable.

D. A state transportation department decides to use sodium road salt after studies show that calcium road salt is ineffective.

The correct answer is **C.** The statement that noble gases are stable is a general principle or well-accepted theory. Thus, the specific conclusion that the noble gas neon is stable can be drawn from this general principle.

Designing an Experiment

According to the scientific method, the following steps are followed after making an observation or asking a question: (1) conduct background research on the topic, (2) formulate a hypothesis, (3) test the hypothesis with an experiment, (5) analyze results, and (6) report conclusions that explain whether the results support the hypothesis. This means after using logical reasoning to formulate a hypothesis, it is time to design a way to test this hypothesis. This is where **experimental design** becomes a factor.

Experimental design is the process of creating a reliable experiment to test a hypothesis. It involves organizing an experiment that produces the amount of data and right type of data to answer the question. A study's validity is directly affected by the construction and design of an experiment. This is why it is important to carefully consider the following components that are used to build an experiment:

- **Independent variable:** This factor does not depend on what happens in the experiment. The independent variable has values that can be changed or manipulated in an experiment. Data from the independent variable is graphed on the x-axis.
- **Dependent variable:** This factor depends on the independent variable. Recognized as the outcome of interest, its value cannot change. It can only be observed during an experiment. Data from the dependent variable is graphed on the y-axis.
- **Treatment group:** This is the group that receives treatment in an experiment. It is the item or subject in an experiment that the researcher manipulates. During an experiment, treatment is directly imposed on a group and the response is observed.
- **Control group:** This is a baseline measure that remains constant. Used for comparison purposes, it is the group that neither receives treatment nor is experimentally manipulated. One type of control is a **placebo**. This false treatment is administered to a

control group to account for the placebo effect. This is a psychological effect where the brain convinces the body that a fake treatment is the real thing. Often, experimental drug studies use placebos.

TEST TIP

It can be hard to remember the differences between an independent and a dependent variable. Use the following mnemonic to help keep those differences clear:

D = dependent | **M** = manipulated variable | **Y** = *y*-axis
R = responding variable | **I** = independent variable | **X** = *x*-axis

Example

A control group

A. modifies the desired outcome of an experiment.

B. fluctuates in value if an experimental factor is manipulated.

C. establishes a baseline measure to compare dependent variables to.

D. depends on the type of independent variable chosen for an experiment.

The correct answer is **C.** A control group functions as a baseline measure or constant that is not influenced by experimental manipulations. It does not receive treatment in a study.

Data Analysis and Interpretation

When researchers test their hypotheses, the next step in the scientific method is to analyze the data and collect empirical evidence. **Empirical evidence** is acquired from observations and through experiments. It is a repeatable form of evidence that other researchers, including the researcher overseeing the study, can verify. Thus, when analyzing data, empirical evidence must be used to make valid conclusions.

While analyzing data, scientists tend to observe cause-and-effect relationships. These relationships can be quantified using correlations. **Correlations** measure the amount of linear association between two variables. There are three types of correlations:

- **Positive correlation:** As one variable increases, the other variable also increases. This is also known as a direct correlation.

FOR EXAMPLE

Studies have shown there is a positive correlation between smoking and lung cancer development. The more you smoke, the greater your risk of developing lung cancer. An example of a negative correlation is the relationship between speed and time when distance is kept constant. The faster a car travels, the amount of time to reach the destination decreases.

- **Negative correlation:** As one variable increases, the other decreases. The opposite is true if one variable decreases. A negative correlation is also known as an inverse correlation or an indirect correlation.
- **No correlation:** There is no connection or relationship between two variables.

From graphs to tables, there are many ways to visually display data. Typically, graphs are a powerful way to visually demonstrate the relationships between two or more variables. This is the case for correlations. A positive correlation is indicated as a positive slope in a graph, as shown below. Negative correlations are indicated as a negative slope in a graph. If there is no correlation between two variables, data points will not show a pattern.

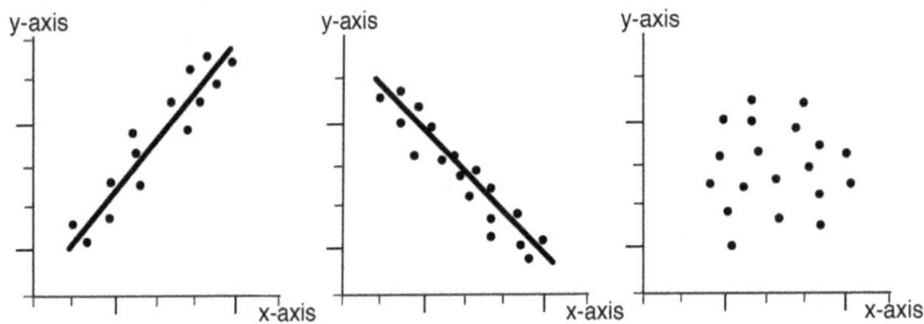

Examples

1. **What is another term used to describe a direct correlation?**

   A. Positive slope B. Negative slope C. Inverse correlation D. Indirect correlation

   The correct answer is **A.** A direct correlation occurs when one variable increases as another increases. Graphically, this is shown as a positive slope.

2. **If a researcher notices a negative slope while analyzing his data, what can he conclude?**

   A. The variables exhibit no correlation.

   B. A different control group should be used.

   C. The variables exhibit a direct correlation.

   D. The variables exhibit an indirect correlation.

   The correct answer is **D.** A negative slope is indicative of an indirect, negative, or inverse correlation.

Scientific Tools and Measurement

Researchers use a wide variety of tools to collect data. The most common types of measuring tools are outlined below:

Barometer	Used to determines the air pressure in a space.
Clock or stopwatch	Used to record time.
Graduated cylinder	Used to measure the volume of liquid.
Ruler	Used to measure the length of an object.
Thermometer	Used to measure temperature. Measurement values may be expressed in degrees Celsius or Fahrenheit.
Triple beam balance	Used to measure the mass of an object or to determine the unit of mass. Electronic balances are used to measure very small masses.

Measured values are often associated with scientific units. Typically, the metric system is preferred when reporting scientific results. This is because nearly all countries use the metric system. Additionally, there is a single base unit of measurement for each type of measured quantity. For example, the base unit for length cannot be the same as the base unit for mass. The following base units are used:

Unit of Measurement	Base Unit Name	Abbreviation
Length	Meter	m
Mass	Gram	g
Volume	Liter	L

Another benefit of the metric system is that units are expressed in multiples of 10. This allows a researcher to express reported values that may be very large or small. This expression is facilitated by using the following metric prefixes, which are added to the base unit name:

Prefix	Abbreviation	Value	Description
kilo	k	1,000	thousand
hecto	h	100	hundred
deka	da	10	ten
BASE	N/A	1	one
deci	d	0.1	tenth
centi	c	0.01	hundredth
milli	m	0.001	thousandth

Example

What base measurement unit is associated with reported values measured by a graduated cylinder?

A. Celsius B. Gram C. Liter D. Meter

The correct answer is **C.** Liter is a base unit for volume. Volume is measured using a graduated cylinder.

Let's Review!

- Formulating a hypothesis requires using either inductive or deductive reasoning.
- A good experimental design properly defines all variables and considers how data will be analyzed.
- Correlations illustrate the cause-and-effect relationships between two variables.
- Positive and negative correlations can be displayed graphically by analyzing the slope of a line.
- Different devices are used to measure objects in an experimental study.
- The metric system is usually used when expressing the units of measured values.

Scientific Notation

This lesson begins by explaining how to convert measurements with very large or very small values into more manageable numbers using scientific notation. It then explores the structure of the atom and describes how to determine the number of protons, neutrons, and electrons in an atom of a specific element. Finally, it describes the relationship between isotopes of the same element and the effects that these isotopes have on the average atomic mass of an element.

Scientific Notation

Scientists often work with very large and very small numbers. For example, the radius of Earth's orbit around the sun is very large: 15,000,000,000,000 centimeters. On the other extreme, the radius of a hydrogen atom is very small: 0.00000000529 centimeters. To make these numbers more manageable, scientists write them using **scientific notation**. Scientific notation is a way to represent numbers and contains three components, which are shown in the diagram below.

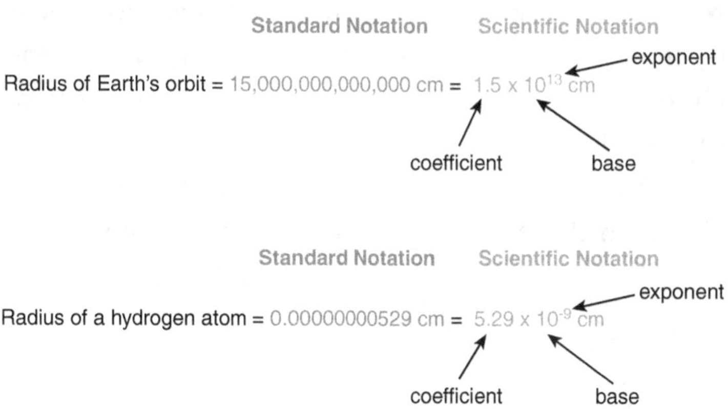

Understanding how these components relate to one another makes it possible to convert between standard notation and scientific notation. The coefficient is a number that has a value of at least 1 but less than 10 and includes all significant digits in the given value. Another way to think about this is that there should always be one non-zero digit before the decimal point.

In scientific notation, the base is always 10.

The exponent indicates the number of places the decimal point needs to move. Notice that when the exponent is positive, the decimal place moves to the right; this is how larger numbers are represented. When the exponent is negative, the decimal place moves to the left; this is how smaller numbers are represented. When the decimal must move beyond the digits that are in the measurement, the "empty" spaces are filled in with zeros.

KEY POINT

When converting from scientific notation to standard notation, a negative exponent requires the decimal point to move to the left, and a positive exponent requires the decimal point to move to the right.

Example

The length of a year is 31,560,000 seconds. What is this value in scientific notation?

A. 0.3156×10^{-6} s B. 3.156×10^{-7} s C. 3.156×10^{7} s D. 31.56×10^{6} s

The correct answer is **C.** The coefficient is a value between 1 and 10 and includes all digits, which is 3.156. Starting with that coefficient, the decimal must be moved seven places to the right to get the value in standard notation, which means that the exponent is a positive seven.

The Atom

All matter is made of atoms. Every atom contains a dense core in the center called a **nucleus.** The nucleus is composed of subatomic particles called **protons** and **neutrons**. Surrounding this core is an area known as the **electron cloud**, in which smaller subatomic particles known as **electrons** are moving.

The Bohr model below shows these components of the atom. In the model, each subatomic particle is marked with a charge. Protons have a positive (+) charge, electrons have a negative (–) charge, and neutrons do not carry any charge; they are neutral. Therefore, the overall charge of an atom depends on the numbers of protons and electrons and is not influenced by the number of neutrons. An atom is neutral if the number of protons is equal to the number of electrons. If there are more protons than electrons, the atom will have an overall positive charge; if there are more electrons than protons, the atom will have an overall negative charge.

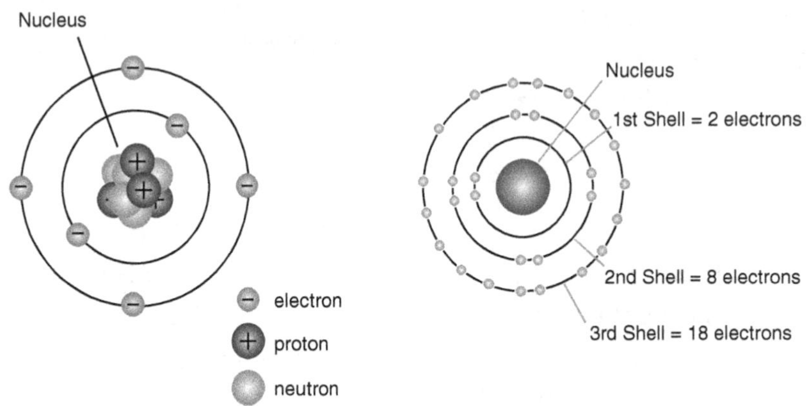

> **COMPARE THE BOHR MODEL TO A REAL ATOM.**
>
> Note that this model is not to scale. The nucleus should be much smaller because it is about 10,000 times smaller than the electron cloud in a real atom. Also, the space between the electrons a real atom is much greater than in the model. In a real atom, the electron cloud is mostly empty space.

To further compare these three subatomic particles, their locations, charges, and masses are shown in the table below. The unit used for mass is the **atomic mass unit (amu)**. The masses of a proton or neutron are considerably larger than the mass of an electron. This difference in mass has important implications. First, because the nucleus is so small relative to the overall size of the atom and contains the more massive protons and neutrons, it is extremely dense. Second, because the electrons are almost 2,000 times less massive than the other subatomic particles, they do not significantly influence the atom's mass.

Subatomic Particle	Symbol	Location	Charge	Mass (amu)
Proton	$p+$	Nucleus	+1	1.0
Neutron	$n0$	Nucleus	0	1.0
Electron	$e-$	Electron cloud	−1	0.00054

One final note about the Bohr model of the atom is that the electrons lie on rings. These rings represent energy levels, sometimes referred to as electron "shells." Electrons that occupy energy levels that are closest to the nucleus have the least energy. Electrons found farther from the nucleus have more energy. A limited number of electrons can occupy each energy level. The first energy level can fit up to 2 electrons. The second energy level can fit up to 8 electrons. The third energy level can fit up to 18 electrons. An atom in its normal state will have electrons lying in the lowest possible energy levels.

While the Bohr model provides a good way to visualize the atom, its representation of the electron cloud is not completely accurate. Electrons move around the nucleus in different energy levels, but this movement is not restricted to specific circular orbits as the Bohr model indicates. The **quantum mechanical model** (also known as the electron cloud model) describes the probable locations of electrons because their exact pathways, locations, and speeds cannot be determined simultaneously.

Example

Which subatomic particles affect the overall charge of the atom?

A. Only protons

B. Protons and neutrons

C. Protons and electrons

D. Protons, neutrons, and electrons

The correct answer is **C**. Because protons are positively charged and electrons are negatively charged, they affect the overall charge of the atom. Neutrons do not affect the charge because they are uncharged.

The Periodic Table of the Elements

The atom is not only the basic building block of matter, but also the smallest unit of an element that can be defined as that element. All known elements are listed in the periodic table.

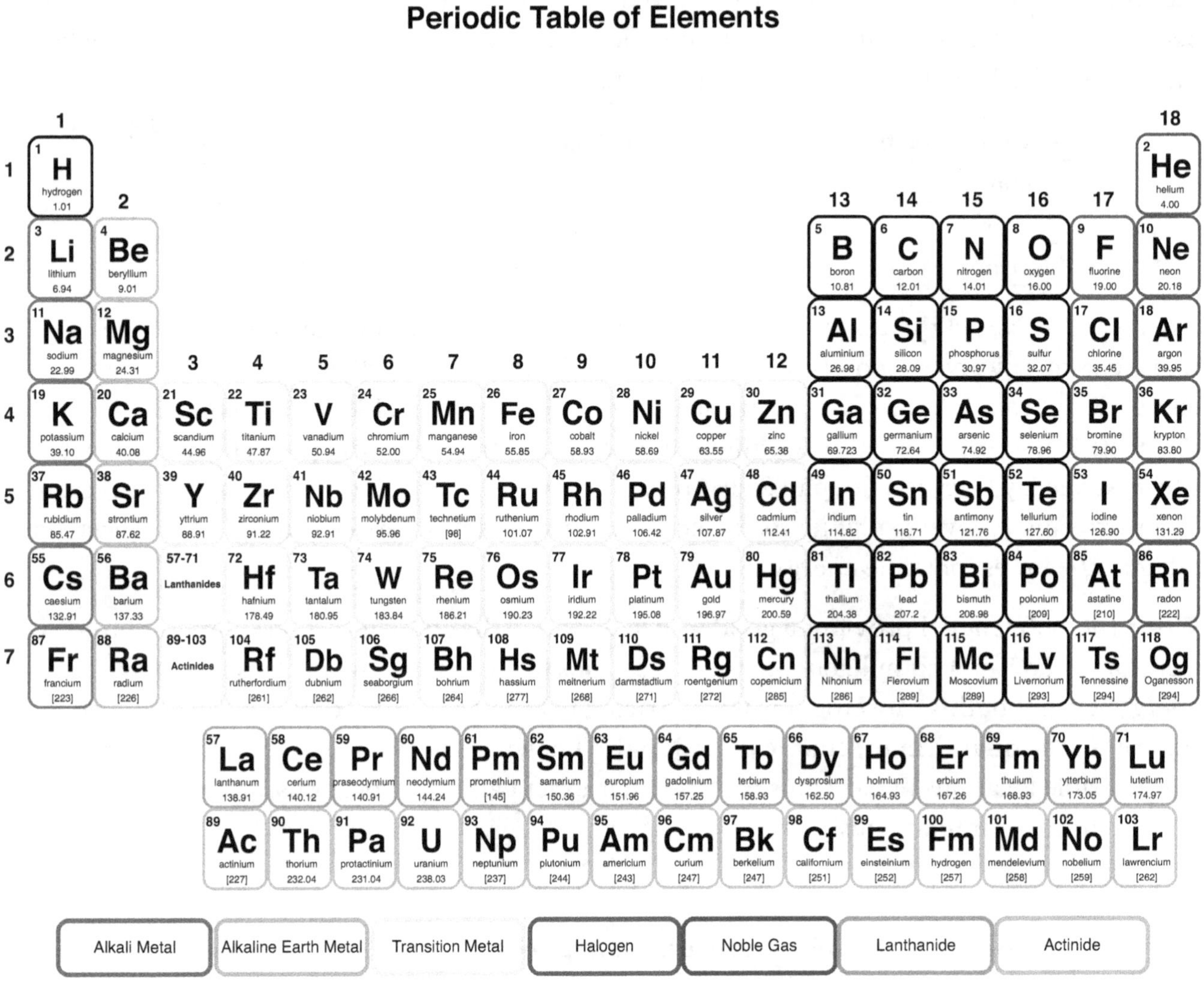

Periodic Table of Elements

	1	2	3	4	5	6	7	8	9	10	11	12	13	14	15	16	17	18
1	1 H hydrogen 1.01																	2 He helium 4.00
2	3 Li lithium 6.94	4 Be beryllium 9.01											5 B boron 10.81	6 C carbon 12.01	7 N nitrogen 14.01	8 O oxygen 16.00	9 F fluorine 19.00	10 Ne neon 20.18
3	11 Na sodium 22.99	12 Mg magnesium 24.31											13 Al aluminium 26.98	14 Si silicon 28.09	15 P phosphorus 30.97	16 S sulfur 32.07	17 Cl chlorine 35.45	18 Ar argon 39.95
4	19 K potassium 39.10	20 Ca calcium 40.08	21 Sc scandium 44.96	22 Ti titanium 47.87	23 V vanadium 50.94	24 Cr chromium 52.00	25 Mn manganese 54.94	26 Fe iron 55.85	27 Co cobalt 58.93	28 Ni nickel 58.69	29 Cu copper 63.55	30 Zn zinc 65.38	31 Ga gallium 69.723	32 Ge germanium 72.64	33 As arsenic 74.92	34 Se selenium 78.96	35 Br bromine 79.90	36 Kr krypton 83.80
5	37 Rb rubidium 85.47	38 Sr strontium 87.62	39 Y yttrium 88.91	40 Zr zirconium 91.22	41 Nb niobium 92.91	42 Mo molybdenum 95.96	43 Tc technetium [98]	44 Ru ruthenium 101.07	45 Rh rhodium 102.91	46 Pd palladium 106.42	47 Ag silver 107.87	48 Cd cadmium 112.41	49 In indium 114.82	50 Sn tin 118.71	51 Sb antimony 121.76	52 Te tellurium 127.60	53 I iodine 126.90	54 Xe xenon 131.29
6	55 Cs caesium 132.91	56 Ba barium 137.33	57-71 Lanthanides	72 Hf hafnium 178.49	73 Ta tantalum 180.95	74 W tungsten 183.84	75 Re rhenium 186.21	76 Os osmium 190.23	77 Ir iridium 192.22	78 Pt platinum 195.08	79 Au gold 196.97	80 Hg mercury 200.59	81 Tl thallium 204.38	82 Pb lead 207.2	83 Bi bismuth 208.98	84 Po polonium [209]	85 At astatine [210]	86 Rn radon [222]
7	87 Fr francium [223]	88 Ra radium [226]	89-103 Actinides	104 Rf rutherfordium [261]	105 Db dubnium [262]	106 Sg seaborgium [266]	107 Bh bohrium [264]	108 Hs hassium [277]	109 Mt meitnerium [268]	110 Ds darmstadtium [271]	111 Rg roentgenium [272]	112 Cn copernicium [285]	113 Nh Nihonium [286]	114 Fl Flerovium [289]	115 Mc Moscovium [289]	116 Lv Livermorium [293]	117 Ts Tennessine [294]	118 Og Oganesson [294]

57 La lanthanum 138.91	58 Ce cerium 140.12	59 Pr praseodymium 140.91	60 Nd neodymium 144.24	61 Pm promethium [145]	62 Sm samarium 150.36	63 Eu europium 151.96	64 Gd gadolinium 157.25	65 Tb terbium 158.93	66 Dy dysprosium 162.50	67 Ho holmium 164.93	68 Er erbium 167.26	69 Tm thulium 168.93	70 Yb ytterbium 173.05	71 Lu lutetium 174.97
89 Ac actinium [227]	90 Th thorium 232.04	91 Pa protactinium 231.04	92 U uranium 238.03	93 Np neptunium [237]	94 Pu plutonium [244]	95 Am americium [243]	96 Cm curium [247]	97 Bk berkelium [247]	98 Cf californium [251]	99 Es einsteinium [252]	100 Fm hydrogen [257]	101 Md mendelevium [258]	102 No nobelium [259]	103 Lr lawrencium [262]

Alkali Metal | Alkaline Earth Metal | Transition Metal | Halogen | Noble Gas | Lanthanide | Actinide

In the periodic table, elements are arranged in rows, also known as **periods**, and columns, also known as **groups**. Both the periods and the groups can be referred to by number. For example, argon is in period 3 and group 18.

Elements with similar properties are put into families that are outlined in different colors in the periodic table above. Note that these families generally correspond to the groups in the periodic table. For example, the elements in group 18 are in a family called the noble gases, while the elements in group 2 are all alkaline earth metals.

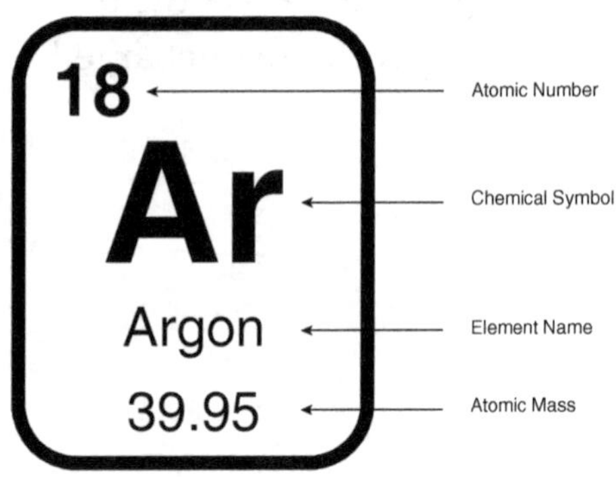

Periodic tables differ in the information they provide, and an example of a block is shown above. This block shows the name of the element and its **chemical symbol**, which is an abbreviation for the name. The chemical symbol is one, two, or three letters with the first letter capitalized and all subsequent letters letter lowercase. The symbol for the element argon is Ar.

DID YOU KNOW?

While many elements have chemical symbols that resemble their names, like argon (Ar), some elements have chemical symbols that are different from their names. This is because the symbols are derived from either the Latin or the Greek names for the elements rather than the English names. The symbol for sodium is Na because the Latin name for the element is natrium.

Each element is assigned an **atomic number**. The atomic number is equal to the number of protons in a single atom of that element and is how an element is identified. Argon, for example, has an atomic number of 18. Therefore, every atom of argon has 18 protons, regardless of how many neutrons or electrons it has.

Example

Which of the following statements is true?

A. A tin atom has 22 protons.

B. An iron atom has 26 protons.

C. A sodium atom has 16 protons.

D. A potassium atom has 15 protons.

The correct answer is **B.** In the periodic table, iron has an atomic number of 26, which means it has 26 protons.

Average Atomic Mass and Mass Number

Some periodic tables also provide the **average atomic mass** of an element in atomic mass units (amu). Because not all atoms of argon have the same mass, the periodic table shows the average mass of all argon atoms. These forms of argon are differentiated based on their **mass numbers**, which are determined by adding the number of protons and neutrons. Argon has three stable forms, called isotopes, which are shown in the table below.

Name	Abundance	Mass (amu)	Mass Number	Number of protons	Number of neutrons
Argon-36	0.337%	35.97	36	18	18
Argon-38	0.063%	37.96	38	18	20
Argon-40	99.6%	39.96	40	18	22

The mass number can be used to determine the number of neutrons, as shown by the equation below. Argon-40 is the most abundant and has a mass number of 40. Its 18 protons contribute 18 to the mass number of the atom. The remaining mass is from the neutrons.

mass number = number of protons + number of neutrons

40 = 18 + number of neutrons

number of neutrons = 40 − 18 = 22 neutrons

To determine the number of electrons, the charge of the atom must be considered. If a charge is not indicated, it can be assumed that the atom in question is neutral. A neutral atom has an equal number of positively charged protons and negatively charged electrons. Therefore, a neutral atom of argon has 18 electrons that balance the charge of its 18 protons, given by the atomic number.

Example

CHECKLIST

Here are reminders for how to determine the numbers of subatomic particles using information found in the periodic table:

Number of protons = atomic number
Number of neutrons = mass number − number of protons (atomic number)
Number of electrons = number of protons (atomic number) in a neutral atom

Using the periodic table, determine how many protons and electrons a neutral atom of potassium has.

A. 19 protons, 19 electrons

B. 19 protons, 20 electrons

C. 19 protons, 39 electrons

D. 39 protons, 39 electrons

The correct answer is **A.** The atomic number of potassium is 19, which means it has 19 protons. Because the atom is neutral, the number of electrons must equal the number of protons.

Isotopes

All atoms of an element have the same number of protons, but the number of neutrons may be different. Atoms that have the same number of protons but different numbers of neutrons are called **isotopes**. Because they have the same number of protons, they are the same element. However, because they contain different numbers of neutrons, their masses and mass numbers are different. The Bohr models for three isotopes of carbon are shown below.

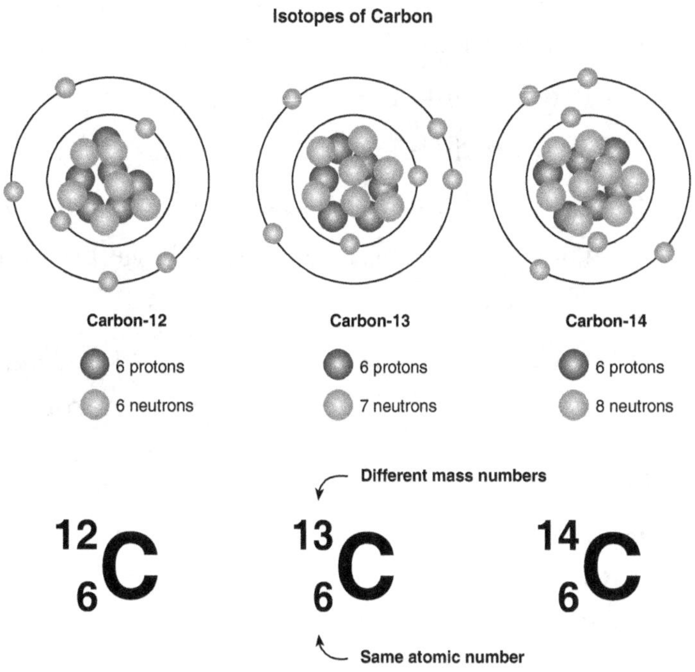

Isotopes of Carbon

Carbon-12
6 protons
6 neutrons

Carbon-13
6 protons
7 neutrons

Carbon-14
6 protons
8 neutrons

Different mass numbers

$^{12}_{6}C$ $^{13}_{6}C$ $^{14}_{6}C$

Same atomic number

All three isotopes have 6 protons because they are all different forms of carbon. They all have 6 electrons because these are neutral atoms of carbon, which means that the positive and negative charges balance each other. The different numbers of neutrons and the different masses differentiate these isotopes.

The isotopes can be named according to their masses. Carbon-12 has a mass number of 12, with 6 protons and 6 neutrons. Carbon-13 has a mass number of 13, with 6 protons and 7 neutrons. Carbon-14 has a mass number of 14, with 6 protons and 8 neutrons. The figure above shows how isotopes can be represented using the element symbols.

Isotopes are present in varying amounts. Carbon-12 makes up 98.93% of all carbon on Earth, and carbon-13 makes up 1.07%. Although carbon-14 exists, its amount is negligible. When calculating the average atomic mass, all isotopes are taken into account. In the periodic table, carbon has an atomic mass of 12.01 amu, which is extremely close to the mass of the most abundant isotope, carbon-12. Though not always true, the average atomic mass of an element is often closest to the mass of the most common isotope.

Example

Atom X has 7 protons and 8 neutrons, and Atom Y has 7 protons and 7 neutrons. Which of the following statements describes the relationship between Atom X and Atom Y?

A. They are different elements because they have different masses.

B. They are different elements because they have different numbers of neutrons.

C. They are isotopes because they have different atomic numbers but the same masses.

D. They are isotopes because they have the same number of protons but different numbers of neutrons.

The correct answer is **D**. Atom X and Y are different isotopes of nitrogen. They both have 7 protons, but the different numbers of neutrons give them different masses.

Let's Review!

- Scientific notation is used to make very large numbers and very small numbers easier to use.
- An atom is composed of protons, neutrons, and electrons. Protons and neutrons are found in the nucleus, and electrons are found in the electron cloud that surrounds the nucleus.
- The number of protons in an atom determines its identity (which element it is).
- The mass number of an atom is determined by adding the number of protons and the number of neutrons.
- The charge of an atom is determined by the numbers of protons and electrons.
- Isotopes are atoms of the same element that have different numbers of neutrons and, therefore, different masses.

TEMPERATURE AND THE METRIC SYSTEM

This lesson introduces the metric system, including how to do metric conversions and use prefixes. It also explores the three different types of temperature systems.

The English and Metric System

A universal language is used in science and research. This scientific language is called the **metric system**. Also known as the International System of Units (SI), the metric system is easy to use, and its design is simple. Prior to the metric system, several different units were used in scientific measurement, which led to confusion. The metric system was created to standardize units and simplify how they are used. By using a universally accepted measurement standard, scientists around the world can easily communicate with one another.

There are two principles of the metric system to keep in mind:

- Only one unit is assigned to a given quantity that is measured. This unit is called the **SI base unit**. The three most common base units are gram (for mass), meter (for length), and liter (for volume).
- The base unit can be expressed in multiples of 10 to account for measured objects that are very large or very small. This means when performing a metric conversion, the base units can either be multiplied or be divided by 10.

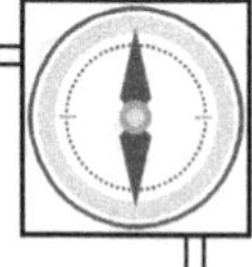

FOR EXAMPLE

A large container that holds 250,000 grams of sand can be said to hold 250 kilograms of sand.

When performing metric conversions, it is important to understand the **metric prefixes**. These are used to distinguish among the base units according to size. The following table provides a list of the most commonly used metric prefixes, including the multiplying factor. Metric prefixes are attached to the beginning of a base unit term. The prefixes can be added to any of the base units.

Metric Prefix	Symbol	Multiplying Factor	Equivalent Value
tera	T	10^{12}	1,000,000,000,000
giga	G	10^{9}	1,000,000,000
mega	M	10^{6}	1,000,000
kilo	k	10^{3}	1,000
hecto	h	10^{2}	100
deca	da	10^{1}	10
deci	d	10^{-1}	0.1
centi	c	10^{-2}	0.01
milli	m	10^{-3}	0.001

Metric Prefix	Symbol	Multiplying Factor	Equivalent Value
micro	μ	10^{-6}	0.000001
nano	n	10^{-9}	0.000000001
pico	p	10^{-12}	0.000000000001
femto	f	10^{-15}	0.000000000000001

The **English system** is another recognized system of measurement. It is not universally accepted, and it consists of several units of measurements that are not functionally related to one another. This means the multiple of 10 cannot be used to convert one English unit to another. The following list provides the equivalent values of commonly used English measurements for length, weight, and volume. These values can be used when performing conversions from one English unit to another.

Length
- 12 inches = 1 foot (ft)
- 3 feet = 1 yard (yd)
- 5,280 feet = 1 mile (mi)

Weight
- 16 ounces (oz) = 1 pound (lb)
- 1 ton = 2,000 pounds

Volume
- 8 ounces = 1 cup (c)
- 2 cups = 1 pint (pt)
- 2 pints = 1 quart (qt)
- 4 quarts = 1 gallon (gal)

DID YOU KNOW?

The English system was created because people needed a way to describe measurements. Many of the measurements were based on the size of body parts and familiar objects. Eventually, this system was standardized into the system used today.

Example

Thalia wants to measure the distance a solar-powered toy car travels over time. What SI base unit should she use?

A. Feet　　B. Inches　　C. Liter　　D. Meter

The correct answer is **D.** Meter is an SI base unit that is used to measure length or distance. When recording the distance the car travels, Thalia would use meters as the unit.

Metric Conversions

Recall that the metric system involves the use of prefixes and base units. The prefixes help a person identify how big or small the measured object is. What happens if one base unit needs to be converted to a different base unit? This is where the concept of using multiples of 10 is important.

When making metric conversions, it is helpful to create a metric staircase, as shown below.

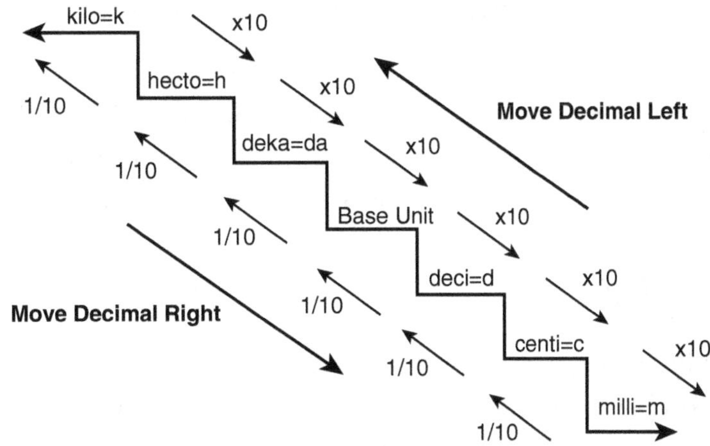

Look at each step on the staircase. It represents a ten-fold change in the metric system. In other words, each step indicates that the decimal place of the measured unit value moves to the left or to the right. Moving to the right (or down the staircase) requires multiplication, which involves using multiples of 10 to convert the larger unit to a smaller unit. When moving to the left (or up the staircase), a smaller unit is converted to a larger unit by dividing using a multiple of 10.

Sometimes, it is necessary to do conversions between the metric and English systems. The following list provides commonly used English measurements and their respective (approximate) metric equivalent values.

Length

- 1 inch = 2.54 centimeters
- 1 yard = 0.91 meters

Weight

- 1 ounce = 28.3 grams
- 2.20 pounds = 1 kilogram

Volume

- 1.06 quart = 1 liter
- 3.79 liters = 1 gallon

KEEP IN MIND

It is helpful to use the following mnemonic to remember the order of the metric prefixes to ensure proper movement of the decimal between units from largest to smallest.

King Henry Doesn't [Usually] Drink Chocolate Milk

Where *king* means "kilo," *Henry* means "hecto," *doesn't* means "deca," *usually* represents the base unit, *drink* means "deci," *chocolate* means "centi," and *milk* means "milli."

FOR EXAMPLE

How many grams are in 2.52 kilograms?

The metric staircase indicates that kilogram is a larger unit than gram. Going down the staircase means the decimal must move to the right to give a value of 2,520 grams. If 2.52 is multiplied by the multiplying factor of 10^3, this will give the same value.

Example

A patient needs a dose of 0.3 g of medicine. How much medicine is this in milligrams?

A. 3 B. 30 C. 300 D. 3,000

The correct answer is **C.** Gram is a larger unit than milligram. Thus, this value must be divided by a factor of 0.001 to get 300 milligrams. If using the metric staircase, the decimal in 0.3 g would move three units to the right to give 300 milligrams.

Temperature Systems

Three temperature scales are commonly used in science: Fahrenheit (F), Celsius (C), and Kelvin (K). **Temperature** measures the amount of kinetic energy that particles of matter have in a substance. Imagine that someone wants to boil a pot of water. Initially, the water molecules move very little. As the temperature rises to water's boiling point, these molecules move faster, bouncing off each other and generating kinetic energy. Movement slows down as the temperature lowers to water's freezing point.

The Fahrenheit temperature scale is part of the English system of measurement. It is not commonly used for scientific purposes like the Celsius (or centigrade) scale is. However, it is important to recognize and know how to use the conversion formulas between Celsius and Fahrenheit. The formulas are shown below:

$$F = \left(\frac{9}{5}\right)C + 32 \text{ and } C = \frac{5}{9}(F - 32).$$

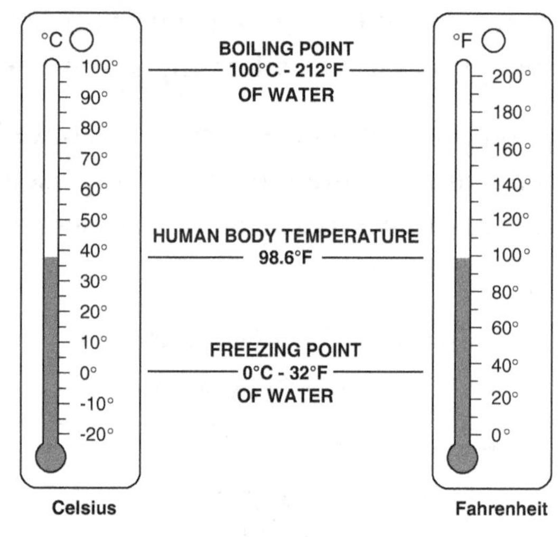

The Fahrenheit scale is based on 32°F for the freezing point of water and 212°F for the boiling point of water. This corresponds to 0°C and 100°C, respectively, on the Celsius scale. The Celsius scale is part of the metric system, which means it is universally accepted when reporting temperature measurements. A thermometer is used to measure temperature. The following thermometers show common temperature values.

Kelvin is another temperature scale that is used. Its degrees are similar in size to degrees Celsius, but its zero is set to an absolute zero, or 0 K. This is the point where all molecular motion ends. On the Kelvin scale, the freezing point of water is 273.15 K. The boiling point is 373.15 K. The following equation is used to convert a Celsius reading to Kelvin:

> **BE CAREFUL!**
> A degree sign is not used in the temperature designation for Kelvin. This symbol is only used with Fahrenheit and Celsius measurements.

$$K = °C + 273$$

Example

On which molecule's boiling and freezing points are the Celsius and Fahrenheit scales based?

A. Alcohol B. Chloride C. Glucose D. Water

The correct answer is **D.** Both the Fahrenheit and Celsius scales are based on the boiling and freezing point of water. The boiling point of water is 212°F (100°C), and the freezing point is 32°F (0°C).

Let's Review!

- The metric system is a universally accepted standard method that is used to determine the units of a given measurement.
- The English system is not universally accepted but provides a collection of measurements whose units are functionally unrelated.
- Meter (length), gram (weight), and liter (volume) are the most common types of SI base units.
- Metric prefixes are added to base units to describe the measurement of an object according to size.
- The metric staircase can be used for metric-metric conversions, and specific equivalent values are used for English-metric conversions.
- Three temperature scales, Celsius, Fahrenheit, and Kelvin, are used in science.
- Formulas are used to convert Celsius values to Fahrenheit or to Kelvin.

Chapter 13 Scientific Reasoning Practice Quiz

1. **Why must researchers consider the placebo effect?**
   A. Monitor the outcome of the experiment
   B. Ensure a proper independent variable is chosen
   C. Account for the body's response to fake treatments
   D. Create a baseline measure for experimental analysis

2. **As a variable increases, another variable increases. This describes a(n)**
   A. positive variation.
   B. negative variation.
   C. inverse correlation.
   D. indirect correlation.

3. **An electric balance measures an object's**
   A. mass.
   B. length.
   C. temperature.
   D. volume.

4. **Which of the following statements describes the mass of an electron?**
   A. The mass of an electron is less than the mass of a proton or neutron.
   B. The mass of an electron is about the same as the mass of a proton or neutron.
   C. The mass of an electron is greater than that of a neutron but less than that of a proton.
   D. The mass of an electron is greater than that of a proton but less than that of a neutron.

5. **Which of the following describes one difference between the two most abundant isotopes of iron, iron-54 and iron-56?**
   A. Iron-56 has more protons than iron-54.
   B. Iron-56 has more neutrons than iron-54.
   C. Iron-54 and iron-56 have different atomic numbers.
   D. Iron-54 and iron-56 contain different numbers of electrons.

6. **Which of the following parts of an atom takes up the most space in terms of area?**
   A. Neutrons
   B. Electron cloud
   C. Individual electrons
   D. Protons and neutrons

7. **Four cups of water are poured into a flask. What is this volume in pints?**
   A. 1
   C. 3
   B. 2
   D. 4

8. **How many ounces are in 3 cups?**
   A. 5
   C. 11
   B. 8
   D. 24

9. **It is advantageous to use the English system when**
   A. converting units using multiples of 10.
   B. describing a reported value using tons.
   C. working with functionally related base units.
   D. communicating information around the world.

Chapter 13 Scientific Reasoning Practice Quiz – Answer Key

1. C. The placebo is a false treatment given to a group to account for the body's psychological response to this type of treatment in a study. **See Lesson: Designing an Experiment.**

2. A. When a variable increases as another variable increases, this relationship is described as a positive correlation, direct correlation, or positive variation. **See Lesson: Designing an Experiment.**

3. A. The mass of an object is determined by using a balance. Electric balances are used to measure a very small mass. **See Lesson: Designing an Experiment.**

4. A. The mass of a proton or neutron is 1.0 amu, and the mass of an electron is much less, 0.00054 amu. **See Lesson: Scientific Notation.**

5. B. Because iron-54 and iron-56 are isotopes of the same element, they have the same number of protons and the same atomic number, but the numbers of neutrons and mass numbers are different. **See Lesson: Scientific Notation.**

6. B. The protons and neutrons are in the nucleus, which is very small and dense. The electron cloud makes up most of the atom in terms of area. **See Lesson: Scientific Notation.**

7. B. Two cups is equivalent to one pint of a solution, so four cups is two pints. **See Lesson: Temperature and the Metric System.**

8. D. There are 8 ounces in 1 cup. Multiplying 3 cups by 8 yields a total of 24 ounces. **See Lesson: Temperature and the Metric System.**

9. B. The English system is not universally accepted and consists of a collection of functionally unrelated units. However, it is useful when reporting values of weight in tons. **See Lesson: Temperature and the Metric System.**

CHAPTER 14 LIFE AND PHYSICAL SCIENCES

AN INTRODUCTION TO BIOLOGY

This lesson introduces the basics of biology, including the process researchers use to study science. It also examines the classes of biomolecules and how substances are broken down for energy.

Biology and Taxonomy

The study or science of living things is called **biology**. Some characteristics, or traits, are common to all living things. These enable researchers to differentiate living things from nonliving things. Traits include reproduction, growth and development, **homeostasis**, and energy processing. Homeostasis is the body's ability to maintain a constant internal environment despite changes that occur in the external environment. With so many living things in the world, researchers developed a **taxonomy** system, which is used for classification, description, and naming. As shown below, there are seven classification levels in the classical Linnaean system.

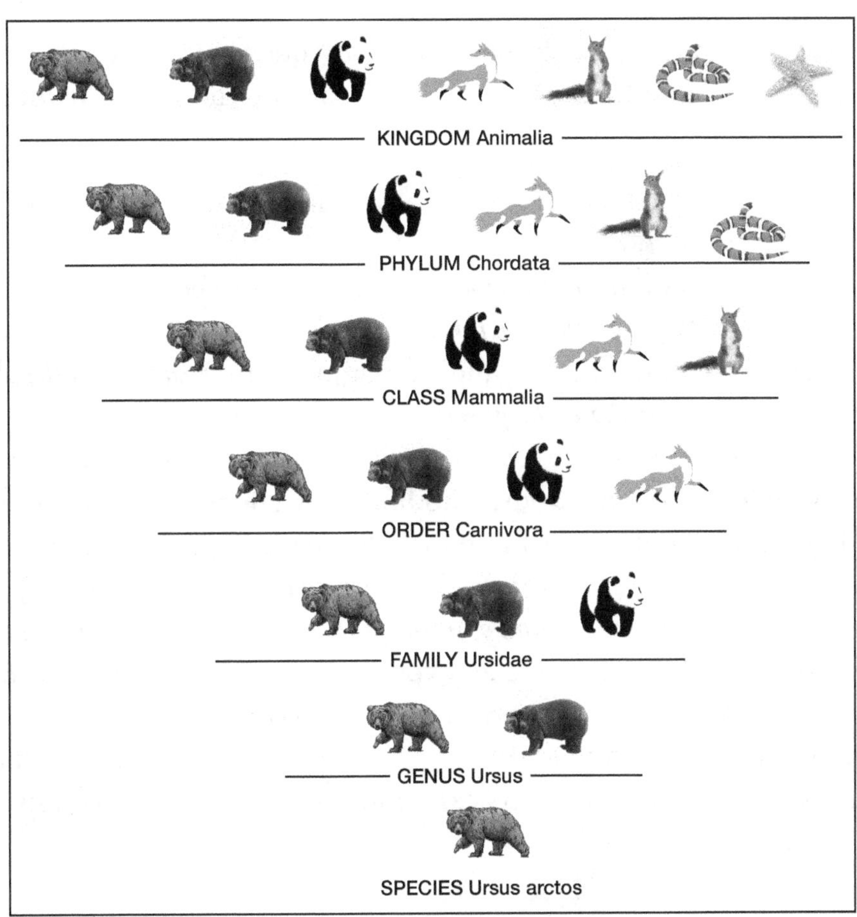

Specificity increases as the levels move from kingdom to species. For example, in the image the genus level contains two types of bears, but the species level shows one type. Additionally, organisms in each level are found in the level above it. For example, organisms in the order level are part of the class level. This classification system is based on physical similarities across living things. It does not account for molecular or genetic similarities.

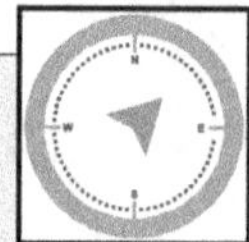

DID YOU KNOW?

Carl Linnaeus only used physical similarities across organisms when he created the Linnaean system because technology was not advanced enough to observe similarities at the molecular level.

Example

A researcher classifies a newly discovered organism in the class taxonomy level. What other taxonomic level is this new organism classified in?

A. Order B. Family C. Species D. Kingdom

The correct answer is **D.** Each level is found in the level above it. The levels above class are phylum and kingdom.

Scientific Method

To develop the taxonomic system, researchers had to ask questions. Researchers use seven steps to answer science questions or solve problems. These make up the **scientific method**, described below:

1. Problem: The question created because of an observation. *Example: Does the size of a plastic object affect how fast it naturally degrades in a lake?*
2. Research: Reliable information available about what is observed. *Example: Learn how plastics are made and understand the properties of a lake.*
3. Hypothesis: A predicted solution to the question or problem. *Example: If the plastic material is small, then it will degrade faster than a large particle.*
4. Experiment: A series of tests used to evaluate the hypothesis. Experiments consist of an **independent variable** that the researcher modifies and a **dependent variable** that changes due to the independent variable. They also include a **control group** used as a standard to make comparisons. *Example: Collect plastic particles both onshore and offshore of the lake over time. Determine the size of the particles and describe the lake conditions during this time period.*
5. Observe: Analyze data collected during an experiment to observe patterns. *Example: Analyze the differences between the numbers of particles collected in terms of size.*
6. Conclusion: State whether the hypothesis is rejected or accepted and summarize all results.
7. Communicate: Report findings so others can replicate and verify the results.

Sometimes, just a few steps of the scientific method are necessary to research a question. At other times, several steps may be repeated as needed. The goal of this method is to find a reliable answer to the scientific question.

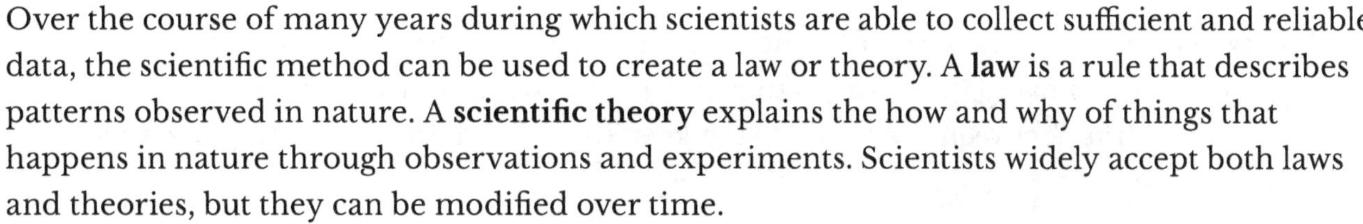

TEST TIP

Using the first letter in each of the steps, you can create a mnemonic device to remember the steps. For example: "**P**eople **R**eally **H**ave **E**lephants **O**n **C**ompact **C**ars." Try creating your own mnemonic device!

Over the course of many years during which scientists are able to collect sufficient and reliable data, the scientific method can be used to create a law or theory. A **law** is a rule that describes patterns observed in nature. A **scientific theory** explains the how and why of things that happens in nature through observations and experiments. Scientists widely accept both laws and theories, but they can be modified over time.

Example

In a study, a researcher describes what happens to a plant following exposure to a dry and hot environment. What step of the scientific method does this most likely describe?

A. Forming a hypothesis

B. Making an observation

C. Communicating findings

D. Characterizing the problem

The correct answer is **B.** The researcher is collecting qualitative data by describing what happens to the plant under specific conditions. This data collection corresponds to the observation step of the scientific method.

Water and Biomolecule Basics

From oceans and streams to a bottle, water is fundamental for life. Without water, life would not exist. Because of water's unique properties, it plays a specific role in living things. The molecular structure of water consists of an oxygen atom bonded to two hydrogen atoms. The structure of water explains some of its properties. For example, water is polar. The oxygen atom is slightly negatively charged, while both hydrogen atoms are slightly positively charged.

As shown below, a single water molecule forms **hydrogen bonds** with nearby water molecules. This type of bonding creates a weak attraction between the water molecules. Hydrogen bonding contributes to water's high boiling point. Water is necessary for biochemical processes like photosynthesis and cellular respiration. It is also a universal solvent, which means water dissolves many different substances.

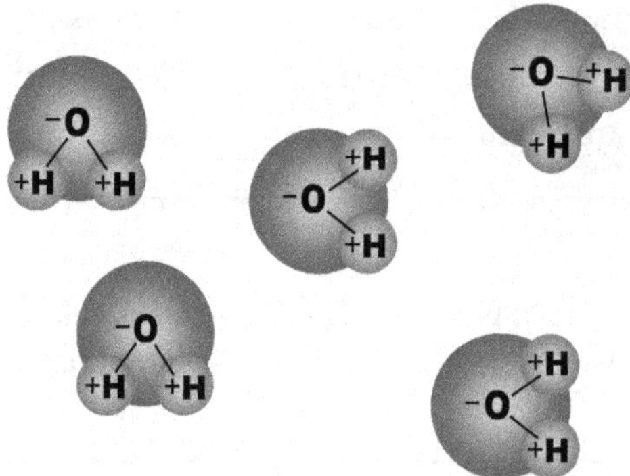

Only two water molecules are needed to show bonding. Remove the partial negative/positive signs and put a – sign next to the oxygen atom and a + sign next to each hydrogen (H) atom. Remove the solid lines between the H and O but keep the dashed line connecting one water molecule to the next.

KEEP IN MIND

It takes a lot of heat to create hot water. This is because of water's high specific heat capacity, which is the amount of heat required to raise the temperature of 1 kilogram of water by 1 degree Celsius. This property of water also makes it ideal for living things.

Biomolecules, or biological molecules, are found in living things. These organic molecules vary in structure and size and perform different functions. Researchers group the wide variety of molecules found in living things into four major classes for organizational purposes: proteins, carbohydrates, lipids, and nucleic acids. Each class of biomolecules has unique **monomers** and **polymers**. Monomers are molecules that covalently bond to form larger molecules or polymers. The table below lists characteristics of each class.

Biomolecule	Monomer(s)	Function	Example
Protein	Amino acid	A substance that provides the overall basic structure and function for a cell	Enzymes
Carbohydrate	Monosaccharides	A form of storage for energy	Glucose Cellulose Starch Disaccharides
Lipid	Glycerol and fatty acids	A type of fat that provides a long-term storage for energy	Fats Steroids Oils Hormones
Nucleic acid	Nucleotides	A substance that aids in protein synthesis and transmission of genetic information	DNA RNA

Example

During protein synthesis in a cell, the primary structure of the protein consists of a linear chain of monomers. What is another way to describe this structure?

A. A linear chain of fatty acids that are hydrogen-bonded together

B. A linear chain of nucleotides that are hydrogen-bonded together

C. A linear chain of amino acids that are covalently bonded together

D. A linear chain of monosaccharides that are covalently bonded together

The correct answer is **C**. The monomers of proteins include amino acids, which are covalently bonded together to form a protein.

The Metabolic Process

Just like water, energy is essential to life. Food and sunlight are major energy sources. Metabolism is the process of converting food into usable energy. This refers to all biochemical processes or reactions that take place in a living thing to keep it alive.

CONNECTIONS

Energy flows through living things. Energy from the sun is converted to chemical energy via photosynthesis. When living things feed on plants, they obtain this energy for survival.

A metabolic pathway is a series of several chemical reactions that take place cyclically to either build or break down molecules. An **anabolic pathway** involves the synthesis of new molecules. These pathways require an input of energy. **Catabolic pathways** involve the breakdown of molecules. Energy is released from a catabolic pathway.

Living things use several metabolic pathways. The most well-studied pathways include glycolysis, the citric acid cycle, and the electron transport chain. These metabolic pathways either release or add energy during a reaction. They also provide a continual flow of energy to living things.

1. **Glycolysis:** This is a catabolic pathway that uses several steps to break down glucose sugar for energy, carbon dioxide, and water. Energy that is released from this reaction is stored in the form of adenosine triphosphate (ATP). Two ATP molecules, two pyruvate molecules, and two NADH molecules are formed during this metabolic pathway.

BE CAREFUL!

Some of these metabolic pathways produce energy in different parts of the cell. Glycolysis takes place in the cytoplasm of the cell. But the citric acid cycle and oxidative phosphorylation occur in the mitochondria.

2. **Citric acid cycle:** The pyruvate molecules made from glycolysis are transported inside the cell's mitochondria. In this catabolic pathway, pyruvate is used to make two ATP molecules, six carbon dioxide molecules, and six NADH molecules.
3. **Electron transport chain and oxidative phosphorylation:** This also takes place in the cell's mitochondria. Many electrons are transferred from one molecule to another in this chain. At the end of the chain, oxygen picks up the electrons to produce roughly 34 molecules of ATP.

The following image provides an overview of **cellular respiration**. Glycolysis, the citric acid cycle, the electron transport chain, and oxidative phosphorylation collectively make up this process. Cellular respiration takes place in a cell and is used to convert energy from nutrients into ATP.

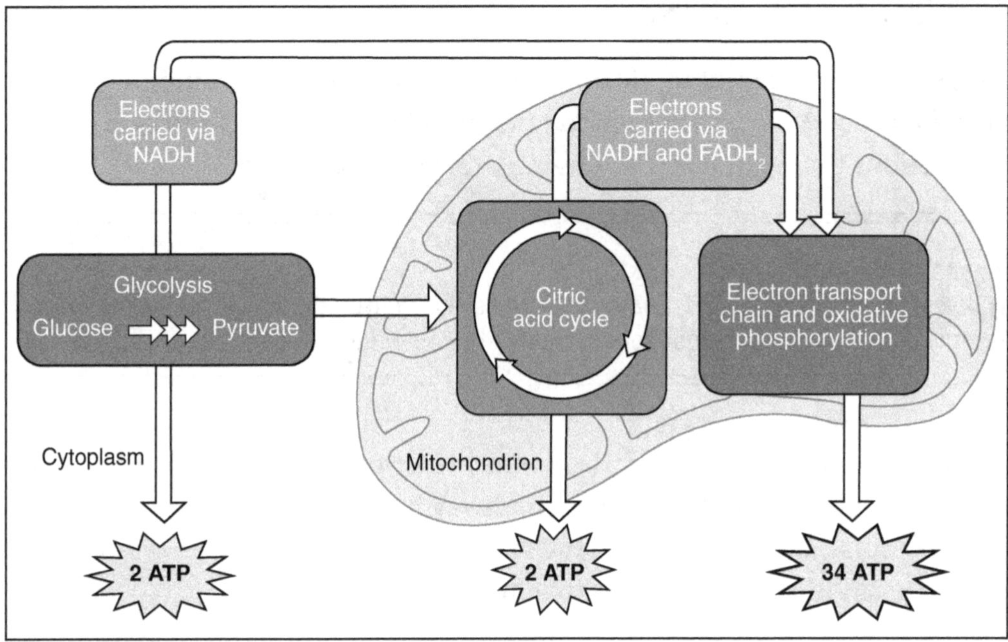

Example

Why are metabolic pathways cyclic?

A. Metabolic reactions generally take place one at a time.

B. All of the products created in metabolic reactions are used up.

C. The reactions are continuous as long as reactants are available.

D. Energy in the form of ATP is sent to different cells for various uses.

The correct answer is **C.** Metabolic reactions are cyclic, which means they keep occurring as long as enough starting materials are available to allow the reaction to proceed.

Let's Review!

- This lesson explored how living things are organized, what the scientific method is, and how biomolecules are classified. It also discussed how living things obtain energy via metabolism.
- Biology is the study of living things. Several characteristics distinguish living things from nonliving things.
- All living things are described, classified, and named using a taxonomic system.
- The scientific method uses seven steps to answer a question or solve a problem.
- Biomolecules are organic molecules that are organized into four classes: proteins, carbohydrates, lipids, and nucleic acids
- Living things rely on various metabolic pathways to produce energy and store it in the form of ATP.

Cell Structure, Function, and Type

This lesson describes the cell structure and two different types of cells. The lesson also explores the functions of various cell parts.

Cell Theory and Types

All living things are made of cells. **Cells** are the smallest structural units and basic building blocks of living things. Cells contain everything necessary to keep living things alive. Varying in size and shape, cells carry out specialized functions. Robert Hooke discovered the first cells in the mid-eighteenth century. Many years later, after advancements in microscopy, the cell theory was formed. This theory, or in-depth explanation, about cells consists of three parts:

1. All living things are composed of one or more cells.
2. Cells are alive and represent the basic unit of life.
3. All cells are produced from preexisting cells.

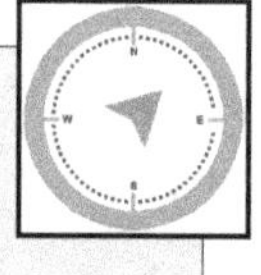

DID YOU KNOW?

More than a trillion cells and at least 200 different types of cells exist in the human body!

Many different types of cells exist. Because of this, cells are classified into two general types: prokaryotic cells and eukaryotic cells. The following comparison table lists key differences between prokaryotes and eukaryotes:

Characteristic	Prokaryote	Eukaryote
Cell size	Around 0.2–2.0 mm in diameter	Around 10–100 mm in diameter
Nucleus	Absent	True nucleus
Organelles	Absent	Several present, ranging from ribosomes to the endoplasmic reticulum
Flagella	Simple in structure	Complex in structure

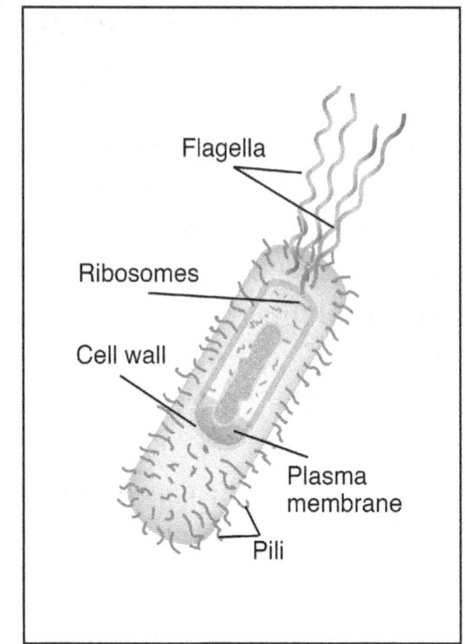

As shown in the image, prokaryotic cells lack nuclei. Their DNA floats in the **cytoplasm**, which is surrounded by a **plasma membrane**. Very simplistic in structure, these cells lack organelles but do have cell walls. **Organelles** are specialized structures with a specific cellular function. They also may have **ribosomes** that aid in protein synthesis. Also, these cells have a **flagellum** that looks like a tail attached to the cell. Flagella aid in locomotion. The **pili**, or hair-like structures surrounding the cells, aid in cellular adhesion. Bacteria and Archaea are the most common prokaryotes. Most prokaryotes are **unicellular**, or made of a single cell, but there are a few **multicellular organisms**.

Eukaryotic cells contain a membrane-bound nucleus where DNA is stored. Membrane-bound organelles also exist in eukaryotic cells. Similar to prokaryotic cells, eukaryotic cells have cytoplasm, ribosomes, and a plasma membrane. Eukaryotic organisms can be either unicellular or multicellular. Much larger than prokaryotes, examples of eukaryotic organisms include fungi and even people.

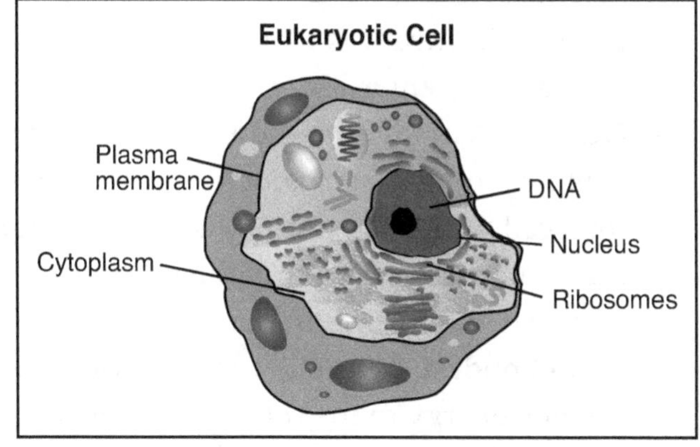

Example

What is an organelle?

A. The building block of all living things

B. A substance that is able diffuse inside a cell

C. The specific receptor found on a cell's surface

D. A membrane-bound structure with a special function

The correct answer is **D.** Organelles such as ribosomes and the nucleus are membrane-bound structures that have specific functions in a cell.

A Peek Inside the Animal Cell

Animal cells are eukaryotic cells. Cheek, nerve, and muscle cells are all examples of animal cells. Because there are many different types, each animal cell has a specialized function. But all animal cells have the same parts, or organelles. Use this image as a guide while going through following list, which describes the organelles found in a eukaryotic (or animal) cell.

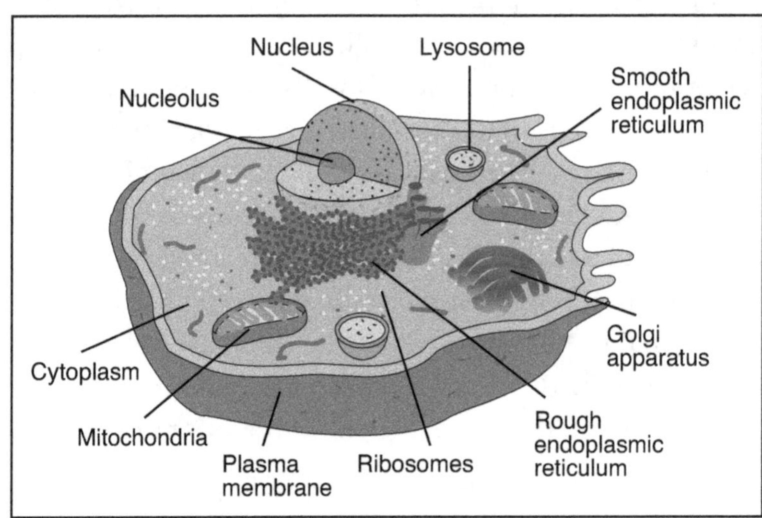

- **Cell membrane:** A double layer that separates the inside of the cell from the outside environment. It is semi-permeable, meaning it only allows certain molecules to enter the cell.
- **Nucleus:** A membrane-bound organelle that contains the genetic material, such as DNA, for a cell. Inside the nucleus is the **nucleolus** that plays a role in assembling subunits required to make ribosomes.
- **Mitochondria:** The cell's powerhouses that provide energy to the cell for it to function. Much of the energy in the form of ATP is produced here.
- **Ribosomes:** The cell's protein factories that can be found floating in the cytoplasm or attached to the endoplasmic reticulum.
- **Vacuoles:** Small sacs in a cell that store water and food for survival. This organelle also stores waste material that is mostly in the form of water.
- **Endoplasmic reticulum:** A network of membranes that functions as a cell's transportation system, shuttling proteins and other materials around the cell. The **smooth endoplasmic reticulum** lacks ribosomes, and the **rough endoplasmic reticulum** has ribosomes.
- **Lysosomes:** Sac-like structures that contain digestive enzymes that are used to break down food and old organelles.
- **Golgi apparatus:** A stack of flattened pouches that plays a role in processing proteins received from the endoplasmic reticulum. It modifies proteins from the endoplasmic reticulum and then packages them into a vesicle that can be sent to other places in the cell.

KEEP IN MIND!

Some of the organelles in animal cells are also present in plant cells. In addition, all organelles are found in the cytoplasm of the cell. The only exception is the nucleus, which it is separated from the cytoplasm because it has its own membrane.

Example

Which two organelles work together to facilitate protein synthesis?

A. Cytoplasm and lysosome

B. Vacuole and mitochondria

C. Nucleus and cell membrane

D. Ribosome and endoplasmic reticulum

The correct answer is **D.** After a protein is synthesized by ribosomes, it is shuttled to the endoplasmic reticulum, where it is further modified and prepared to be transported by vesicles to other places in the cell.

Plant Cells

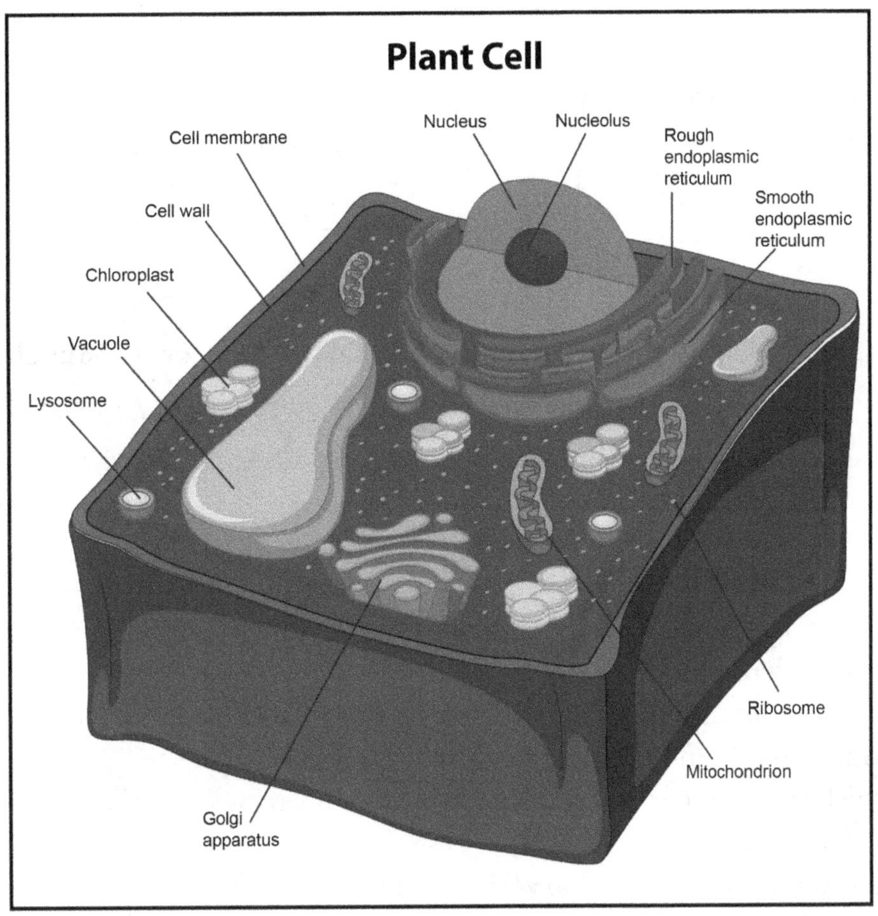

Recall that plant cells are also eukaryotic cells. Structurally, these cells are similar to animal cells because some of the parts in a plant cell are also found in an animal cell. However, there are some notable differences. The following image shows the structure of a plant cell.

First, only plant cells have a **cell wall**. The purpose of this structure is to provide protection and support to plant cells. The cell wall also enforces the overall structural integrity of the plant cell, and it is found outside the cell membrane. The next organelle is a chloroplast. It is found in the cytoplasm of only plant cells. **Chloroplasts** are photosynthetic compounds used to make food for plant cells by harnessing energy from the sun. These organelles play a role in photosynthesis.

Chloroplasts and mitochondria are both designed to collect, process, and store energy for the cell. Thus, organisms are divided into autotrophs or heterotrophs based on how they obtain energy. **Autotrophs** are organisms that make energy-rich biomolecules from raw material in nature. They do this by using basic energy sources such the sun. This explains why most autotrophs rely on photosynthesis to transform sunlight into usable food that can produce energy necessary for life. Plants and certain species of bacteria are autotrophs.

Animals are **heterotrophs** because they are unable to make their own food. Heterotrophs have to consume and metabolize their food sources to absorb the stored energy. Examples of heterotrophs include all animals and fungi, as well as certain species of bacteria.

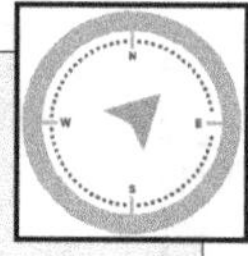

DID YOU KNOW?

More than 99% of all energy for life on Earth is provided through the process of photosynthesis.

Example

Kelp use chlorophyll to capture sunlight for food. What are these organisms classified as?

A. Autotrophs
B. Chemotrophs
C. Heterotrophs
D. Lithotrophs

The correct answer is **A.** Kelp is an autotroph because it uses chlorophyll to trap energy from the sun to make food.

Let's Review!

- This lesson focused on the cell theory, different cell types, and the various cell parts found in plant and animal cells.
- The cell theory is an in-depth explanation, supported with scientific data, to prove a cell is a living thing and has unique characteristics.
- Cells are the basic building blocks of life. Coming in various sizes and shapes, cells have specialized functions.
- Two broad types of cells are prokaryotic and eukaryotic cells.
- Prokaryotes are single-celled organisms that lack a nucleus, while eukaryotes are multicellular organisms that contain a nucleus.
- Chloroplasts and cell walls are only found in plant cells.
- Both animal and plant cells have similar organelles such as ribosomes, mitochondria, and an endoplasmic reticulum.
- Living things can be classified as autotrophs or heterotrophs based on how they obtain energy.

Cellular Reproduction, Cellular Respiration, and Photosynthesis

This lesson introduces basic processes including cellular reproduction and division, cellular respiration, and photosynthesis. These processes provide ways for cells to make new cells and to convert energy to and from food sources.

Cell Reproduction

Cells divide primarily for growth, repair, and reproduction. When an organism grows, it normally needs more cells. If damage occurs, more cells must appear to repair the damage and replace any dead cells. During reproduction, this process allows all living things to produce offspring. There are two ways that living things reproduce: asexually and sexually.

Asexual reproduction is a process in which only one organism is needed to reproduce itself. A single parent is involved in this type of reproduction, which means all offspring are genetically identical to one another and to the parent. All prokaryotes reproduce this way. Some eukaryotes also reproduce asexually. There are several methods of asexual reproduction.

Binary fission is one method. During this process, a prokaryotic cell, such as a bacterium, copies its DNA and splits in half. Binary fission is simple because only one parent cell divides into two daughter cells (or offspring) that are the same size.

Sexual reproduction is a process in which two organisms produce offspring that have genetic characteristics from both parents. It provides greater genetic diversity within a population than asexual reproduction. Sexual reproduction results in the production of **gametes**. These are reproductive cells. Gametes unite to create offspring.

Example

Binary fission is a method

A. where one daughter cell is produced.

B. required to produce reproductive cells.

C. that represents a form of asexual reproduction.

D. where two parent cells interact with each other.

The correct answer is **C.** Binary fission is a method organisms use to reproduce asexually. It involves a single parent cell that splits to create two identical daughter cells.

When the Cell Cycle Begins

For a cell to divide into more cells, it must grow, copy its DNA, and produce new daughter cells. The **cell cycle** regulates cellular division. This process can either prevent a cell from dividing or trigger it to start dividing.

> **KEEP IN MIND**
> The cell cycle is a circular process. This means after two daughter cells are made, they can participate in the cell cycle process, starting it over from the beginning.

The cell cycle is an organized process divided into two phases: **interphase** and the **M (mitotic) phase**. During interphase, the cell grows and copies its DNA. After the cell reaches the M phase, division and of the two new cells can occur. The G_1, S, and G_2 phases make up interphase.

- **G1:** The first gap phase, during which the cell prepares to copy its DNA
- **S:** The synthesis phase, during which DNA is copied
- **G2:** The second gap phase, during which the cell prepares for cell division

It may appear that little is happening in the cell during the gap phases. Most of the activity occurs at the level of enzymes and macromolecules. The cell produces things like nucleotides for synthesizing new DNA strands, enzymes for copying the DNA, and tubulin proteins for building the mitotic spindle. During the S phase, the DNA in the cell doubles, but few other signs are obvious under the microscope. All the dramatic events that can be seen under a microscope occur during the M phase: the chromosomes move, and the cell splits into two new cells with identical nuclei.

Example

For an organism, the cell cycle is needed for

A. competition. B. dispersal. C. growth. D. parasitism.

The correct answer is **C.** The cell cycle is the process during which a cell grows, copies its own DNA, and physically separates into new cells. With help from the cell cycle, more cells can be provided to help an organism grow.

Mitosis

Mitosis is a form of cell division where two identical nuclei are produced from one nucleus. DNA contains the genetic information of the cell. It is stored in the nucleus. During mitosis, DNA in the nucleus must be copied, or replicated. Recall that this happens during the S phase of the cell cycle. During the M phase, this copied DNA is divided into two complete sets, one of which goes to a daughter cell.

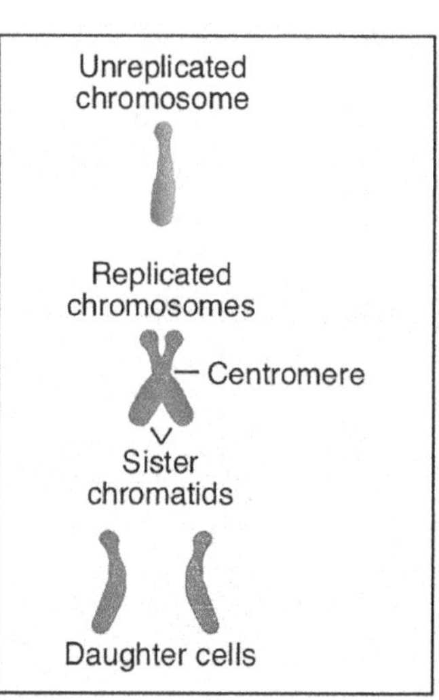

When DNA replicates, it condenses to form **chromosomes** that resemble an X. The DNA forms chromosomes by wrapping around proteins called histones. As shown below, it takes two identical sister chromatids to form a chromosome. A **centromere** holds the sister chromatids together.

Four phases take place during mitosis to form two identical daughter cells:

1. **Prophase:** The nuclear membrane disappears, and other organelles move out of the way. The spindle, made of microtubules, begins to form. During **prometaphase**, the microtubules begin to attach to the centromeres at the center of the chromosome.
2. **Metaphase:** Spindle fibers line the chromosomes at the center of the cell. This is because they are pulled equally by the spindle fibers, which are attached to the opposite poles of the cell.
3. **Anaphase:** The chromosomes are pulled to the opposite poles of the cell.
4. **Telophase:** The chromosomes de-condense, the nuclear membrane reappears, and other parts of the cell return to their usual places in the cell.

The cell divides into two daughter cells by way of **cytokinesis**. The illustration below demonstrates the process of mitosis.

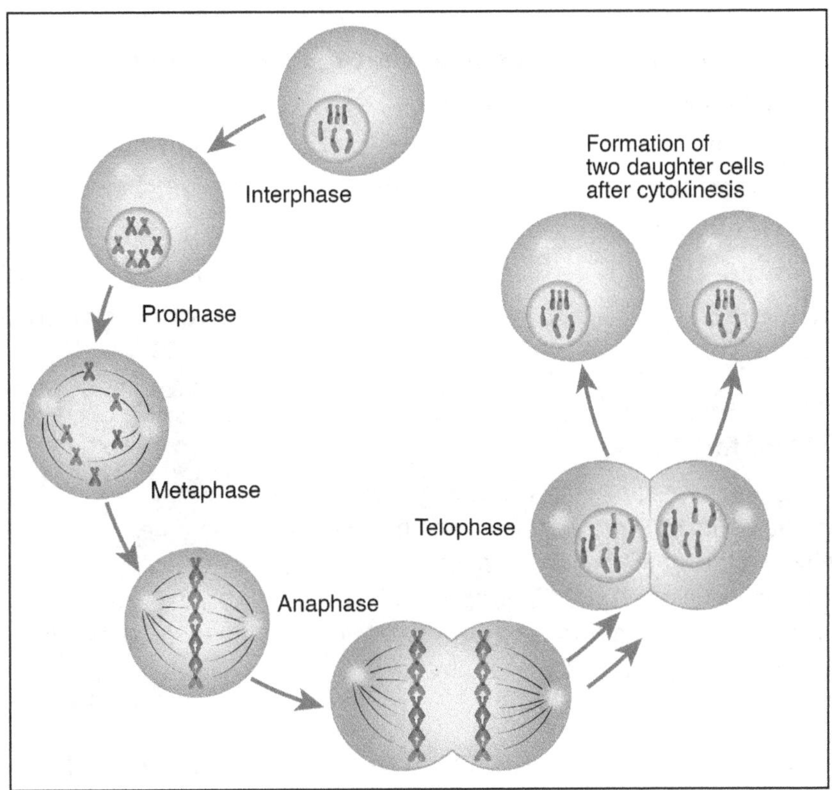

TEST TIP

There is a popular mnemonic to help remember the order of the phases for mitosis:

[Please] Pee on the MAT.

The "please" refers to prophase, while "pee" refers to prometaphase. MAT stands for metaphase, anaphase, and telophase, respectively.

Example

Before mitosis occurs

1. the spindle fibers must elongate.
2. DNA must wrap around histones.
3. chromosomes must split into chromatids.
4. the cell cycle process must be suspended.

The correct answer is **B.** After DNA replicates, it wraps around proteins called histones to form a chromosome. The chromosome must be formed for mitosis to occur.

Meiosis

Meiosis, sexual cell division in eukaryotes, involves two phases of mitosis that take place one after the other but without a second replication of DNA. This provides the reduction in chromosome number from $2n$ to n needed for fertilization to restore the normal $2n$ state. Diploid multicellular organisms use meiosis, which reduces the number of chromosomes by half. Then, when two haploid (n) sex cells (sperm, egg) unite, the normal number of chromosomes is restored. Diploid organisms, such as humans and oak trees, have two copies of every chromosome per cell ($2n$), as opposed to n, when one copy of every chromosome is present per cell.

DID YOU KNOW?

During prophase I of meiosis, **crossing over** occurs to increase genetic diversity. Corresponding chromosomes from the mother and the father of the organism undergoing meiosis are physically bound, and *X*-shaped structures called **chiasmata** form. These are where corresponding DNA from the different parental chromosomes are exchanged, resulting in increased diversity.

The process of meiosis is divided into two rounds of cell division: meiosis I and meiosis II. The phases that occur in mitosis (prophase, metaphase, anaphase, and telophase) also occur during each round of meiosis. Also, cytokinesis occurs after telophase during each round of cell division. However, DNA replication does not happen when meiosis I proceeds to meiosis II. The result of meiosis is one diploid cell that divides into four haploid cells, as shown in the following image.

Cytokinesis looks different in plant and animal cells. Plant cells build a new wall, or cell plate, between the two cells, while animal cells split by slowly pinching the membrane toward the center of the cell as the cell divides. Microtubules are more important for cytokinesis in plant cells, while the actin cytoskeleton performs the pinching-off operation during animal cytokinesis.

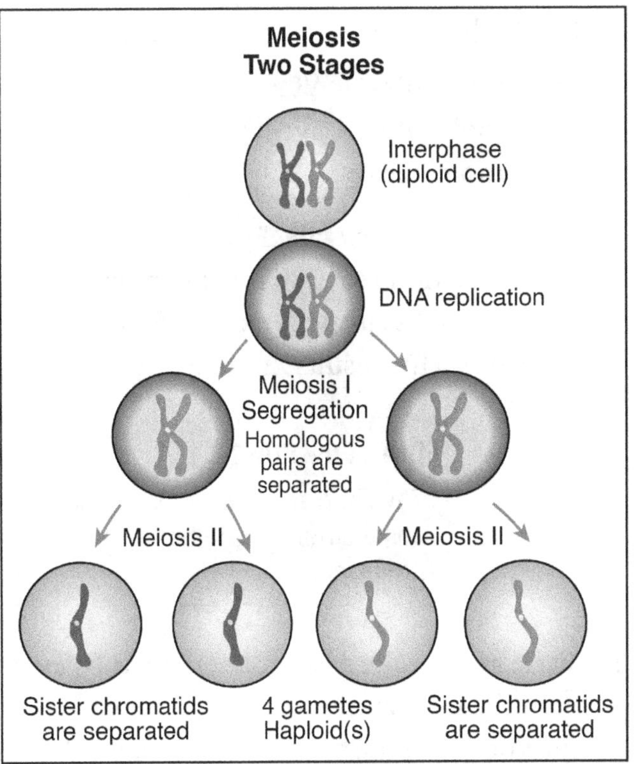

Example

How many rounds of cell division occur during meiosis?

A. 1
B. 2
C. 3
D. 4

The correct answer is **B.** A difference between mitosis and meiosis is that meiosis requires two rounds of cell division. At the end of both rounds, four haploid daughter cells have been produced.

KEY POINT

Meiosis and mitosis both require cytokinesis to physically separate a cell into daughter cells. Also, the sequence of events that occur in mitosis are the same in meiosis. However, there are two primary differences between the types of cell division: (1) meiosis has two rounds of cell division, and (2) daughter cells are genetically identical to the parent cell in mitosis but are not genetically identical in meiosis.

Cell Respiration

Once cells have been made, they need to be powered. Plants and some other cells can capture the energy of light and convert it into stored energy in ATP. However, most prokaryotic cells and all eukaryotic cells can perform a metabolic process called **cellular respiration**. Cellular respiration is the process by which the mitochondria of a cell break down glucose to produce energy in the form of ATP. The following is the general equation for cellular respiration:

$$O_2 + C_6H_{12}O_6 \rightarrow CO_2 + H_2O + ATP$$

Reactions during cellular respiration occur in the following sequence:

1. **Glycolysis:** One molecule of glucose breaks down into two smaller sugar molecules called **pyruvate**. This is an anaerobic process, which means it does not need oxygen to be present.

Glycolysis takes place in the cell's cytoplasm. End product yield from this reaction per one glucose molecule is

- two molecules of ATP
- two molecules of pyruvate
- two molecules of NADH

2. **Oxidation of pyruvate:** Pyruvate is converted into **acetyl coA** in the mitochondrial matrix. This transition reaction must happen for pyruvate to enter the next phase of cellular respiration. Pyruvate is **oxidized**, which means it loses two electrons and a hydrogen molecule. This results in the formation of NADH and loss of CO_2.

DID YOU KNOW?

The citric acid cycle is not identical for all organisms. Plants have some differences in terms of the enzymes used and energy carriers produced.

3. **Citric acid cycle:** Also called the **Krebs cycle**, during this cycle an acetyl group detaches from the coenzyme A in the acetyl coA molecule. This process is **aerobic**, which means it must occur in the presence of oxygen. The net yield per one glucose molecule is
   - two molecules of ATP
   - six molecules of NADH
   - two molecules of $FADH_2$
   - four molecules of CO_2

4. **Electron transport chain:** This process happens in the inner mitochondrial membrane. It consists of a series of enzymatic reactions. Both NADH and $FADH_2$ molecules are passed through a series of enzymes so that electrons and protons can be released from them. During this process, energy is released and used to fuel **chemiosmosis**. During chemiosmosis, protons are transported across the inner mitochondrial membrane to the outer mitochondrial compartment. This flow of protons drives the process of ATP synthesis. This step of cellular respiration creates an approximate net yield of 34 ATP per glucose molecule. Six molecules of water are also formed at the end of the electron transport chain.

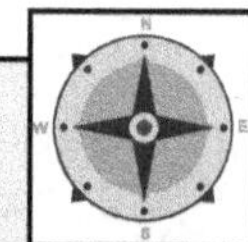

KEEP IN MIND

Cellular respiration requires oxygen, but there are forms of **fermentation** that extract energy from food without using oxygen. Fermentation can be either alcoholic (makes ethanol as an end product, like yeast in the brewing of beer) or lactic acid type. Lactic acid is produced in a person's muscles during strenuous activity when the body cannot move enough oxygen to the cells.

Example

Before a molecule of glucose can be run through the citric acid cycle, it must experience

A. ATP production.

B. NADH production.

C. pyruvate oxidation.

D. oxygen deprivation.

The correct answer is **C.** A glucose molecule must first experience pyruvate oxidation because one CO_2 molecule must be removed from each pyruvate molecule after glycolysis and before the citric acid cycle.

Photosynthesis

Photosynthesis is the process plants use to make a food source from energy. This process can be thought of as the reverse of cellular respiration. Instead of glucose being broken down into carbon dioxide to create energy-containing molecules, energy is captured from the sun and used to turn carbon dioxide into glucose (and other organic chemicals the plant needs). The energy source is the sun. The reaction for photosynthesis is shown below:

$$CO_2 + H_2O \rightarrow C_6H_{12}O_6 + O_2$$

Energy is captured from the sun and used to turn carbon dioxide into glucose (and other organic chemicals). **Chloroplasts** are **organelles** in plants that contain green chlorophyll, which helps the plants absorb light from the sun.

The photosynthetic reaction involves two distinct phases: light reactions and dark reactions. Light-dependent reactions require light to produce ATP and NADPH. During dark reactions, also known as the **Calvin cycle**, light is not required. These reactions use ATP and NAPDH to produce sugar molecules like glucose.

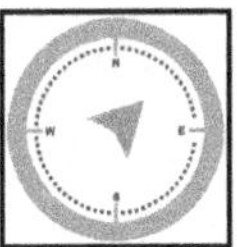

DID YOU KNOW?

Some plants skip photosynthesis! These plants are parasites. They lack chlorophyll, so they attach to nearby plants, stealing water and sugar from their hosts.

Let's Review!

- Cells are needed for growth, repair, and reproduction.
- Mitosis is a form of cell division where one parent cell divides into identical two daughter cells.
- Meiosis involves two rounds of cell division to divide two parent cells into four haploid cells.
- Cells are powered by cellular respiration and photosynthesis, which make ATP and organic chemicals.
- Cellular respiration goes from glycolysis to the citric acid cycle to the electron transport chain.
- Photosynthesis proceeds from the light reactions to the dark reactions, which are known as the Calvin cycle.

Genetics and DNA

The lesson introduces genetics, which is the study of heredity. Heredity is the characteristics offspring inherit from their parents. This lesson also examines Gregor Mendel's theories of heredity and how they have affected the field of genetics.

Gregor Mendel and Garden Peas

From experiments with garden peas, Mendel developed a simple set of rules that accurately predicted patterns of heredity. He discovered that plants either **self-pollinate** or **cross-pollinate**, when the pollen from one plant fertilizes the pistil of another plant. He also discovered that traits are either **dominant** or **recessive**. Dominant traits are expressed, and recessive traits are hidden.

Mendel's Theory of Heredity

To explain his results, Mendel proposed a theory that has become the foundation of the science of genetics. The theory has five elements:

1. Parents do not transmit traits directly to their offspring. Rather, they pass on units of information called **genes**.
2. For each trait, an individual has two factors: one from each parent. If the two factors have the same information, the individual is **homozygous** for that trait. If the two factors are different, the individual is **heterozygous** for that trait. Each copy of a factor, or **gene**, is called an **allele**.
3. The alleles determine the physical appearance, or **phenotype**. The set of alleles an individual has is its **genotype**.
4. An individual receives one allele from each parent.
5. The presence of an allele does not guarantee that the trait will be expressed.

Punnett Squares

Biologists can predict the probable outcomes of a cross by using a diagram called a **Punnett square**. In the Punnett square illustrated at the right, the yellow pea pods are dominant, as designated by a capital Y, and the green pea pods are recessive, as designated with a lowercase y. In a cross between one homozygous recessive (yy) parent and a heterozygous dominant parent (Yy), the outcome is two heterozygous dominant offspring (Yy) and two homozygous recessive offspring (yy), which gives a ratio of 2:2.

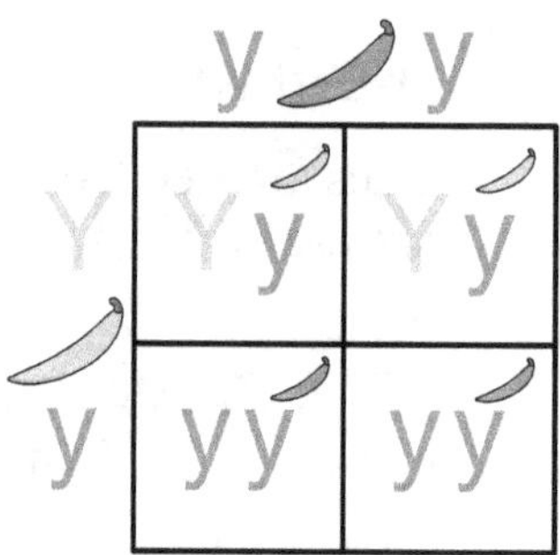

Example

In the Punnett square below, homozygous green pea pods are crossed with dominant yellow pea pods. What is the probability of a homozygous green pea pod?

A. 25%
B. 50%
C. 75%
D. 100%

The correct answer is **B.** There is a 2 out of 4, or 50%, chance of a homozygous green pea pod.

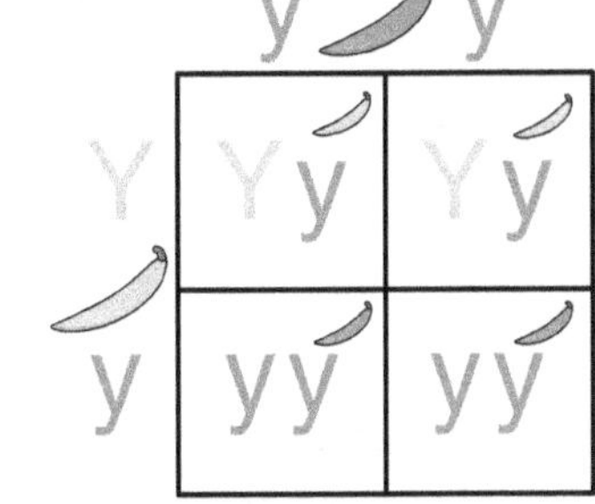

Chromosomes

A **gene** is a segment of DNA, deoxyribonucleic acid, which transmits information from parent to offspring. A single molecule of DNA has thousands of genes. A **chromosome** is a rod-shaped structure that forms when a single DNA molecule and its associated proteins coil tightly before cell division.

Chromosomes have two components:

- **Chromatids:** two copies of each chromosome
- **Centromeres:** protein discs that attach the chromatids together

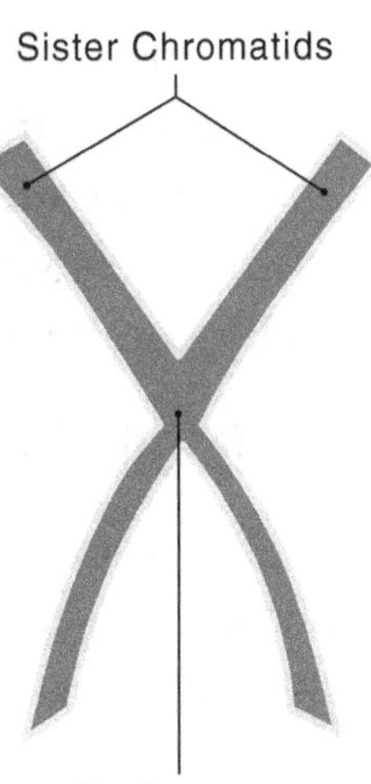

Human cells have 23 sets of different chromosomes. The two copies of each chromosome are called **homologous** chromosomes, or homologues. An offspring receives one homologue from each parent. When a cell contains two homologues of each chromosome, it is termed **diploid (2n)**. A **haploid (n)** cell contains only one homologue of each chromosome. The only haploid cells humans are the sperm and eggs cells known as **gametes**.

Example

What is the difference between a diploid cell and a haploid cell?

A. A haploid cell is only found in skin cells.
B. A diploid cell is only found in heart cells.
C. A diploid cell has a full number of chromosomes, and a haploid cell does not.
D. A haploid cell has a full number of chromosomes, and a diploid cell does not.

The correct answer is **C.** Diploid cells have a full number of chromosomes, and haploid cells have half the number of chromosomes.

Deoxyribonucleic Acid

The **DNA molecule** is a long, thin molecule made of subunits called **nucleotides** that are linked together in a **nucleic acid** chain. Each nucleotide is constructed of three parts: a **phosphate group**, **five-carbon sugar**, and **nitrogen base**.

The four nitrogenous bases are

- adenine (A);
- guanine (G);
- thymine (T); and
- cytosine (C).

Adenine and guanine belong to a class of large, organic molecules called **purines**. Thymine and cytosine are **pyrimidines**, which have a single ring of carbon and nitrogen atoms. Base pairs are formed as adenine pairs with thymine and guanine pairs with cytosine. These are the only possible combinations.

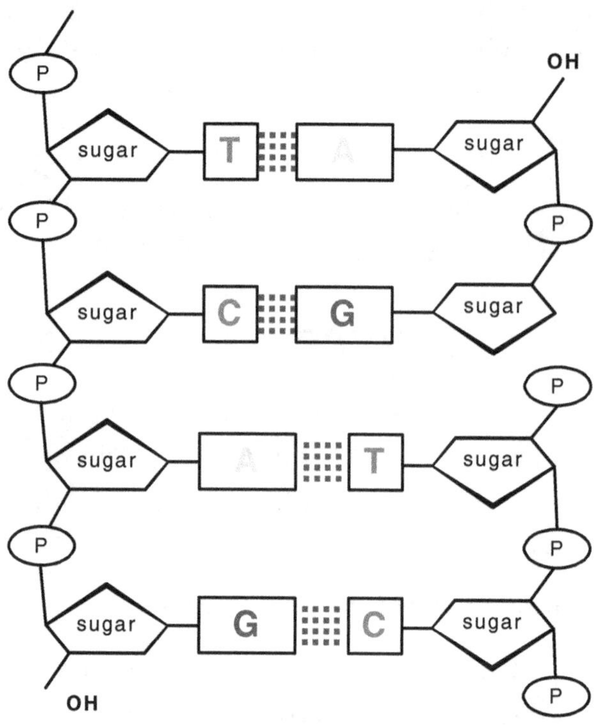

DNA Replication

The process of synthesizing a new strand of DNA is called **replication**. A DNA molecule replicates by separating into two strands, building a complementary strand, and twisting to form a double helix.

Transcription

The first step in using DNA to direct the making of a protein is **transcription**, the process that "rewrites" the information in a gene in DNA into a molecule of messenger RNA. Transcription manufactures three types of RNA:

- Messenger RNA (mRNA)
- Transfer RNA (tRNA)
- Ribosomal RNA (rRNA)

Messenger RNA is an RNA copy of a gene used as a blueprint for a protein. In eukaryotes, transcription does not produce mRNA directly; it produces a pre-mRNA molecule. **Transfer RNA** translates mRNA sequences into amino acid sequences. **Ribosomal RNA** plays a structural role in ribosomes.

Transcription proceeds at a rate of about 60 nucleotides per second until the **RNA polymerase** (an enzyme) reaches a **stop codon** on the DNA called a **terminator** and releases the RNA molecule.

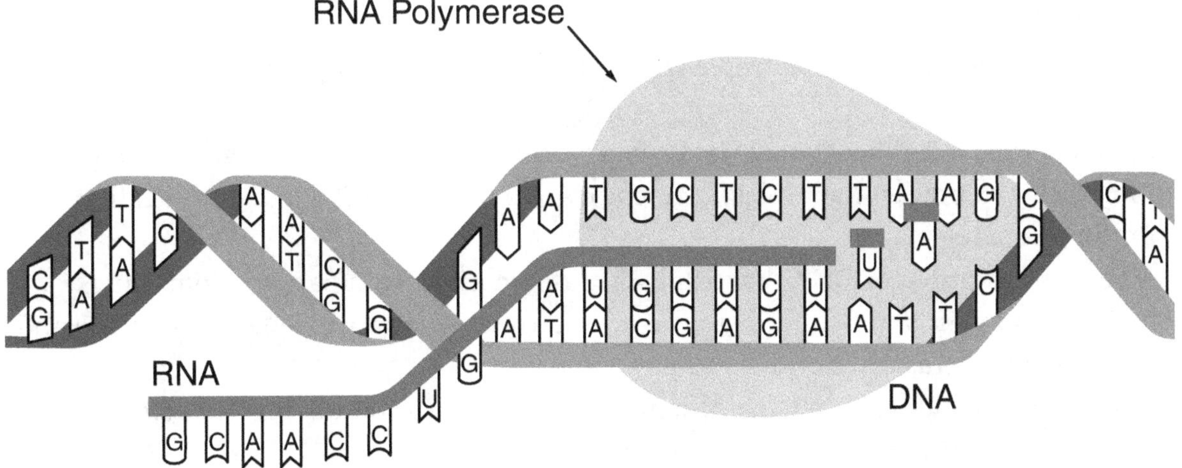

Translation

The components necessary for **translation** are located in the cytoplasm. Translation is the making of proteins by mRNA binding to a ribosome with the start codon that initiates the production of amino acids. A **peptide bond** forms and connects the amino acids together. The sequence of amino acids determines the protein's structure, which determines its function.

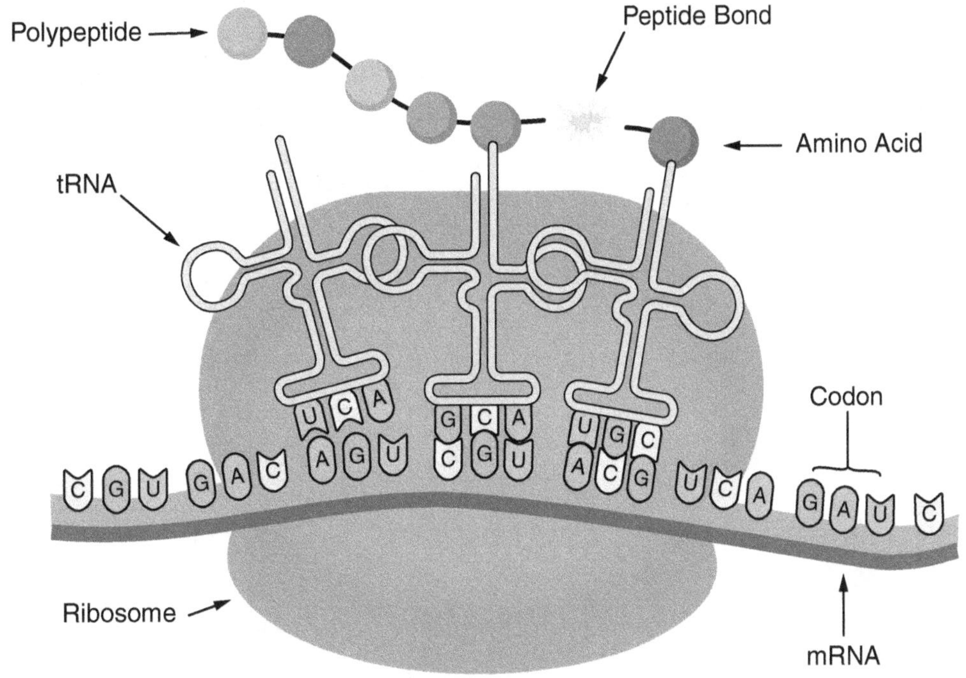

Example

Which type of RNA acts as an interpreter molecule?

A. mRNA B. pre-mRNA C. rRNA D. tRNA

The correct answer is **D.** Transfer RNA (tRNA) acts as an interpreter molecule, translating mRNA sequences into amino acid sequences.

Let's Review!

- Gregor Mendel developed a simple set of rules that accurately predicts patterns of heredity.
- Mendel proposed a theory that has become the foundation of the science of genetics.
- Biologists can predict the probable outcomes of a cross by using a diagram called a Punnett square.
- A gene is a segment of DNA that transmits information from parent to offspring
- A chromosome is a rod-shaped structure that forms when a single DNA molecule and its associated proteins coil tightly before cell division.
- Deoxyribonucleic acid is a long, thin molecule made of subunits called nucleotides that are linked together in a nucleic acid chain.
- Replication is the process of synthesizing a new strand of DNA.
- Transcription is the first step in using DNA to direct the making of a protein.
- Translation is the process of making proteins.

Chapter 14 Life and Physical Sciences Practice Quiz

1. **Which of the following helps differentiate a non-living thing from a living thing?**

   A. Energy processing
   B. Behavior in nature
   C. Occurrence in nature
   D. Description of habitat

2. **What standard is used to make comparisons in experiments?**

   A. Sample size
   B. Control group
   C. Dependent variable
   D. Independent variable

3. **What is the most basic unit of structure in living things?**

   A. Cell
   B. Organelle
   C. Oxygen
   D. Pigment

4. **A researcher discovers a cell that is less than 0.5 millimeters in diameter. This cell has pili surrounding its cell wall. What does the researcher classify this cell as?**

   A. Autotroph
   B. Eukaryote
   C. Heterotroph
   D. Prokaryote

5. **A chemist decides to study reactions occurring in a cell's cytoplasm. Which of the following reactions does she observe?**

   A. Mitosis
   B. Cell cycle
   C. Glycolysis
   D. Carbon cycle

6. **Which process involves crossing over?**

   A. Mitosis
   B. Meiosis
   C. Calvin cycle
   D. Cell respiration

7. **If an organism has a total of 12 chromosomes, 12 is the ______ number of chromosomes.**

   A. diploid
   B. equivalent
   C. haploid
   D. neutral

8. **The sequence of amino acids in a gene determines**

   A. the primary structure of a codon.
   B. the primary structure of a protein.
   C. the primary structure of a nucleotide.
   D. the primary structure of a nucleic acid.

Chapter 14 Life and Physical Sciences Practice Quiz – Answer Key

1. A. There are several features that scientists use to identify living things. These features include: how living things process energy, growth and development, reproduction, and homeostasis. **See Lesson: An Introduction to Biology.**

2. B. A control group is a factor that does not change during an experiment. Due to this, it is used as a standard for comparison with variables that do change such as a dependent variable. **See Lesson: An Introduction to Biology.**

3. A. The most basic unit and building block of all living things is the cell. **See Lesson: Cell Structure, Function, and Type.**

4. D. Common characteristics of prokaryotic cells are that they are small and have hair-like structures called pili that surround their cell wall. **See Lesson: Cell Structure, Function, and Type.**

5. C. The first step of cellular respiration is glycolysis. This process happens in the cell's cytoplasm, where glucose is broken down to pyruvate, yielding two molecules of ATP. **See Lesson: Cellular Reproduction, Cellular Respiration, and Photosynthesis.**

6. B. Meiosis is a form of cell division that occurs when DNA from homologous chromosomes is exchanged. This exchange, or crossing over, increases genetic diversity in a population. **See Lesson: Cellular Reproduction, Cellular Respiration, and Photosynthesis.**

7. A. Diploid refers to the full number of chromosomes. **See Lesson: Genetics and DNA.**

8. B. The sequence of amino acids in a gene determines the primary structure of a protein. **See Lesson: Genetics and DNA.**

CHAPTER 15 CHEMISTRY

STATES OF MATTER

This lesson explains the differences between solids, liquids, gases, and plasmas. It also describes how a sample can change from one state of matter to another.

States of Matter

On Earth, substances are found in four states of matter: solid, liquid, gas, and plasma. Many properties of these states of matter are familiar. For example, solids are rigid and hard, liquids can flow inside their containers, and gases can spread throughout an entire room. But what happens at the molecular level may not be as familiar. The differences among them can be explained by the amount of energy that the particles have and the strength of the cohesive forces that hold the particles together. **Cohesion** is the tendency of particles of the same kind to stick to each other and is an important property to consider when looking at states of matter. The motion and density of particles in a substance and the tendency of a substance to take the shape and volume of its container differentiate states of matter.

Solids have the lowest energy. The particles are packed close together, and their structure is relatively rigid. Strong cohesive forces prevent particles from moving very far or very fast. Therefore, both the shape and volume of a solid are fixed.

> **DID YOU KNOW?**
> While particles are generally more tightly packed in solids than in other states, water is an exception. When liquid water freezes, it expands. The molecules are pushed apart as strong intermolecular forces, known as hydrogen bonds, allow the particles to form crystals. This property of water is important in many processes on Earth.

In **liquids**, particles have more energy than in solids and can overcome the cohesive forces to some degree. Since particles can move more freely, they flow and take the shape of their container. However, cohesive forces are strong enough to somewhat restrict the movement of particles. While the shape of the liquid is not fixed, the volume is.

Gases have more energy than solids or liquids. In a gas, the cohesive forces are very weak because the particles move very quickly. Gas particles move more freely than liquids, which means that gas particles can not only take the shape of the container, but also spread to occupy the entire volume of the container.

CONNECTIONS

Gases and liquids are considered fluids because of their ability to "flow" and take the shape of their containers.

In **plasma**, the particles have so much energy that the electrons separate from their nuclei. The result is a substance composed of moving positively and negatively charged particles. Although plasmas are less common in everyday life than the other states of matter, there are a few familiar examples. First, the hottest parts of the sun are made of plasma because of the high temperature (up to 15,000,000 K). Also, neon signs glow when plasma is produced by passing an electric current through a gas.

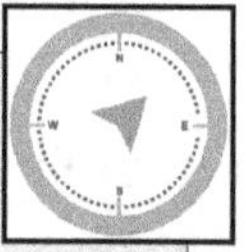

DID YOU KNOW?

Not all neon signs contain neon. Other noble gases (helium, argon, and xenon) can be used to produce different colors of light.

Example

In which state of matter are particles moving slowest?

A. Solid B. Liquid C. Gas D. Plasma

The correct answer is **A.** Because solid particles have less energy than particles in other states of matter, they have the most restricted movement.

Phase Changes

Whenever a substance transforms from one state of matter to another, it undergoes a phase change. These processes are physical changes because the chemical composition of the substance remains the same; only its appearance is different. The six most common phase changes are summarized in the diagram and chart below. Note that the states of matter are arranged in order of increasing energy from left to right.

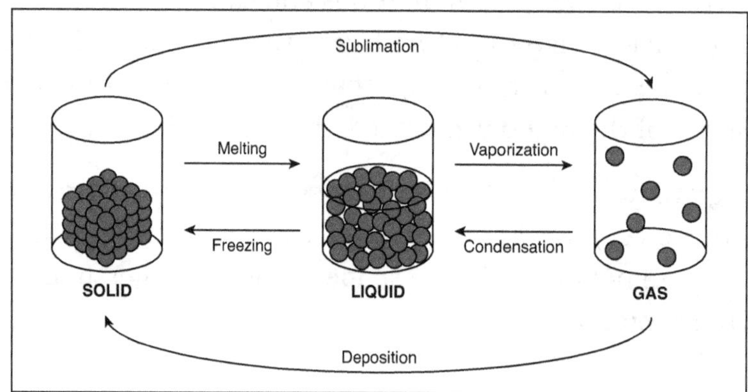

Phase Change	Name	Absorb or Release Energy
solid to liquid	melting	absorb
liquid to gas	vaporization	absorb
solid to gas	sublimation	absorb
liquid to solid	freezing	release
gas to liquid	condensation	release
gas to solid	deposition	release

All phase changes require the system to either absorb or release energy. Any phase change that moves to the right in the diagram above requires energy to be added to the system because the substance has more energy at the end of the phase change. The phase changes are **melting**, **vaporization (boiling)**, and **sublimation**. When energy is added, particles move faster and can break away from each other more easily as they move to a state of matter with a higher amount of energy. This is most commonly done by heating the substance.

Any phase change that moves to the left in the diagram requires energy to be removed from the system because the substance has less energy at the end of the phase change. These phase changes are **freezing**, **condensation**, and **deposition**. When the particles release energy, they move more slowly. The cohesive forces bring these particles closer together as they move to a state of matter with a lower amount of energy. This is most commonly done by cooling the substance.

The temperatures at which phase changes occur depends the strength of the cohesive forces between particles. For substances like metals that have high melting and boiling points, it takes a relatively large amount of energy to overcome the intermolecular forces enough to change states of matter. Similarly, substances with low melting and boiling points, like the gases that make up Earth's atmosphere, do not require as much energy to overcome their intermolecular forces.

Example

Which of the following phase changes requires a substance to release energy?

A. Boiling B. Condensation C. Melting D. Sublimation

The correct answer is **B.** During condensation, a gas turns to a liquid. For this to occur, high-energy particles in the gas must release some energy for the cohesive forces to bring the particles closer together.

Heating and Cooling Curves

When studying phase changes, one can examine the heating or cooling curve of a substance. Heating and cooling curves are plots of temperature versus time that occur as energy is added to or removed from the system at a constant rate.

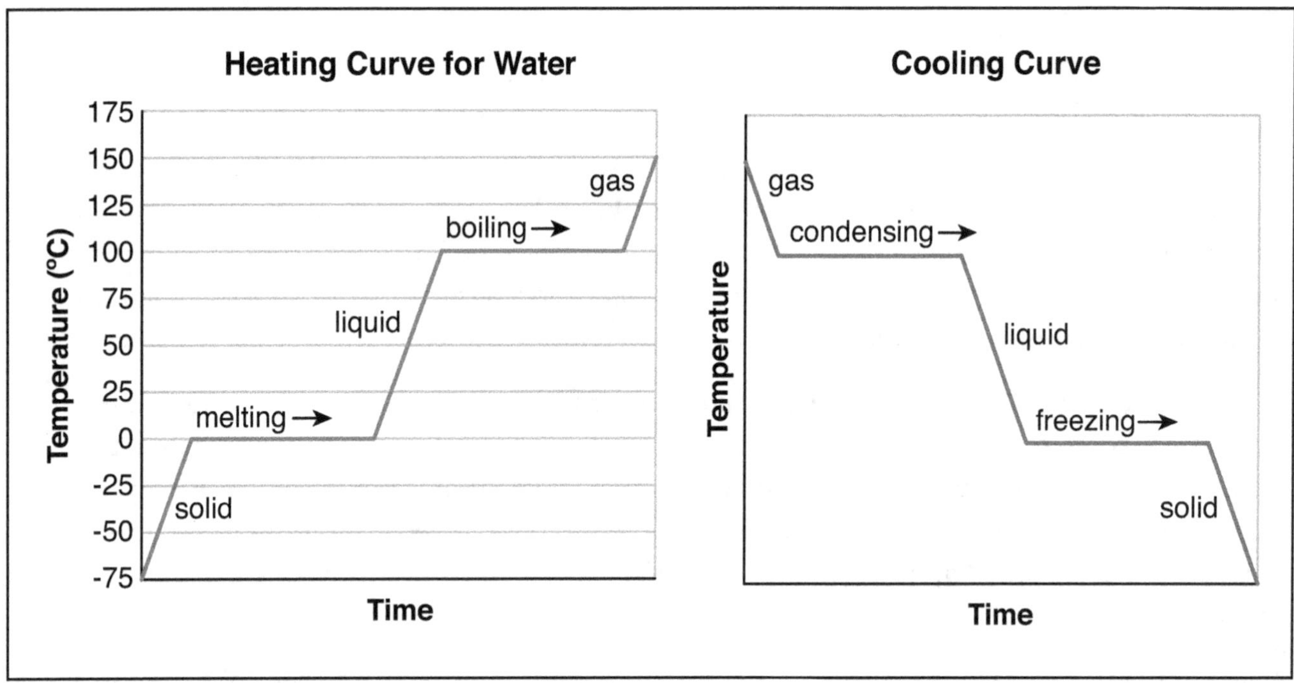

The heating curve for water is shown above. Notice that at the beginning of the experiment, the substance is a solid. As heat is added, the temperature of the solid increases until it reaches its melting point, 0°C. The temperature remains constant at the melting point until the entire sample has changed to a liquid. Note that even though heat is still being added, the temperature is not increasing. This is because the added energy is used to disrupt the cohesive forces in the solid, allowing the particles to move more freely as the substance changes to a liquid.

Once the sample is completely melted, the temperature increases again. It increases until the boiling point, 100°C, is reached. Heat is still being added, but the temperature remains constant as the substance boils. This time, the added energy is being used to break the intermolecular bonds in the liquid as the particles transform into a gas and move farther away from each other. It is not until the phase change is complete and the sample is entirely gas that the temperature starts increasing again.

KEEP IN MIND

The temperature of a substance is a measure of the kinetic energy of the particles that make up a substance. In other words, temperature is related to how fast the particles are moving.

A cooling curve has the opposite shape of a heating curve, as seen in the graph above. In these experiments, the sample starts as a high-temperature gas. As heat is removed, the temperature of the gas decreases to its boiling point. At this point, the temperature remains constant until the entire sample is liquid. The liquid then cools to a lower temperature until it reaches the freezing point. The temperature remains constant as the substance freezes, and once it is completely solid, the temperature decreases again.

KEY POINT!

As a substance undergoes a phase change, its temperature remains constant. The only time a substance experiences an increase or decrease in temperature is when it is entirely in one state of matter.

Example

If a sample of water is losing energy but its temperature is not changing, what may be happening?

A. Freezing B. Melting C. Sublimation D. Vaporization

The correct answer is **A.** When a substance is freezing, the liquid particles lose enough energy to become a solid. The temperature will not change until the phase change is complete.

Let's Review!

- Solids, liquids, gases, and plasmas differ from one another in the amount of energy that the particles have and the strength of the cohesive forces that hold the particles together.
- A substance can undergo a phase change if it either absorbs or releases enough energy.
- Heating and cooling curves show the temperature of a substance as heat is consistently added or removed.
- As a substance changes states, its temperature remains constant. Any energy that is absorbed or released is used to change the way in which the particles interact with one another.

Properties of Matter

This lesson introduces the properties of matter, which are fundamental to the understanding of chemistry.

Matter and Its Properties

Aluminum, clothing, water, air, and glass are all different kinds of matter. **Matter** is anything that takes up space and has mass. A golf ball contains more matter than a table-tennis ball. The golf ball has more mass. The amount of matter that an object contains is its **mass**.

Table sugar is 100 percent sugar. Table sugar (sucrose) is an example of a substance. A **substance** is matter that has a uniform and definite composition. Lemonade is not a substance because not all pitchers of lemonade are identical. Different pitchers of lemonade may have different amounts of sugar, lemon juice, or water and may taste different.

All crystals of sucrose taste sweet and dissolve completely in water. All samples of a substance have identical physical properties. A **physical property** is a quality or condition of a substance that can be observed or measured without changing the substance's composition. Some physical properties of matter are color, solubility, mass, odor, hardness, density, and boiling point.

Just as every substance has physical properties, every substance has chemical properties. For example, when iron is exposed to water and oxygen, it corrodes and produces a new substance called iron (III) oxide (rust). The chemical properties of a substance are its ability to undergo chemical reactions and to form new substances. Rusting is a chemical property of iron. **Chemical properties** are observed only when a substance undergoes a change in composition, which is a chemical change.

Physical vs. Chemical Properties

Physical Properties	Chemical Properties
• Color • Shape • Size • Density • Amount • Volume	• Flammability • Rusting • Burning • Corrosion • Reactivity

Intensive and Extensive Properties

Intensive properties do not depend on the amount of matter that is present. Intensive properties do not change according to the conditions. They are used to identify samples because their characteristics do not depend on the size of the sample. In contrast, **extensive** properties do depend on the amount of a sample that is present. A good example of the difference between the two types of properties is that mass and volume are extensive properties, but their ratio (density) is an intensive property. Notice that mass and volume deal with amounts, whereas density is a physical property.

Intensive Properties
versus
Extensive Properties

Intensive Properties	Extensive Properties
Intensive properties are physical properties that do not depend on the amount of matter	Extensive properties are physical properties that depend on the amount of matter
Independant of the amount of matter	Depend of the amount of matter
Some examples include melting point, boiling point, density, etc.	Some examples include volume, mass, energy, etc.

Example

Which of the following explains the difference between chemical and physical properties?

A. Physical properties can easily change, while chemical properties are constant.

B. Chemical properties always involve a source of heat, and physical properties always involve light.

C. Chemical properties involve a change in the chemical composition of a substance, while physical properties can easily be observed.

D. Physical properties involve a change in the chemical composition of a substance, while chemical properties can easily be observed.

The correct answer is **C**. A physical property is a quality or condition of a substance that can be observed or measured without changing the substance's composition, while a chemical property is one where a change in chemical composition has occurred.

Phase Changes

There are six phase changes: condensation, evaporation, freezing, melting, sublimation, and deposition.

Condensation is the change of a gas or vapor to a liquid. A change in the pressure and the temperature of a substance causes this change. The condensation point is the same as the boiling point of a substance. It is most noticeable when there is a large temperature difference between an object and the atmosphere. Condensation is also the opposite of evaporation.

Evaporation is the change of a liquid to a gas on the surface of a substance. This is not to be confused with boiling, which is a phase transition of an entire substance from a liquid to a gas. The evaporation point is the same as the freezing point of a substance. As the temperature increases, the rate of evaporation also increases. Evaporation depends not only on the temperature, but also on the amount of substance available.

Freezing is the change of a liquid to a solid. It occurs when the temperature drops below the freezing point. The amount of heat that has been removed from the substance allows the particles of the substance to draw closer together, and the material changes from a liquid to a solid. It is the opposite of melting.

Melting is the change of a solid into a liquid. For melting to occur, enough heat must be added to the substance. When this is done, the molecules move around more, and the particles are unable to hold together as tightly as they can in a solid. They break apart, and the solid becomes a liquid.

Sublimation is a solid changing into a gas. As a material sublimates, it does not pass through the liquid state. An example of sublimation is carbon dioxide, a gas, changing into dry ice, a solid. It is the reverse of deposition.

Deposition is a gas changing into a solid without going through the liquid phase. It is an uncommon phase change. An example is when it is extremely cold outside and the cold air comes in contact with a window. Ice will form on the window without going through the liquid state.

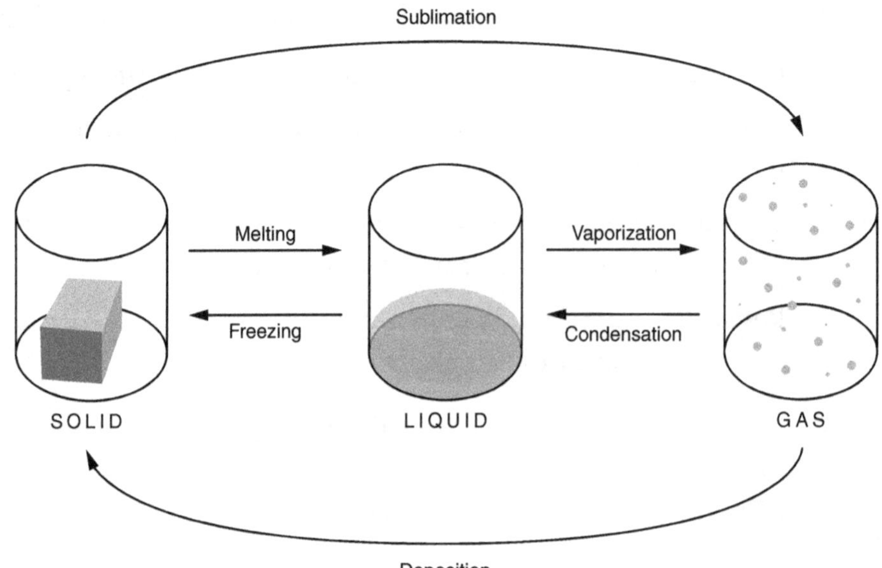

Example

Which of the six types of phase changes is the opposite of sublimation?

A. Condensation B. Deposition C. Evaporation D. Freezing

The correct answer is **B.** Sublimation is the changing of a solid to a gas, and deposition is the changing of a gas to a solid.

Adhesiveness and Cohesiveness

Because of polarity, water is attracted to water, a property called **cohesion**. The typical water molecule has a polar configuration, as seen below.

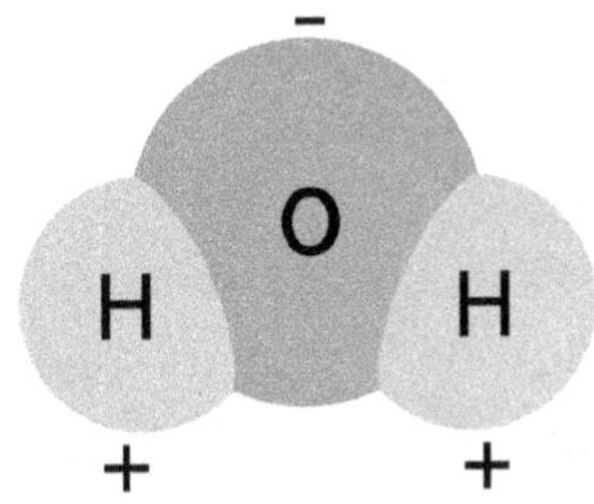

Notice that there is a negative end and a positive end. This means it is a polar molecule. In a **polar molecule**, one end of the molecule is slightly negative and one end is slightly positive.

Inside a plant, water has to travel up, against gravity, to reach all the leaves. Because the water molecules are attracted to each other, or demonstrate **cohesion**, they also adhere to the sides of the xylem vessels that transport water up to where it is needed in the plant. This is possible because of **adhesion**. Adhesion is water's ability to be attracted to other substances.

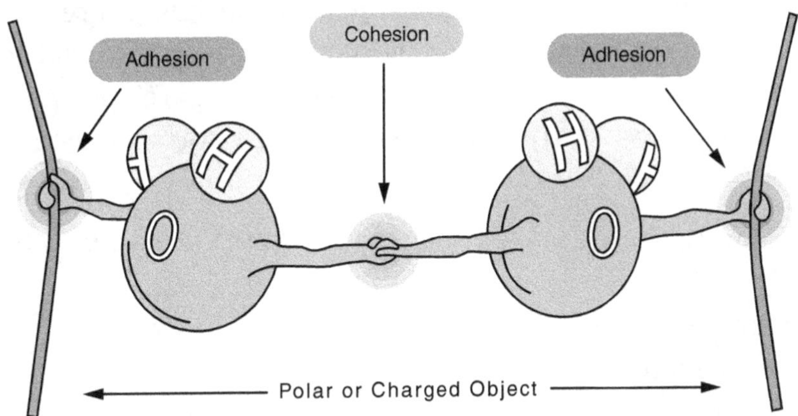

Example

What property allows water to flow against the force of gravity?

A. Adhesion B. Cohesion C. Polarity D. Xylem

The correct answer is **A.** Adhesion is water's ability to be attracted to other substances. Because of adhesion, water is able to move upward.

Diffusion and Osmosis

When a bottle of perfume is opened, perfume molecules diffuse throughout a room. **Diffusion** is the tendency of molecules and ions to move toward areas of lower concentrations until the concentration is uniform throughout the room (that is, it reaches equilibrium). This random movement of individual particles has an important consequence. Because the movement is random, a particle is more likely to move from an area where there are a lot of molecules (area of high concentration) to an area where there are fewer molecules (an area of lower concentration). In the human lungs, oxygen diffuses into the bloodstream because there is a higher concentration of oxygen molecules in the lungs' air sacs than there is in the blood.

Solute and solvent particles tend to diffuse from areas where their concentration is high to areas where their concentration is lower. Imagine that a membrane separates two regions of liquid. As long as solute particles and solvent (water) molecules can pass freely through the membrane, diffusion will equalize the amount of solute and solvent on the two sides. The sides will reach equilibrium.

But what if a polar solute that cannot pass through the membrane is added to one side? This situation is common in cells. An amino acid cannot cross a lipid bilayer, and neither can an ion or a sugar molecule. Unable to cross the membrane, the polar solute particles form hydrogen bonds with the water molecules surrounding them. These "bound" water molecules are no longer free to diffuse through the membrane. The polar solute has reduced the number of free water molecules on that side of the membrane. This means the opposite side of the membrane (without solute) has more free water molecules than the side with the polar solute. As a result, water molecules move by diffusion from the side without the polar solute to the side with the polar solute.

Eventually, the concentration of free water molecules will equalize on the sides of the membrane. At this point, however, there are more water molecules (bound and unbound) on the side of the membrane with the polar solute. Net water movement through a membrane in response to the concentration of a solute is called **osmosis**. Stated another way, osmosis is the diffusion of water molecules through a membrane in the direction of higher solute concentration.

OSMOSIS and DIFFUSION

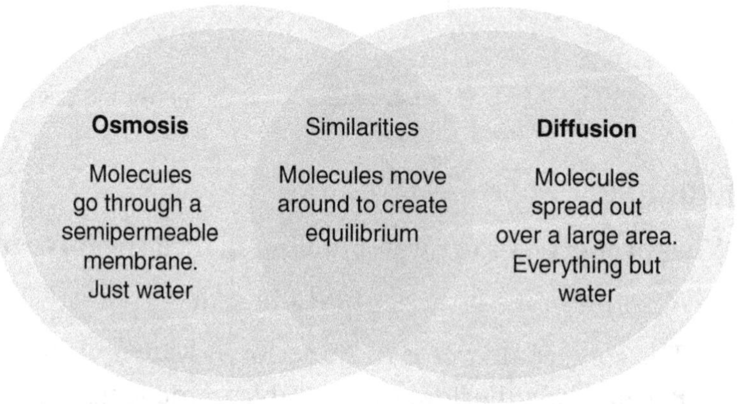

Osmosis
Molecules go through a semipermeable membrane. Just water

Similarities
Molecules move around to create equilibrium

Diffusion
Molecules spread out over a large area. Everything but water

Example

What is the goal of osmosis?

A. The water will equalize on both side of the semipermeable membrane.

B. The concentration of solutes will diffuse through the semipermeable membrane.

C. The concentration of free water molecules will equalize on both sides of the membrane

D. The solute particles will flow from an area of high concentration to an area of lower concentration.

The correct answer is **C.** As a result of osmosis, the concentration of free water molecules will equalize on both sides of the membrane.

Let's Review!

- Matter is anything that takes up space and has mass.
- The difference between physical and chemical properties is that chemical properties involve a change in a substance's chemical composition and physical properties do not.
- The difference between extensive and intensive properties is based on whether the properties depend on the amount of substance that is present.
- Cohesiveness is the attraction of water to itself, and adhesiveness is the attraction of water to other substances.
- Osmosis is the diffusion of water and the movement of molecules from an area of high concentration to an area of lower concentration.

Chemical Bonds

This lesson introduces bonding and explains the three ways in which atoms can become stable. The rest of the lesson examines different types of bonds in more detail.

Introduction to Bonding

Chemical elements found in the periodic table have different levels of reactivity. The number of **valence electrons** in an atom is the most important factor in determining how an element will react. Valence electrons, which are found in an atom's outermost energy level, are involved in forming chemical bonds. The periodic table below shows the Bohr models of select elements. The valence electrons appear in red.

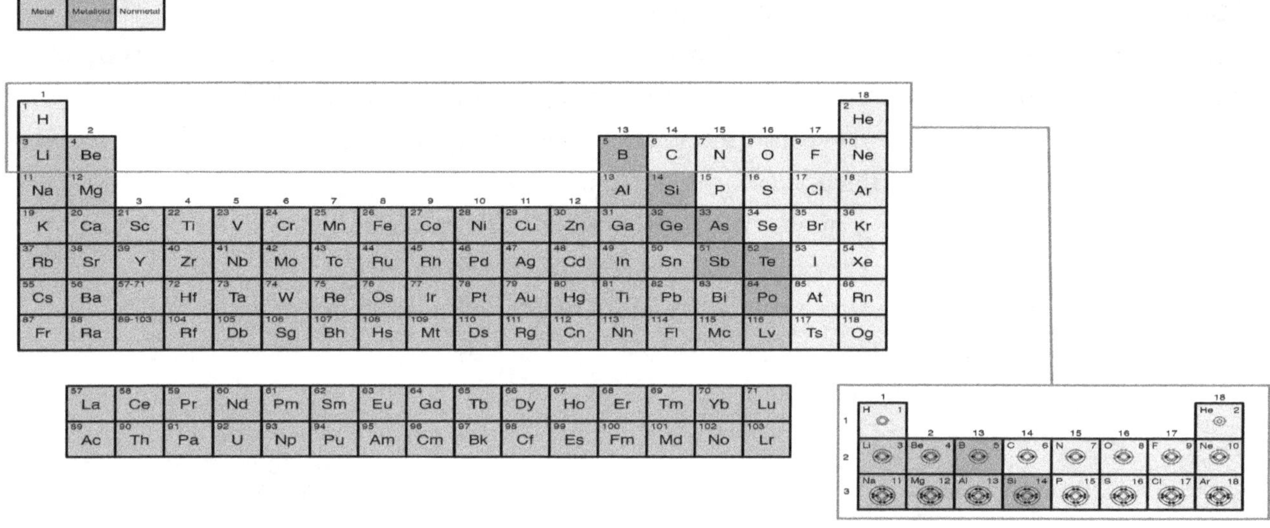

The **octet rule** states that atoms will lose, gain, or share electrons to obtain a stable electron configuration of eight valence electrons. In other words, if an atom needs to become stable, it will react with another atom, which can result in the formation of a chemical compound. Note that the elements in group 18, the noble gases, have eight valence electrons. Helium is an exception and is stable with two valence electrons. Because they have a stable electron configuration, the noble gases do not need to react with other elements to become stable. As a result, they are found in nature as single elements rather than in compounds.

KEY POINT!

The goal of forming chemical bonds is to become stable by having eight electrons in the outer shell. This is easy to remember because it is described in the *octet* rule. The prefix *octa-* means "eight," and it can be seen in other words, such as *octopus* and *octagon*.

Elements in other groups will react to become stable in predictable ways, depending on how many valence electrons they have. In the periodic table above, elements are classified as metals, nonmetals, or metalloids. Compared to other elements, metals have fewer valence electrons and tend to lose them to become stable. Notice that removing the red valence electrons from the outermost energy level exposes another energy level. This becomes the valence shell, and the atom is stable because it has eight valence electrons.

Nonmetals and metalloids have a relatively high number of valence electrons. Except for the noble gasses, these elements tend to gain or share electrons to become stable.

Ionic compounds are formed when electrons are transferred from a metal (which loses one or more electrons) to a nonmetal (which gains one or more electrons). **Covalent compounds** are formed when two nonmetals or metalloids share electrons.

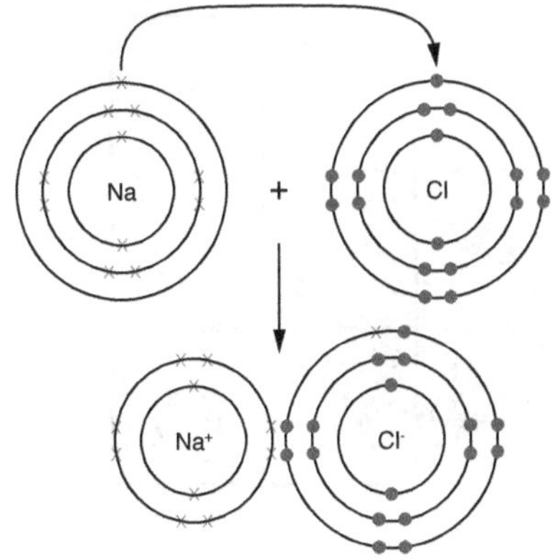

Ionic Bond

TEST TIP

A quick way to determine if atoms are held together by ionic or covalent bonds is to examine the types of elements involved. If a metal and a nonmetal bond, an ionic bond forms. If two nonmetals or metalloids bond, a covalent bond forms.

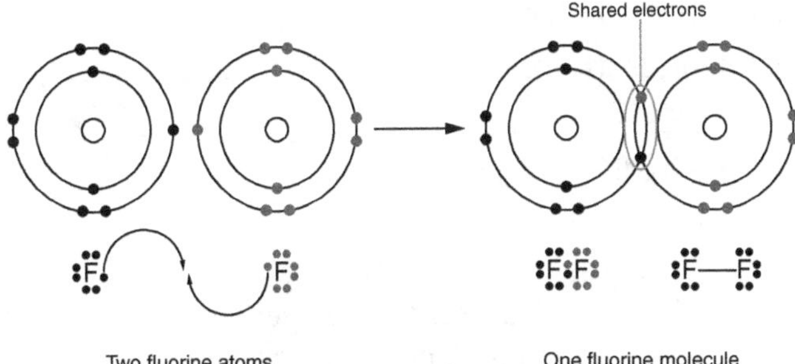

Two fluorine atoms

One fluorine molecule

Covalent Bond

Example

In the compound sodium bromide (NaBr), electrons are __________. In the compound carbon tetrabromide (CBr_4), electrons are __________.

A. shared, shared

B. shared, transferred

C. transferred, shared

D. transferred, transferred

The correct answer is **C**. Electrons are transferred when an ionic compound like sodium bromide forms. Electrons are shared when a covalent compound like carbon tetrabromide forms.

Ion Formation

If an atom has an equal number of positively charged protons and negatively charged electrons, it is neutral and has no **net charge.** When electrons are transferred, atoms end up with either more protons than electrons or more electrons than protons. The atoms are considered **ions** because they have a net positive or negative charge.

> **KEEP IN MIND**
> Protons are positively charged subatomic particles and can be represented by the symbol *p+*. Electrons are negatively charged subatomic particles and can be represented by the symbol *e-*.

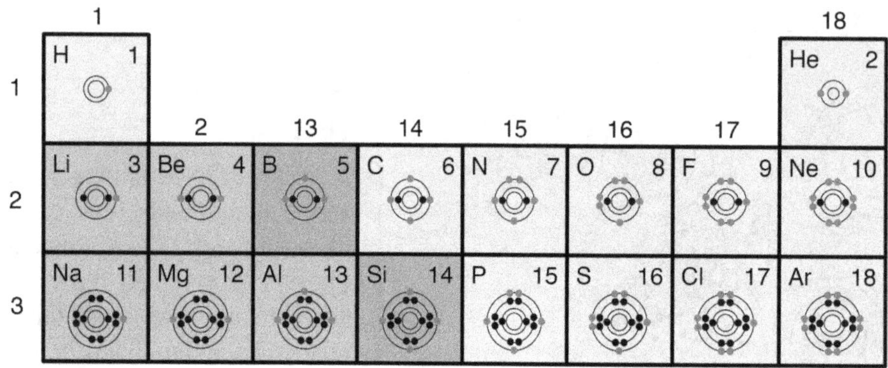

When a metal such as sodium reacts to become stable, it loses its valence electrons. At first, it is a neutral atom with 11 protons and 11 electrons. When it loses an electron, the number of protons does not change, and the atom has 11 protons and 10 electrons. Because there is one more positively charged proton, a **cation** forms. A cation is an ion with a net positive charge.

When a nonmetal such as chlorine reacts to become stable, it gains a valence electron. At first, it is a neutral atom with 17 protons and 17 electrons. When it gains an electron, the number of protons does not change, and the atom has 17 protons and 18 electrons. Because there is one more negatively charged electron, an **anion** forms. An anion is an ion with a net negative charge.

> **BE CAREFUL!**
> When an atom *gains* electrons, it has a net *negative* charge because it gains negatively charged particles. When an atom *loses* electrons, it has a net *positive* charge. After the loss, there are more protons than electrons, which means there are more positively charged particles.

The way in which an element reacts can be predicted based on that element's position in the periodic table. The table below summarizes the reactivity of elements according to their group number. Elements in each group have a specific number of valence electrons, which dictates what the atoms need to do to obtain a valence shell with eight electrons. Some will lose electrons, and others will gain electrons. This, along with the number of electrons that must be transferred, determines the charge of the stable ion that forms.

Group	1	2	13	14	15	16	17	18
Valence *e*-	1	2	3	4	5	6	7	8
Lose/Gain *e*-	Lose 1	Lose 2	Lose 3	Lose/Gain 4	Gain 3	Gain 2	Gain 1	N/A
Charge	+1	+2	+3	+/-4	-3	-2	-1	N/A

Example

What will strontium do to form a stable ion with a +2 charge?

A. Gain two protons

B. Lose two protons

C. Gain two electrons

D. Lose two electrons

The correct answer is **D**. Atoms gain or lose electrons, not protons, to form ions. Like other metals in group 2, strontium will lose its two valence electrons to become stable.

Ionic Bonding

An ionic compound is composed of a cation and an anion. An ionic bond is formed from the cation's attraction to the oppositely charged anion. The figure at the right shows how transferring an electron from sodium to chlorine results in the formation of an ionic bond.

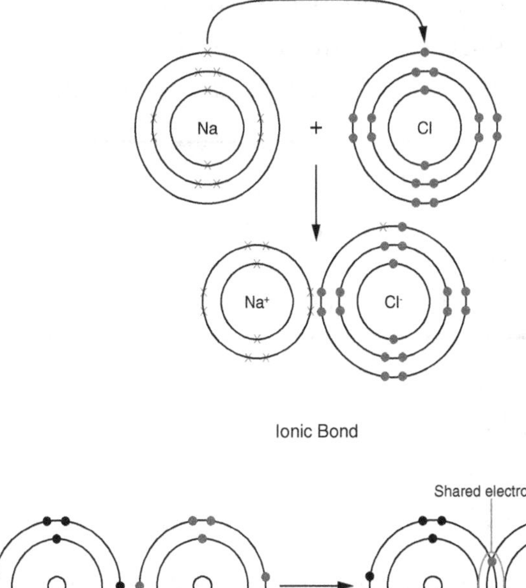

Ionic Bond

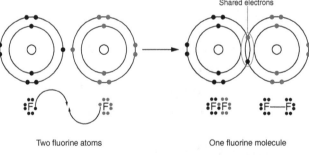

Two fluorine atoms

One fluorine molecule

Covalent Bond

Notice that the charges on sodium (Na^+) and chlorine (Cl^-) ions have the same magnitude (they both have a value of 1). Therefore, the charge of one sodium ion balances the charge of one chlorine ion. When an ionic compound is formed from ions that have equal but opposite charges, the elements will be present in a 1:1 ratio. Examples are shown in the table below.

Compound Name	Cation	Anion	Compound Formula
Potassium fluoride	K^+	F^-	KF
Magnesium oxide	Mg^{2+}	O^{2-}	MgO
Aluminum nitride	Al^{3+}	N^{3-}	AlN

In some cases, atoms need to lose or gain two, three, or, in rare cases, four electrons to become stable. For example, magnesium must give up two electrons to become stable. Because chlorine only needs one electron, magnesium can give an electron to two different chlorine atoms. Then, one magnesium cation with a +2 charge (Mg^{2+}) bonds with two chloride anions (Cl^{-}) to form magnesium chloride, ($MgCl_2$). The subscript 2 indicates that there are two chloride ions in this compound.

Compound Name	Cation	Anion	Compound Formula
Calcium bromide	Ca^{2+}	Br^{-}	$CaBr_2$
Aluminum fluoride	Al^{3+}	F^{-}	AlF_3
Rubidium oxide	Rb^{+}	O^{2-}	Rb_2O
Sodium phosphide	Na^{+}	P^{3-}	Na_3P
Aluminum oxide	Al^{3+}	O^{2-}	Al_2O_3
Calcium phosphide	Ca^{2+}	P^{3-}	Ca_3P_2

Similarly, when oxygen and lithium react, the oxygen atom receives an electron from each of two lithium atoms. This transfer results in two lithium cations (Li^{+}) and an oxygen anion (O^{2-}). They attract each other to form the compound lithium oxide with a formula of Li_2O. Other examples are shown in the table below. Notice that in all ionic compounds, the total positive charge balances out the total negative charge, resulting in a neutral compound.

KEY POINT!

Regardless of how many electrons are transferred, ionic compounds have net charges of zero. They are all neutral because the positive cations attract as many anions as they need to balance their charges, and vice versa.

Example

What is the formula for the compound formed between calcium and oxygen?

A. CaO
B. CaO_2
C. Ca_2O
D. Ca_3O_2

The correct answer is **A.** Calcium is in group 2 and will lose its two valence electrons to become stable. Oxygen is in group 16 and, because it has six valence electrons, will gain two electrons to complete its octet. Therefore, one calcium ion requires one oxide ion to balance its charge to form a neutral ionic compound.

Covalent Bonding

When a nonmetal atom reacts with a nonmetal or metalloid, the atoms share electrons to obtain eight valence electrons each. An example can be seen in the model below. Both the Bohr models and the electron dot structures of the fluorine atoms show their seven valence electrons. After each atom shares an electron with the other, shown by the arrows, a covalent bond forms. In the newly formed fluorine molecule, both fluorine atoms have the stable electron configuration of eight valence electrons. The shared electrons can be represented by two dots or by a line in between the fluorine atoms.

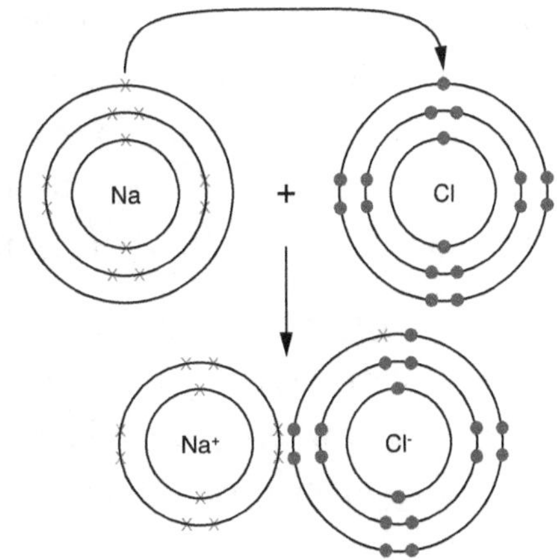

Ionic Bond

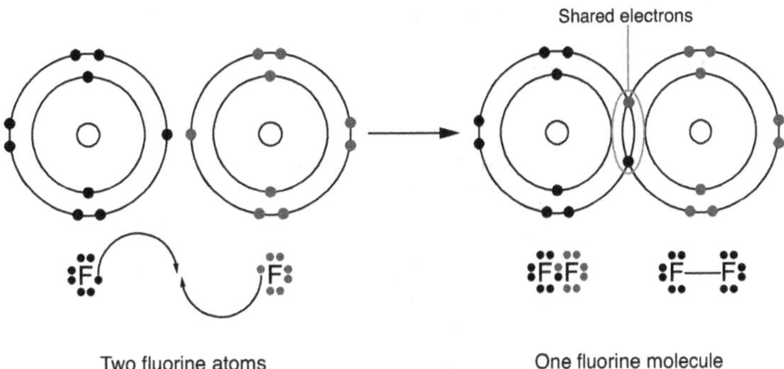

Two fluorine atoms

One fluorine molecule

Covalent Bond

Covalent compounds can be modeled in **Lewis structures**. Lewis structures for methane, ammonia, and water are shown below. In a Lewis structure, covalent bonds, also called shared electrons, are represented by lines between two atoms. Valence electrons that are not involved in bonding, also called **lone-pair electrons**, are represented by dots.

> **KEEP IN MIND**
>
> Each line (bond) in a Lewis structure represents two electrons, one from each atom involved in the bond.

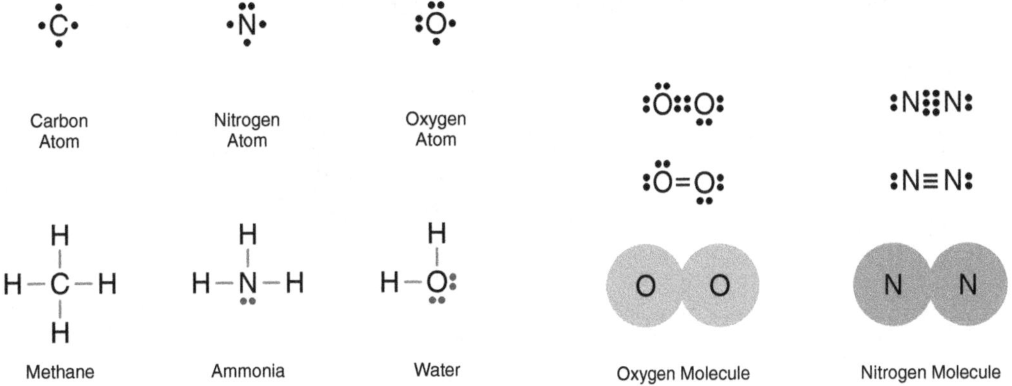

The number of bonds that an atom forms depends on the number of valence electrons that the atom has as a single atom. In a molecule of methane (CH_4), one carbon atom bonds to four hydrogen atoms. A single neutral carbon atom has four valence electrons and can share each one with a different hydrogen atom. In the end, it has four covalent bonds. Because each covalent bond involves two electrons, carbon has a total of eight valence electrons and is stable.

Similarly, in a molecule of ammonia (NH_3), one nitrogen atom bonds to three hydrogen atoms. Nitrogen shares six electrons total and has two remaining lone-pair electrons that are not involved in bonding for a total of eight. In a water molecule, an oxygen atom bonds to two hydrogen atoms. Oxygen has four shared electrons and four lone-pair electrons for a total of eight.

Example

In the Lewis structure of a fluorine molecule shown below, how are the eight valence electrons of each fluorine atom arranged?

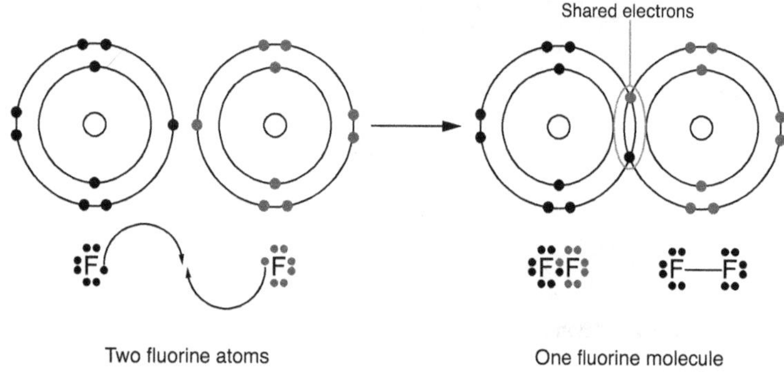

Covalent Bond

A. 2 are shared, 6 are lone-pair.

B. 4 are shared, 4 are lone-pair.

C. 6 are shared, 2 are lone-pair.

D. 8 are shared, none are lone-pair.

The correct answer is **A**. A fluorine atom forms a single covalent bond with another fluorine atom, which means that two electrons are being shared. The other six valence electrons are lone-pair electrons and are represented by dots around the atom.

Types of Covalent Bonds

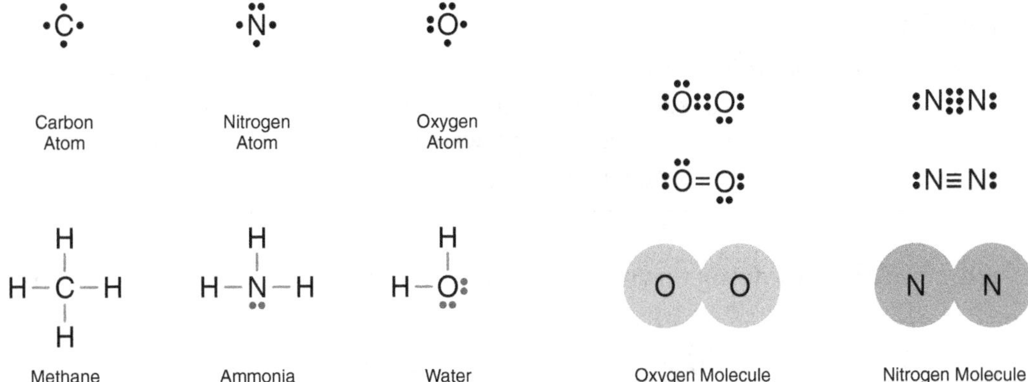

In methane, ammonia, and water, atoms are joined by **single covalent bonds** in which the atoms share two electrons. However, two atoms may need to share more than one pair of electrons to be stable. For example, two oxygen atoms form a **double bond**, in which two pairs of electrons (four electrons total) are shared. Similarly, two nitrogen atoms form a molecule with a **triple bond**, in which three pairs of electrons (six electrons total) are shared.

As more pairs of electrons are shared, the length of the bond decreases, and the bond strength increases. Single bonds are the longest and weakest bonds. They require the least energy to break because there is not as much energy stored in them.

> **CONNECTION**
>
> A pair of shared electrons between two atoms can be compared to a rubber band stretching between two objects. Having two or three rubber bands, rather than one, increases the strength of the "bond" that holds them together, making it harder to separate the objects.

Regardless of how many electrons are shared, the strength of a covalent bond comes from the positively charged nuclei of both atoms attracting the negatively charged electrons that are being shared. However, not all atoms attract shared electrons equally. This property is known as **electronegativity**, the tendency of an atom to attract shared electrons in a covalent bond. It is a measure of how hard an atom is pulling on shared electrons. Electronegativity increases going from left to right in the periodic table. Nonmetal atoms pull harder on electrons and do not tend to give them up. Therefore, the halogens in group 17 have the highest electronegativity of all elements.

If the two atoms share electrons equally, the bond is classified as **nonpolar covalent**. This occurs if the two atoms have similar electronegativities, which means that neither atom pulls significantly harder on the shared electrons than the other. If the two atoms share electrons unequally, the bond is **polar covalent**. This occurs if the electronegativity of one atom is significantly higher than the other, causing it to pull significantly harder on the shared electrons.

Example

> **CONNECTION**
> The sharing of electrons is like a game of tug-of-war in which two opposing teams are pulling on a rope in opposite directions. In a nonpolar bond, the opposing teams are pulling with the same force, and the rope is not moving toward one team or the other. In a polar bond, one team is winning by pulling the rope closer to its side.

An atom of which of the following elements has the strongest pull on shared electrons in a covalent bond?

A. Aluminum B. Chlorine C. Sodium D. Sulfur

The correct answer is **B.** The element with the highest electronegativity will have the strongest pull on shared electrons in a covalent bond. Electronegativity increases moving from left to right across the periodic table, so the element farthest to the right in the period, chlorine, has the highest electronegativity.

Let's Review!

- As stated in the octet rule, any atom that does not have a stable electron configuration of eight valence electrons will lose, gain, or share electrons to become stable.
- Exceptions to the octet rule include hydrogen and helium, which are stable when they have two valence electrons.
- Ionic bonds are formed when electrons are transferred from a metal atom to a nonmetal atom.
- Covalent bonds are formed when two atoms share electrons. When two atoms need to share more than one pair of electrons, multiple bonds form. If two pairs are shared, a double bond forms. If three pairs are shared, a triple bond forms.
- The difference in the electronegativities of the two atoms determines if electrons are shared equally, forming a nonpolar covalent bond, or shared unequally, forming a polar covalent bond.

CHEMICAL SOLUTIONS

This lesson discusses the properties of different types of mixtures, focusing on solutions. Then, it examines aspects of chemical reactions, including the components of the reactions and the types of changes that occur.

Solutions

When elements and compounds are physically (not chemically) combined, they form a **mixture**. When the substances mix evenly and it is impossible to see the individual components, the mixture is described as **homogeneous**. When the substances mix unevenly and it is possible to see the individual components, the mixture is described as **heterogeneous**.

Solubility is the ability of a substance to dissolve in another substance. For example, salt and sugar are both substances that can dissolve in water. They are **soluble**. In contrast, sand does not dissolve in water. It is **insoluble**. Individual particles of sand can be seen in water, but individual particles of salt are completely mixed in.

When one substance dissolves in the other, a type of homogeneous mixture called a **solution** forms. The substance that is being dissolved is the **solute**. The substance in which the solute is dissolved is the **solvent**, which makes up a greater percentage of the mixture than the solute. When salt dissolves in water, salt is the solute, and water is the solvent. Saltwater is an example of an **aqueous solution**, which forms when any substance dissolves in water.

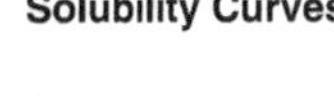

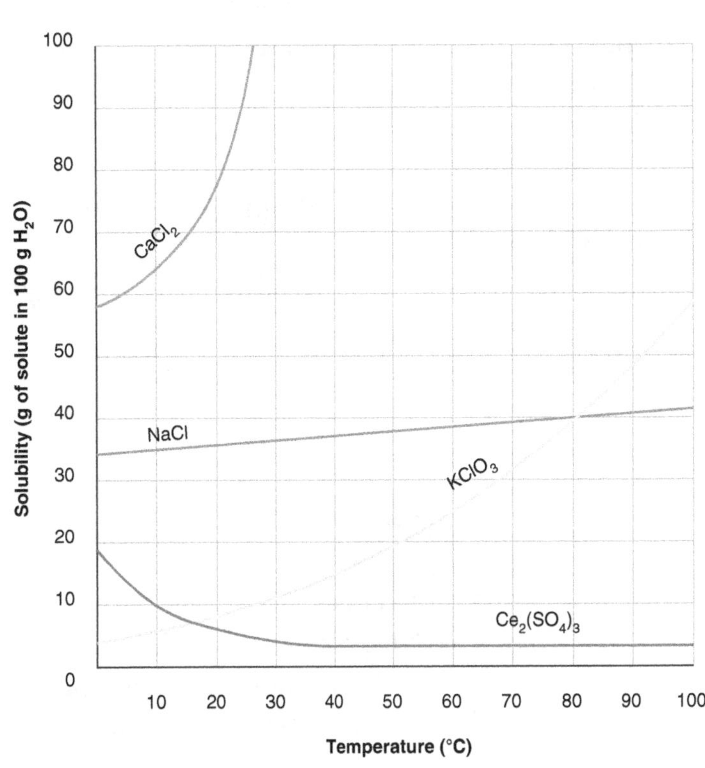

The **concentration** of a solution is the amount of solute in a given volume of solution and can be expressed in several ways:

- **Molarity** (number of moles of a substance in one liter of solution)
- **Molality** (number of moles of a substance per kilogram of solvent)
- **Percent composition by mass** (mass of a solute per unit mass of the solution)
- **Mole fraction** (moles of a solute divided by the total number of moles in the solution)

Solubility can also refer to the *amount* of a substance that can dissolve. Even for soluble substances, there is a limit to how much of it can dissolve. The lines in the graph below show these limits for different substances at different temperatures in 100 grams of water. The area below a line represents masses of solute that dissolve in 100 grams of water. This type of solution is **unsaturated** because more solute can be dissolved. At the line, the solution is **saturated** because the limit has been reached. Any solute added above that mass will remain undissolved.

Example

> **CONNECTION**
>
> The term *saturated* is also used in everyday life to describe things, such as sponges or clothing that have soaked up all the water that they can absorb.

A beaker contains 50 mL of oil and 50 mL of water. No matter how much the mixture is stirred, the oil and the water still separate into two layers. Which statement accurately describes this mixture?

A. Oil is insoluble in water.

B. It is an unsaturated solution.

C. It is a homogeneous mixture.

D. Water is a good solvent for oil.

The correct answer is **A.** Because the oil will not mix into the water, it is insoluble.

Chemical Reactions

A chemical reaction involves elements and compounds that combine, break apart, rearrange, or change form in some way. **Reactants** are the substances that are present at the beginning of the reaction and undergo a change. **Products** are the substances that are formed from the reactants. Chemical reactions can be described by chemical equations, an example of which is shown below.

Coefficient　　　　　　　　Coefficient

$$CH_4(g) + 2O_2(g) \longrightarrow CO_2(g) + 2H_2O(g)$$

Reactant side　　　　　　　　Product side

In this reaction, methane (CH_4) is burned in the presence of oxygen (O_2) to form carbon dioxide (CO_2) and water (H_2O). In the chemical equation, the formulas of the reactants (CH_4 and O_2) and

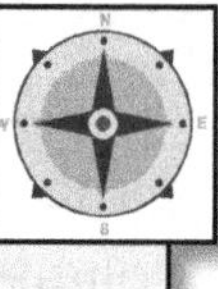

> **KEEP IN MIND**
>
> Reactants will always be on the left side of the arrow, and products will always be on the right side.

products (CO_2 and H_2O) are used. If there is more than one reactant or more than one product, their formulas are separated by a plus sign (+). The reactants and products are separated by an arrow.

The state of matter may also be shown in the chemical equation in parentheses after the substance formula. Substances can be solid, liquid, or gas, indicated by (*s*), (*l*), or (*g*), respectively. If a substance is dissolved in water, forming an aqueous solution, that state is indicated by (*aq*) in a chemical equation.

Finally, coefficients may appear in chemical equations. These coefficients indicate how many particles (atoms or molecules) of each substance react or form. When there is no coefficient present, only one particle is involved. In the example above, one molecule of methane (CH_4) reacts with two molecules of oxygen (O_2). One molecule of carbon dioxide (CO_2) is produced, along with two molecules of water (H_2O).

Example

The equation describing the formation of ammonia (NH3) from nitrogen and hydrogen is shown below. Which of the following statements is true?

$3H_2(g) + N_2(g)\ 2NH_3(g)$

A. NH_3 is the reactant, and H_2 and N_2 are products.

B. H_2 and N_2 are the reactants, and NH_3 is the product.

C. N and H_3 are the reactants, and H_2 and N_2 are products.

D. H_2 and N_2 are the reactants, and N and H_3 are the products.

The correct answer is **B.** Two reactants, H_2 and N_2, are found on the left side of the arrow. One product, NH_3, is found on the right side of the arrow.

Types of Reactions

Chemical reactions can be classified according to the reactants and products involved. This lesson will cover five types of reactions: synthesis, decomposition, single-replacement, double-replacement, and combustion. The first four types are outlined in the table below.

Type of Reaction	Model	Example
Synthesis	A + B AB	$2H_2(g) + O_2(g)\ 2H_2O(g)$
Decomposition	AB A + B	$2H_2O_2(aq)\ 2H_2O(l) + O_2(g)$
Single-Replacement	AB + C AC + B	$2HCl(aq) + Zn(s)\ ZnCl_2(aq) + H_2(g)$
Double-Replacement	AB + CD AD + CB	$AgNO_3(aq) + NaCl(aq)\ AgCl(s) + NaNO_3(aq)$

Synthesis reactions involve two or more reactants (A and B) combining to form one product (AB). In the example provided, hydrogen (H_2) and oxygen (O_2) begin as separate elements. At the end of the reaction, the hydrogen and oxygen atoms are bonded in a molecule of water (H_2O).

Decomposition reactions have only one reactant (AB) that breaks apart into two or more products (A and B). In the example above, hydrogen peroxide (H_2O_2) breaks apart into two smaller molecules: water (H_2O) and oxygen (O_2).

Single-replacement reactions involve two reactants, one compound (AB) and one element (C). In this type of reaction, one element replaces another to form a new compound (AC), leaving one element by itself (B). In the example, zinc replaces hydrogen in hydrochloric acid (HCl). As a result, zinc forms a compound with chlorine, zinc chloride ($ZnCl_2$), and hydrogen (H_2) is left by itself.

Double-replacement reactions involve two reactants, both of which are compounds made of two components (AB and CD). In the example, silver nitrate, composed of silver (Ag^{1+}) and nitrate (NO_3^{1-}) ions, reacts with sodium chloride, composed of sodium (Na^{1+}) and chloride (Cl^{1-}) ions. The nitrate and chloride ions switch places to produce two compounds that are different from those in the reactants.

Combustion reactions occur when fuels burn, and they involve specific reactants and products, as seen in the examples below. Some form of fuel that contains carbon and hydrogen is required. Examples of such fuels are methane, propane in a gas grill, butane in a lighter, and octane in gasoline. Notice that these fuels all react with oxygen, which is necessary for anything to burn. In all combustion reactions, carbon dioxide, water, and energy are produced. When something burns, energy is released, which can be felt as heat and seen as light.

Fuel	Reaction
Methane (CH_4)	$CH_4 + 2O_2\ CO_2 + 2H_2O$ + energy
Propane (C_3H_8)	$C_3H_8 + 5O_2\ 3CO_2 + 4H_2O$ + energy
Butane (C_4H_{10})	$2C_4H_{10} + 13O_2\ 8CO_2 + 10H_2O$ + energy
Octane (C_8H_{18})	$2C_8H_{18} + 25O_2\ 16CO_2 + 18H_2O$ + energy

DID YOU KNOW?

The fuels used in combustion reactions belong to a class of compounds called *hydrocarbons* because they are composed of hydrogen and carbon atoms. Hydrocarbons can be found in crude oil and include fossil fuels such as coal and natural gas. They are referred to as *fossil fuels* because they formed from the decomposition of organisms that died millions of years ago.

Example

Which of the following equations shows a decomposition reaction?

A. $3H_2 + N_2 \ 2NH_3$

B. $2KClO_3 \ 2KCl + 3O_2$

C. $2C_2H_2 + 5O_2 \ 4CO_2 + 2H_2O$

D. $2Na + ZnCl_2 \ Zn + 2NaCl$

The correct answer is **B.** This reaction starts with a single compound as a reactant that breaks down into two smaller products.

Energy Diagrams

Energy diagrams can be used to show how the energy of the species in a reaction changes over time. The reactants have a certain amount of energy stored in their bonds, and the products usually have a different amount of energy. If energy is released, the products have less energy than the reactants, and the reaction is **exothermic**. If energy is absorbed, the products have more energy than the reactants, and the reaction is **endothermic**. The shapes of the energy diagrams are shown below.

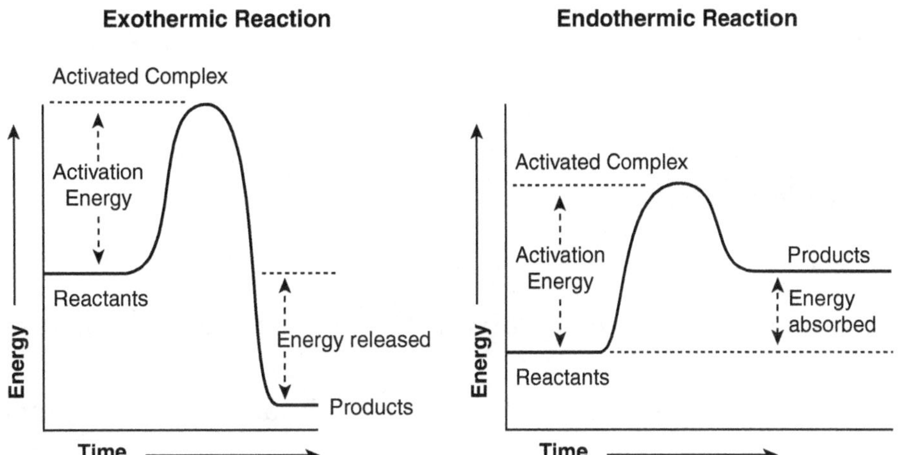

In every reaction, an **activated complex** must form between reactants. This complex can also be referred to as a transition state because it is required to convert, or provide a transition between, the reactants and products. In energy diagrams like the ones above, the activated complex has more energy than both the reactants and the products. The **activation energy** is the amount of energy required to transform the reactants into the activated complex, which then breaks apart to form the products.

> **CONNECTION**
>
> The difference between *endothermic* and *exothermic* reactions can be remembered by thinking about the meanings of the prefixes of these terms. In an *exo*thermic reaction, energy is released or "exits" the system. In an *endo*thermic reaction, energy "goes in."

The components of an energy diagram are as follows:

- Energy of reactants - energy of substances at the beginning of the reaction
- Energy of products - energy of substances at the end of the reaction
- Energy of the activated complex - energy of the substance represented by the maximum in the energy diagram
- Activation energy - difference in energy between the reactants and the activated complex
- Amount of energy released/absorbed - difference in energy between the reactants and products

Example

When iron reacts with oxygen, iron (III) oxide (Fe_2O_3), also known as rust, forms according to the equation below. The iron (III) oxide has less energy than the iron and oxygen. How is reaction classified, and why?

$4Fe(s) + 3O_2(g)\ 2Fe_2O_3(s)$

A. It is exothermic because energy is released.

B. It is exothermic because energy is absorbed.

C. It is endothermic because energy is released.

D. It is endothermic because energy is absorbed.

The correct answer is **A**. It is exothermic because the reactants must release energy to form a product that has less energy.

Let's Review!

- A solution is a type of homogeneous mixture that is formed when a solute dissolves in a solvent.
- The concentration of a solution is the amount of a substance in a given amount of solution.
- Chemical reactions occur when reactants combine, break apart, or rearrange to form products.
- Chemical equations represent chemical reactions using formulas and symbols.
- Chemical reactions can be classified as synthesis, decomposition, single-replacement, double-replacement, or combustion based on the reactants and products.
- Energy diagrams show how the energy of the species involved in the reaction changes as the reaction progresses.

ACIDS AND BASES

This lesson introduces the properties of acids and bases, including the various theories that define them. It also covers acid-base reactions and the pH scale.

Nature of Acids and Bases

Acids are compounds that contain at least one hydrogen atom or proton (H^+), which, when dissolved in water, can form a hydronium ion (H_3O^+). Acids dissolved in water generally have the following properties:

- Taste sour
- Turn litmus red
- Act corrosive

Acids are found in a variety of substances, from vinegar to apple juice. The following table provides a list of common acids and their sources or applications.

Name of Acid	Chemical Formula	Sources or Applications
Citric acid	$C_6H_8O_7$	Citrus fruits such as oranges and lemons
Lactic acid	$C_3H_6O_3$	Yogurt and buttermilk
Acetic acid	$C_2H_4O_2$ or CH_3COOH	Nail polish remover and vinegar
Hydrochloric acid	HCl	Stomach
Phosphoric acid	H_3PO_4	Detergents and soft drinks
Nitric acid	HNO_3	Fertilizers

Bases are compounds that form hydroxide ions (OH^-) in a water solution. They also accept hydronium ions from acids. Bases dissolved in water generally have the following properties:

- Slippery in solution
- Very corrosive
- Turn litmus blue
- Taste bitter

Like acids, bases have many applications. The following table provides examples of common bases and how they are used.

Name of Base	Chemical Formula	Applications
Sodium hydroxide	$NaOH$	Soap, oven cleaners, and textiles
Potassium hydroxide	KOH	Soap and textiles
Ammonia	NH_3	Cleaning agents and fertilizers
Magnesium hydroxide	$Mg(OH)_2$	Laxatives and antacids

Acidic solutions have more hydrogen ions than hydroxide ions, whereas basic solutions have more hydroxide ions than hydrogen ions. All water solutions have both ion types, but the relative numbers dictate whether an aqueous solution is acidic, basic, or neutral. Anything that is dissolved in water is an **aqueous solution**. Neutral solutions are neither acidic nor basic, meaning that an equal number of hydrogen and hydroxide ions are present. Pure water is an example of a neutral solution.

KEEP IN MIND

Substances that form ions in aqueous solutions are called **electrolytes**. As electrolytes, acids and bases are conductors of electricity in solution. This is because they contain dissolved ions.

Water is the primary solvent used to create an aqueous solution. Thus, it is important to understand how pure water behaves in solution. A small fraction of water molecules breaks down to form hydronium and hydroxide ions. When two water molecules interact, one water molecule gives up a positively charged hydrogen ion to form a hydroxide ion. A hydronium ion forms when a water molecule accepts a hydrogen ion. The following equation illustrates this reaction:

$$2H_2O \rightarrow H_3O^+ + OH^-$$

Examples

1. **Which of the following is an acid?**

   A. KNO_3 B. $BaCl_2$ C. NaOH D. H_3PO_4

   The correct answer is **D**. Phosphoric acid (H_3PO_4) is a common acid that is capable of donating one of its hydrogen atoms to form a hydronium ion.

2. **Which is a characteristic of a basic solution?**

   A. Tastes sour
   B. Accepts OH^- ions
   C. Turns litmus blue
   D. Contains a lot of H_3O^+ ions

   The correct answer is **C**. A basic solution is made using water as a solvent. Basic solutions turn litmus paper from red to blue.

Acid and Base Classification

Recall that an acid produces hydrogen ions, and a base produces hydroxide ions. These compounds are defined as **Arrhenius** acids and bases. The Arrhenius theory explains how acids and bases form ions when dissolved in water. Take, for example, the acid HCl, shown in the equation below. When forming an aqueous solution of HCl, this acid dissociates, or splits, into hydrogen ions and chloride ions in water.

$$HCl\,(g) \rightarrow H^+\,(aq) + Cl^-\,(aq)$$

An Arrhenius base dissociates into hydroxide ions (OH-) in an aqueous solution. This is the case for sodium hydroxide, NaOH, as shown in the following equation:

$$NaOH\,(s) \rightarrow Na^+\,(aq) + OH^-(aq)$$

> **BE CAREFUL!**
> Free H+ ions do not float in an aqueous solution. Rather, they bind with water to form H_3O^+. However, it is not uncommon to see the two formulas, H+ and H_3O^+, used interchangeably in chemical reactions.

One limitation of this theory is that it does not account for acids and bases that lack a hydrogen or hydroxide ion in their molecular structure. Another way to define acids and bases is by using the Brønsted-Lowry theory. A Brønsted-Lowry **acid** is a hydrogen ion donor that increases the concentration of hydronium ions in solution. A Brønsted-Lowry **base** is a hydrogen ion acceptor that increases hydroxide ion concentration in solution. The term *proton* is used interchangeably with the term *hydrogen ion*.

When a base accepts a hydrogen ion, it produces a conjugate acid. When an acid donates a hydrogen ion, it produces a conjugate base. In the following example, ammonia is the base, but its conjugate acid is ammonium ion. What is the conjugate base for the acid?

$$\underset{\text{base}}{NH_3} + \underset{\text{acid}}{H_2O} \longrightarrow \underset{\text{conjugate acid}}{NH_4^+} + \underset{\text{conjugate base}}{OH^-}$$

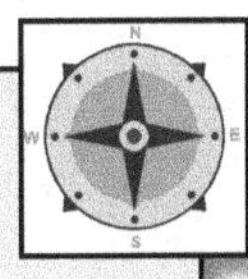

> **KEEP IN MIND**
> When substances such as pure water act as an acid or a base, they are **amphoteric**.

The last theory about acids and bases is called the Lewis theory. This theory is based on electron movement during an acid-base reaction. A **Lewis acid** accepts a pair of electrons, while a **Lewis base** donates an electron pair.

Example

What is the conjugate acid in the following equation?

$$CH_3COOH + H_2O \rightleftharpoons H_3O^+ + CH_3COO^-$$

A. H_3O^+ B. H_2O C. CH_3COO^- D. CH_3COOH

The correct answer is **A**. A conjugate acid is a substance that accepts a proton from a base. In this case, the base H_2O accepts a proton to form the conjugate acid, hydronium ion (H_3O^+).

Acid-Base Reactions

In an aqueous solution, a base increases the hydroxide concentration (OH^-), while an acid increases the hydrogen ion (H^+) concentration. Sometimes, **neutralization reactions** also occur. This type of reaction happens when an acid and a base react with each other to form water and salt. Salt is typically defined as an **ionic compound** that includes any cation except H^+ and any anion except OH^-. Consider the following example of a neutralization reaction between hydrobromic acid (HBr) and potassium hydroxide (KOH).

$$HBr + KOH \longrightarrow KBr + H_2O$$

> **BE CAREFUL!**
> Not all neutralization reactions proceed in the manner where all reactants are in the aqueous phase. In some chemical reactions, one reactant may be a solid. The neutralization reaction can still proceed to completion.

In the above equation, one molecule of water forms in addition to the salt potassium bromide (KBr). There are instances where acid-base reactions must be balanced because more than one molecule of an acid or a base react to form products. This is the case for the reaction between hydrochloric acid and magnesium hydroxide, as shown below.

$$2HCl + Mg(OH)_2 \longrightarrow MgCl_2 + 2H_2O$$

When two molecules of hydrochloric acid react with magnesium hydroxide, two water molecules and one molecule of salt, $MgCl_{2,}$ form.

Example

Which is a product of a neutralization reaction?

A. Acid B. Base C. Proton D. Salt

The correct answer is **D**. When an acid and a base react, they form a salt and water. This type of reaction is called a neutralization reaction.

Acid and Base Strength and pH

Acids and bases can be classified according to their strength. This strength refers to how readily an acid donates a hydrogen ion. The strength of a base is determined by how readily it removes a hydrogen ion from a molecule, or **deprotonates**. Strong acids are also known as strong electrolytes, which means that they completely ionize in solution. Weak acids are weak electrolytes because they partially ionize in solution. The following diagram shows what happens to a strong or weak acid in an aqueous solution.

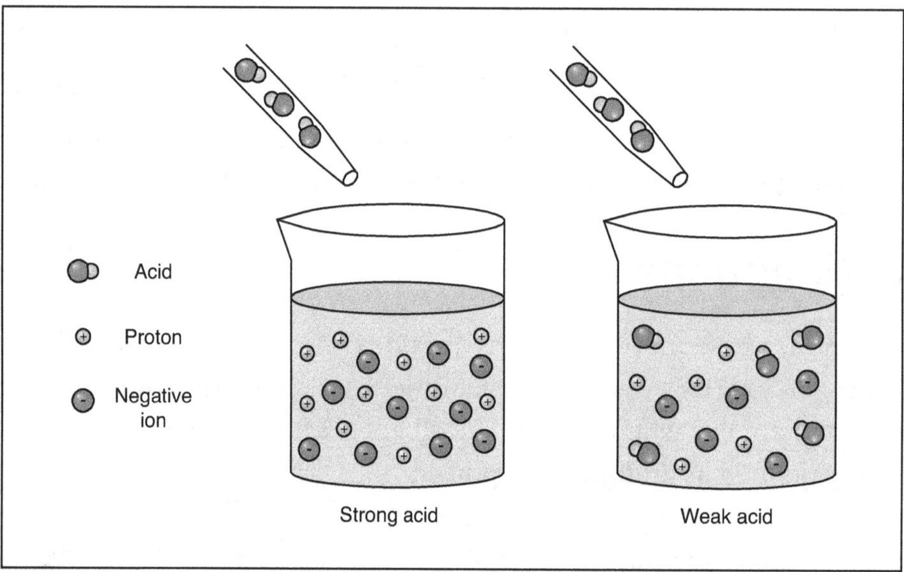

The maximum number of ions is produced when strong acids ionize. As shown in the following equations, the weak acid reaction is reversible (and incomplete) in aqueous solutions. This explains why weak acids produce fewer ions than strong acids.

Strong acid in solution

$$HNO_3 \longrightarrow H^+ + NO_3^-$$

Weak base in solution

$$NH_3 + H_2O \rightleftarrows NH_4^+ + OH^-$$

Like strong acids, strong bases fully dissociate in solution. They produce metal ions and hydroxide ions. Like weak acids, weak bases partially dissociate and participate in reversible reactions. The following table provides a list of common strong acids and bases and common weak acids and bases.

BE CAREFUL!
Ammonia is a weak base even though it does not have a hydroxide ion (OH^-) in its chemical formula. It will accept a proton and form hydroxide ions in aqueous solutions.

Strong Acid	Weak Acid	Strong Base	Weak Base
Hydrochloric acid (HCl)	Hydrofluoric acid (HF)	Sodium hydroxide (NaOH)	Ammonia (NH_3)
Nitric acid (HNO_3)	Carbonic acid (H_2CO_3)	Potassium hydroxide (KOH)	Methylamine (CH_3NH_2)
Perchloric acid ($HClO_4$)	Phosphoric acid (H_3PO_4)	Calcium hydroxide ($Ca(OH)_2$)	Hydrazine (N_2H_4)
Sulfuric acid (H_2SO_4)	Acetic acid ($C_2H_4O_2$ or CH_3COOH)	Lithium hydroxide (LiOH)	Pyridine (C_5H_5N)

Researchers can determine the strength of an acid or a base by measuring the **pH** of a solution. The pH value describes how acidic or basic a solution is. On pH scale, shown below, if the number is less than 7 the solution is acidic. A pH greater than 7 means the solution is basic. When the pH is exactly 7, the solution is neutral.

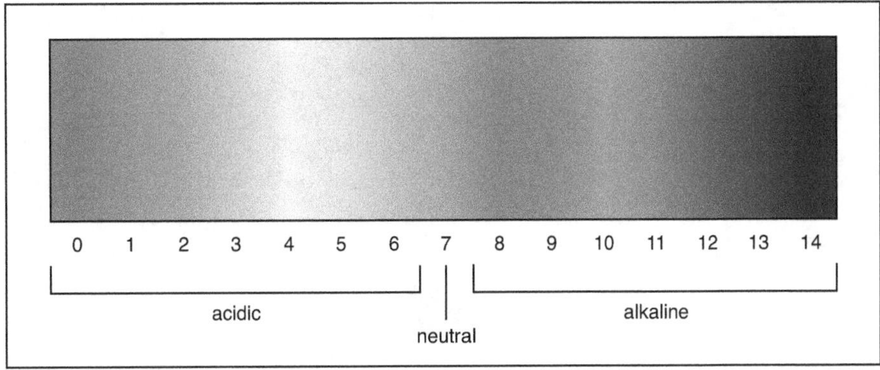

Example

Which of the following measured pH values means a solution is basic?

A. 2 B. 5 C. 7 D. 9

The correct answer is **D.** When the pH of an aqueous solution is greater than 7, which is the case for a solution that has a pH of 9, the solution is basic.

Let's Review!

- Acids and bases exhibit unique properties when dissolved in water.
- Arrhenius acids donate hydrogen ions, and Arrhenius bases accept hydrogen ions in solution.
- Brønsted-Lowry acids donate protons (or hydrogen ions), and Brønsted-Lowry bases accept protons (or hydrogen ions).
- Lewis acids are electron pair acceptors, and Lewis bases are electron pair donors.
- A neutralization reaction occurs when an acid and a base react to form a salt and water.
- Strong acids completely ionize in solution, and strong bases fully dissociate in solution.
- Weak acids and weak bases only partially dissociate in solution.
- The pH of a solution determines how acidic or basic it is.

Chapter 15 Chemistry Practice Quiz

1. **A stick of butter is melted in a dish in the microwave. After it melts, which of the following statements describes the butter?**

   A. It has both the shape and volume of the dish.

   B. It has the shape but not the volume of the dish.

   C. It has the volume but not the shape of the dish.

   D. It has neither the shape nor the volume of the dish.

2. **In the cooling curve for any substance, the freezing point is equal to the ______ in the heating curve of the same substance under the same conditions.**

   A. boiling point

   B. melting point

   C. temperature at which the liquid changes to gas

   D. temperature at which the gas changes to liquid

3. **What is the difference between evaporation and boiling?**

   A. Evaporation occurs throughout a substance, and boiling occurs on the bottom of it.

   B. Evaporation occurs on the surface of a substance, and boiling occurs throughout it.

   C. Evaporation occurs on the bottom of a substance, and boiling occurs on the surface of it.

   D. Evaporation occurs on the surface of a substance, and boiling occurs on the bottom of it.

4. **Which of the following represents a substance?**

   A. Cup of water

   B. Bowl of stew

   C. Slice of pizza

   D. Bowl of salad

5. **Which of the following elements will gain three electrons to become stable?**

   A. Aluminum

   B. Boron

   C. Oxygen

   D. Phosphorus

6. **What type of bond forms between calcium and iodine, and why?**

   A. Ionic, because it involves two nonmetals

   B. Covalent, because it involves two nonmetals

   C. Ionic, because it involves a metal and a nonmetal

   D. Covalent, because it involves a metal and a nonmetal

7. **A spoonful of sugar is added to a hot cup of tea. All the sugar dissolves. How can the resulting solution be described?**
   A. Saturated and homogeneous
   B. Saturated and heterogeneous
   C. Unsaturated and homogeneous
   D. Unsaturated and heterogeneous

8. **Sugar is dissolved in water. Which of the following statements best describes the components of this solution?**
   A. Sugar and water are both solutes.
   B. Sugar and water are both solvents.
   C. Sugar is the solute, and water is the solvent.
   D. Sugar is the solvent, and water is the solute.

9. **The strength of a base is determined by its ability to**
   A. turn litmus paper blue.
   B. feel slippery to the touch.
   C. completely ionize in water.
   D. dissociate into hydroxide ions.

10. **Which of the following determines the strength of an acidic solution?**
   A. Litmus paper that turns red
   B. Litmus paper that turns blue
   C. Measured pH value equal to 7
   D. Measured pH value less than 7

Chapter 15 Chemistry Practice Quiz – Answer Key

1. B. As the butter melts, it goes from a solid to a liquid, which takes the shape but not the volume of its container. **See Lesson: States of Matter.**

2. B. Any substance will melt and freeze at the same temperature, assuming these processes are carried out under the same conditions. This is the temperature at which the substance transitions between solid and liquid states. **See Lesson: States of Matter.**

3. B. Evaporation occurs on the surface of a substance, and boiling occurs throughout a substance. **See Lesson: Properties of Matter.**

4. A. A substance has is the same throughout and water is the only option that fits that definition. **See Lesson: Properties of Matter.**

5. D. Phosphorus is in group 15, which means it has five valence electrons. Gaining three would give it eight valence electrons, making the atom stable. **See Lesson: Chemical Bonds.**

6. C. Calcium is a metal, and iodine is a nonmetal. When these elements bond, valence electrons are transferred from calcium atoms to iodine atoms, creating an ionic bond. **See Lesson: Chemical Bonds.**

7. C. Because more solute could be added and dissolve, the solution has not yet reached its limit and is considered unsaturated. Because all the solute dissolves, the particles in the mixture are evenly distributed as a homogenous mixture. **See Lesson: Chemical Solutions.**

8. C. Generally, the solute dissolves in the solvent to form a solution. To make sugar water, the sugar dissolves in water. **See Lesson: Chemical Solutions.**

9. D. A weak base only partially dissociates in solution. A strong base fully dissociates, or contributes the maximum number of hydroxide ions, in solution. **See Lesson: Acids and Bases.**

10. D. Both litmus paper and a pH scale can be used to indicate whether a solution is acidic. However, a pH scale can also determine the strength of an acid. **See Lesson: Acids and Bases.**

Chapter 16 Physics

This lesson introduces the basics of motion and the application of simple physical principles and basic vector math to problems involving moving bodies. It culminates with an introduction to projectile motion and a presentation of Newton's laws of motion, which summarize the classical view of physics.

Nature of Motion

The space that people perceive is filled with objects of various sizes and shapes, but these objects are not always in the same places. They change their distances and orientations relative to observers and to one another, although these changes do not take place all at once. Such changes are called **motion**, and they are measured as differences in position or orientation over time.

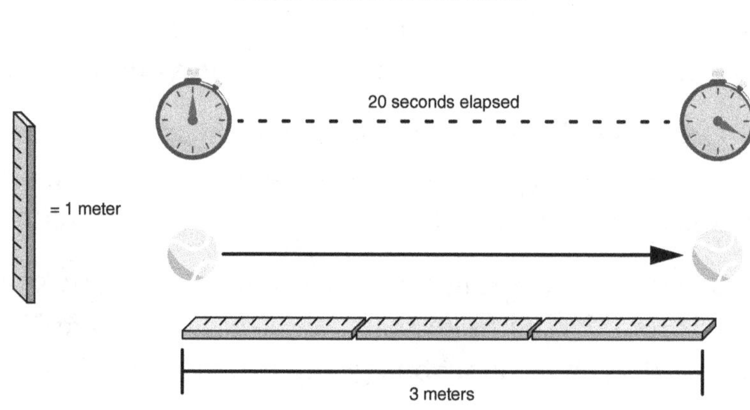

Systematically measuring motion requires standards of **distance** and **time**—two concepts that people use and understand in everyday situations but may have difficulty defining independently. Instead of tackling the philosophical problem of what time and distance are, most people take the pragmatic approach to using these concepts by employing a generally agreed-upon standard. For example, in the metric (SI) system, the **meter** (m) is the fundamental unit of length. Comparing the relative locations of objects to that standard enables an observer to measure the distance between them and report it in a way that others can understand.

Time is more esoteric. A standard for time requires reference to some periodic event (a concept that is itself based on some understanding of time). For example, the revolution of Earth around the sun (a year), the full rotation of Earth on its axis (a day), or even something as mundane as the drip of a faucet (a duration that depends on numerous factors) are periodic events that can be used as standards for time. In the metric (SI) system, the fundamental unit of time is the **second** (s). The critical point is that the event be periodic. Because it occurs at unchanging intervals, it provides a common standard of time to which everyone can refer.

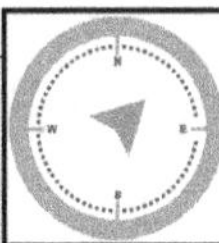

DID YOU KNOW?

Time and distance are concepts that you use every day, but they are difficult to define because they are fundamental to human experience. Try thinking about how you would explain time or distance without referring to time or distance.

Example

Which approach would best serve as a common standard for measuring motion?

A. Comparing changes in distance using a peach and a sundial

B. Comparing changes in distance using a yardstick and a heartbeat

C. Comparing changes in distance using a quarter and a dripping faucet

D. Comparing changes in distance using an index card and a metronome

The correct answer is **D.** To measure motion in a way that is meaningful to others and consistent in different locations and on different days, the standards of time and distance must be consistent and reproducible. Although a quarter, a yardstick, and an index card all have consistent dimensions, peaches vary. A sundial and a metronome can provide consistent indications of time's passage, but heartbeats and dripping faucets vary. Thus, the best answer is an index card and a metronome.

Vectors and Scalars

Determining the change in the distance or orientation of an object with respect to some standard of time yields a measurement of the object's motion. Motion has two general characteristics: its direction and its quickness. Therefore, **vectors** are helpful in quantifying motion. A vector is a quantity that has a direction and a length (or magnitude) but no defined location. It is often depicted as an arrow that begins at one point (called the **tail**) and ends at another point (called the **head**). Because a vector has no location, it can move anywhere and remain the same vector. Variables representing vectors often appear in boldface (e.g., ***v***) or with a small arrow above them (e.g., $\vec{v}$).

In a rectangular coordinate system, one representation of a vector is the coordinates of the head when the tail is at the origin. For example, a vector in two dimensions might be expressed as (3, −5). Because vectors have no location, however, the same vector can have its tail elsewhere. To return it to the origin, subtract the coordinates of the tail from the respective coordinates of the head to yield the

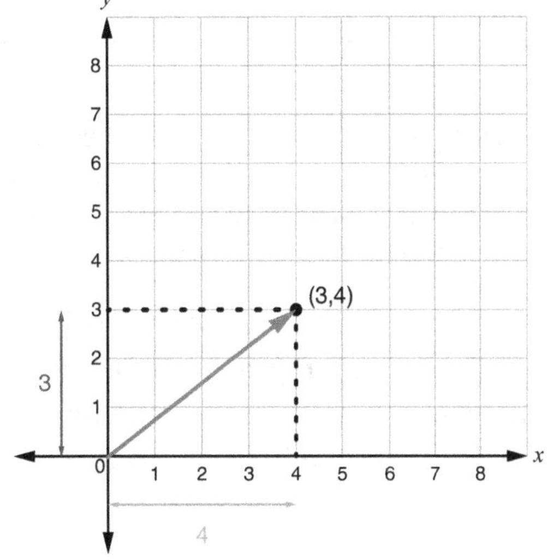

Length of (3,4) is

$\sqrt{3^2 + 4^2} = \sqrt{9 + 16}$

$= \sqrt{25} = 5$

standard vector form. To find the length of a vector expressed in standard form, square each of the coordinates, add them, and take the square root of the sum. This process is an application of the Pythagorean theorem for right triangles.

In contrast with a vector is a **scalar,** which has a magnitude but no direction. A simple number such as 5 or 10.2 is a scalar. The length of a vector, for example, is a scalar.

Example

What is the length of a vector that has its head at (1, 3) and its tail at (–2, 7)?

A. 1 B. 5 C. 9 D. 25

The correct answer is **B.** First, convert the vector to standard form by subtracting the tail coordinates from the corresponding head coordinates: (1 – [–2], 3 – 7) = (3, –4). Then, calculate the length by squaring each coordinate, adding them, and taking the square root of the sum: $\sqrt{(3)^2 + (-4)^2} = \sqrt{9 + 16} = \sqrt{25} = 5$

Basic Vector Operations

Adding two or more vectors yields a **resultant.** Graphically, adding two vectors involves placing the tail of one on the head of the other (and continuing this process when adding more vectors). The resultant is a new vector starting at the tail of the first and ending at the head of the second. Because the resultant vector is the same regardless of which way the vectors are added, vector addition is **commutative** (meaning $\vec{a} + \vec{b} = \vec{b} + \vec{a}$). Adding vectors in coordinate form just requires adding the respective coordinates of each. For example, (7, 1) + (2, –3) = (7 + 2, 1 + [–3]) = (9, –2).

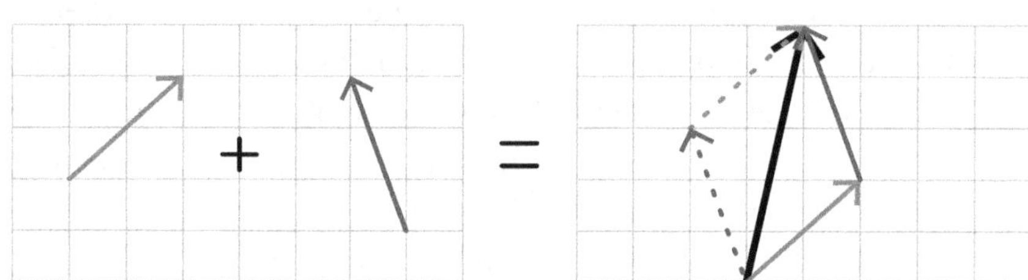

Subtracting vectors follows similar rules: for example, (7, 1) – (2, –3) = (7 – 2, 1 – [–3]) = (5, 4).

KEY POINT!

Remember that because vectors have no location, they can be moved as necessary to aid in visualization, addition, or any number of purposes. As long as two vectors have the same direction and length (magnitude), they are the same vector.

To multiply a vector by a scalar, multiply each coordinate in the vector by that scalar. To divide a vector by a scalar, divide each coordinate by that scalar. Dividing a vector by its length (or, equivalently, multiplying by the reciprocal of its length) yields a new vector that has the same direction as the original but a length 1. Such a vector is called a **unit vector.** These rules also allow vector subtraction to be expressed as vector addition: $\vec{a}-\vec{b} = \vec{a} + ([-1] \times \vec{b}) = \vec{a} + (-\vec{b})$. They also enable easier graphical addition of vectors.

Example

If $\vec{u} = \left(2,\ 5\right)$ and $\vec{v} = \left(3,-1\right)$, what is $2\vec{u}-3\vec{v}$?

A. (−5, 13) B. (−1, 6) C. (1, −6) D. (13, 7)

The correct answer is **A.** First, perform the multiplication of each vector by its respective scalar: $2\vec{u}-3\vec{v} = 2(2,\ 5)-3(3,-1) = (4,\ 10)-\left(9,-3\right)$ Next, either convert to addition or simply subtract the respective coordinates: $(4,\ 10)-(9,-3) = (4-9,\ 10-[-3]) = \left(-5,\ 13\right)$

Velocity and Acceleration

Because motion has a direction and a magnitude of some type, vectors are a way to quantify it. One measurement of how quickly an object is moving is **speed:** the distance from one point to another divided by the travel time. For instance, if a plane moves 252 meters in 2.00 seconds, its speed is 252 meters ÷ 2.00 seconds = 126 meters per second (m/s). But for passengers on that plane, the direction of flight is just as important as the speed. Thus, multiplying the speed by a unit vector in the direction of travel yields a vector called **velocity.**

The rate at which velocity changes is called **acceleration.** Like velocity, acceleration has a magnitude and a direction, so it can be expressed as a vector. (Note that the term *acceleration* can also mean the magnitude of the acceleration vector, which is a scalar. The context of the problem will generally clarify whether the term refers to a vector or a scalar.) For instance, if a truck moving in a straight line is speeding up, its acceleration is in the same direction as its velocity; if the truck is slowing down, its acceleration is in the direction opposite to its velocity. Quantitatively, the magnitude of the acceleration is the difference in speed divided by the elapsed time.

KEEP IN MIND

These simple mathematical definitions of *velocity* and *acceleration* assume constant speed and acceleration scalars, respectively, over the time period in the calculation. If the speed or acceleration is changing, they yield *average* values for that time period.

KEY POINT!

The *velocity* of an object is a vector: it quantifies both the magnitude and the direction of the object's motion. The *speed* of an object is a scalar: it is just the magnitude of its motion. Therefore, two objects can have the same speed but different velocities.

Example

A runner finishes a 1,600-meter race in 5 minutes and 20 seconds. What was his average speed?

A. 1 m/s B. 5 m/s C. 64 m/s D. 320 m/s

The correct answer is **B.** The average speed of the runner is the distance divided by the running time. Before calculating the speed, convert the time to seconds: because 5 minutes is equal to 300 seconds, the total time is 320 seconds. $\frac{1{,}600 \text{ m}}{320 \text{ s}} = 5 \text{ m/s}$

Projectile Motion

One special case of motion involves an object moving under the influence of gravity—for example, when a player hits a baseball or a cannon fires a cannonball. Ignoring any other forces (including air resistance), such an object moves in two dimensions, generally combining a horizontal component of motion and a vertical component. It experiences downward acceleration of 9.8 meters per square second (m/s²) but no horizontal acceleration.

Given a horizontal speed v_x and an initial horizontal position (coordinate) x_i, the object's horizontal position (assuming a starting time of $t = 0$) is $x(t) = x_i + v_x t$. However, the object's vertical distance from its starting point is complicated by the acceleration due to gravity. Some basic calculus shows that given an initial vertical speed v_y and an initial vertical position (coordinate) y_i, the object's vertical position (assuming a starting time of $t = 0$) is $y(t) = -\frac{1}{2}gt^2 + v_y t + y_i$. Note that g is the acceleration due to gravity (9.8 m/s²) and that the quadratic term is negative because gravity accelerates an object downward. Plotting the coordinates of the object at various times shows that it traces a parabola.

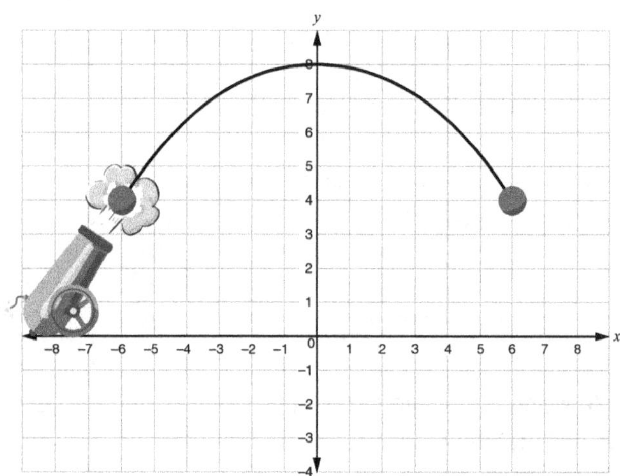

BE CAREFUL!

Make sure you know the height of the ground when analyzing projectile motion. Generally, an object won't be able to go any lower than ground level!

Example

A child throws a ball directly upward from the ground with an initial speed of 45 meters per second. How long will the ball take to return to the ground?

A. 1.4 seconds B. 2.0 seconds C. 3.0 seconds D. 9.2 seconds

The correct answer is **D.** Because the ball has no horizontal velocity, just use the equation for height with respect to time. The initial vertical velocity is 45 meters per second, and the initial height of the ball is 0. Also recall that the acceleration due to gravity is 9.8 m/s².

$$y(t) = -\frac{1}{2}gt^2 + v_y t + y_i = -\frac{1}{2}(9.8)t^2 + (45)t + 0 = -4.9t^2 + 45t$$

Next, set the height *y* equal to 0 and solve for *t* by factoring.

$$y(t) = 0 = -4.9t^2 + 45t \; 0 = t(-4.9t + 45)$$

Note that the ball is at ground level at $t = 0$ (the factor *t*), but the solution to this problem is for *t* greater than 0 (the factor $-4.9t + 45$). Set the latter equal to 0 and solve for *t*.

$$-4.9t + 45 = 0 \; 4.9t = 45 \; t = 9.2$$

The solution is 9.2 seconds.

Newton's Laws of Motion

Newton's laws of motion summarize the qualitative characteristics of moving objects. These laws refer to two important concepts in physics: **force** and **mass.** A force is a "push" or "pull" that an object experiences or exerts on another object; it is also a vector with a direction and magnitude. Mass is in some sense resistance to movement (or "displacement") by a force; it is a scalar. Thus, given a certain force, an object with less mass will move more than an object with more mass.

Newton's first law of motion, which deals with **inertia,** states that an object in motion will remain in motion unless a **net force** acts on it and that an object at rest will remain at rest unless a net force acts on it. Note that *net force* just means the object feels some force: it is the resultant of all forces acting on the object. If two people push with the same force against a cart but direct their efforts in precisely opposite directions, the cart will feel no net force. Another way to understand this law is that an object's velocity will stay the same unless a force acts on the object.

Newton's second law of motion relates an object's mass, its acceleration, and the (net) force acting on it. This law says the force on an object (a vector $\vec{F}$) produces acceleration of the object ($\vec{a}$) that is proportional to the object's mass (*m*). Hence the well-known equation $\vec{F} = m\vec{a}$ (or $F = ma$ when dealing only in magnitudes—that is, scalars—not directions.) In SI units, the force is in newtons (N), the mass is in kilograms (kg), and the acceleration is in meters per square second (m/s²). Qualitatively, this law says that accelerating more-massive objects requires a greater force than accelerating less-massive objects.

Newton's third law of motion states that when an object exerts a force on another object, it experiences a force of equal magnitude but opposite direction from that other object. This law is sometimes expressed by saying that for every action, there is an equal and opposite reaction.

Example

A 2.0-kilogram object experiences a net force of 144 newtons. What is its acceleration?

A. 36 m/s² B. 72 m/s² C. 140 m/s² D. 290 m/s²

The correct answer is **B**. Use Newton's second law of motion: $F = ma$. (Vectors are unnecessary because the problem only deals with scalars.) Plug in the numbers and solve for a, noting that it will be in meters per square second.

$F = ma$ 144 N = (2.0 kg)a $a = \frac{144 \text{ N}}{2.0 \text{ kg}} = 72 \text{ m/s}^2$

Let's Review!

- Motion is the change in an object's position or orientation over time.
- Measurement of motion requires a consistent, accessible standard of distance and time.
- A vector is a quantity with magnitude and direction but no location; a scalar has a magnitude but no direction.
- The standard notation form of a vector is the coordinates of its head when its tail is at the origin of the coordinate system. If the vector is shown elsewhere, subtract the coordinates of the tail from the respective coordinates of the head to get the standard form.
- To multiply a scalar and a vector, multiply each coordinate of the vector by the scalar: $a \times (x, y) = (ax, ay)$.
- To calculate the resultant, or sum, of two vectors, add the respective coordinates of those vectors: $(a, b) + (c, d) = (a + c, b + d)$.
- To find the length of a vector, square its coordinates, add them, and take the square root.
- Vector addition is commutative: $\vec{a} + \vec{b} = \vec{b} + \vec{a}$.
- Velocity is a vector that represents how quickly an object is moving. Speed is the magnitude of that vector (it is a scalar).
- Acceleration is a vector that represents how quickly the velocity is changing.
- Projectile motion is the motion of an object under the influence of gravity. Such an object follows a parabolic path. Its horizontal position at time t, given initial horizontal velocity v_x and initial horizontal position x_i, is $x(t) = x_i + v_x \times t$. Its vertical position at time t, given initial vertical velocity v_y and initial vertical position y_i, is $y(t) = -\frac{1}{2}gt^2 + v_y t + y_i$.
- Newton's laws of motion summarize motion in classical physics.
- Newton's first law is that an object at rest stays at rest and an object in motion stays in motion, unless a net force acts on the object.
- Newton's second law is that the net force, object mass, and acceleration are related by $\vec{F} = m \times \vec{a}$ (or $F = m \times a$ when dealing only in magnitudes).
- Newton's third law is that an object exerting a force on another object feels the same force, but in the opposite direction.

Friction and Types of Motion

This lesson discusses different types of motion. Then, it examines uniform circular (rotational) motion and centripetal acceleration. It also introduces the concept of friction and its effect on motion in real-world situations.

Types of Motion

According to Newton's first law of motion, an object moving with a given velocity (even if it is zero) will maintain that velocity indefinitely unless some net force acts on it. Absent any net force, the object will move in one direction along a line (assuming a nonzero speed). In this case, the object exhibits **linear motion** because its movement is in only one spatial dimension. If a force acts on the object and that force is parallel with the dimension in which the object is moving, the acceleration will be parallel or antiparallel (exactly opposite in direction) to the velocity. Thus, even though the object will speed up or slow down, its motion will remain linear.

If a force acts on an object in a direction that is not parallel to the object's velocity, the object no longer moves along a line; it exhibits **nonlinear motion.** Passengers riding in a car, for example, can tell the difference between linear and nonlinear motion by the direction of the force they feel as they ride. If the car speeds up or slows down linearly, they will feel only a backward force (positive acceleration) or a forward force (negative acceleration, or deceleration). If it turns (nonlinear motion), the passengers will feel a force toward either side as the car turns in some direction.

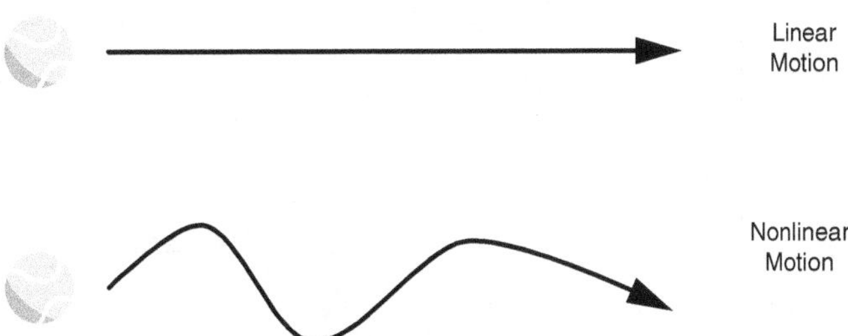

In general, mathematically analyzing nonlinear motion requires vector calculus. However, in certain cases, nonlinear motion can be described using only algebra. One case is **rotational motion**, which involves objects spinning on an axis or moving in a circle around some central point. Because rotational motion involves circular geometry, it is also commonly called **circular motion**.

Example

An object has a constant nonzero speed but a randomly varying velocity. Which term best describes its motion?

A. Linear B. Nonlinear C. Rotational D. Stationary

The correct answer is **B.** If the object has a fixed speed greater than zero but its velocity changes randomly, then its direction of motion changes randomly. Therefore, the object is exhibiting nonlinear motion. Because the changes are random, however, it cannot be rotational motion, which is nonlinear but also determinate with regard to changes in velocity.

Uniform Circular Motion

An object that rotates about an axis or revolves circularly around some point exhibits **rotational motion** (or **circular motion**). A simple case that provides a foundation for more-complex analysis is an object moving in a circle around some point outside its surface. For example, consider a ball tied to the end of a stick by a string. If someone holds the stick and causes the ball to move a circle, the ball will always be a fixed distance from the end of the stick—that distance is the length of the string. If such an object moves with a constant speed, its movement is called **uniform circular motion.**

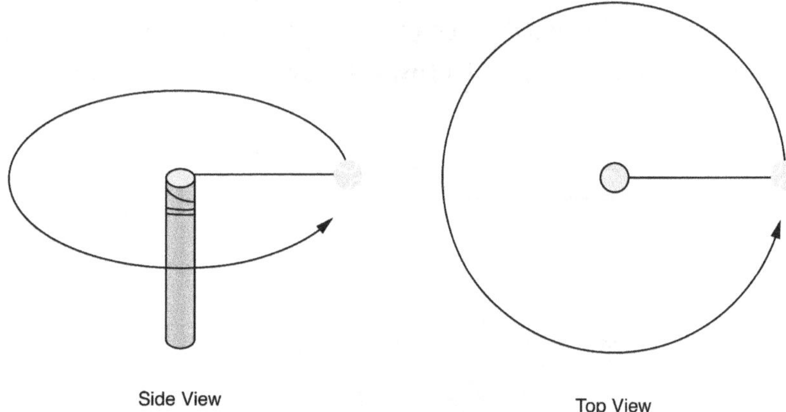

The speed of an object in uniform circular motion is, like in linear motion, a distance divided by the time required to traverse that distance. A simple expression is the circumference of the circle divided by the time the object takes to go around one full time. Given a radius r and a time T to go around the circle, the speed v is $v = \frac{2\pi r}{T}$

This time T is also called the object's **period**, and its inverse $\left(\frac{1}{T}\right)$ is the **frequency**, often expressed as f. The frequency measures how often the object completes a revolution around the circle, and its unit (when T is in seconds) is hertz (Hz). Another useful quantity is the **angular frequency**, $2\pi f$, which is often expressed as ω and may also use hertz. Employing this definition, the velocity is ωr. Therefore, the velocity v is also equal to $2\pi fr$.

DID YOU KNOW?

In the case of a ball on a string, if at any point the string is cut, removing the force acting on the ball, the ball will immediately begin moving linearly at the same speed with which it was moving circularly. Its direction will be tangential to the circle—that is, the direction of its velocity at the moment the string is cut.

Example

An electron in a magnetic field moves in a circle of radius 0.030 meters. If the angular frequency of its rotational motion is 2,400 hertz, what is its velocity?

A. 1.3×10^{-5} m/s B. 72 m/s C. 452 m/s D. 80,000 m/s

The correct answer is **B.** The velocity of the electron is the following: $v = \frac{2\pi r}{T}$ Because $\frac{2\pi}{T}$ is equal to $2\varpi f$, it is the angular frequency (ω). Thus, the velocity in meters per second is $v = \omega r = (2{,}400 \text{ hertz})(0.030 \text{ m}) = 72 \text{ m/s}$

Centripetal Acceleration

Although the *speed* of an object in uniform circular motion is constant, its *velocity* is always changing: it is at all points tangent to the circular path. By Newton's first law of motion, therefore, the object is experiencing acceleration and thus a force. This acceleration—called **centripetal acceleration**—always points toward the center of the circle. A simple example is a planet, such as Earth, orbiting a star. The star exerts a gravitational force that pulls the planet toward the star, and the planet moves (ideally) in a circle around the star. The derivation of centripetal acceleration (a_c) is complicated, but the formula is simple given a speed v and a radius r: $a_c = \frac{v^2}{r}$

TEST TIP

If you are unsure whether you correctly remember a formula, such as centripetal acceleration, you can increase your confidence by checking the units. For instance, using metric units, acceleration is in units of m/s^2. Velocity squared yields units of m^2/s^2, and the radius is in units of m. Dividing the squared velocity units by the radius units yields m/s^2, which is the same as for acceleration. This check is not sufficient to prove the formula is correct, but it can identify an erroneous formula.

By Newton's second law of motion, the **centripetal force** F_c on an object of mass m is therefore $F_c = ma_c = \frac{mv^2}{r}$

Centrifugal force is a "ghost" force. For example, a passenger in a car that turns right feels a leftward force. But by Newton's first law of motion, the passenger's body tries to keep moving straight when the car turns right, causing the car to push the passenger to the right. The feeling, however, is of another force pushing the passenger leftward into the car rather than the car pushing the passenger rightward toward the center of rotational motion. The centrifugal force is therefore equal in magnitude but opposite in direction to the centripetal force.

Example

A 75-kilogram passenger on a rotating theme-park ride experiences a centripetal force of 230 newtons. If she is 12 meters from the center of rotation, what is her velocity?

A. 6.1 m/s B. 6.2 m/s C. 37 m/s D. 38 m/s

The correct answer is **A.** Use the formula for centripetal force with respect to mass, velocity, and radius of rotation: $F_c = \frac{mv^2}{r}$ $v^2 = \frac{F_c r}{m}$ $v = \sqrt{\frac{F_c r}{m}}$ Use the given quantities to get the velocity in meters per second: $v = \sqrt{\frac{(230)(12)}{75}} = \sqrt{37} = 6.1$ m/s

Friction

Newton's first law of motion seems to break down in everyday life: rolling cars come to a stop, falling objects stop accelerating at a certain speed despite the force of gravity, and so on. The cause of the apparent breakdown is another force that resists the motion of objects: **friction**. For example, a plane that turns off its engines loses horizontal speed because of **air resistance**, which is a type of friction. A heavy piece of furniture is often difficult to slide across a floor because it experiences friction wherever it touches the floor. Friction can also act on nonmoving objects. For instance, it can prevent an object from sliding down an incline despite the force of gravity.

Because friction is a force, it causes acceleration. For moving objects, the friction force generally has a direction opposite that of the velocity. When an object decelerates because of friction, byproducts of this deceleration can be motion of something else (such as waves or eddies when the object is moving in water) or **heat**. Heat is another type of motion that involves movement of the atoms and molecules that constitute matter. For example, people with cold hands may rub them together briskly to warm them. For stationary objects, the force of friction is opposite to what would otherwise be a net force, such as gravity.

KEEP IN MIND

Calculating the friction force can be difficult because it involves many factors, such as the roughness of surfaces (in the case of sliding objects) and the fluid characteristics of air (in the case of air resistance). For this reason, problems often assume friction is negligible—an assumption that often still allows a good approximation of the solution.

A common example of friction is an object sliding on a surface. The force due to friction is proportional to the object's mass because the mass determines the object's **weight** (which is the force it experiences from gravity). The weight of an object causes it to "push" against the surface, and when the object slides, that vertical push creates the resistance to horizontal motion (that is, friction) because of surface imperfections and irregularities.

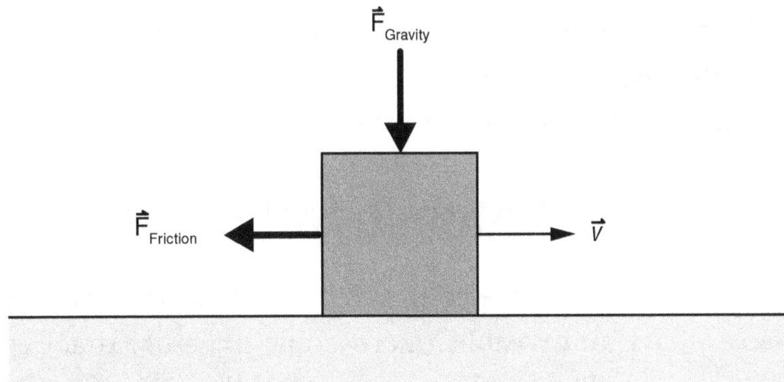

Example

A car is moving east at 20 meters per second. In what direction is the force of friction?

A. East B. North C. South D. West

The correct answer is **D.** Friction is generally in the direction opposite to the direction of motion—hence, a car that coasts in neutral, for example, will slow down without changing direction. For a car moving east, the friction force is directed west. The car's speed is unimportant to determining the direction of the force of friction.

Let's Review!

- Linear motion is movement along a line; the velocity and acceleration may vary, but they are always parallel to the line.
- Nonlinear motion is movement that is not confined to a line; the velocity and acceleration can be any quantity.
- Rotational (circular) motion is movement around an axis or along a circular path.
- The period (T) of an object in uniform circular motion is the time it takes to travel once around the circle. The inverse of the period is the frequency (f), and the angular frequency (ω) is $2\pi f$.
- Centripetal acceleration (a_c) is the acceleration an object experiences when in uniform circular motion. It is equal to $\frac{v^2}{r}$, where v is the object's velocity and r is the radius of the circle of motion.
- The centripetal force on an object in uniform circular motion is the object's mass times its centripetal acceleration.
- Centrifugal force is a "ghost force" in which an object undergoing centripetal acceleration "feels" like it is being pushed away from the center of rotation.
- Friction is resistance to motion. It is a force that is generally directed opposite to a moving object's velocity.
- Friction causes heat and/or motion of surrounding materials as a byproduct of its force on a moving object.
- Friction can prevent motion by acting opposite to other forces, such as gravity.

WAVES AND SOUND

This lesson reviews a simple model of the atom and its role in the materials of everyday life. It then discusses waves in general and mechanical and electromagnetic waves in particular and applies these principles to optics.

Matter and Atomic Structure

The materials that are common to human experience (through sight, touch, and the other senses) have an invisible, microscopic structure that experimenters can probe using scientific instruments. The fundamental unit of this structure is the **atom,** which comprises a central, heavy **nucleus** (plural **nuclei**) surrounded ("orbited") by lighter **electrons.** The nucleus is composed of **protons,** which carry a positive electric charge, and **neutrons,** which carry no electric charge (they are electrically neutral). Together, the protons and neutrons are sometimes called **nucleons.** Electrons carry a negative electric charge. Below is a simple representation of the structure of an atom.

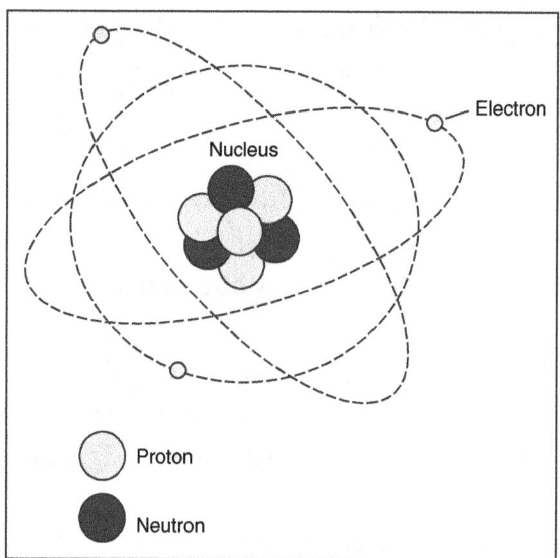

Electric charge (or just "charge") is a property of matter that relates to attraction or repulsion through the **electric force.** Charge comes in two known varieties; although scientists use *positive* and *negative* to describe charge, these terms are just conventions that have some mathematical utility. They do not describe a fundamental "signed" property of charge. The main qualitative rule is that like charges repel and unlike charges attract.

The electric force holds the atom together through the attraction of the negatively charged electrons to the positively charged nucleus. When an atom has the same number of electrons as protons, it is electrically neutral because the amount of charge on an electron is the same as that on a proton, but they are unlike, causing electrical attraction. The result is the simplistic model of an atom that shows electrons orbiting the nucleus like planets orbit the sun.

The number of protons in a nucleus determines the **element** that the atom represents: hydrogen (1 proton), helium (2), carbon (6), oxygen (8), iron (26), and so on. The number of neutrons in a nucleus can vary. Instances of an element with different neutron counts are called **isotopes** of that element. As a rule, isotopes of common elements have about as many neutrons as protons.

If the number of electrons in an atom differs from the number of protons, that atom has a net electric charge: positive if it has more protons than electrons, and negative if it has more electrons than protons. An atom with a net electric charge is called an **ion.**

Although not all matter is composed of atoms—physicists claim to have discovered a variety of particles that can exist apart from atoms—an understanding of atomic structure informs numerous fields, including chemistry and semiconductor physics. Moreover, the nucleons of an atom appear to have a deeper internal structure, a topic that researchers are exploring.

Example

A certain isotope of magnesium has 13 neutrons and 12 protons. If an atom of this isotope is electrically neutral, how many electrons does it have?

A. 12 B. 13 C. 25 D. 50

The correct answer is **A.** An electrically neutral atom must have the same number of protons as electrons. Because they carry no charge, neutrons have no electrical effect on the atom.

Properties of Waves

A universally recognizable example of waves is in water—whether in the ocean, a pool, or a small container. It is possible to visualize many aspects of invisible and conceptual, or mathematical, waves by observing how waves act in water. For example, the highest part of an ocean wave is the **crest** (or **peak**), the lowest part is the **trough,** and half the distance between these two points is the **amplitude.** (The full distance between the crest and trough is called the **peak-to-peak amplitude.**) The distance between successive peaks or successive troughs is called the **wavelength.** These parameters describe the spatial (space-related) characteristics of the wave. But waves also generally have temporal (time-related) characteristics. For example, given some fixed point in space, the time between the arrival of successive waves is the **period,** and its reciprocal is the **frequency**—often expressed in hertz (Hz), or inverse seconds (s^{-1}).

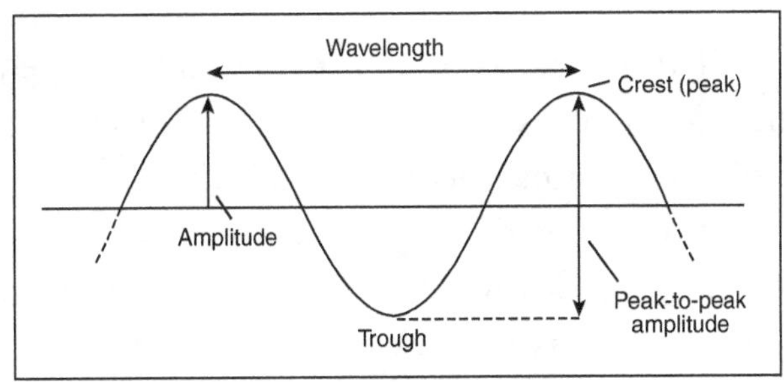

The wavelength (λ), frequency (f), and **wave speed** (v) are related by the equation $v = \lambda f$.

Although these spatial and temporal properties are the most intuitive, waves can have other, less intuitive properties. For instance, if a light source increases and decreases in intensity over time, its intensity can be described as a wave whose frequency is temporal and whose amplitude is intensity (rather than height). Mechanical (e.g., sound and water) and electromagnetic (e.g., visible light and radio) waves are additional examples.

Water waves also demonstrate some of the general behaviors of waves. When they strike a wall or other fairly stationary object, for example, the result is **reflection**: some or all of the wave "bounces" off the object. Waves that pass through a medium with changing material properties may bend, a phenomenon called **refraction.** The changing depth of the ocean floor, for instance, causes ocean waves to bend and usually arrive perpendicular to shore, regardless of their original direction. Another behavior of waves is **diffraction**: wa`ves traveling in a certain direction can "turn" around sharp edges.

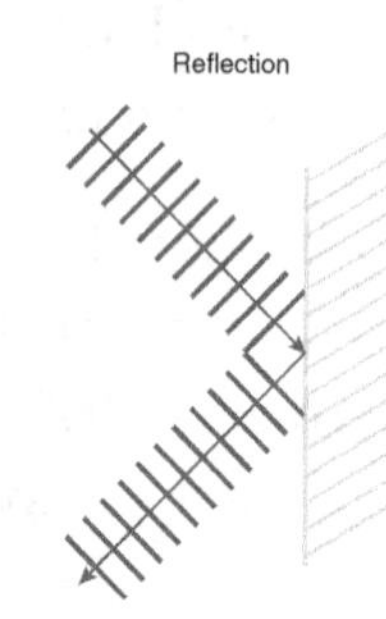

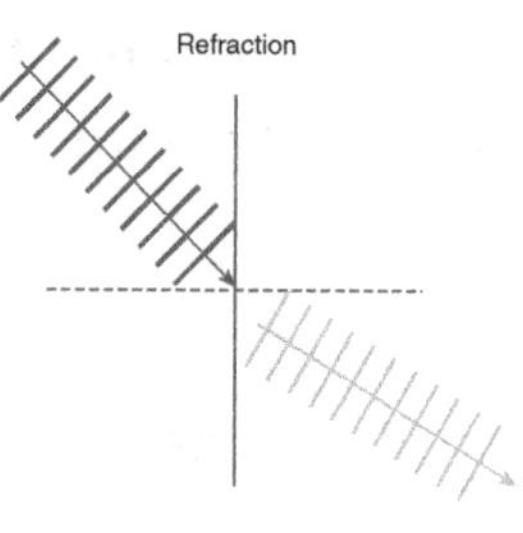

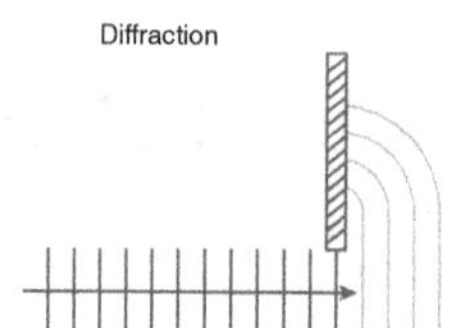

Example

An oceanographer has set a post in the water near shore to study waves before a hurricane. If she finds that the waves are 75 feet apart and a trough arrives every 25 seconds, what is the frequency?

A. 0.013 Hz
B. 0.040 Hz
C. 25 Hz
D. 75 Hz

The correct answer is **B.** The frequency of a wave is the reciprocal of its period: the time between arrival of successive troughs or peaks. In this case, the frequency is $\frac{1}{25\text{ s}} = 0.040\text{ s}^{-1} = 0.040\text{ Hz}$.

Mechanical Waves

Waves that propagate in matter—for example, water waves—are called **mechanical waves.** They can involve variation in height, as in water waves, or variation in pressure, as in acoustic/sound waves. Earthquakes involve mechanical waves similar to sound waves: these seismic waves cause the ground to shake as they travel from the source of the quake.

In the case of sound, what the ear detects as **pitch** is essentially the frequency of the wave, and the **volume** is essentially the amplitude. Characteristics of the wave, including its speed, depend on the properties of the **medium** (or substance/material) that carries it. In the case of sound, for example, the wave speed depends on the **density** of the medium—how many atoms are packed into a unit volume—and the **compressibility** of the medium—how much the medium can be compacted given a certain force or pressure. The denser and less compressible a material, the faster sound waves will travel through it. Because water is denser and less compressible than air, for instance, sound travels faster in the former than in the latter. Similarly, waves in a rope will travel faster if the rope is taut than if it is loose.

Depending on the type of mechanical wave and the medium through which it travels, the wave speed may be apparent to the human senses. For example, at a sufficiently large distance from the observer, an event such as a hammer strike or gunfire is visible before it is audible. This delay occurs because light travels much faster than sound. Therefore, distant events are often seen before they are heard.

Mechanical waves exhibit the same phenomena as other waves, such as reflection, refraction, and diffraction.

Example

If a sound wave in air at a certain temperature and humidity has a frequency of 125 Hz and a wavelength of 9.00 feet, what is its wave speed?

A. 0.0720 feet per second

B. 13.9 feet per second

C. 134 feet per second

D. 1,125 feet per second

The correct answer is **D.** The wave speed v is related to the frequency f and wavelength λ by the formula $v = \lambda f$. Multiply the frequency (which is in hertz, or inverse seconds) by the wavelength to get the wave speed in feet per second.

Electromagnetic (Light) Waves

Electromagnetic waves exhibit the same behavior as other waves, but unlike mechanical waves, they require no medium to propagate. (That is, they can propagate in a vacuum.) Electromagnetic waves result from the movement—specifically, the acceleration—of a charge. Examples include visible light, radio waves, X-rays, microwaves, and infrared radiation.

As their name implies, electromagnetic waves involve variation in the **electric field** and the **magnetic field** around the source charge(s). These fields mutually oscillate in a manner similar to that of mechanical waves, although the oscillation is in field intensity and direction rather than, for example, wave height or material pressure.

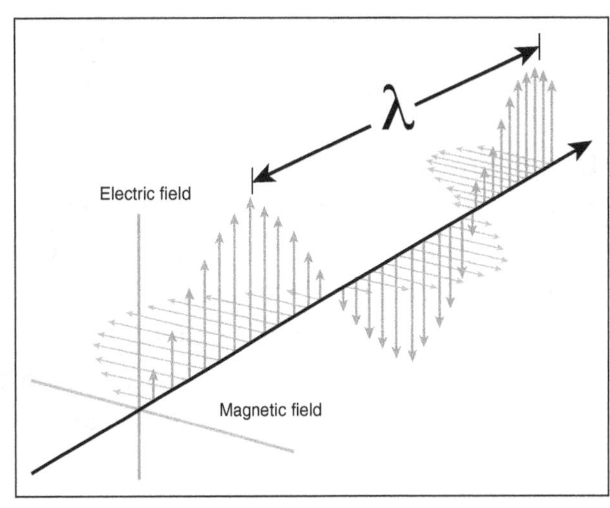

In a vacuum, the speed of an electromagnetic wave (or the **speed of light,** sometimes labeled c) is a constant: approximately 186,000 miles per second, which is much faster than the speed of sound in air—roughly 0.2 miles per second, or about 770 miles per hour. When traveling in a material, the speed of an electromagnetic wave decreases by a factor of $1/n$, where n is the material's **refractive index** (or **index of refraction**). Therefore, the speed of light v in a material of refractive index n is $v = c/n$. The refractive index depends on the electrical and magnetic properties of the material.

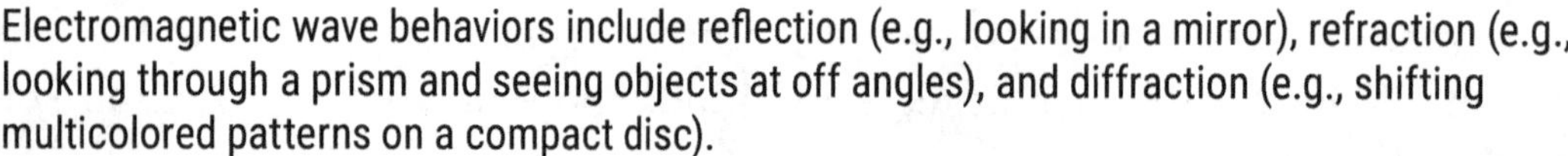

CONNECTIONS

Electromagnetic wave behaviors include reflection (e.g., looking in a mirror), refraction (e.g., looking through a prism and seeing objects at off angles), and diffraction (e.g., shifting multicolored patterns on a compact disc).

Example

A radio wave is passing through a material with a refractive index of 2.00. What is its speed?

A. 2,000 miles per second

B. 93,000 miles per second

C. 186,000 miles per second

D. 372,000 miles per second

The correct answer is **B.** The speed of light in a medium (material) is the speed of light in a vacuum (c = 186,000 miles per second) divided by the refractive index (2.00, in this case). The result is 93,000 miles per second.

Optics

In situations where the dimensions of a problem are much larger than the wavelength of the electromagnetic waves, those waves can often be accurately approximated as **rays**: directed line segments that represent the waves. Some simple rules enable analysis of electromagnetic-wave behavior in media that involve mirrors and in materials with different refractive indices. This model is a straightforward, often effective way to study **optics**, which is the subset of physics that examines the behavior of light.

DID YOU KNOW?

A laser acts as like nearly ideal ray because it maintains a very narrow beam over long distances. When used with caution (specifically, eye protection), low-power lasers are excellent for clearly seeing the principles of optics in action.

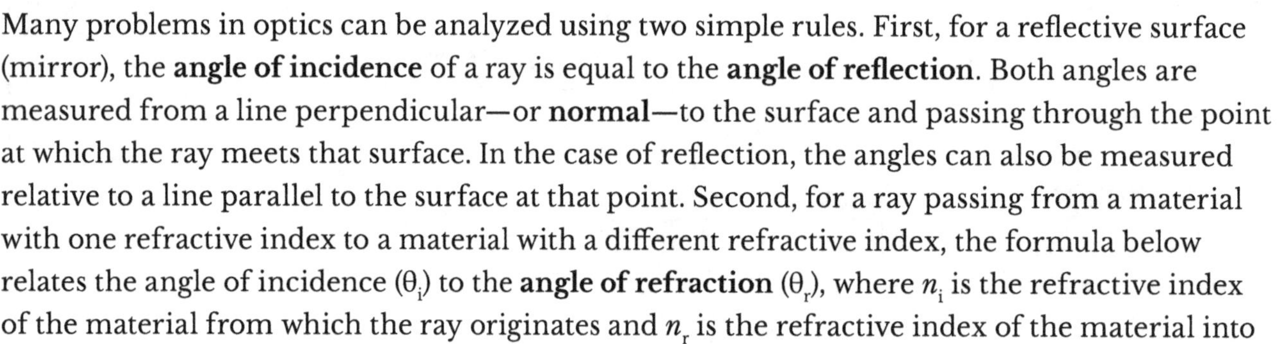

Many problems in optics can be analyzed using two simple rules. First, for a reflective surface (mirror), the **angle of incidence** of a ray is equal to the **angle of reflection**. Both angles are measured from a line perpendicular—or **normal**—to the surface and passing through the point at which the ray meets that surface. In the case of reflection, the angles can also be measured relative to a line parallel to the surface at that point. Second, for a ray passing from a material with one refractive index to a material with a different refractive index, the formula below relates the angle of incidence (θ_i) to the **angle of refraction** (θ_r), where n_i is the refractive index of the material from which the ray originates and n_r is the refractive index of the material into which the ray transmits. This relationship is called **Snell's law** and is responsible for the magnification of objects using lenses.

$$\frac{\sin\theta_i}{\sin\theta_r} = \frac{n_r}{n_i}$$

Example

If a light ray hits a mirror with a 30° angle of incidence relative to the normal, what is its angle of reflection relative to the normal?

A. 30°
B. 40°
C. 60°
D. 90°

The correct answer is **A.** The angle of incidence is equal to the angle of reflection, as long as both angles are measured from the same line (normal or parallel).

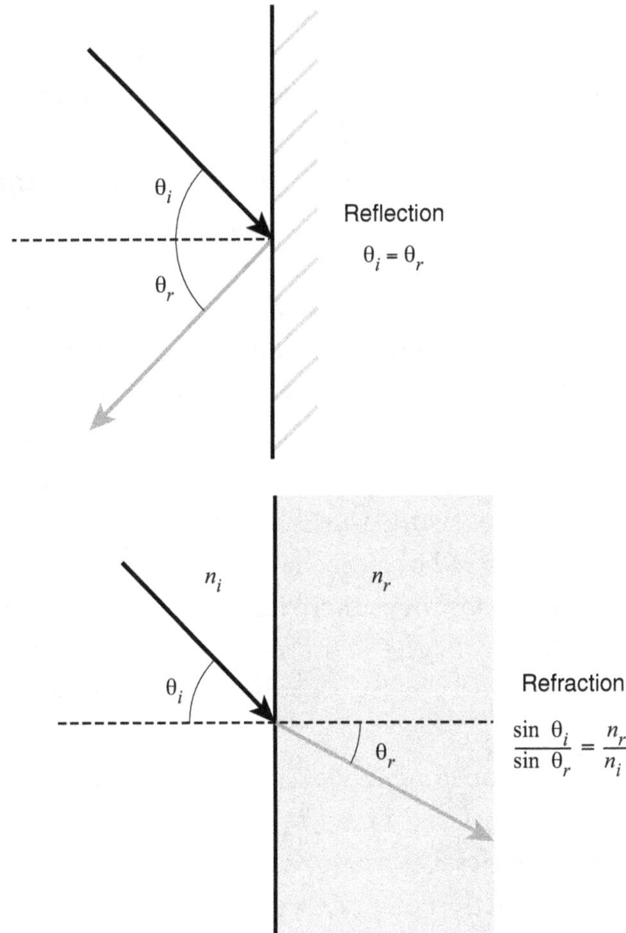

Let's Review!

- The matter that appears in everyday life is largely composed of atoms; each atom has a central nucleus made of positively charged protons and uncharged neutrons that is surrounded by "orbiting" negatively charged electrons.
- The elements are each a type of atom with a different number of protons in its nucleus. A given element with a given number of neutrons is an isotope.
- The electric force binds the electrons to the nucleus of an atom.
- Waves occur throughout nature in different forms, but they have common properties and behaviors.
- A wave is defined by its amplitude, frequency, and wavelength. The wave speed is equal to the product of the frequency and the wavelength ($v = \lambda f$).
- Common wave behaviors include reflection (when the wave "bounces" off an object), refraction (when it bends in a medium), and diffraction (when it turns around an edge).
- Mechanical waves are waves in a material—solid, liquid, or gas. Examples include sound waves, seismic waves, and ocean waves.
- The speed of a mechanical wave depends on the compressibility and density of a material. As these values increase, so does the wave speed.
- Electromagnetic waves are a back-and-forth oscillation of the electric and magnetic fields owing to acceleration of a charge. They can propagate without a medium (that is, in a vacuum).
- The speed of an electromagnetic wave in a material is equal to the speed of light in a vacuum (c) divided by the refractive index of that material.
- In optics, the angle of incidence of a light ray is equal to the angle of reflection.
- Refraction of a ray is described by Snell's law:
- $\frac{\sin\theta_i}{\sin\theta_r} = \frac{n_r}{n_i}$,
- where θ_i is the angle of incidence, θ_r is the angle of refraction, n_i is the refractive index in the material from which the ray is traveling, and n_r is the refractive index in the material to which the ray is traveling.

Kinetic Energy

This lesson introduces the concept of mechanical energy as the sum of kinetic energy and potential energy. The lesson also examines objects in motion and the effects of changing velocities and forces on moving objects. Finally, the lesson discusses how the force of gravitation affects objects in the universe.

Mechanical Energy

Energy is the ability to do work. Mechanical energy can be divided into two types: kinetic energy and potential energy.

Kinetic energy of an object is represented by the equation $KE = \frac{1}{2}mv^2$, where m is the mass of the object and v is the velocity. The kinetic energy is proportional to the object's mass. A 7.26 kg shot thrown through the air has much more kinetic energy than a 145 g baseball with the same velocity. The kinetic energy of an object is also proportional to the square of the velocity of the object. A car traveling at 40 m/s has four times the kinetic energy of the same car moving at 20 m/s. This is the result of the squared velocity term in the formula. Kinetic energy, like work, is measured in **joules**.

Consider a group of boulders perched high on a cliff. These boulders have energy in a stored condition because gravity could cause them to fall. This is called gravitational potential energy (there are other types of stored energy, such as chemical and electrical). Potential energy of an object is stored energy due to the object's configuration or position relative to a force acting on it. The formula for calculating gravitational potential energy is $PE = mgh$, where m is the mass of the object, g is the acceleration of gravity on Earth (9.8 m/s^2), and h is the object's height above Earth's surface. The unit for potential energy is also **joules**. Potential energy is an energy of position because much of the way this quantity can be changed is due to height.

Falling objects provide an interesting case for mechanical energy calculations. If we assume that there is no wind resistance, then all potential energy an object has before falling turns into kinetic energy as the object falls. Once the object impacts Earth's surface, there are different calculations to be done. We will simplify things by considering the object at the moment before impact.

Example

If a boulder falls off a 65 m high cliff, at what height, in meters, does the boulder have zero potential energy?

A. 0 B. 0.010 C. 32 D. 65

The correct answer is **A**. Potential energy is defined as $PE = mgh$. Only at $h = 0$ will the equation equal 0.

Linear Momentum and Impulse

The **momentum** of an object depends upon its mass and velocity. **Momentum** is defined as $\boldsymbol{p} = \boldsymbol{mv}$, where $\boldsymbol{m}$ is the mass and $\boldsymbol{v}$ is the velocity. The unit for momentum is kg·m/s and does not have a special name. This concept can be illustrated by a simple example: Most people would rather try stopping a child's tricycle rolling at 0.5 miles per hour than a loaded dump truck at the same speed. The difference is the dump truck's greater momentum as a result of its much larger mass.

Newton's second law of motion explains how the momentum of an object is changed by a net force acting upon it. Newton's second law of motion, $\boldsymbol{F} = \boldsymbol{ma}$, can be rewritten by using the definition of acceleration as the change in velocity divided by the time interval.

$$F = ma = m\left(\frac{\Delta v}{\Delta t}\right)$$

Multiplying both sides of the equation by the time interval results in the following equation:

$$F\Delta t = m\Delta v$$

The left side, $F\Delta t$, is the product of the average force and the time interval over which it acts. This product is called the **impulse**, and an impulse is found by determining the area under the curve of a force-time graph, as shown below.

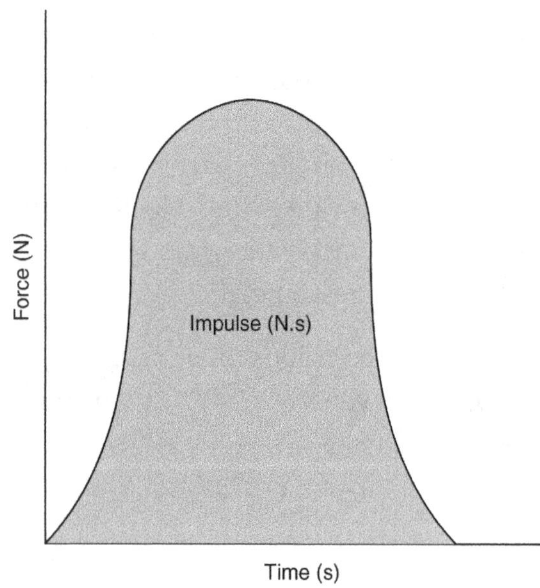

Impulse-Momentum Theorem: $F\Delta t = p2 - p1$

This equation is called the **impulse-momentum theorem**. The impulse on an object is equal to the change in momentum that it causes. If the force is constant, the impulse is just the product of the force and the time interval over which it acts.

What happens to a driver when a crash suddenly stops a car? An impulse is needed to bring the driver's momentum to zero. The steering wheel can exert a large force during a short period of time. An airbag reduces the force exerted on the driver by greatly increasing the length of the time over which the force is exerted.

Refer to the equation: $F = (m\Delta v)/\Delta t$. In the equation, Δv is the same with or without the airbag. However, the airbag reduces F by increasing Δt. Less force on a person during a crash is a good thing.

Example

What is the mass of a student's phone, in grams, if a pillow on the floor provides 7.71 N in 0.100 s while reducing the falling phone's speed from 4.43 m/s to rest?

A. 0.174 B. 1.74 C. 17.4 D. 174

The correct answer is **D.** Use the impulse-momentum theorem to solve for mass.
$\frac{F \bullet \Delta t}{v} = m$; $\frac{7.71\ \text{N} \bullet 0.100\ \text{s}}{4.43\ \frac{\text{m}}{\text{s}}} = 0.174\ \text{kg} = 174\ \text{g}$

Universal Gravitation

Newton used mathematical arguments to show that if the path of a planet is an ellipse, then the magnitude of the force, *F*, on the planet resulting from the sun must vary inversely with the square of the distance between the center of the planet and center of the sun.

Newton later stated that the sight of a falling apple made him think about the motion of planets. He recognized that the apple fell straight down because Earth attracted it. He wondered whether this force might extend beyond the trees to the clouds, to the moon, and beyond. Could gravity also be the force that attracts the planets to the sun? Newton hypothesized that the force on the apple must be proportional to its mass. In addition, according to Newton's third law of motion, the apple would also attract Earth. Thus, the force of attraction must be proportional to the mass of Earth. The attractive force that exists between all objects is known as **gravitational force.**

Newton assumed that the same force of attraction would act between any two masses, ml and m2. He proposed his **law of universal gravitation**, which is represented by the following equation:

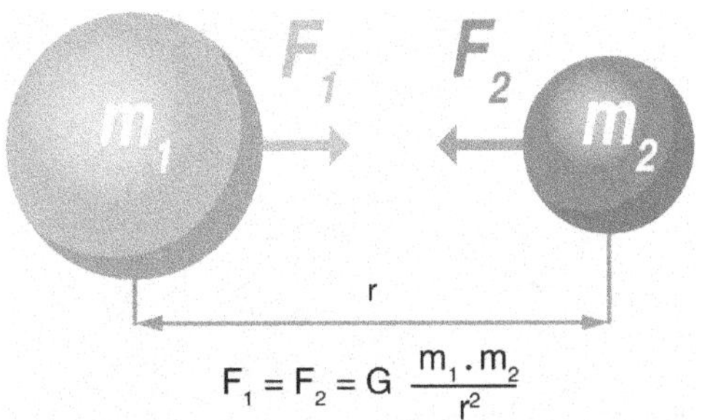

In the equation, ***r*** is the distance between the centers of the masses, and ***G*** is a universal constant—that is, it is the same everywhere. The gravitational constant G = 6.67×10^{-11} N·m²/kg². The force of gravitation is directly proportional to the masses of the objects. However, force is inversely proportional to the square of the distance between the objects.

Example

What is the force of gravitational attraction, in newtons, between Mars (6.39×10^{23} kg) and its inner moon Phobos (10.6×10^{15} kg) 6.00×10^{6} m away?

A. 1.25×10^{16} B. 4.37×10^{16} C. 2.42×10^{17} D. 8.93×10^{18}

The correct answer is **A.** Use the formula to calculate the force: $F = G\left(\frac{m_1 m_2}{r^2}\right)$ $F =$ Skipping unsupported tag: span$\left(6.67 \times 10^{-11} \frac{\text{N} \bullet \text{m}^2}{\text{kg}^2}\right)\left(\frac{(6.39 \times 10^{23}\,\text{kg})(10.6 \times 10^{15}\,\text{kg})}{(6.00 \times 10^{6}\,\text{m})^2}\right) = 1.25 \times 10^{16}\,\text{N}$.

Let's Review!

- Kinetic energy, or the energy of motion, of an object is represented by the equation $KE = \frac{1}{2}mv^2$.
- The potential energy of an object is stored energy due to the object's configuration or position relative to a force acting on it. Gravitational potential energy is defined as $PE = mgh$. Near Earth's surface, gravitational acceleration is measured to be $g = 9.8$ m/s^2.
- Newton's second law of motion explains how the momentum of an object is changed by a net force action on it.
- The impulse on an object is equal to the change in momentum that it causes.
- The attractive force that exists between all objects is known as gravitational force. That force is directly related to the product of the two masses and inversely related to the square of the distance between the masses.
- $F = G\left(\frac{m_1 m_2}{r^2}\right)$ *where* $G = 6.67 \times 10^{-11} \frac{N \bullet m^2}{kg^2}$

ELECTRICITY AND MAGNETISM

This lesson reviews the nature and relationship of electricity and magnetism and how these forces enable many modern technologies.

Electric Forces and Fields

Objects that have an **electric charge** attract or repel other electrically charged objects depending on whether the charges are like (repel) or unlike (attract). **Coulomb's law** describes the **electric force** F_E that an object carrying charge Q_1 exerts on an object carrying charge Q_2:

$$F_E = k\frac{Q_1 Q_2}{r^2}$$

where r is the distance between the objects and k is the electric constant. When using SI units—that is, the force is measured in newtons (N), distance in meters (m), and charge in coulombs (C)—k is approximately 9×10^9. To aid the math, electric charge is described as either positive (like the charge on a proton) or negative (like the charge on an electron).

When studying and describing light (and other electromagnetic waves), defining the **electric field** is helpful. The electric field is the force that an object with a charge of 1 coulomb experiences at a given distance r from an object with charge Q. The formula for this field (E) is similar to Coulomb's law:

$$E = k\frac{Q}{r^2}$$

The field is measured in newtons per coulomb.

Generally, the electric force and field are vectors, meaning they have both a magnitude and direction. Correctly adding forces therefore requires adding the vectors, not just the magnitudes. As a result, for example, if two forces acting on a charged object have equal magnitudes but opposite directions, their sum is zero—the object experiences no net force.

BE CAREFUL!

Charged objects only exert a force on other charged objects. Uncharged objects—for example, neutrons and many everyday objects—neither experience nor exert an electric force (at least under typical conditions).

KEEP IN MIND

Generally, if Coulomb's law yields a negative value for the electric force, that force is attractive; if it yields a positive value, that force is repulsive.

Example

What is the magnitude of the attractive electric force, in newtons, that an object with a charge 5.0 C exerts on another object with a charge –8.0 C that is 1.2×10^2 meters away?

A. -2.7×10^{-3}

B. -3.3×10^{-1}

C. -2.6×10^{7}

D. -3.0×10^{9}

The correct answer is **C.** Using Coulomb's law: $F_E = k\frac{Q_1 Q_2}{r^2}$ $F_E = \left(9 \times 10^9\right)\frac{(5.0) \times (-8.0)}{(1.2 \times 10^2)^2}$ $F_E = (9 \times 10^9)\frac{-40}{1.4 \times 10^4} = -2.6 \times 10^7$ *newtons*

Magnetism

Magnetism manifests through forces and fields in a manner similar to electricity, but the mathematics are more complicated. Qualitatively, a simple model of magnetism is relatively easy to understand. **Magnetic fields** and **magnetic forces** arise from moving charges—that is, any charged object with a nonzero velocity produces a magnetic field (and thus can exert a magnetic force on another moving charge). For instance, a wire that carries an **electric current**—which is the movement of negatively charged electrons through the wire—creates a magnetic field around that wire. The movement of electrons around the nucleus of an atom also creates a magnetic field, and in some elements (such as iron), the result can be powerful magnetic properties. Earth has a magnetic field that allows navigation using a compass, which uses a small magnetic needle to detect the direction of the field.

Like electric charge, magnetism has two "polarities" (or **poles**) called **north** and **south**. Unlike electric charge, however, a magnetic object (or **magnet**) always has a magnetic north and a magnetic south—north and south never exist by themselves. (Positive and negative electric charges can exist by themselves.) In addition, like polarities repel, and unlike polarities attract.

BE CAREFUL!

Remember that any motion of charge creates a magnetic field, but only charge *acceleration* creates electromagnetic waves.

DID YOU KNOW?

Because electric currents create magnetic fields, they can deflect a compass needle. For instance, if you connect a wire across the terminals of a battery, causing an electric current to flow, you can see the effect of magnetism if you bring a compass near it. An accidental observation of this phenomenon led to the discovery of the link between electric current and magnetism.

Example

Which of the following events produces a magnetic field?

A. An accelerating electron

B. A wire in an electric field

C. A neutron moving through space

D. A positively charged object in a stationary position

The correct answer is **A.** Magnetic fields result from moving charges. Of the possible choices, only A involves a charged object (neutrons have no net charge) that is also in motion.

Electric and Magnetic Flux

Electric flux is the "flow" of the electric field through a given surface. To envision this concept, drawing **electric field lines** is helpful. Field lines show the direction of the electric force in space—specifically, the path a positive "test charge" would follow if it were initially stationary at some arbitrary point in space. By convention, field lines are generally shown flowing out from positive charges and in to negative charges. The illustration below shows a positive charge in empty space, a negative charge in empty space, and a positive and negative charge in close proximity.

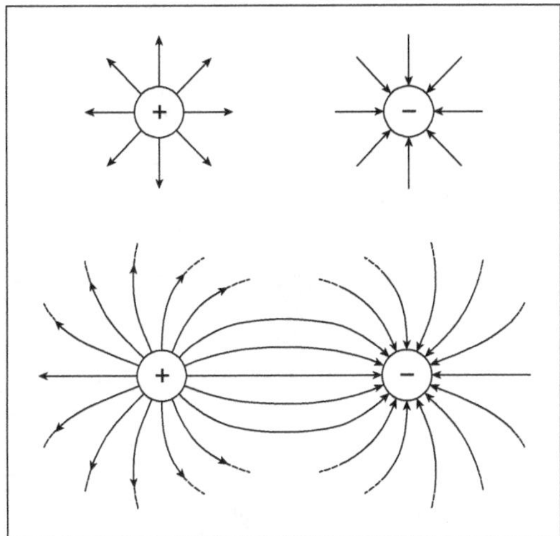

The more field lines that flow through an area, the greater the flux. Higher field-line density indicates a stronger field or force in that region. Although field lines are conceptual rather than physical, they are a helpful way to represent how electricity and magnetism permeate the space around charged objects.

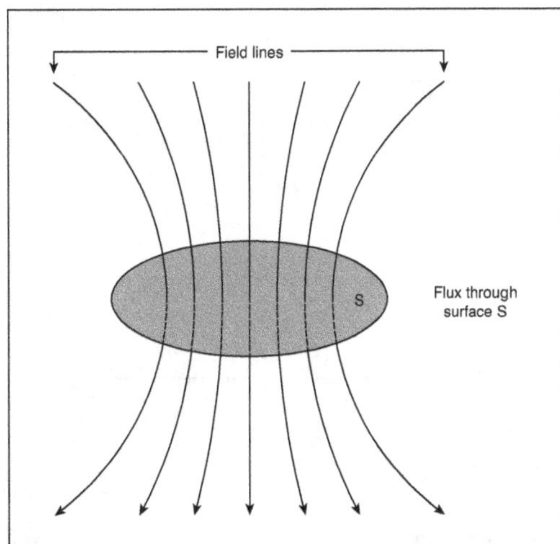

Magnetic flux and **magnetic field lines** are analogous to electric flux and field lines, but they represent magnetism rather than electricity. The same general principles apply.

One aspect of electricity and magnetism underlying much of today's technology is **electromagnetic induction.** This phenomenon occurs when an electrical conductor such as a wire experiences a changing magnetic field: the result is an electric force in that conductor. The strength of the electric force around a conducting loop is proportional to the rate at which the magnetic flux through that loop is changing. For example, spinning a coil of wire positioned between powerful magnets (or vice versa) is essentially how power companies produce electricity. Electrically driven motors apply the same principles, but in reverse.

Example

A positively charged object is inside a sphere that has no effect on electric fields. In what direction will the electric flux be?

A. Into the sphere
B. Out of the sphere
C. Along the surface of the sphere
D. Both into and out of the sphere

The correct answer is **B.** The electric flux is the "flow" of the electric field and is closely related to the field lines. Because the field lines go out from positive charges, the flux will be out of the sphere in this case.

Electric Circuits

Electric circuits are a critical component of many modern technologies, including computing technology and electrical power distribution. An **electric circuit** (or just *circuit*) is a closed "loop" in which electric charge experiences an electric force around the loop. Important parameters in a circuit are voltage, current, and resistance. **Voltage,** also called the **electric potential difference,** is the amount of energy required to move a unit of charge between two points in a circuit. **Current** is the amount of charge flowing through a given surface per second. **Resistance** is a measure of how much an electrical component impedes the flow of current.

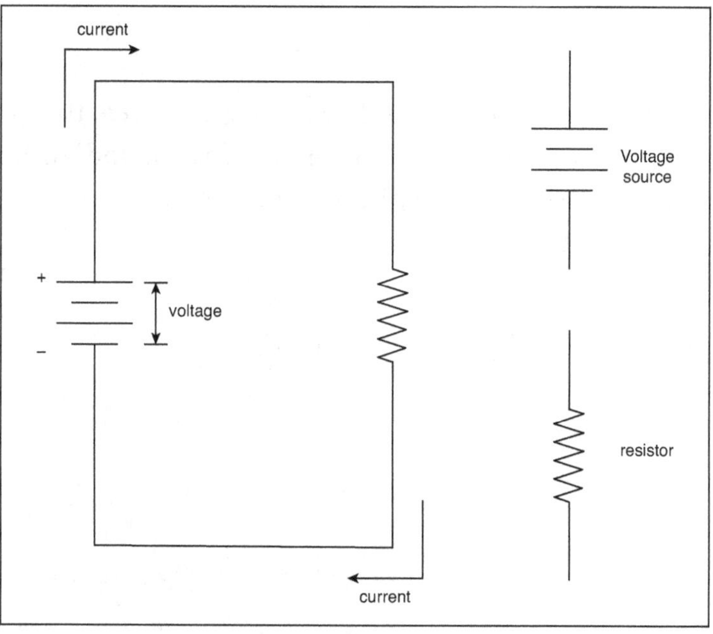

A simple example of a circuit includes a **voltage source** (for example, a battery) and a **resistor** (for example, a light bulb) connected by metal wires. A simple voltage source has two **terminals:** it maintains an electric potential difference across those terminals so that charge will try to flow from the higher-voltage ("positive") terminal to the lower-voltage ("negative") terminal.

Voltage is usually measured in **volts** (V); current is usually measured in **amperes** (A) or **amps,** which are coulombs per second; and resistance is usually measured in **ohms** (Ω). Materials, such as metal, that allow the free flow of electric charge are called **conductors.** Materials, such as many plastics, that do *not* allow the free flow of electric charge are called **insulators.**

DID YOU KNOW?

By convention, current is defined as the flow of positive charge. But because *negative* charge (electrons) is what actually flows in basic circuits, the mathematical assignment of a negative sign to the electron's charge created a historical dilemma. Mathematically, the flow of positive charge in one direction is equal to the flow of negative charge in the opposite direction, so the common practice is to discuss the flow of positive charge even though electrons often constitute the current.

Example

Which of the following best describes an electric current?

A. The storage of electric charge

B. The movement of electric charge

C. The energy required to move electric charge

D. The impedance of electric charge's movement

The correct answer is **B.** Electric current is the flow of electric charge.

Ohm's Law

Circuit analysis can become extremely complex when the circuit involves many components, but a ew basic principles can aid the process, especially for simple circuits. One example is **Ohm's law,** which relates the current I through and voltage V across a component with a given resistance R: $V = IR$.

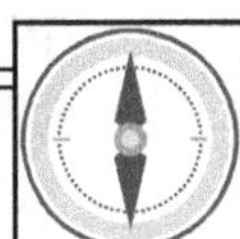

FOR EXAMPLE

If a circuit involves a 10-volt battery connected to a 100-ohm resistor, you can find the current through the resistor using Ohm's law:

$$V = IR$$

$$I = \frac{V}{R} = \frac{10 \text{ volts}}{100 \text{ ohms}} = 0.1 \text{ amps}$$

Two important rules also help in analyzing circuits. The first rule is that at any point (or **node**) in the circuit, the current flowing into that point must equal the current flowing out of that point. Thus, if three wires join at a node, the sum of the currents flowing in must equal the sum of the currents flowing out. The second rule is that for any closed loop in the circuit, the sum of the voltages around the loop must equal zero. For this rule, going around the entire loop in the same direction is critical. One convention is that going from a higher voltage to a lower voltage represents a positive voltage change (or voltage "drop"), whereas going from a lower voltage to a higher voltage represents a negative voltage change. Thus, in a circuit containing just a battery and a resistor, the voltage change across the resistor must be equal in magnitude but opposite in sign to the voltage change across the battery (when going either clockwise or counterclockwise around the circuit).

Example

If 0.2 amps are flowing through a 1,000-ohm resistor, what is the voltage across that resistor?

A. 0.0002 volts B. 200 volts C. 1,000 volts D. 5,000 volts

The correct answer is **B.** Use Ohm's law: $V = IR$ $V = (0.2 \text{ amps}) \times (1{,}000 \text{ ohms}) = 200 \text{ volts}$

Let's Review!

- Electric charges, which can be either positive or negative, create electric fields and exert an electric force on other charges.
- The electric force between two charges (Q_1 and Q_2) obeys Coulomb's law: $F_E = k\frac{Q_1 Q_2}{r^2}$, where k is the electric constant (about 9×10^9 when working in SI units) and r is the distance between the charges.
- The electric field from a charge Q is $E = k\frac{Q}{r^2}$.
- Magnetic fields and forces result from moving charges (an electric current). Magnets have north and south polarities, but unlike electricity where negative and positive charges can appear separately, these magnetic polarities always appear together.
- Electric flux is the "flow" of the electric field, which can be visualized using electric field lines.
- Magnetic flux is the "flow" of the magnetic field, which can be visualized using magnetic field lines.
- Changing magnetic flux through a surface creates an electric field through that surface—a phenomenon that enables electricity generation.
- Electric circuits involve current flowing through resistors and other electrical components, driven by an electric potential difference (voltage).
- The voltage across a resistor is equal to the product of the resistance and the current (Ohm's law). Common units for these parameters are volts, amperes, and ohms.

Chapter 16 Physics Practice Quiz

1. **A vector has its tail at (9, 4) and its head at (0, 3). Which representation of the vector is correct?**

   A. (−9, −1)
   B. (−9, 1)
   C. (−9, 7)
   D. (−9, 12)

2. **Which statement about an object undergoing projectile motion is true? (Assume ideal conditions with no friction.)**

   A. The object's vertical velocity is constant.
   B. The object's vertical acceleration is zero.
   C. The object's horizontal velocity is constant.
   D. The object's horizontal acceleration is nonzero.

3. **Which of the following best describes the behavior of an object in uniform circular motion?**

   A. Constant speed, constant velocity, constant acceleration vector
   B. Changing speed, changing velocity, constant acceleration vector
   C. Constant speed, constant velocity, changing acceleration vector
   D. Constant speed, changing velocity, changing acceleration vector

4. **Surface imperfections cause a horizontally sliding block to come to a halt. Which of the following remains as a result?**

   A. Heat
   B. Velocity
   C. Air resistance
   D. Horizontal force

5. **Which term best describes two atoms that have the same number of protons but different numbers of neutrons?**

   A. Elements
   B. Ions
   C. Isotopes
   D. Nuclei

6. **Which statement about a magnesium ion is correct?**

   A. The number of protons differs from the number of neutrons.
   B. The number of protons differs from the number of electrons.
   C. The number of electrons differs from the number of neutrons.
   D. The numbers of protons, electrons, and neutrons are all the same.

7. **What did Newton hypothesize when he watched the apple fall to the ground?**

   A. The force on the apple must be equal to its mass.
   B. The force on the apple must be unrelated to its mass.
   C. The force on the apple must be proportional to its mass.
   D. The force on the apple must be inversely proportional to its mass.

8. **The chemical bonds found in sugar are an example of what type of energy?**

   A. Kinetic
   B. Magnetic
   C. Potential
   D. Thermal

9. **Which situation represents an attractive magnetic force?**

   A. Two north poles in close proximity
   B. Two south poles in close proximity
   C. Any two magnetic poles in close proximity
   D. A north pole and a south pole in close proximity

10. **A scientist is using a compass to detect magnetic fields. Which experiment will deflect the compass needle?**

    A. Holding a charged object stationary near the compass
    B. Moving a charged object quickly away from the compass
    C. Holding an uncharged object stationary near the compass
    D. Moving an uncharged object quickly away from the compass

CHAPTER 16 PHYSICS PRACTICE QUIZ – ANSWER KEY

1. A. The standard form of a vector is the head coordinates minus the tail coordinates: (0 – 9, 3 – 4) = (–9, –1). **See Lesson: Nature of Motion.**

2. C. An object undergoing projectile motion (in ideal conditions) has a constant horizontal velocity but a changing vertical velocity due to gravity. Thus, its horizontal acceleration is zero, but its vertical acceleration is nonzero. Only answer C is true. **See Lesson: Nature of Motion.**

3. D. An object in uniform circular motion has a constant speed, but as it moves, its velocity and its acceleration vector change direction. **See Lesson: Friction.**

4. A. Once the block has come to a stop, it no longer has any velocity or acceleration. It is therefore experiencing no net force. Likewise, without any velocity, air resistance no longer applies. But as the block slowed, it created heat because of friction, and that heat remains—just like when people who feel cold rub their hands together briskly to warm them up. **See Lesson: Friction.**

5. C. If two atoms have the same number of protons, they are the same element. If two atoms of the same element have different numbers of neutrons, they are isotopes. **See Lesson: Waves and Sounds.**

6. B. An ion is an atom with a net electric charge. Therefore, the number of protons must be different from the number of electrons. Neutrons have no electric charge and therefore have no bearing on the atom's net charge. **See Lesson: Waves and Sounds.**

7. C. He hypothesized that the force on the apple must be proportional to its mass. **See Lesson: Kinetic Energy.**

8. C. When the bonds are broken, the potential energy stored in them is converted to kinetic energy. **See Lesson: Kinetic Energy.**

9. D. As with electric charge, magnetic polarities (or poles) attract if they are different and repel if they are like. Therefore, a north pole attracts a south pole (and vice versa), but north poles repel each another, as do south poles. **See Lesson: Electricity and Magnetism.**

10. B. A magnetic field will deflect the compass needle. Magnetic fields result from moving charges, eliminating answers C and D (which involve uncharged objects). Answer B involves a moving charged object, which will deflect the compass needle. **See Lesson: Electricity and Magnetism.**

CHAPTER 17 EARTH AND SPACE SCIENCES

ASTRONOMY

Are you ready to embark upon a journey through space and time? For centuries, scientists have sought to answer questions about our planet and its place in the universe. Astronomy is the study of the moon, stars, and other objects in space. Modern astronomy can be dated back to the time of the ancient Greeks, when scientists began using mathematics to explain what they observed in the night sky.

The Solar System

Our solar system is made up primarily of the sun and eight planets. All of the objects in our solar system revolve around the sun. By mass alone, the sun makes up 99.8 percent of our solar system.

The eight planets of our solar system are categorized in two groups. The inner planets, the four planets closest to the sun, are small and dense and have rocky surfaces, while the outer planets are larger, are farther away from the sun, and do not have solid surfaces. Pluto, once considered one of the outer planets, is now categorized as a dwarf planet.

- Inner planets: Mercury, Venus, Earth, and Mars
- Outer planets: Jupiter, Saturn, Uranus, and Neptune

Stars

When humans began observing the night sky, they imagined that the twinkling lights they saw formed pictures of people and animals. Today, we call these lights, stars, and the patterns that they form constellations.

Stars are balls of very hot gases that form when gravity pulls a cloud of gas, called a nebula, together with dust. When the mass of gas and dust becomes dense enough, enormous amounts of energy are released, resulting in the light that we see from Earth. Scientists characterize stars based on their color, temperature, size, and chemical composition.

Stars are grouped together in clusters called star systems. Galaxies are large groups of stars and star systems bound together with dust and gas by gravity. Our solar system is located in a galaxy called the Milky Way. Many galaxies, including the Milky Way, are bound by gravity to hundreds or even thousands of other galaxies in regions of space called galaxy clusters.

Most of the stars in our galaxy are main sequence stars, or stars that are in their longest stage of life. Most are also dwarf stars, or small stars with relatively low luminosity. Giant stars, in contrast, are very large and are brighter than the sun.

The Universe

Astronomers define the universe as all of space and everything in it, such as planets, stars, galaxies, and other matter. Most of the matter in the universe is actually dark matter, so called because it does not interact with light and is therefore difficult to measure. The universe also contains cosmic phenomena called black holes, or regions in space with gravity so intense that nothing—not even light—can escape.

How did it all start? The leading theory, called the Big Bang Theory, is that the universe began in an instant, billions of years ago, with an explosion or a big bang. After that explosion, the universe cooled and expanded, inflating over time to become the cosmos that we know today.

Because the distances between objects in space are so large, astronomers use a special unit of measurement, called a light-year, to evaluate them. A light-year is the distance that light travels in space in one Earth year, about 9.5 trillion kilometers. The sun is approximately 150 million kilometers, or 8 light-minutes, away from Earth, whereas the North Star, also called Polaris, is 2 billion kilometers or 320 light-years away.

Let's Review!

- The solar system is made up of the sun and eight planets: Mercury, Venus, Earth, Mars, Jupiter, Saturn, Uranus, and Neptune.
- Stars are made up of gas and dust that have been pulled together by gravity.
- The universe consists of space and everything in it, such as planets, stars, galaxies, and other matter.

GEOLOGY

Geology is the study of Earth and its physical components and how these components interact over time. Geologists use the information they learn to better understand Earth's history and predict future geological processes.

Earth's Spheres

Earth is made up of four distinct zones, or spheres, that each have unique characteristics: geosphere (land), hydrosphere (water), biosphere (living things), and atmosphere (air).

Geosphere

The geosphere is the region of Earth that contains the crust and core of the planet and everything within them. This includes all of the natural, lifeless matter from the rocks at the top of Mount Everest, to the sand at the bottom of the ocean floor, to the molten magma in Earth's center.

Hydrosphere

The hydrosphere is all of the water on the planet, whether it is in liquid, solid, or gaseous form. Ninety-seven percent of the water on the planet is saltwater, while the remaining three percent is freshwater in the form of rivers, streams, groundwater, and glaciers.

Biosphere

If it is alive, it is part of Earth's biosphere. This includes humans, plants, animals, bacteria, fungi, protists, and microorganisms, as well as any organic matter that has not yet decomposed.

Atmosphere

The atmosphere contains all of Earth's gases, including the air we breathe. The atmosphere absorbs the heat from the sun that is reflected off Earth, controlling the temperature as well as weather patterns on the planet.

Earth's Internal Layers

Earth's internal layers are divided into three sections: the crust, the mantle, and the core.

Crust

The crust is Earth's outermost layer. It is further divided into two categories—the thin oceanic crust that lies under the ocean basins and the thicker continental crust that forms the foundation for land on Earth.

Mantle

Earth's mantle is the filling sandwiched between the crust and the core. It is 2,890 kilometers thick and can be divided into the upper mantle and the lower mantle. The upper mantle is closer to the crust. The temperatures in this region are cooler, resulting in rocks that are hard and brittle. The lower mantle is characterized by warmer temperatures and rock that is hot and soft.

Core

The core is the innermost region of the planet. It is divided into the outer core, which contains molten rock, and the inner core, which is under so much pressure that it prevents rock from becoming liquid. The core is Earth's source of internal heat.

Plate Tectonics

Plate tectonics is the geological theory that the geosphere can be broken down into seven distinct large plates—the African, North American, South American, Eurasian, Australian, Antarctic, and Pacific plates—as well as several smaller plates.

According to the plate tectonics theory, these plates are all moving in different directions and at different speeds in such a way that they sometimes crash into or pull away from one another, causing such phenomena as earthquakes, volcanic eruptions, and rifts.

The regions where plates crash into one another are called convergent boundaries, while divergent boundaries occur when plates pull apart from one another. Places where plates slide past, or "side-swipe," one another are called transform boundaries.

Let's Review!

- Earth is made up of four distict zones: the geosphere, the hydrosphere, the biosphere, and the atmosphere.
- The Earth is divided into three sections: the crust, the mantle, and the core.
- Plate tectonics is the theory that divides the geosphere into seven distict large plates: the African, North American, South American, Eurasian, Australian, Antarctic, and Pacific plates, as well as several smaller plates.

METEOROLOGY

Meteorology is the study of Earth's atmosphere with a focus on predicting weather patterns.

Earth's Resources

All of the resources on Earth can be classified into two categories: renewable and nonrenewable. Renewable resources are natural resources that can be replenished over time, while nonrenewable resources cannot. All fossil fuels, a significant source of energy for people around the world, are nonrenewable and are therefore finite.

Renewable Energy Resources

- Biomass
- Hydropower
- Geothermal
- Wind
- Solar

Nonrenewable Energy Resources

- Crude oil
- Natural gas
- Coal
- Uranium

The Water Cycle

The water cycle describes how water changes form and moves throughout Earth's spheres. The cycling of water into and out of the atmosphere plays a major role in Earth's weather patterns. The three main phases of the water cycle are evaporation, condensation, and precipitation.

Evaporation

In its liquid form, water can be found in rivers, lakes, streams, and oceans. When heat from the sun causes the water on Earth to warm up, some of it may evaporate into its gaseous form and enter the atmosphere. This is called evaporation.

Condensation

Once in the atmosphere, gaseous water begins to cool and change back into its liquid form. This process is called condensation, and it is responsible for the development of clouds.

Precipitation

When enough water has accumulated in the atmosphere, it may fall back to Earth in the form of precipitation. This precipitation may return directly to the oceans, lakes, and rivers, or it may fall on land where it will become groundwater that plants and animals (including humans) drink.

Weather vs. Climate

Weather and climate are often confused, but the terms describe two different phenomena. Weather is what is happening in the atmosphere right now and what will happen in the near future. It is defined in terms of temperature, humidity, precipitation, cloud cover, and wind speed and direction.

In contrast, climate is an accumulation of weather statistics that occur over months or years. Meteorologists use climate data to explain daily weather and make predictions about extreme weather patterns.

Climate Patterns

A climate pattern is any regular cycle that occurs within climate over a period of time. Climate patterns include regular occurrences, such as the yearly change of seasons, and more periodic events, such as El Niño.

The circulation of the atmosphere in the form of wind is the result of Earth's rotation in combination with the influx of energy from the sun. As hot air rises around the equator, it travels north and south toward Earth's poles and circulates within distinct cells.

Together with the tides, or the rise and fall of sea levels produced by gravity and Earth's rotation, atmospheric circulation transfers energy and heat throughout the planet.

Erosion sometimes occurs as a result of this flow of wind and water. When earthen materials, such as soil or rock, are transferred from one location to another as a result of wind or water, it is called erosion.

Let's Review!

- There are two types of resources on Earth: renewable and nonrenewable.
- Renewable resources can be replenished over time, while nonrenewable resources cannot.
- Water changes forms as it moves through Earth's spheres in a water cycle.
- The three main phases of the water cycle are: evaporation, condensation, and precipitation.
- Weather is the term used to define what is happening in the atmosphere right now and what will happen in the near future.
- Climate is the term used to define the accumulation of weather statistics that occur over months and years.
- A climate pattern is a regular cycle that occurs within climate over a period of time.

Chapter 17 Earth and Space Sciences Practice Quiz

1. **What is the name for the four planets in our solar system that are closest to the sun?**

   A. Inner planets

   B. Outer planets

   C. Interior planets

   D. Adjacent planets

2. **What are main sequence stars?**

   A. Stars that are very small and dim

   B. Stars that are in their longest stage of life

   C. Stars that are very large and brighter than the sun

   D. Groups of stars and star systems that are bound together by gravity

3. **Which components are part of the geosphere?**

   A. The gases on Earth

   B. The water on Earth

   C. The living things on Earth

   D. The crust and core of Earth

4. **What is the name for Earth's innermost layer?**

   A. Core

   B. Crust

   C. Center

   D. Mantle

5. **Which of the following is a renewable energy resource?**

   A. Coal

   B. Wind

   C. Crude oil

   D. Natural gas

6. **What is climate?**

   A. The rise and fall of sea levels

   B. The circulation of the atmosphere

   C. Current and future happening in the atmosphere

   D. An accumulation of weather statistics over months or years

CHAPTER 17 EARTH AND SPACE SCIENCES PRACTICE QUIZ – ANSWER KEY

1. **A.** Mercury, Venus, Earth, and Mars are the four planets closest to the sun and are called the inner planets. **See Lesson: Astronomy.**

2. **B.** Main sequence stars are stars that are in their longest stage of life. **See Lesson: Astronomy.**

3. **D.** The geosphere comprises the crust and the core of Earth and everything within them. **See Lesson: Geology.**

4. **A.** The core is the innermost region of the planet. **See Lesson: Geology.**

5. **B.** Wind is not finite and is therefore a renewable resource. **See Lesson: Meteorology.**

6. **D.** Climate describes the accumulation of weather statistics that occurs over months or years. **See Lesson: Meteorology.**

SECTION V. WRITING

CHAPTER 18 ESSAY WRITING

THE WRITING PROCESS

Effective writers break the writing task down into steps to tackle one at a time. They allow a certain amount of room for messiness and mistakes in the early stages of writing but attempt to create a polished finished product in the end.

KEEP IN MIND . . .

If your writing process varies from the steps outlined below, that's okay—as long as you can produce a polished, organized text in the end. Some writers like to write part or all of the first draft before they go back to outline and organize. Others make a plan in the prewriting phase, only to change the plan when they're drafting. It is not uncommon for writers to compose the body of an essay before the introduction, or to change the thesis statement at the end to make it fit the essay they wrote rather than the one they intended to write.

The point of teaching the writing process is not to force you to follow all the steps in order every time. The point is to give you a sense of the mental tasks involved in creating a well-written text. If you are drafting and something is not working, you will know you can bounce back to the prewriting stage and change your plan. If you are outlining and you end up fleshing out one of your points in complete sentences, you will realize you still need to go back to finish the rest of the plan before you continue drafting.

In other words, it is fine to change the order of steps from the writing process,* or to jump around between them. Published writers do it all the time, and you can too.

*But almost everyone really does benefit from saving the editing until the end.

The Writing Process

A writer goes through several discrete steps to transform an idea into a polished text. This series of steps is called the **writing process**. Individual writers' processes may vary somewhat, but most writers roughly follow the steps below.

Prewriting is making a plan for writing. Prewriting may include brainstorming, free writing, outlining, or mind mapping. The prewriting process can be messy and include errors. Note that if a writing task requires research, the prewriting process is longer because you need to find, read, and organize source materials.

Drafting is getting the bulk of the text down on the page in complete sentences. Although most writers find drafting difficult, two things can make it easier: 1) prewriting to make a clear plan, and 2) avoiding perfectionism. Drafting is about moving ideas from the mind to the page, even if they do not sound right or the writer is not sure how to spell a word. For writing tasks that involve research, drafting also involves making notes about where the information came from.

Revising is making improvements to the content and structure of a draft. Revising may involve moving ideas around, adding information to flesh out a point, removing chunks of text that are redundant or off-topic, and strengthening the thesis statement. Revising may also mean improving readability by altering sentence structure, smoothing transitions, and improving word choice.

Editing is fixing errors in spelling, grammar, and punctuation. Many writers feel the urge to do this throughout the writing process, but it saves time to wait until the end. There is no point perfecting the grammar and spelling in a sentence that is going to get cut later.

For research projects, you also need to craft **citations**, or notes that tell readers where you got your information. If you noted this information while working on your prewriting and first draft, all you need to do now is format it correctly. (If you did not make notes as you worked, you will have to search laboriously through all your research materials again.) If you are using MLA or APA styles, citations are included in parentheses at the ends of sentences. If you are using Chicago style, citations appear in footnotes or endnotes.

Prewriting Techniques

Prewriting encompasses a wide variety of tasks that happen before you start writing. Many new writers skip or skimp on this step, perhaps because a writer's prewriting efforts are not clearly visible in the final product. But writers who spend time gathering and organizing information tend to produce more polished work.

Thinking silently is a valid form of prewriting. So is telling someone about what you are planning to write. For very short pieces based on your prior knowledge, it may be enough to use these—but most long writing tasks go better if you also use some or all of the strategies below.

Gathering Information

- **Conducting research** involves looking for information in books, articles, websites, and other sources. Internet research is almost always necessary, but do not overlook the benefits of a trip to a library, where you can find in-depth printed sources and also get help from research librarians.
- **Brainstorming** is making a list of short phrases or sentences related to the topic. Brainstorming works best if you literally write down every idea that comes to mind, whether or not you think you can use it. This frees up your mind to find unconscious associations and insights.
- **Free writing** is writing whatever comes to mind about your topic in sentences and paragraphs. Free writing goes fast and works best if you avoid judging your ideas as you go.

Organizing information

- **Mind mapping** arranges ideas into an associative structure. Write your topic, main idea, or argument in a circle in the middle of the page. Then draw lines and make additional circles for supporting points and details. You can combine this step with brainstorming to make a big mess of ideas, some of which you later cross out if you decide not to use them. Or you can do this after brainstorming, using the ideas from your brainstormed list to fill in the bubbles.

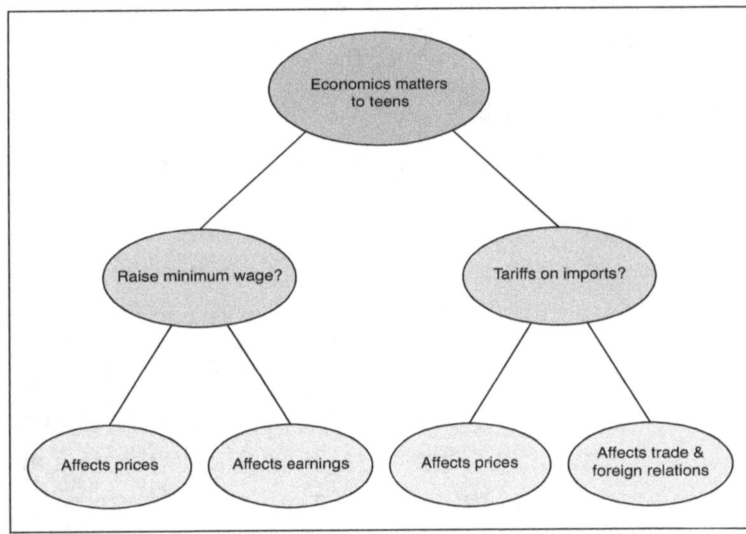

- **Outlining** arranges ideas into a linear structure. It starts with an introduction, includes supporting points and details to back them up, and ends with a conclusion. Traditionally, an outline uses Roman numerals for main ideas and letters for minor ideas.

Example:

I. Introduction - Economics should be a required subject in high school because it affects political and social issues that matter to students.

II. Domestic Issues - Minimum wage
  a. How do people decide if the minimum wage should be raised?
  b. They need to know how changes to the minimum wage affect workers, businesses, and prices.

III. Foreign Issues - Tariffs
  a. How do people decide if they favor taxes on imports?
  b. They need to know how tariffs affect prices and trade.

IV. Conclusion – These issues affect how much money high school graduates can earn and what they can afford to buy.

Paragraph Organization

Paragraphs need to have a clear, coherent organization. Whether you are providing information, arguing a point, or entertaining the reader, the ultimate goal is to make it easy for people to follow your thoughts.

Introductions

The opening of a text must hook the reader's interest, provide necessary background information on the topic, and state the main point. In an academic essay, all of this typically happens in a single paragraph. For instance, an analytical paper on the theme of unrequited love in a novel might start with a stark statement about love, a few sentences identifying the title and author of the work under discussion, and a thesis statement about the author's apparently bleak outlook on love.

Body Paragraphs

In informational and persuasive writing, body paragraphs should typically do three things:

1. Make a point.
2. Illustrate the point with facts, quotations, or examples.
3. Explain how this evidence relates to the point.

Body paragraphs need to stay on topic. That is, the point needs to relate clearly to the thesis statement or main idea. For example, in an analytical paper about unrequited love in a novel, each body paragraph should say something different about the author's bleak outlook on love. Each paragraph might focus on a different character's struggles with love, presenting evidence in the form of an example or quotation from the story and explaining what it suggests about the author's outlook. When you present evidence like this, you must introduce it clearly, stating where it came from in the book. Don't assume readers understand exactly what it has to do with your main point; spell it out for them with a clear explanation.

The structure above is useful in most academic writing situations, but sometimes you need to use other structures:

Chronological – Describe how events happen in order.
Sequential – Present a series of steps.
Descriptive – Describe a topic in a coherent spatial order, e.g. from top to bottom.
Cause/Effect – Present an action and its results.
Compare/Contrast – Describe the similarities and differences between two or more topics.

Conclusions

Like introductions, conclusions have a unique structure. A conclusion restates the thesis and main points in different words and, ideally, adds a bit more. For instance, it may take a broader outlook on the topic, giving readers a sense of why it matters or how the main point affects the world. A text should end with a sentence or two that brings the ideas together and makes the piece feel finished. This can be a question, a quotation, a philosophical statement, an intense image, or a request that readers take action.

Let's Review!

- The writing process includes prewriting, drafting, revision, and editing.
- For projects that involve research, writers must include the creation of citations within the writing process.
- Effective writers spend time gathering and organizing information during the prewriting stage.
- Writers must organize paragraphs coherently so that readers can follow their thoughts.

Essay Revisions and Transitions

A well-written essay should be easy to follow and convincing. The words should be well-chosen, and the transitions should be smooth.

Content, Organization, and Coherence

To revise an essay effectively, you must read through your own work with a critical eye. As you read, consider the content, organization, and flow of ideas.

Content

Every time you write, you are setting out to communicate something. Check to make sure you have clearly and succinctly stated an argument or main point, usually in a one-sentence thesis statement at the end of the first paragraph. Does your essay follow through on this point? By the end, you should have defended or developed it completely without leaving any holes or veering off onto other subjects. If you have not done this, add or delete information.

Organization

The ideas in your essay need to appear in an order that makes sense and avoids repetition. As you revise, check to make sure your ideas flow in a logical order, and move sentences around if they do not. Some topics lend themselves naturally to a particular type of organization. For instance, sometimes you will use chronological order, or you will outline causes first and effects second.

However, many analytical and persuasive papers do not fall into one natural organization. In this case, just choose an order that makes sense to you. In an argumentative paper, for instance, you could place your strongest arguments first and last, with the less impactful ones in the middle. No matter what, be sure each paragraph makes a point that is clearly distinguishable from the points in the other paragraphs. Do not just repeat the same idea in different words.

Coherence

When the ideas in an essay flow in a logical and consistent way that readers can easily follow, we say the writing has **coherence.** A well-written essay makes it possible for readers to follow the writer's thoughts. Make sure you have clear topic sentences in each paragraph to link back to the main idea. Do not bounce off onto new subtopics without explaining how they relate. Within paragraphs, explain your points and evidence explicitly. Do not leave gaps or make readers guess how one point relates to another.

Rhetorical Effectiveness and Use of Evidence

When you revise a persuasive essay, you must evaluate your work for **rhetorical effectiveness.** In other words, you need to make sure it is convincing. The cornerstones of rhetorically effective writing are reason, trust, and emotions.

Every good argument is grounded in logic and reasoning. When you offer opinions, you should present facts and logic to back them up. For example, if you are arguing that young children should not be required to do hours of homework every night, you could cite a study showing that kids under twelve did not learn more when they spent additional time doing homework outside of class.

Good arguments must also inspire trust. One of the primary ways to do this is to use credible sources and identify them clearly. The evidence above would generally be considered trustworthy if the study was conducted by a Harvard professor with a doctorate in education. It is a good idea to share information like this in an essay. It is not a good idea to use evidence if it comes from a source that is not credible.

It is also appropriate to engage the emotions in persuasive writing. In an essay opposing homework, you could call on readers' nostalgia and sense of fun by briefly describing the enjoyable activities kids could do instead of homework. But be careful. Good writing never uses personal attacks or scare tactics. In other words, it would be inappropriate to call people who believe in homework "fun killers" or to make an exaggerated suggestion that kids forced to do too much homework will suffer deep psychological damage.

Using Evidence

There are several rules of thumb for using evidence to back up your ideas.

- It must genuinely back up your thesis. Imagine you are arguing that kids under 12 should not do homework at all, and you find a study that says elementary school kids who did three hours of homework per night did not learn any more than kids who did only one hour. The study supports limited homework; it does not clearly support your thesis.
- If evidence comes from an outside source, it must be introduced and cited correctly. In general, you should name and share the credentials of your source the first time you introduce it. Afterward, you may refer to the same source by last name only.
- You need to explain how the evidence fits the argument. Readers may not understand what you are thinking about the evidence you present unless you spell it out for them.
- You need the right amount of evidence—not too much, not too little. Back up every opinion. One to three pieces of evidence per point should suffice. Do not continue piling on additional evidence to support a point you have already defended.

Word Choice

After you have revised for major issues like content, organization, and evidence, it is time to consider your word choice. This means you should attempt to use the right word at the right time. Below are several thoughts to consider as you hone your word choice.

Simplicity

The first goal of writing is to be understood. Many students try to use the biggest words they can, but it is usually a better style choice to choose an ordinary word. Do not use fancy vocabulary unless you have a good reason.

Precision

Sometimes the need for precision is a good reason for choosing a fancier word. There are times when it is best to say you hurt your knee, and there are times when it is best to say you injured your anterior cruciate ligament. Consider what your readers need to know and why. An audience of doctors might need or appreciate the medical terminology, whereas a general audience would likely be better served by the simpler language.

Tone

You can establish a clear tone by considering and manipulating the connotations of the words you use. Many words have a positive or negative connotation, whereas others are more neutral. *Cheap* has a negative tone, whereas *economical* is positive and *inexpensive* is neutral. If you are writing about making a purchase, choosing one or another of these words can subtly convey your attitude about what you bought.

Formality

Our language contains many levels of formality. Academic writing usually calls for slightly more formal language than daily speech. In academic writing, you should avoid slang, contractions, and abbreviations like *idk* or *tfw* that are commonly used in text messages and on the Internet. Depending on the writing task, you may also choose more formal words like *purchase* rather than less formal words like *buy.*

Inclusivity

Aim to use language that includes everyone, not language that plays into stereotypes and gender biases. Avoid referring to the entire human race as *man* or *mankind.* Use gender-neutral words like *firefighter* over gender-specific words like *fireman.* Do not assume people are male or female just because they belong to a certain profession. For example, do not automatically refer to a doctor as *he* or a preschool teacher as *she.* Note that using plurals can make it possible to write around gendered pronouns entirely. That is, if you refer to doctors or preschool teachers in the plural, you can refer back to them neutrally as *they.*

Transitions

At the very end of your revision process, read your work and make sure that your ideas flow smoothly from one to the next. Use connecting words and phrases, or **transitions**, to link ideas and help readers follow the flow of your thoughts. The number of possible ways to transition between ideas is almost limitless. Below are a few common transition words, categorized by the way they link ideas.

Type of Transition	Example
Time and sequence transitions help show when events happened in time.	first, second, next, now, then, at this point, after, afterward, before this, previously, formerly, thereafter, finally, in conclusion
Addition or emphasis transitions let readers know when you are building on an established line of thought or stressing an important idea.	moreover, also, likewise, furthermore, above all, indeed, in fact
Example transitions introduce ideas that illustrate a point.	for example, for instance, to illustrate, to demonstrate
Causation transitions indicate a cause-and-effect relationship.	as a result, consequently, thus, therefore
Contrast transitions indicate a difference between ideas.	nevertheless, despite, in contrast, however

Different types of transitions are necessary in different parts of an essay. Within a paragraph, you should use short transitions of one or two words to show how the information in one sentence is linked to the information preceding it. But when you are starting a new paragraph or making another major shift in thought, you may take time to explain relationships more thoroughly.

Between Sentences: Clara was in a minor car accident last week. *Afterward,* she experienced headaches and dizziness that worsened over time.

Between Paragraphs: *Because of her worsening headaches and dizziness,* Clara has found it increasingly difficult to work at her computer.

Note that longer transitions are long because they have content to explain how ideas relate. Some long transitions, such as the very wordy "due to the fact that" take up space without adding more meaning than simpler words like "because." Very long-winded transitions are considered poor style.

Let's Review!

- When you revise an essay, consider content, organization, and coherence first.
- Rhetorically effective writing appeals to the reader's reason and inspires trust and emotions appropriately.
- Use clear evidence to back up every opinion in your writing.
- Aim to use exactly the right words for the writing task at hand.
- Use appropriate transitions to create a smooth flow of ideas.

ACTIVE AND PASSIVE VOICE

Active and passive voice are two different styles of writing that are used to create a certain effect. This lesson will cover how to recognize, form, and use (1) active voice and (2) passive voice in writing.

Active Voice

Active voice is most often used in non-scientific academic writing. In active voice, the subject of the sentence performs the action of the verb.

Active voice sentences are more concise. Using the active voice prevents wordy and convoluted sentences and makes the meaning clear. The subject is acting on something and not being acted on.

- The dog bit the boy.
- Half of the class failed the exam.
- The actress joined the cast of the play.
- He turned on the window fan.

Passive Voice

Passive voice is used in scientific writing. In passive voice, the subject is being acted upon as the subject receives the action of the verb.

The words "by the" indicate the subject in a passive voice sentence. Passive voice will always include a form of the verb "to be."

Passive voice in academic writing can make the essay seem uninteresting, but sometimes passive voice can be a stylistic choice. Scientific writing uses passive voice to remain objective.

- The boy was bitten by the dog.
- The exam was failed by half of the class.
- The cast of the play was joined by the actress.
- The window fan was turned on by him.

Let's Review!

- In **active voice**, the subject performs the action of the verb. These sentences are clearer and more concise.
- In **passive voice**, the subject is acted upon. The subject receives the action of the verb. The use of the verb "to be" and the words "by the" indicate passive voice.

THE WRITING SECTION

The Writing Section of the ACT exam consists of a 40-minute test that assesses your writing skills. This optional test builds on the skills required in the English and reading tests by allowing you to demonstrate practical knowledge of the conventions of standard written English. You will be asked to read a prompt and write a persuasive essay that develops your perspective about the issue.

You will be assessed on your ability to clearly state a main idea, provide specific examples and details to back up your main idea, and follow the conventions of standard English. You will not be allowed to outside resources, such as a dictionary, but you may use plain scratch paper (provided at the testing center) to plan your essay and write your rough draft(s).

How to Write a Persuasive Essay

The purpose of a persuasive essay is **to convince the reader** to think or act in a particular way.

A successful persuasive essay should:

- Clearly state the issue and your position on it in the introduction
- Use language appropriate to the audience you are trying to convince
- Support your position with facts, statistics, and reasons
- Answer possible objections to your position
- Show clear reasoning
- Conclude with a summary of your position or a call to action

A persuasive essay follows the traditional 5-paragraph essay structure and should contain an introductory paragraph, body paragraphs, and a concluding paragraph.

Paragraph 1:

The first goal of your **introductory paragraph** is to introduce your topic. The introduction should contain a strong opening sentence that hooks the reader. If your goal is to urge the reader to act a certain way, you must capture their interest and make them want to read your position. Start off with an anecdote, and unusual detail related to your subject, a quotation, a question, or some other strong statement that will grab the reader's attention.

The second goal of your introductory paragraph is to express your opinion about the topic. Your thesis statement should clearly state your position, or an opinion, about the subject. Your position statement should be clear and direct so the reader understands what you are trying to accomplish with your essay.

Paragraphs 2, 3, and 4:

The **body paragraphs** are where you will develop your position about your subject. This is where you state any facts, examples, and explanations that support your main ideas. Each body paragraph should contain one well-developed example. Your examples can come from just about anywhere: business, current events, entertainment, history, politics, pop culture, science, even your own personal experience.

Your goals for each body paragraph are to: introduce an example, describe the example, explain how the example fully supports your thesis. Be sure to use transition words at the beginning of each body paragraph to introduce your next example.

Paragraph 5:

The ultimate goal of your persuasive paper is to convince your audience to act or think about your given subject in a particular way. In your **concluding paragraph**, you should introduce the opposing side to your argument. Then refute their position by reinforcing the validity of your thesis. Use a strong ending sentence to emphasize the main point of your essay.

Sample Essay Prompts

Before you sit for your exam, practice writing sample essays to become familiar with the process and comfortable with the format. Below are three sample essay prompts. Choose at least 2 topics and write practice essays.

Try to follow the paragraph organization as outlined above. Then, once you have written your draft, review the rules of grammar and conventions of English (spelling, punctuation, capitalization) in the English and reading sections of this study guide to help you fine-tune your writing. If the opportunity permits, ask a teacher, relative, or friend read your essay and offer feedback on your work.

Essay Prompts:

1. **Is society too dependent on technology?** Text messaging has become a valuable way of communicating in today's society. However, some people spend too much time sending messages by phone instead of interacting with others face to face. Addressing an audience of your peers, explain why you agree or disagree with this observation.

2. **Should the minimum wage be increased?** Many business owners argue that raising the minimum wage would result in hardship and cause them to raise their prices. But many workers argue raising the minimum wage is necessary to help low-income workers dig out of poverty.

3. **Are security cameras an invasion of privacy?** While security cameras are in place to protect both businesses and the general public, some argue cameras have gone too far and actually invade privacy because people are constantly under surveillance.

SECTION VI. FULL-LENGTH PRACTICE EXAMS

ACT PRACTICE EXAM 1

SECTION I. ENGLISH

1. **Select the part of speech of the underlined word in the following sentence.**

   He hit the ball <u>so</u> hard that he was sure it was a home run!

   A. Verb
   B. Adverb
   C. Adjective
   D. Pronoun

2. **Which word in the following sentence is an adjective?**

   It was a late flight.

   A. It
   B. was
   C. late
   D. flight

3. **How many adjectives are in the following sentence?**

   The children love to play with the cute, furry kitten.

   A. 0
   B. 1
   C. 2
   D. 3

4. **Which word in the following sentence is an adverb?**

   That racecar is incredibly fast!

   A. That
   B. is
   C. incredibly
   D. fast

5. **Select the correct word to complete the following sentence.**

   Tam performed badly, but I was even _____.

   A. worse
   B. worst
   C. badder
   D. more bad

6. **Which word(s) in the following sentence should be capitalized?**

   My friend's birthday is december 25. she does not like that her birthday is on christmas.

   A. christmas
   B. december
   C. december and christmas
   D. december, she, and christmas

7. **Choose the correct sentence.**

   A. The Victorian era is marked by strict modesty.
   B. The Victorian Era is marked by strict modesty.
   C. The victorian era is marked by strict modesty.
   D. the victorian era is marked by strict modesty.

8. **Fill in the blank with the correctly capitalized form.**

   In the 2018 Super Bowl, the _______ played against the _______.

   A. philadelphia eagles, new england patriots
   B. Philadelphia eagles, New England patriots
   C. Philadelphia Eagles, New England Patriots
   D. Philadelphia Eagles, new england Patriots

9. Which of the following is correct?

A. senate
B. congress
C. White House
D. Supreme court

10. Identify the conjunction in the following sentence.

I walked home even though my feet really hurt.

A. home
B. even though
C. my
D. really hurt

11. Which word is not a preposition?

A. It
B. At
C. For
D. In

12. What part of speech are the underlined words in the following sentence?

Twelve students passed the exam, but seven did not, so the teacher is letting them retake it.

A. Adjective
B. Preposition
C. Conjunction
D. Adverb

13. What is the object of the underlined preposition?

I found our cat under the table by the window next to the TV.

A. our cat
B. the table
C. the window
D. the TV

14. Identify the subordinating conjunction in the following sentence.

Don't leave until we get there.

A. until
B. we
C. get
D. there

15. Select the context clue from the following sentence that helps you define the word emulate.

Felicia always tried to emulate her big sister, so she would often imitate the way she spoke, moved, and how she dressed.

A. "tried"
B. "often"
C. "imitate "
D. "way"

16. Select the word from the following sentence that has more than one meaning.

Javier was overjoyed when he finally finished his application for college.

A. Overjoyed
B. Finally
C. Application
D. College

17. Select the correct definition of the underlined word having multiple meanings in the sentence.

Natalie's fingers were calloused after practicing her bass.

A. Kind of fish
B. Low and deep sound
C. Lowest male singing voice
D. A guitar with four strings that makes low sounds

18. Select the meaning of the underlined word in the sentence based on the context clues.

Sheila has such an exuberant personality; she always has a smile on her face.

A. Sincere
B. Cheerful
C. Appealing
D. Interesting

19. **Select the word from the following sentence that has more than one meaning.**

They need to prune the bushes every year or else they will lose their shape.

A. Need
B. Prune
C. Lose
D. Shape

20. **Identify the verb, if any, that has a direct object in the following sentence.**

Dr. Popov sat and squinted as he viewed cells through the microscope.

A. sat
B. squinted
C. viewed
D. There is no direct object.

21. **Identify the direct object in the following sentence, if there is one.**

Max tried so hard, but he did not succeed.

A. so
B. hard
C. not
D. There is no direct object.

22. **Select the part of speech that cannot be found in the following sentence.**

I subscribe to National Geographic, and I read it every month.

A. Indirect object
B. Direct object
C. Verb
D. Pronoun

23. **Identify the indirect object in the following sentence, if there is one.**

Snowflakes fell softly to the ground.

A. Snowflakes
B. softly
C. ground
D. There is no indirect object.

24. **Select the verb that acts on the underlined direct object in the following sentence.**

James Madison and Thomas Jefferson were among the men who helped to write the Constitution.

A. were
B. among
C. helped
D. write

25. **Which word in the following sentence is not a modifier?**

That young woman arrived late yesterday.

A. young
B. woman
C. late
D. yesterday

26. **What type of error can be found in the following sentence?**

The report earned an A that I wrote on the Korean War.

A. Run-on sentence
B. Incorrect subject-verb agreement
C. Misplaced modifier
D. Pronoun error

27. **How many modifiers describe the underlined word in the following sentence?**

Pass that large silver bowl.

A. 1
B. 2
C. 3
D. 4

28. **Identify the likely misplaced modifier in the following sentence.**

The man in blue wore a large, gaudy hat on his head, which was ugly.

A. in blue
B. large
C. gaudy
D. which was ugly

29. Which word or phrase does the underlined modifier describe?

A <u>great</u> time was had by all.

A. A
B. time
C. was had
D. by all

30. Select the correct words to complete the following sentence.

I have _____ due tomorrow.

A. many homework
B. many homeworks
C. a lot of homework
D. a lot of homeworks

31. What part of speech is the underlined word in the following sentence?

Professor Allen estimated that his research could be completed in two weeks, but he soon realized that his <u>estimate</u> was incorrect.

A. Verb
B. Noun
C. Adverb
D. Adjective

32. Which type of noun is the underlined word?

One thing I cannot tolerate is <u>dishonesty</u>.

A. Plural noun
B. Proper noun
C. Abstract noun
D. Concrete noun

33. What is the plural form for the noun *crisis*?

A. Crisii
B. Crisis
C. Crises
D. Crisises

34. Select the pronoun that could be used in the following sentence.

I recognized two people, one of ____ I had worked with before.

A. him
B. who
C. them
D. whom

35. How many pronouns are in the following sentence?

She and I used to be friends until I dated her brother and it didn't end well.

A. 3
B. 4
C. 5
D. 6

36. Which word in the following sentence is a possessive pronoun?

Are you sure that it's yours?

A. it's
B. you
C. that
D. yours

37. What is the role of the pronoun *him* in a sentence?

A. Object
B. Subject
C. Possessive
D. Any of these

38. What is missing from the following sentence?

Classical music helps with studying, I always listen to it before a test.

A. There needs to be a colon after studying.
B. There needs to be a semicolon after studying.
C. There should be an exclamation point at the end.
D. Nothing is missing.

39. What is the mistake in the following sentence?

The video game was intense; I needed state of the art weapons and armor to slay a dragon.

A. The semicolon is misplaced.

B. *Video game* should be hyphenated.

C. *State of the art* should be hyphenated.

D. There should be a comma between *weapons* and *and*.

40. Which of the following sentences is correct?

A. It was good, wasn't it?

B. Anne did you like the movie?

C. It had action drama and romance.

D. Before the movie we went to dinner.

41. Which is the sentence with the correct use of punctuation?

A. The book was amazing she couldn't put it down;

B. The book was amazing; she couldn't put it down.

C. The book was amazing; so she couldn't put it down.

D. The book was amazing so; she couldn't put it down.

42. Which of the following prefixes means with?

A. bio-

B. per-

C. con-

D. trans-

43. Select the meaning of the underlined word in the sentence.

The teacher listened to the student's excuse with an incredulous smile.

A. Forced

B. Amused

C. Insincere

D. Disbelieving

44. Which of the following root words means to say?

A. vis

B. vid

C. dict

D. script

45. Monochromatic most nearly means

A. having one color.

B. having many parts.

C. having a lot of time.

D. having too much heat.

46. What is the best definition of the word rupture?

A. To seep

B. To heal

C. To swell

D. To burst

47. People have ____ arms and legs.

A. to

B. tu

C. too

D. two

48. Every runner needs a good _____ of shoes.

A. pair

B. piar

C. pear

D. pare

49. Which of the following spellings is correct?

A. Argument

B. Arguemint

C. Arguement

D. Arguemant

50. What is the correct plural of half?

A. Half

B. Halfs

C. Halfes

D. Halves

51. **Which subject is third person singular?**
    - A. I
    - B. He
    - C. We
    - D. You

52. **Select the verb to complete the following sentence.**

    Do you think the automobile or the personal computer ____ changed our lives more?
    - A. have
    - B. haves
    - C. has
    - D. his

53. **Select the subject and verb that complete the sentence correctly.**

    ____ some birds.
    - A. There
    - B. There's
    - C. There is
    - D. There are

54. **Select the subject with which the underlined verb must agree.**

    Anyone who has skates is invited to join us.
    - A. Anyone
    - B. who
    - C. skates
    - D. us

55. **Which part of the following sentence is the predicate? .**

    My granddaughter was born on January 18.
    - A. My granddaughter
    - B. was
    - C. was born on January 18
    - D. January 18

56. **Which word is an antonym of <u>mollify</u>?**
    - A. Enrage
    - B. Regale
    - C. Berate
    - D. Advocate

57. **Doctor : Pediatrician :: Instrument : ____________**
    - A. Harp
    - B. Harmony
    - C. Musician
    - D. Orchestra

58. **Adding which prefix to <u>partisan</u> would make the antonym of the word?**
    - A. Non-
    - B. Multi-
    - C. Trans-
    - D. Inter-

59. **The following words have the same denotation. Which of the words has a negative connotation?**
    - A. Ruthless
    - B. Ambitious
    - C. Motivated
    - D. Determined

60. **Which of the following words in the list of synonyms shows the weakest degree of meaning?**
    - A. Blissful
    - B. Ecstatic
    - C. Content
    - D. Delighted

61. **Identify the dependent clause in the following sentence.**

    Joe always did his homework before he went to bed.
    - A. Went to bed
    - B. Before he went to bed
    - C. Joe always did his homework
    - D. Did his homework

62. **Fill in the blank with the correct subordinating conjunction.**

    We will throw a pizza party _____ you win the game.
    - A. if
    - B. that
    - C. since
    - D. because

63. **Identify the independent clause in the following sentence.**

Although most people understand the benefits of exercise, people do not exercise as much as they should.

A. Although most people understand
B. The benefits of exercise
C. People do not exercise as much as they should
D. People do not exercise

64. **Fill in the blank with the correct coordinating conjunction.**

Julia wanted the new iPhone, _____ she could not afford it.

A. so
B. or
C. but
D. and

65. **How would you connect the following clauses?**

The trial must begin.

She shows up or not.

A. The trial must begin and she shows up or not.
B. The trial must begin which she shows up or not.
C. The trial must begin because she shows up or not.
D. The trial must begin whether she shows up or not.

66. **Which of the following is an example of a compound sentence?**

A. Monte cannot run in the race tomorrow, he injured his ankle.
B. Monte injured his ankle and cannot run in the race tomorrow.
C. Monte injured his ankle, so he cannot run in the race tomorrow.
D. Monte cannot run in the race tomorrow since he injured his ankle.

67. **Which of the following options would give this sentence a parallel structure?**

Traveling gives people memorable experiences, exposes them to different cultures, and ____________________.

A. broadens their perspective
B. to broaden their perspective
C. broadening their perspective
D. will broaden their perspective

68. **Which of the following is an example of a simple sentence?**

A. Calcium for bones.
B. Calcium makes bones strong.
C. Calcium is necessary it makes bones strong.
D. Calcium is good for bones, so people need it.

69. **Which sentence combines all of the information below using a parallel structure?**

New York City is exciting. New York City is full of different cultures. New York City has so much to offer.

A. New York City is exciting, diverse, and interesting.

B. New York city has a lot of excitement, diverse, and interesting.

C. New York City is exciting, has different cultures, and interesting.

D. New York city is full of excitement, having different cultures, and it has so much to offer.

70. Which of the following uses a conjunction to combine the sentences below so the focus is on Tony preparing for his job interview?

Tony prepared well for his job interview. Tony ended up getting an offer.

A. Tony ended up getting an offer; he prepared for his job interview.

B. Tony prepared well for his job interview, he ended up getting an offer.

C. Tony prepared well for his job interview and he ended up getting an offer.

D. Tony ended up getting an offer because he prepared for his job interview.

71. Select the <u>simple past tense</u> verb form to complete the following sentence.

The farmer's market ____ strawberries for 99 cents a pound yesterday.

A. sells

B. sold

C. has sold

D. was selling

72. Select the helping verb that completes the following sentence.

Millions of people watched the news story on TV as it ____ unfolding.

A. is

B. did

C. was

D. would

73. Which exclamation contains a verb?

A. Oh no!

B. Not me!

C. So true!

D. That's great!

74. What verb tense are the underlined words in the following sentence?

I <u>am going</u> out.

A. Past perfect

B. Present perfect

C. Past progressive

D. Present progressive

75. Select the sentence that best describes something that is happening at this moment.

A. The chef roasts a chicken.

B. The chef roasted a chicken.

C. The chef is roasting a chicken.

D. The chef was roasting a chicken.

SECTION II. MATH

1. **How many whole numbers are less than 3 but greater than −3?**

   A. 2
   B. 3
   C. 4
   D. 5

2. **Which procedure is impossible?**

   A. Adding two negative numbers
   B. Subtracting a negative number from zero
   C. Adding two quantities with different units
   D. Placing negative numbers on the number line

3. **Evaluate the expression 15 × (−15).**

   A. −225
   B. −30
   C. −1
   D. 0

4. **Evaluate the expression 26 ÷ 9.**

   A. 2
   B. 2R8
   C. 3R1
   D. 35

5. **A circle has an area of 12 square feet. Find the diameter to the nearest tenth of a foot. Use 3.14 for π.**

   A. 1.0
   B. 2.0
   C. 3.0
   D. 4.0

6. **A circular dinner plate has a diameter of 13 inches. A ring is placed along the edge of the plate. Find the circumference of the ring in inches. Use 3.14 for π.**

   A. 31.4
   B. 40.82
   C. 62.8
   D. 81.64

7. **Select the square with the correct lines of symmetry.**

   A.
   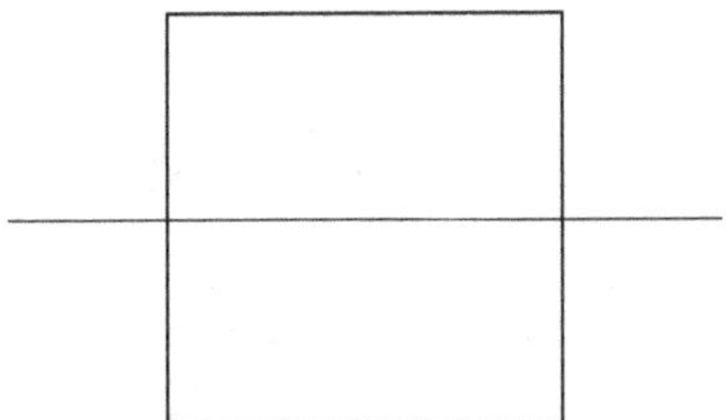

   B.
   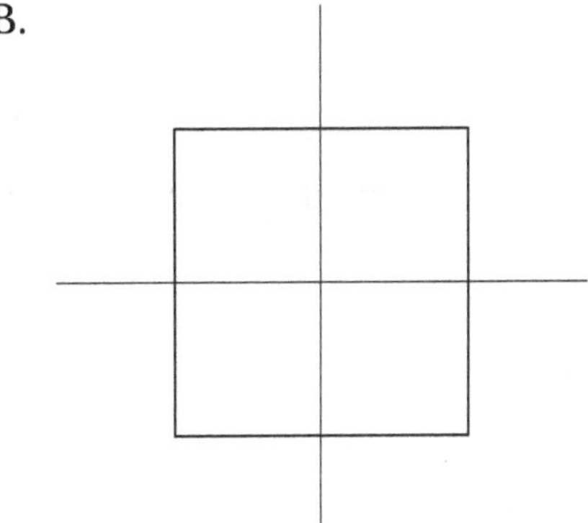

   C.
   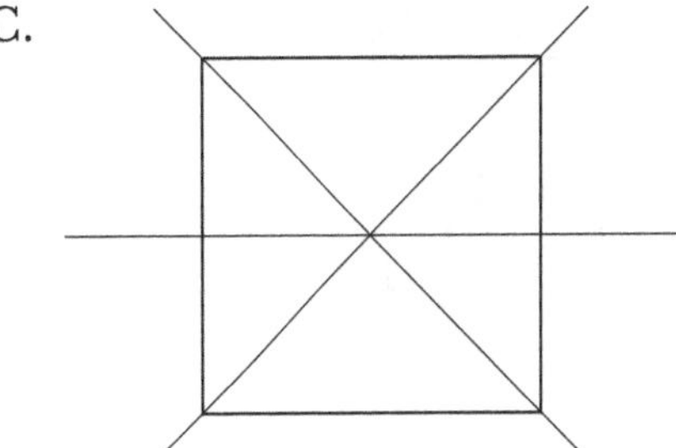

   D.
   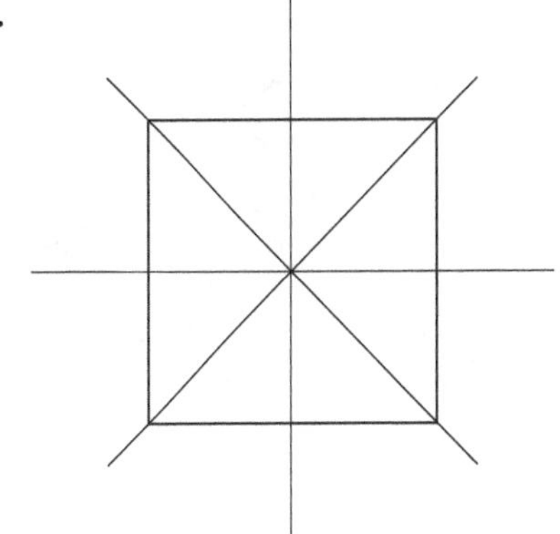

8. Find the area in square centimeters of a circle with a diameter of 16 centimeters. Use 3.14 for π.

A. 25.12 C. 100.48

B. 50.24 D. 200.96

9. Select the drawing of $\overrightarrow{AB}$ and $\overrightarrow{CD}$ intersecting at *D*.

A.

B.

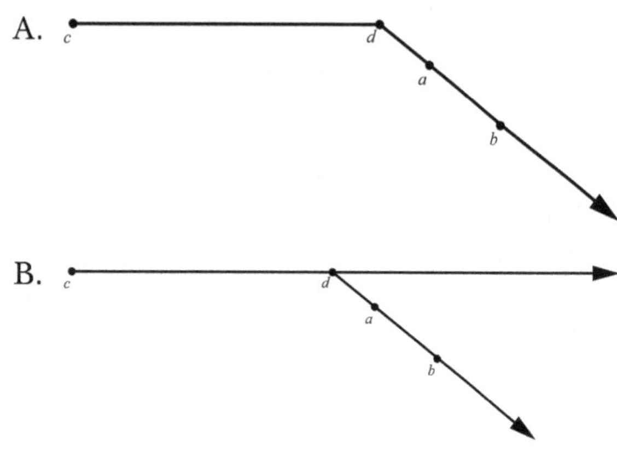

C.

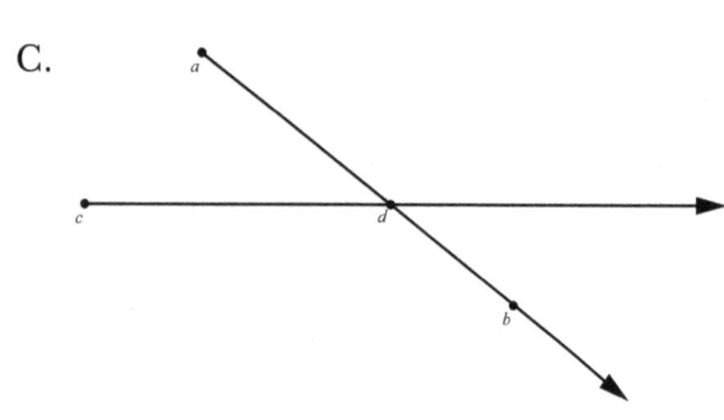

D.

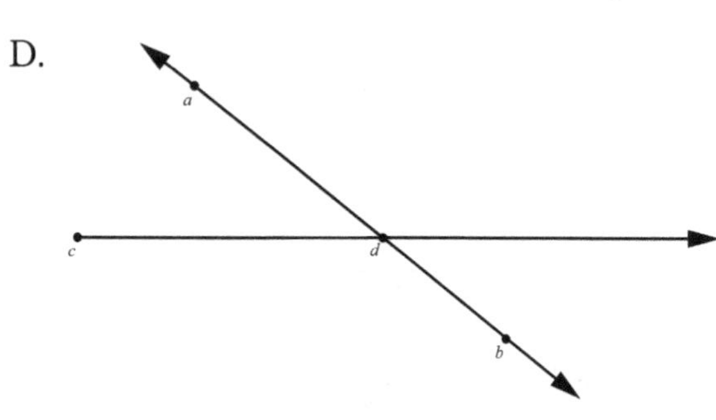

10. Δ*JKL* has points *J* (5, –3), *K* (–2, 4), and *L* (3, 0). After a transformation, the points are *J′* (5, 3), *K′* (–2, –4), and *L′* (3, 0). What is the transformation between the points?

A. Reflection across the x-axis

B. Reflection across the y-axis

C. Reflection across the $y = x$

D. Reflection across the $y = -x$

11. Change 0.375 to a fraction. Simplify completely.

A. $\frac{3}{8}$ C. $\frac{1}{2}$

B. $\frac{2}{5}$ D. $\frac{7}{16}$

12. Write $\frac{1}{5}$ as a percent.

A. 15% C. 25%

B. 20% D. 30%

13. Change $\frac{5}{11}$ to a decimal. Simplify completely.

A. $0.\overline{4}$ C. $0.\overline{5}$

B. $0.\overline{45}$ D. $0.\overline{54}$

14. Solve the equation for the unknown, $\frac{c}{-4} = -12$.

A. –16 C. 3

B. –8 D. 48

15. Solve the inequality for the unknown, $3(x + 1) + 2(x + 1) \geq 5(3 - x) + 4(x + 2)$.

A. $x \geq 0$ C. $x \geq 2$

B. $x \geq 1$ D. $x \geq 3$

16. Solve the equation for *P*, $A = P + Prt$.

A. $A(1 + rt) = P$

B. $Art = P$

C. $Art + 1 = P$

D. $\frac{A}{1 + rt} = P$

17. **Solve the system of equations,**

$$\begin{aligned} 2y + x &= -20 \\ y &= -x - 12 \end{aligned}.$$

A. (4, 8) C. (-4, 8)

B. (4, -8) D. (-4, -8)

18. **Solve the system of equations,**

$$\begin{aligned} -2x + 2y &= 28 \\ 3x + y &= -22 \end{aligned}.$$

A. (9, 5) C. (9, -5)

B. (-9, -5) D. (-9, 5)

19. **Solve the system of equations by graphing,** $\begin{aligned} 2x + y &= 4 \\ 4x + y &= 14 \end{aligned}.$

A.

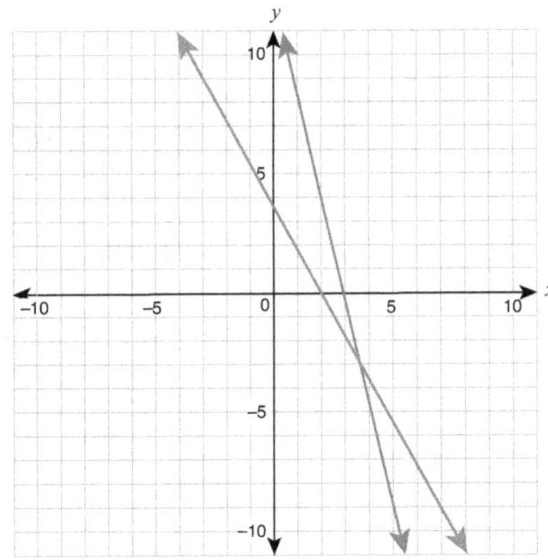

B.

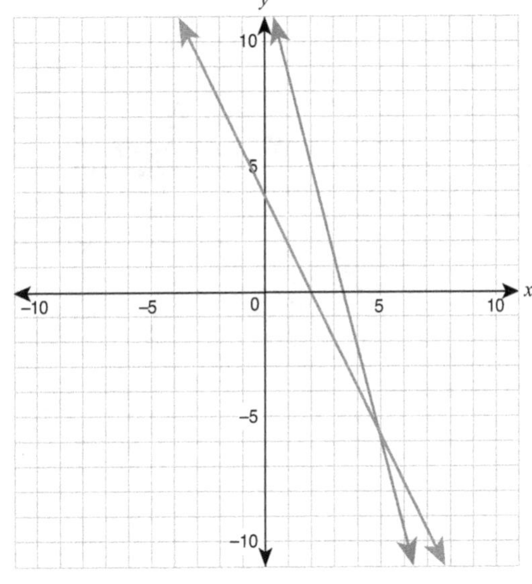

C.

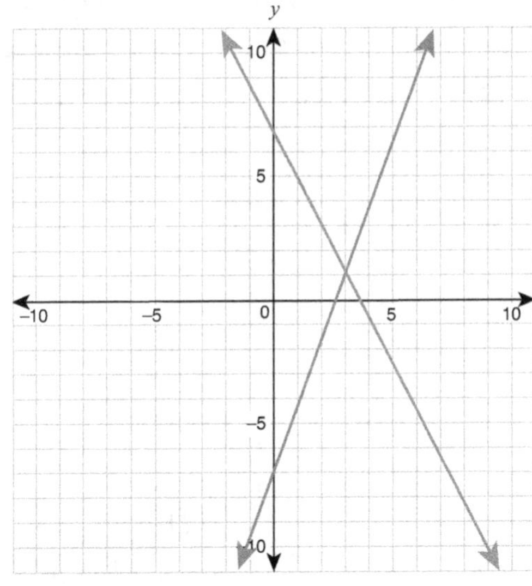

D.

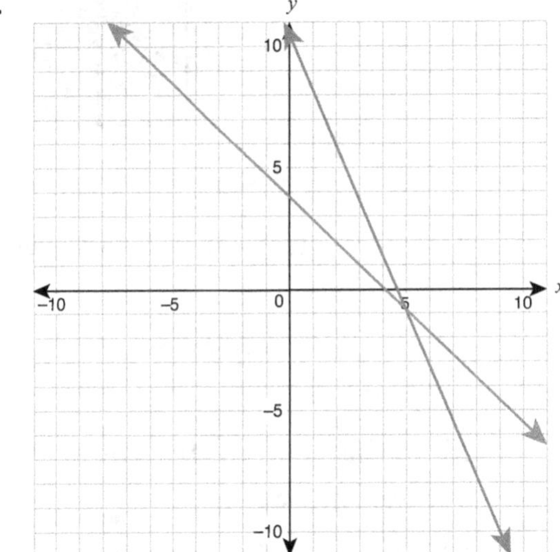

20. **How many prime numbers are less than 20 but greater than 0?**

A. 8 C. 10

B. 9 D. 11

21. **Which number is a multiple of 123?**

A. −123 C. 247

B. 1 D. 359

22. The histogram below shows the amount a family spent on groceries during the year. Which statement is true for the histogram?

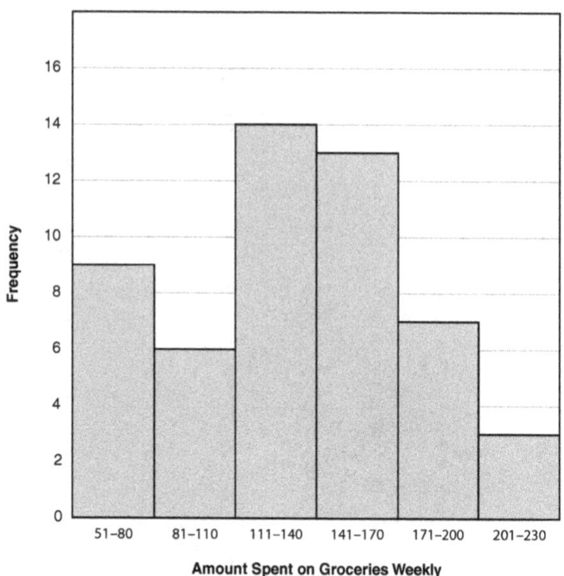

A. The lowest frequency is between $80 and $110.

B. The highest frequency is between $140 and $170.

C. More than half of the amount spent is greater than $140.

D. More than half of the amount spent is between $110 and $170.

23. A soccer team has scored 1, 1, 2, 2, 3, 3, 4, 4, 5 goals in its first 9 games. During the next game, the team scores 8 goals. Compare the mean and the standard deviation before and after the next game.

A. The mean and standard deviation increase.

B. The mean and standard deviation decrease.

C. The mean increases, but the standard deviation does not change.

D. The mean decreases, but the standard deviation does not change.

24. Find the median for the data set 34, 31, 37, 35, 38, 33, 39, 32, 36, 35, 37, and 33.

A. 34

B. 35

C. 36

D. 37

25. The data below shows the number of minutes available to eat breakfast for a group of employees.

10, 20, 40, 30, 50, 60, 50, 40, 30, 20, 40, 30, 10, 20, 30, 50, 40, 10, 10, 20, 30, 40, 20, 50, 40, 30

Select a dot plot for the data.

A. **Minutes to Eat Breakfast**

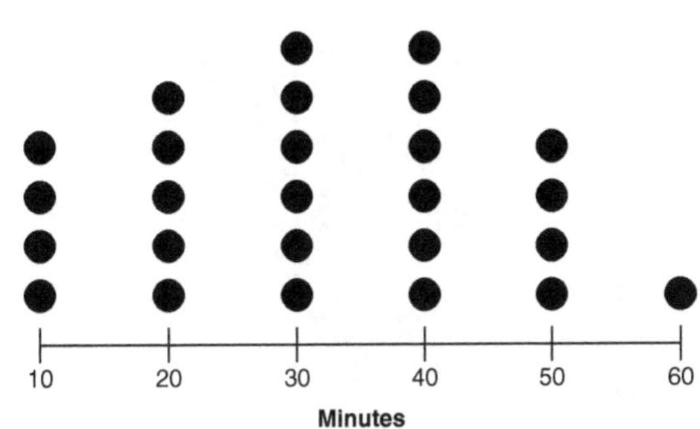

B. **Minutes to Eat Breakfast**

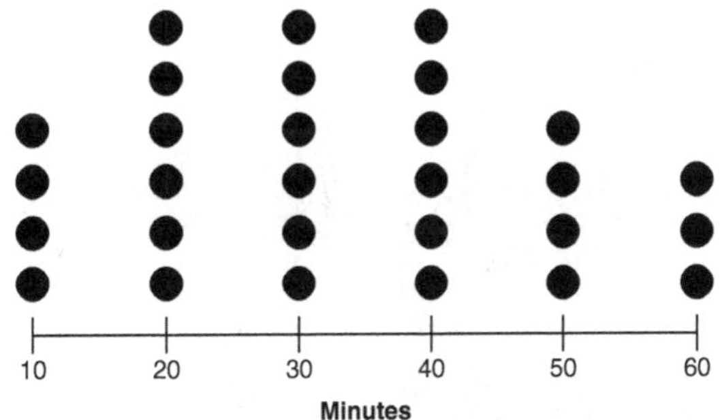

C. **Minutes to Eat Breakfast**

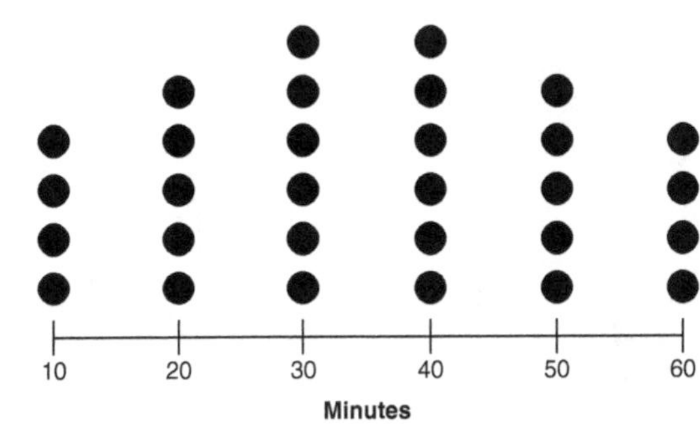

D. **Minutes to Eat Breakfast**

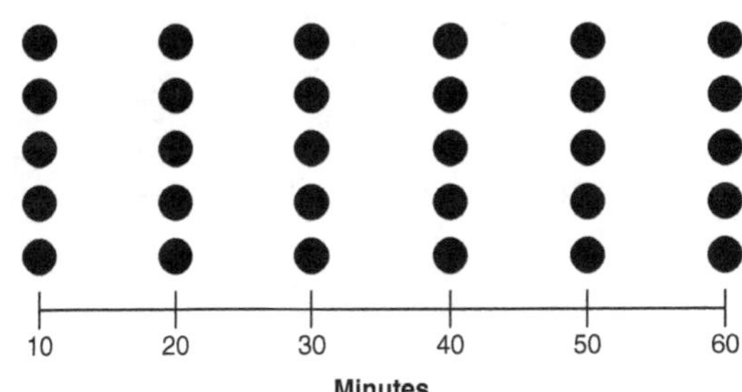

26. The bar chart shows the number of items collected for a charity drive. What is the total number of items collected for the three highest classes?

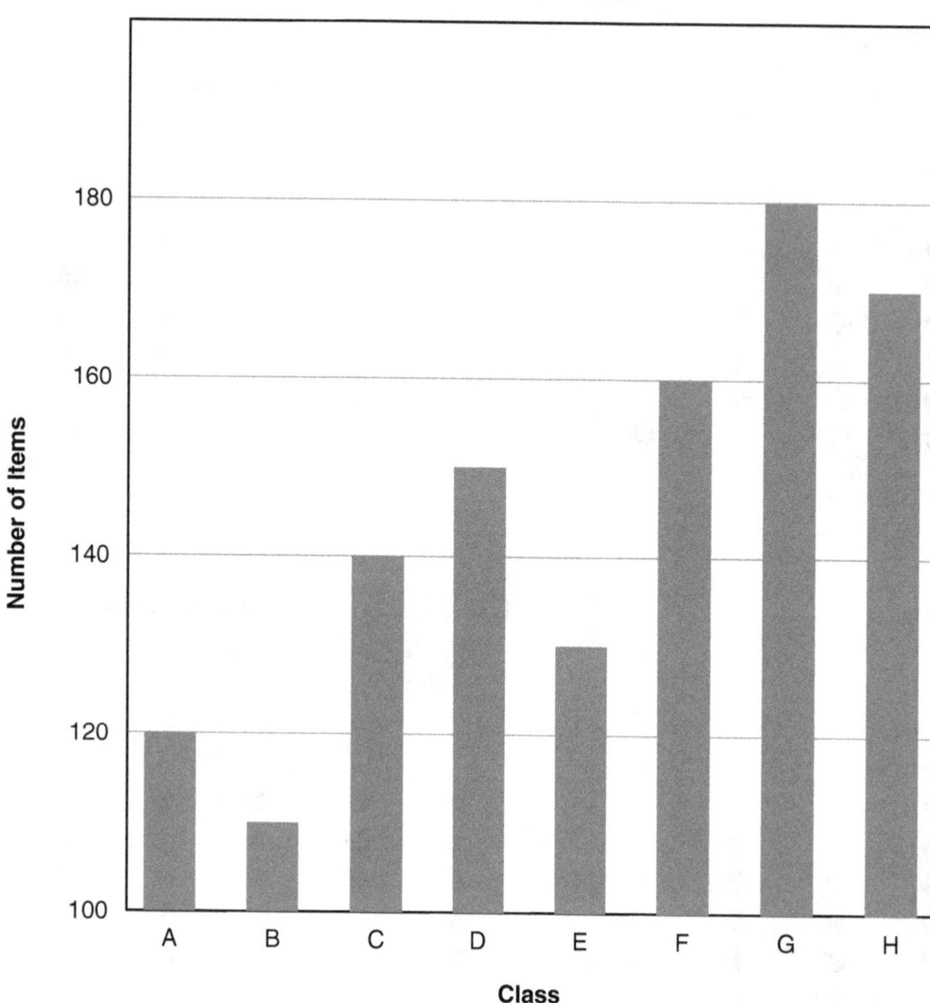

A. 500
B. 510
C. 520
D. 530

27. Find the range for the data set 34, 45, 27, 29, 36, 60, 52, 48, 41, 65, 44, 50, 64, 58, 47, and 31.

A. 3
B. 5
C. 36
D. 38

28. A rectangular pyramid has a length of 10 centimeters, a width of 11 inches, and a height of 12 inches. Find the volume in cubic inches.

A. 220
B. 440
C. 660
D. 880

29. A sphere has a volume of 972π cubic millimeters. Find the radius in millimeters.

A. 3
B. 9
C. 27
D. 81

30. Find the height in centimeters of a cylinder with a volume of 800π cubic centimeters and a radius of 10 centimeters.

A. 8
B. 10
C. 40
D. 80

31. Divide $1\frac{2}{3} \div 3\frac{7}{12}$.

A. $\frac{20}{43}$
B. $3\frac{7}{18}$
C. $3\frac{3}{4}$
D. $5\frac{35}{36}$

32. Multiply $\frac{6}{7} \times \frac{7}{10}$.

A. $\frac{1}{17}$
B. $\frac{1}{3}$
C. $\frac{3}{5}$
D. $\frac{13}{17}$

33. Multiply $3\frac{1}{5} \times \frac{5}{8}$.

A. 1
B. 2
C. 3
D. 4

34. Multiply, $(5x-3)(5x+3)$.

A. $25x^2-9$
B. $25x^2+9$
C. $25x^2+30x-9$
D. $25x^2+30x+9$

35. Perform the operation, $(-3x^2-2xy+4y^2)+(5x^2+3xy-3y^2)$.

A. $2x^2-xy+y^2$
B. $-2x^2-xy+y^2$
C. $-2x^2+xy+y^2$
D. $2x^2+xy+y^2$

36. Apply the polynomial identity to rewrite x^3+125.

A. $(x+5)(x^2-5x+25)$
B. $(x-5)(x^2-10x+25)$
C. $(x+5)(x^2+10x+25)$
D. $(x-5)(x^2+10x+25)$

37. Simplify $\left(\frac{x^3y^{-2}}{x^{-2}y^3}\right)^5$.

A. $\frac{1}{x^{25}y^{25}}$
B. $\frac{y^{25}}{x^{25}}$
C. $\frac{x^{25}}{y^{25}}$
D. $x^{25}y^{25}$

38. One athlete had a salary of about 3×10^7 dollars per year and another athlete had a salary of about 2×10^6 dollars per year. How many times larger is the salary of the first athlete?

A. 2
B. 5
C. 10
D. 15

39. Solve $x^3 = -216$.

A. -6
B. -4
C. 4
D. 6

40. If a survey finds that 120 people are in group X and 230 people are in group Y, what is the ratio of people in group Y to people in group X or group Y?

A. 12:35
B. 12:23
C. 23:35
D. 35:23

41. The number 22 is what percent of 54?

A. 22%
B. 29%
C. 41%
D. 76%

42. If 35% of a cattle herd is Ayrshire and the rest is Jersey, and it has 195 Jerseys, how many cattle are in the herd?

A. 230
B. 263
C. 300
D. 557

43. A regular hexagon has a side length of 5 inches and an apothem of 2 inches. Find the area in square inches.

A. 30
B. 40
C. 50
D. 60

44. A wedge of cheese is in the shape of a right triangular prism. The area of the base is 30 square inches. What is the height in inches of the cheese if the volume is 150 cubic inches?

A. 2.5
B. 5
C. 7.5
D. 10

45. A house is located at (15,30). The next house is 100 meters away. What could be the coordinate of the second house?

A. (15, 30)
B. (30, 15)
C. (115, 15)
D. (115, 30)

46. Solve the equation by completing the square, $x^2-2x-37 = 0$.

A. $-1 \pm \sqrt{37}$
B. $1 \pm \sqrt{37}$
C. $-1 \pm \sqrt{38}$
D. $1 \pm \sqrt{38}$

47. Solve the equation by factoring, $x^2-5x-50 = 0$.

A. –10, –5
B. –10, 5
C. 10, –5
D. 10, 5

48. Solve the equation by any method, $x^2 + 17x + 20 = 0$.

A. −15.73 and −1.27
B. 15.73 and −1.27
C. −15.73 and 1.27
D. 15.73 and 1.27

49. In a word game, a player loses 8 points when using an invalid word. If there were 65 invalid words, how many points were lost during the game?

A. −520
B. −480
C. −73
D. −57

50. A service group collects trash from area roadways for four straight weeks. The amount of trash they pick up is about $19\frac{1}{2}$, $15\frac{1}{3}$, $20\frac{7}{10}$, and $16\frac{3}{5}$ pounds. Estimate the total number of pounds collected.

A. 70
B. 71
C. 72
D. 73

51. In a game, positive and negative points can be scored. For 10 turns, the point total is −5, +4, −7, −2, 0, +3, +5, −6, −4, +2. What is the average point total?

A. −2
B. −1
C. 1
D. 2

52. Convert 15,000 grams to metric tons.

A. 0.00015 metric ton
B. 0.0015 metric ton
C. 0.015 metric ton
D. 0.15 metric ton

53. Identify 3:00 p.m. in military time.

A. 0300
B. 0600
C. 1200
D. 1500

54. Identify 1435 in 12-hour clock time.

A. 12:35 a.m.
B. 2:35 a.m.
C. 12:35 p.m.
D. 2:35 p.m.

55. There is an election at a school where 4 candidates out of 10 will be elected. Which object and results are the most appropriate for a simulation?

A. Toss a coin
B. Ten-sided number cube and use multiples of 2
C. Eight-section spinner and use the odd numbers
D. Throw two six-sided number cubes and use the results of 1 and 6

56. A survey group wants to know the percentage of voters in a town who favor building a new shopping center. What is the survey group's population?

A. All eligible voters in the town

B. All people who live in the town

C. All interviewed people in the town

D. All voters 35 years and older in the town

57. A school wants to know the daily attendance of all classes. What data would be good for a census?

A. Attendance on Fridays

B. Attendance every day

C. Attendance for math classes

D. Attendance after holiday breaks

58. Which option results in the largest loss on a product?

A. 30% of gaining $2 million and 70% of losing $1 million

B. 60% of gaining $1 million and 40% of losing $2 million

C. 30% of gaining $3 million and 70% of losing $1.5 million

D. 60% of gaining $1.5 million and 40% of losing $2.5 million

59. If a letter is chosen at random from the word SUBSTITUTE, what is the probability that the letter chosen is "S" or "T"?

A. $\frac{1}{5}$

C. $\frac{2}{5}$

B. $\frac{3}{10}$

D. $\frac{1}{2}$

60. A spinner contains numbers 1–20. What is the probability of spinning a multiple of 3 or a multiple of 5?

A. $\frac{3}{10}$

C. $\frac{9}{20}$

B. $\frac{1}{5}$

D. $\frac{11}{20}$

SECTION III. READING

1. **If you are using a book for research but it contains more information than you need, which text feature is most likely to help you find the most important pages to read?**

   A. Index
   B. Italics
   C. Sidebars
   D. Endnotes

Read the following passage and answer questions 2-4.

Every time I visit the bookstore, I find a new science fiction title about post-apocalyptic survivors taking refuge in New York City's subway tunnels. Some of these survival stories are fun to read, but they have a pesky plausibility problem: if society collapses, those subway tunnels won't be there anymore—at least not for long. On a typical day in a functioning New York City, a crew of engineers works around the clock to pump about 13 million gallons of water out of the subway system, and a major rain event pushes that number up fast. What happens if you take the engineers—and the electricity to work the sump pumps—out of the equation? The first big storm will flood those tunnels, probably for good. At that point, any survivors left underground will have to grow gills or head for the surface.

2. **Which of the following is the best title for this passage?**

   A. A Visit to a Bookstore
   B. The Science of Growing Gills
   C. A Refuge in Fiction, But Not in Fact
   D. The Best Science Fiction of the Year

3. **Which graphic element would most clearly illustrate the author's point?**

   A. A schematic showing the depth and volume of all of New York City's subway tunnels
   B. A graph comparing the ridership of New York City's subways with those of other major American cities
   C. A table showing how much water runs through the New York City subway system in varying conditions
   D. A New York City subway map showing emergency exits and detailing procedures for exiting the system during a flood

4. **Which information would belong in a sidebar alongside this text?**

   A. An illustration showing how a family of people might look if they all had gills behind their ears
   B. A description of a subway's electrified third rail and an explanation of how it works to power the train
   C. A list of science fiction novels about people living in subway tunnels in a post-apocalyptic world
   D. A description of the job qualifications of a subway engineer who works the pumps to keep the tunnels functional

5. **Which sentence does *not* display gender bias?**

   A. The parent who feeds her infant organic foods cares for her infant's physical growth.

   B. The parent who feeds his infant organic foods cares for his infant's physical growth.

   C. The parent who feeds an infant organic foods cares for the infant's physical growth.

   D. The parent who feeds their infant organic foods cares for her infant's physical growth.

Read the following passage and answer questions 6-8.

It is a well-known fact that CAT News is a so-called "fake news" site presenting highly biased and negatively influential stories to its viewers. Watching a CAT News broadcast feels like stepping into a slightly deranged and extremely angry alternate universe. Cynical exaggerations of violence dupe naïve viewers into believing the world is falling apart outside the confines of their gated retirement communities.

6. **One assumption behind the argument in this passage is that:**

   A. there were riots in Burgertown, Arizona.

   B. some reports by CAT News are exaggerated.

   C. no violent drug dealers cross the border illegally.

   D. many CAT News viewers are wealthy and elderly.

7. **The opening sentence of this paragraph should raise a careful reader's suspicions because it:**

   A. points out bias in the news.

   B. presents an opinion as a fact.

   C. uses quotation marks to indicate irony.

   D. falsely suggests a cause-and-effect relationship.

8. **Which detail from the passage suggests that it may be highly biased?**

   A. It suggests that undocumented immigrants are innocent victims.

   B. It says all CAT News employees are "deranged and extremely angry."

   C. It criticizes a news organization that is obviously reputable.

   D. It portrays CAT News viewers as unintelligent and out of touch.

9. **In which of the following situations would it be best to use informal language?**

   A. Buying a suit

   B. A birthday party

   C. A meeting at work

   D. Going to a work lunch

10. **Which of the following sentences uses the MOST formal language?**

    A. We connect blonde hair with silliness.

    B. We believe blonde hair means silliness.

    C. Blonde hair is often associated with silliness.

    D. People think blonde hair means silliness.

11. Which of the following sentences uses the MOST informal language?

A. You need to bandage that wound.

B. I won't do it.

C. Traveling for leisure is the best way to travel.

D. The young girl had an illness.

12. In which of the following situations would you use formal language?

A. Texting a friend.

B. A family reunion.

C. Skyping your grandparents.

D. At a Parent-Teacher meeting.

Please read the text below and answer questions 13-17.

It is perhaps unsurprising that fad diets are so common given the level of obesity in American society. But over the long term, most fad diets are harmful both to the health and to the waistline. Many such diets advocate cutting out one major nutrient, such as fats or carbohydrates. Others suggest fasting over long periods or eating from fixed menu options that may not meet the body's needs. Most of these diets are highly impractical, and many lead directly or indirectly to binge eating and other unhealthy behaviors.

13. The topic of this paragraph is:

A. fasting.

B. obesity.

C. fad diets.

D. binge eating.

14. The topic sentence of this paragraph is:

A. But over the long term, most fad diets are harmful both to the health and to the waistline.

B. Many such diets advocate cutting out one major nutrient, such as fats or carbohydrates.

C. It is perhaps unsurprising that fad diets are so common given the level of obesity in American society.

D. Most of these diets are highly impractical, and many lead directly or indirectly to binge eating and other unhealthy behaviors.

15. If the author added a description of a man who attempted several fad diets and ended up heavier than ever, what type of information would this be?

A. A main idea

B. A topic sentence

C. A supporting detail

D. An off-topic sentence

16. **Read the following description of the paragraph:**

    The author argues unfairly against fad diets without taking their good qualities into account.

    Why is this *not* a valid description of the main idea?

    A. It is not accurate; the author of the paragraph is stating facts, not opinions.

    B. It is not objective; the person summarizing the main idea is adding a judgment.

    C. It is not accurate; the author of the paragraph does not argue against fad diets.

    D. It is not objective; the person summarizing the main idea ignores a sentence about the benefits of dieting.

17. **Why doesn't a statistic about early childhood obesity rates belong in this paragraph?**

    A. It does not directly support the main idea that fad diets are harmful.

    B. Readers might feel hopeless to solve the problem the author identifies.

    C. Statistics should never be used as supporting details in persuasive writing.

    D. It would act as a second topic sentence and confuse readers about the main idea.

The diagram below provides information about the parts of a neuron (brain cell). Study the image and answer questions 18-19.

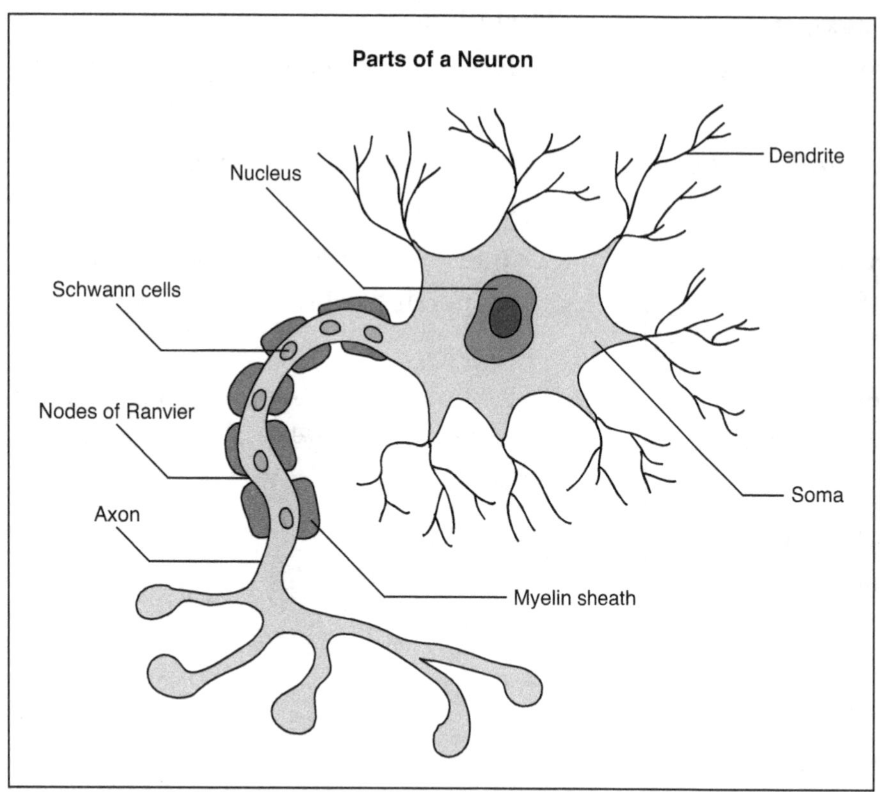

18. What is the small, root-like part of the neuron on the top right called?

A. Axon
B. Nucleus
C. Dendrite
D. Myelin sheath

19. Which question can be answered by consulting this diagram?

A. Why does the brain contain neurons?
B. Where is a nucleus located in a neuron?
C. What is the function of a myelin sheath?
D. How does a neuron interact with other cells?

A high school student is presenting research on how gender affects participation in her political science class. Study the graphic elements below and answer questions 20-22.

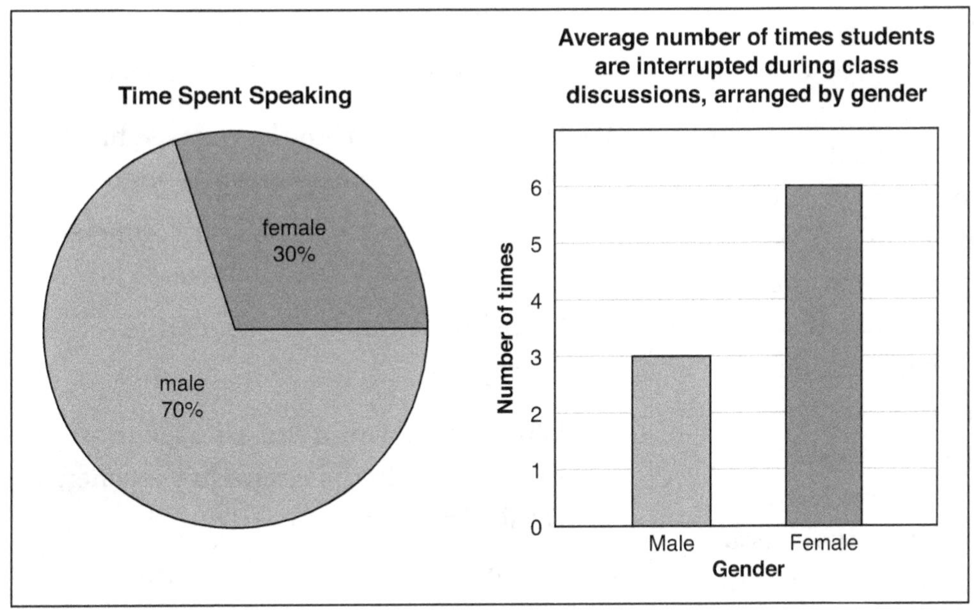

20. Male students spend ______ of class time speaking.

    A. 3%
    B. 6%
    C. 30%
    D. 70%

21. Which statement accurately describes the average number of interruptions during each class discussion?

    A. Male students are interrupted an average of six times.
    B. Female students are interrupted an average of six times.
    C. Male students interrupt others an average of three times.
    D. Female students interrupt others an average of three times.

22. Which argument does the information in the graphs best support?

    A. Female students do not have as many ideas about political science as male students.
    B. The class should make a greater effort to give students of both genders a fair chance to speak.
    C. Contrary to popular belief, male students face greater gender discrimination in school settings.
    D. There is no substantial difference between male and female students' class participation in discussions.

Read the passage and answer questions 23-26.

Dear Dr. Rodriguez,

I am writing to request that you change my daughter Amelia's chemistry grade. Amelia is a brilliant and capable girl who does not deserve an F in your class. Incidentally, I am sure you recall our family's substantial donation to your school district last year. I was led to believe we would no longer be troubled by petty grade issues or incompetent teachers after I wrote that check. In fact, I feel compelled to forward this message to your superiors to make certain the issue is dealt with promptly, and to ensure that we have no future misunderstandings.

Sincerely,

Violetta D. Johannsen

23. Which adjective best describes the tone of this passage?

A. Friendly
B. Arrogant
C. Hopeless
D. Respectful

24. Which phrase from the passage has an openly hostile and superior tone?

A. I am writing to request
B. brilliant and capable
C. incompetent teachers
D. to make certain

25. What mood would this passage most likely evoke in the chemistry teacher, Dr. Rodriguez?

A. Fury
B. Glee
C. Calm
D. Respect

26. Which transition word or phrase from the passage adds emphasis to the writer's point?

A. And
B. After
C. In fact
D. Incidentally

Read the following text and answer questions 27-30.

Fly Lake is the heart and soul of our town, and it needs our help. The environmental problems are obvious everywhere. The parking lot and path to the lake are strewn with beer cans and other litter. A half-dead grove of oaks bears the scars of a careless visitor's untended fire. Other trees are tagged with spray-painted graffiti. Any visitor who bothers to walk past this depressing scene all the way to the edge of the lake will notice piles of discarded fishing gear—but the fishing is terrible these days. Beneath the surface, hardly anything is still swimming. The lake has long been a source of recreation, tourist revenue, and food for the people of our town, but if current trends continue, it will no longer be able to fulfill any of these roles. For the greater good, we need funding and workers to clean up Fly Lake.

27. This passage is best described as:

A. narrative.
B. technical.
C. persuasive.
D. expository.

28. Which two organizational schemes best describe the structure of the text?

A. Cause/effect and sequence
B. Problem-solution and description
C. Cause/effect and compare/contrast
D. Problem-solution and compare/contrast

29. If this text were to continue for a few more paragraphs, which genre label would best apply to it?

A. Essay
B. Fable
C. History
D. Memoir

30. Which statement best expresses the unstated theme of the passage?

A. People who litter should pay hefty fines.
B. Caring for the environment benefits everyone.
C. If you start a campfire, don't be careless with it.
D. Worthless human beings scar and defile the earth.

Read the following passage and answer questions 31-35.

A growing focus on STEM—science, technology, engineering, and math—has brought funding and excitement for these subjects into schools. Meanwhile, the push for standardized testing is requiring teachers to devote a large proportion of class time to reading and math test preparation. One consequence of these dual trends is that schools are skimping on social studies instruction.

Mindful world citizens need, at a minimum, a general awareness of foreign cultures, a passing familiarity with geography, and a basic understanding of history. If you're not sure your child's school is instilling these basic foundations of knowledge, you need to support your kids' learning yourself. Daunting as this may sound, it doesn't need to take an inordinate amount of time and effort.

A good first step is to keep a globe or world map in a prominent location in your home. Whenever possible, refer to this resource in conversation. For instance, if your child is interested in a particular animal, point out where in the world it lives. If older children ask questions about the news, show them where current events are happening. If your budget allows it, keep a good children's atlas handy too. This will allow your conversations to go into greater depth if your children show interest.

Children have ever-greater access to high-quality fiction about people and cultures around the world. If you're reading together about a foreign place or time—or if you see your older child picking up a historical or multicultural book—take a moment to find a children's nonfiction book on the same subject. If you don't have time to do this research during a family library trip, most libraries allow patrons to browse and order books online.

31. This article is written for:

A. parents
B. children
C. teachers
D. policymakers

32. The author of this article assumes that:

A. parents are eager to support their children's education.
B. parents have unlimited time to support their kids' education.
C. teachers do not like helping children learn about social studies.
D. teachers all prefer STEM subjects and reading over social studies.

33. A careful reader of this article can infer that the author wants children to grow up to become:

A. STEM employees.
B. successful teachers.
C. multicultural patrons.
D. mindful world citizens.

34. Which conclusion is not supported by the article?

A. The author thinks teachers have limited time and energy.
B. The author thinks people benefit from understanding history.
C. The author thinks many parents read regularly with their kids.
D. The author thinks STEM instruction is a waste of children's time.

35. Which sentence from the article shows the author's awareness that modern parents are often busy people?

A. A good first step is to keep a globe or world map in a prominent location in your home.

B. If you don't have time to do this research during a family library trip, most libraries allow patrons to browse and order books online.

C. If you're not sure your child's school is instilling these basic foundations of knowledge, you need to support your kids' learning yourself.

D. A growing focus on STEM—science, technology, engineering, and math—has brought funding and excitement for these subjects into schools.

Read the following text and answer questions 36-40.

WiseWear gear provides you with cutting-edge technology to enhance your performance and optimize your training. WiseWear products include sensors to track your heart rate, activity level, and calorie burn during workouts. Information is automatically uploaded to your phone and organized so you can track your improvement over time with just a tap of the screen.

Concerned about comfort? We've got you covered. WiseWear clothing is made with high-tech synthetic compression fabrics to promote circulation and wick away sweat while you work out.

Top-level pro athletes, like ultra-marathoner Uri Schmidt, rely on WiseWear for training and competition. Shouldn't you do the same?

36. The purpose of this passage is to:

A. decide.

B. inform.

C. persuade.

D. entertain.

37. With which statement would the author of this passage most likely agree?

A. Americans who work out put too much emphasis on performance and not enough on enjoyment.

B. People who do not buy high-end exercise gear do not deserve to get a good workout and stay healthy.

C. The best way to achieve a healthy body is to follow a simple exercise plan and avoid hyped-up gadgets.

D. Consumers want help pushing their bodies to the limit and gathering information about their exercise performance.

38. Which detail from the passage, if true, is factual?

A. WiseWear transforms the user into a better and more informed athlete.

B. WiseWear gear is the most comfortable exercise clothing on the market.

C. WiseWear products contain sensors that track the user's body signals.

D. WiseWear users are bound to improve at the sport of their choice over time.

39. The author of the passage includes details about WiseWear's comfort and ease of use in order to appeal to the reader's:

A. reason.

B. trust.

C. feelings.

D. knowledge.

40. The author most likely includes the detail about a famous ultra-marathoner in order to make readers:

A. understand that WiseWear gear is factually the best on the market.

B. take a weak position when they attempt to argue against the point.

C. trust that scientists have really studied WiseWear gear and proven it worthy.

D. feel an association between WiseWear products and a person they admire.

SECTION IV. SCIENCE

1. **Which is a classification level in the Linnaean system?**

   A. Achaea
   B. Domain
   C. Genus
   D. Ursidae

2. **Which statement confirms that the cell membrane is selectively permeable?**

   A. Receptors are found on a cell's surface.
   B. Cells communicate with each other using cell signals.
   C. Environmental changes can cause a cell to expand or shrink.
   D. Sodium ions must travel through ion channels to enter the cell.

3. **Where does enzyme synthesis occur in a cell?**

   A. Cytoplasm
   B. Mitochondrion
   C. Nucleus
   D. Ribosome

4. **Why does photosynthesis need ATP?**

   A. Make membranes
   B. Establish a gradient
   C. Produce chloroplasts
   D. Create sugar molecules

5. **How many net ATP molecules are generated by the process of glycolysis?**

   A. 2
   B. 6
   C. 32
   D. 34

6. **During the G2 phase, more copies of tubulin are made to separate**

   A. histones.
   B. chromosomes.
   C. daughter cells.
   D. sister chromatids.

7. **What does a barometer measure?**

   A. Mass
   B. Air pressure
   C. Temperature
   D. Volume of a liquid

8. **What is a treatment group?**

   A. A type of placebo
   B. A baseline measure
   C. The outcome of interest
   D. The variable being manipulated

9. **What is the function of a peptide bond?**

   A. To connect proteins together
   B. To connect nucleotides together
   C. To connect amino acids together
   D. To connect nucleic acids together

10. **The DNA base cytosine only pairs with ______.**

    A. adenine
    B. cytosine
    C. guanine
    D. thymine

11. **The only haploid cells are the sperm and egg cells, which are known as ______.**

    A. alleles
    B. centromeres
    C. gametes
    D. zygotes

12. Fats and steroids belong to what biomolecule class?

A. Lipids
B. Proteins
C. Nucleic acids
D. Carbohydrates

13. Which of the following is a weak base?

A. Vinegar
B. Ammonia
C. Pure water
D. Sodium hydroxide

14. What happens to a Brønsted-Lowry base in an aqueous solution?

A. Donates hydrogen ions
B. Accepts a pair of electrons
C. Dissociates to hydronium ions
D. Increases hydroxide ion concentration

15. Which of the following statements is true regarding the number of valence electrons in different elements?

A. The number of valence electrons increases going from left to right on the periodic table.
B. The number of valence electrons decreases going from left to right on the periodic table.
C. The number of valence electrons increases going from top to bottom on the periodic table.
D. The number of valence electrons decreases going from top to bottom on the periodic table.

16. How do zinc and sulfur react to form a compound?

A. Zinc and sulfur will share electrons.
B. Sulfur will transfer electrons to zinc.
C. Zinc will transfer electrons to sulfur.
D. Zinc and sulfur do not react with each other.

17. Which of the following describes one way that a chlorine atom can become stable?

A. It can gain one electron to form a cation.
B. It can lose one electron to form a cation.
C. It can gain one electron to form an anion.
D. It can lose one electron to form an anion.

18. When an antacid tablet is placed in water, fizzing is observed. The chemical equation for the reaction that occurs is shown below. Which compound is being released in the bubbles?

$$C_6H_8O_7(aq) + 3NaHCO_3(aq)\ 3CO_2(g) + 3H_2O(l) + NaC_6H_5O_7(aq)$$

A. CO_2
B. H_2O
C. $C_6H_8O_7$
D. $NaC_6H_5O_7$

19. What products are formed in all combustion reactions?

A. CH and O_2
B. CO_2 and O_2
C. H_2O and O_2
D. H_2O and CO_2

20. Which of the following equations shows a double replacement reaction?

A. $CaO + H_2O\ Ca(OH)_2$

B. $2Na + ZnCl_2\ Zn(s) + 2NaCl$

C. $Pb(NO_3)_2 + 2KI\ PbI_2 + 2KNO_3$

D. $2C_4H_{10} + 13O_2\ 8CO_2 + 10H_2O$

21. What would happen if an amino acid could not pass through a lipid bilayer?

A. The solutes would be targeted by nearby ions.

B. The solutes on one side would form a channel to move through.

C. The amino acid solutes would bond with water and move through the bilayer.

D. The polar solute particles would form hydrogen bonds with the water molecules surrounding them.

22. What is polar molecule?

A. A molecule that contains oxygen

B. A molecule that is repulsed by water

C. A molecule that is attracted to water

D. A molecule that has slight charges on each end

23. An atom has 3 protons, 4 neutrons, and 3 electrons. Which element is it?

A. Beryllium

B. Carbon

C. Lithium

D. Neon

24. Which of the following numbers has the smallest magnitude?

A. 5.14×10^{-27}

B. 4.65×10^{-19}

C. 2.87×10^{-16}

D. 5.29×10^{-7}

25. In which of the following phases are particles of a substance generally closest together?

A. Gas

B. Liquid

C. Plasma

D. Solid

26. In which of the following situations does helium have the greatest amount of energy?

A. Helium is liquid at temperatures below -270°C.

B. Helium gas is used to blow up a birthday balloon.

C. Helium is used in yellow-orange neon lights in plasma form.

D. Helium is stored as a liquid for use as a coolant in space applications.

27. How many kilograms are in 1,800 grams?

A. 0.18

B. 1.8

C. 18

D. 180

28. If a bag is filled with 5.0 liters of saline, how many quarts of saline are in the bag?

A. 1.1

B. 2.2

C. 4.7

D. 5.3

29. In a certain circuit, three wires connect at a node. If one of those wires carries 3 amps into the node and another carries 1 amp out of the node, what current does the third wire carry?

A. 2 amps into the node

B. 2 amps out of the node

C. 4 amps into the node

D. 4 amps out of the node

30. A 200-volt source is connected to a single 1,000-ohm resistor. What is the voltage drop across the resistor?

A. 0.2 volts
B. 5 volts
C. 200 volts
D. 1,000 volts

31. The friction force in newtons on a certain type of sliding block is 0.050 times the block's mass in kilograms. What is the minimum horizontal force that must be applied to slide a 230-kilogram block?

A. 2.2×10^{-4} N
B. 12 N
C. 230 N
D. 4,600 N

32. A satellite is 6.7×10^6 meters from the center of Earth. If it maintains a circular orbit, what is its speed? (The acceleration due to gravity is 9.8 m/s^2.)

A. 8.3×10^2 m/s
B. 8.1×10^3 m/s
C. 6.8×10^5 m/s
D. 6.6×10^7 m/s

33. An object in uniform circular motion with a radius of 42 meters has an angular frequency of 0.29 hertz. What is its velocity?

A. 0.0069 m/s
B. 1.9 m/s
C. 12 m/s
D. 140 m/s

34. What is the mass of a student who jumps off the 3.0 m high bleachers after the school team wins the state championship if that student's potential energy was 1900 J?

A. 32 kg
B. 65 kg
C. 78 kg
D. 97 kg

35. Which of the following can be used to describe climate patterns?

A. The circulation in the atmosphere
B. The transfer of energy and heat throughout the planet
C. Thestudy of what is happening in the atmosphere right now
D. Any regular cycle that occurs within climate over a period of time.

36. If the velocity of an object is decreased by half, by what factor is the kinetic energy reduced?

A. 2
B. 4
C. 6
D. 8

37. What are main sequence stars?

A. Stars that are very dim
B. Stars that are in their longest stage of life
C. Stars that are very large and brighter than the sun
D. Groups of stars and star systems that are bound together by gravity

38. Which situation best illustrates Newton's first law of motion?

A. A ball that is on a flat surface accelerates as a piston pushes it.
B. A ball that is rolling on a flat surface maintains the same velocity.
C. A ball that is on a sloped surface rolls down the slope because of gravity.
D. A ball that is stationary on a flat surface does not fall despite the downward force of gravity.

39. If the vertical distance between the crest and trough of a wave is 10.0 meters, what is the wave's amplitude?

A. 2.50 meters
B. 5.00 meters
C. 10.0 meters
D. 20.0 meters

40. Which components are part of Earth's biosphere?

A. The gases on Earth
B. The water on Earth
C. The living things on Earth
D. The crust and core of Earth

ACT Practice Exam 1
Answer Key with Explanatory Answers

Section I. English

1. B. *So* is an adverb that describes the adverb *hard*. (*Hard* describes the verb *hit*.) **See Lesson: Adjectives and Adverbs.**

2. C. *Late* is an adjective that describes the noun *flight*. **See Lesson: Adjectives and Adverbs.**

3. C. *Cute* and *furry* are adjectives that describe the noun *kitten*. **See Lesson: Adjectives and Adverbs.**

4. C. *Incredibly* is an adverb that describe the adjective *fast*. **See Lesson: Adjectives and Adverbs.**

5. A. *Worse* is a comparative form of the adverb *badly*. **See Lesson: Adjectives and Adverbs.**

6. D. *december, she, and christmas*. All months and holidays are capitalized. She is the beginning of a sentence and needs to be capitalized. **See Lesson: Capitalization.**

7. B. The Victorian Era is marked by strict modesty. All specific historical time periods are capitalized. **See Lesson: Capitalization.**

8. C. *Philadelphia Eagles, New England Patriots*. Cities, regions, and sports teams are meant to be capitalized. **See Lesson: Capitalization.**

9. C. White House. The White House is capitalized because it is an important governmental building. **See Lesson: Capitalization.**

10. B. *Even though* is a subordinating conjunction. It connects the clauses *I walked home* and *my feet really hurt*. **See Lesson: Conjunctions and Prepositions.**

11. A. *It* is a pronoun, not a preposition. **See Lesson: Conjunctions and Prepositions.**

12. C. *But* and *so* are coordinating conjunctions. These two conjunctions connect three independent clauses in this sentence. **See Lesson: Conjunctions and Prepositions.**

13. B. *The table* is the object of the preposition *under*. **See Lesson: Conjunctions and Prepositions.**

14. A. *Until* is a subordinating conjunction, connecting the main clause *don't leave* and the dependent clause *we get there*. **See Lesson: Conjunctions and Prepositions.**

15. C. The meaning of emulate in this context is "to try to be like someone you admire." The word "imitate" helps you figure out the meaning of emulate. **See Lesson: Context Clues and Multiple Meaning Words.**

16. C. The word "application" has more than one meaning. **See Lesson: Context Clues and Multiple Meaning Words.**

17. D. The meaning of <u>bass</u> in the context of this sentence is "a guitar with four strings that makes low sounds." **See Lesson: Context Clues and Multiple Meaning Words.**

18. B. The meaning of <u>exuberant</u> in the context of this sentence is "cheerful." **See Lesson: Context Clues and Multiple Meaning Words.**

19. B. The word "prune" has more than one meaning. **See Lesson: Context Clues and Multiple Meaning Words.**

20. C. *Cells* is the direct object of the verb *viewed.* **See Lesson: Direct Objects and Indirect Objects.**

21. D. Neither the verb tried nor the verb succeed has a direct object. *So* and *hard* are adverbs. **See Lesson: Direct Objects and Indirect Objects.**

22. A. There is no indirect object in this sentence. **See Lesson: Direct Objects and Indirect Objects.**

23. D. There is no indirect object. **See Lesson: Direct Objects and Indirect Objects.**

24. D. *The Constitution* is a direct object of the verb *write.* **See Lesson: Direct Objects and Indirect Objects.**

25. B. *Woman* is not a modifier. **See Lesson: Modifiers.**

26. C. *That I wrote on the Korean War* should modify *report,* so it should be placed after that word. **See Lesson: Modifiers.**

27. C. *That, large,* and *silver* describe *bowl.* **See Lesson: Modifiers.**

28. D. *Which was ugly* most likely refers to *hat,* so it should be placed after that word, not after *head.* **See Lesson: Modifiers.**

29. B. The adjective *great* describes *time.* **See Lesson: Modifiers.**

30. C. *a lot of homework. Homework* is a non-count noun and cannot be made plural by adding *-s.* **See Lesson: Nouns.**

31. B. The word *estimated* in this sentence functions as a verb, but here *estimate* is a noun. **See Lesson: Nouns.**

32. C. *Dishonesty* does not physically exist; it is an abstract noun. **See Lesson: Nouns.**

33. C. *crises.* **See Lesson: Nouns.**

34. D. The pronoun *whom* should be used as the object of the preposition *of.* **See Lesson: Pronouns.**

35. C. *She, I, I, her,* and *it* are pronouns. **See Lesson: Pronouns.**

36. D. *Yours* is a possessive pronoun. **See Lesson: Pronouns.**

37. A. *Him* is an object pronoun. **See Lesson: Pronouns.**

38. B. *There needs to be a semicolon after studying.* A semicolon is used to connect two related sentences. **See Lesson: Punctuation.**

39. C. *State of the art should be hyphenated.* It is a compound word before a noun and needs to be hyphenated. **See Lesson: Punctuation.**

40. A. *It was good, wasn't it?* Commas are used before question tags. **See Lesson: Punctuation.**

41. B. *The book was amazing; she couldn't put it down.* Semicolons are used to connect two related sentences without using a coordinating conjunction. **See Lesson: Punctuation.**

42. C. The prefix that means "with" is *con.* **See Lesson: Root Words, Prefixes, and Suffixes.**

43. D. The root *cred* means "believe," the prefix *in* means "not," and the suffix *ous* means "full of or possessing," so, incredulous means disbelieving. **See Lesson: Root Words, Prefixes, and Suffixes.**

44. C. The root that means "to say" is *dict.* **See Lesson: Root Words, Prefixes, and Suffixes.**

45. A. The root *chrom* means "color" and the prefix *mono* means "one," so monochromatic means to having one color. **See Lesson: Root Words, Prefixes, and Suffixes.**

46. D. The root *rupt* means "break," so rupture means to burst. **See Lesson: Root Words, Prefixes, and Suffixes.**

47. D. *Two* is the correctly spelled form of the number. **See Lesson: Spelling.**

48. A. *Pair* is spelled correctly and has the appropriate meaning for the sentence. **See Lesson: Spelling.**

49. A. *Argument* is the only correct spelling. **See Lesson: Spelling.**

50. D. With a word ending in -f, you drop the -f and add -ves. **See Lesson: Spelling.**

51. B. *He* is third person singular. **See Lesson: Subject and Verb Agreement.**

52. C. *The automobile* and *the personal computer* are both singular subjects connected by *or,* so they take a singular verb form. **See Lesson: Subject and Verb Agreement.**

53. D. *Birds* is plural, so the verb should take the plural form *are.* **See Lesson: Subject and Verb Agreement.**

54. A. The verb *is* agrees with the subject *anyone. Who has skates* is a relative clause; it is not the main subject. **See Lesson: Subject and Verb Agreement.**

55. C. The subject is *my granddaughter*, and the predicate is *was born on January 18.* **See Lesson: Subject and Verb Agreement.**

56. A. An antonym of mollify is enrage. **See Lesson: Synonyms, Antonyms, and Analogies.**

57. A. A pediatrician is an example of a doctor in the same way that a harp is an example of an instrument. **See Lesson: Synonyms, Antonyms, and Analogies.**

58. A. Adding "non" would make the word nonpartisan, which is the antonym for partisan. **See Lesson: Synonyms, Antonyms, and Analogies.**

59. A. Ruthless has a negative connotation. **See Lesson: Synonyms, Antonyms, and Analogies.**

60. C. Content is the word that shows the weakest degree in the list of synonyms. **See Lesson: Synonyms, Antonyms, and Analogies.**

61. B. Before he went to bed. It is dependent because it does not express a complete thought and relies on the independent clause. The word "before" also signifies the beginning of a dependent clause. **See Lesson: Types of Clauses.**

62. A. If. The word "if" signifies the beginning of a dependent clause and is the only conjunction that makes sense in the sentence. **See Lesson: Types of Clauses.**

63. C. People do not exercise as much as they should. It is independent because it has a subject, verb, and expresses a complete thought. **See Lesson: Types of Clauses.**

64. C. But. It is the only conjunction that fits within the context of the sentence. **See Lesson: Types of Clauses.**

65. D. The trial must begin whether she shows up or not. With an independent and dependent clause, a subordinating conjunction is used to connect them. "Whether" is the only choice that makes sense. **See Lesson: Types of Clauses.**

66. C. This is a compound sentence joining two independent clauses with a comma and the conjunction *so.* **See Lesson: Types of Sentences.**

67. A. *Broadens their perspective* would be parallel in structure to the other items since they are longer phrases and use the same verb form. **See Lesson: Types of Sentences.**

68. B. This is a simple sentence since it contains one independent clause consisting of a simple subject and a predicate. **See Lesson: Types of Sentences.**

69. A. This sentence combines the information using parallel structure. **See Lesson: Types of Sentences.**

70. D. The subordinate conjunction "because" combines the sentences and puts the focus on Tony preparing for his job interview. **See Lesson: Types of Sentences.**

71. B. *Sold* is the simple past tense form. **See Lesson: Verbs and Verb Tenses.**

72. C. *Was unfolding* (past progressive) is the correct verb tense to use in this sentence. **See Lesson: Verbs and Verb Tenses.**

73. D. *That's great* contains the contraction *That is*. *Is* is a verb. **See Lesson: Verbs and Verb Tenses.**

74. D. *Am going* is present progressive tense. **See Lesson: Verbs and Verb Tenses.**

75. C. This sentence is in present progressive tense, and it describes something that is happening at this moment. **See Lesson: Verbs and Verb Tenses.**

Section II. Math

1. B. The correct solution is 3. The whole numbers include 0, 1, 2, 3,.... All whole numbers are greater than −3, but only 0, 1, and 2 are less than 3. **See Lesson: Basic Addition and Subtraction.**

2. C. The correct solution is adding two quantities with different units. To add quantities, they must have the same unit. For instance, adding a quantity of meters to a quantity of grams is impossible. **See Lesson: Basic Addition and Subtraction.**

3. A. When multiplying signed numbers, remember that the product of a negative and a positive is negative. Other than the sign, the process is the same as multiplying whole numbers. **See Lesson: Basic Multiplication and Division.**

4. B. Because 26 is not evenly divisible by 9, the best answer in this case has a remainder. The division algorithm is used to obtain this result. **See Lesson: Basic Multiplication and Division.**

5. D. The correct solution is 4.0 because $A = \pi r^2; 12 = 3.14 r^2; 3.82 = r^2;\ r \approx 2.0$. The diameter is twice the radius, or about 4.0 feet. **See Lesson: Circles.**

6. B. The correct solution is 40.82 because $C = \pi d \approx 3.14(13) \approx 40.82$ inches. **See Lesson: Circles.**

7. D. The correct solution is the square with four lines of symmetry. There is a horizontal line, a vertical line, and two diagonals of symmetry that map the rectangle onto itself. **See Lesson: Congruence.**

8. D. The correct solution is 200.96. The radius is 8 centimeters and $A = \pi r^2 \approx 3.14(8)^2 \approx 3.14(64) \approx 200.96$ square centimeters. **See Lesson: Circles.**

9. C. The two rays intersect at point *D*. **See Lesson: Congruence.**

10. A. The correct solution is a reflection across the x-axis because the points (x, y) become $(x, -y)$. **See Lesson: Congruence.**

11. A. The correct solution is $\frac{3}{8}$ because $\frac{0.375}{1} = \frac{375}{1000} = \frac{3}{8}$. **See Lesson: Decimals and Fractions.**

12. B. The correct answer is 20% because $\frac{1}{5}$ as a percent is $0.2 \times 100 = 20\%$. **See Lesson: Decimals and Fractions.**

13. B. The correct answer is $0.\overline{45}$because $\frac{5}{11} = 5.00 \div 11 = 0.\overline{45}$. **See Lesson: Decimals and Fractions.**

14. D. The correct solution is 48 because both sides of the equation are multiplied by −4. **See Lesson: Equations with One Variable.**

15. D. The correct solution is $x \geq 3$.

$3x + 3 + 2x + 2 \geq 15 – 5x + 4x + 8$	Apply the distributive property.
$5x + 5 \geq -x + 23$	Combine like terms on both sides of the inequality.
$6x + 5 \geq 23$	Add x to both sides of the inequality.
$6x \geq 18$	Subtract 5 from both sides of the inequality.
$x \geq 3$	Divide both sides of the inequality by 6.

See Lesson: Equations with One Variable.

16. D. The correct solution is $\frac{A}{1+rt} = P$.

$A = P(1 + rt)$	Factor P from the left side of the equation.
$\frac{A}{1 + rt} = P$	Divide both sides of the equation by $1 + rt$.

See Lesson: Equations with One Variable.

17. D. The correct solution is (-4, -8).

	The second equation is already solved for y.
$2(-x-12) + x = -20$	Substitute $-x-12$ in for y in the first equation.
$-2x-24 + x = -20$	Apply the distributive property.
$-x-24 = -20$	Combine like terms on the left side of the equation.
$-x = 4$	Add 24 to both sides of the equation.
$x = -4$	Divide both sides of the equation by -1.
$y = -(-4)-12$	Substitute -4 in the second equation for x.
$y = 4-12 = -8$	Simplify using order of operations.

See Lesson: Equations with Two Variables.

18. D. The correct solution is (-9, 5).

$-6x-2y = 44$	Multiply all terms in the second equation by -2.
$-8x = 72$	Add the equations.
$x = -9$	Divide both sides of the equation by -8.
$3(-9) + y = -22$	Substitute -9 in the second equation for x.
$-27 + y = -22$	Simplify using order of operations.
$y = 5$	Add 27 to both sides of the equation.

See Lesson: Equations with Two Variables.

19. B. The correct graph has the two lines intersect at (5, -6). **See Lesson: Equations with Two Variables.**

20. A. Start by eliminating 1, which is not a prime number. The number 2 is the only even prime; the other even numbers are composite. Therefore, consider only odd numbers greater than 2. The prime numbers less than 20 but greater than 2 are 3, 5, 7, 11, 13, 17, and 19. The total is eight. **See Lesson: Factors and Multiples.**

21. A. Any product of a number and an integer is a multiple of that number. Since 123×-1 is -123, one multiple of 123 is -123. **See Lesson: Factors and Multiples.**

22. D. The correct solution is more than half of the amount spent is between \$110 and \$170. There are 14 weeks where the amount spent is between \$110 and \$140 and 13 weeks where the amount spent is between \$140 and \$170. This is 27 weeks, which is more than half the data set. **See Lesson: Interpreting Categorical and Quantitative Data.**

23. A. The correct solution is the mean and standard deviation increase. The game with 8 goals increases the mean from 2.8 to 3.3 and increases the standard deviation from 1.315 to 2.002. **See Lesson: Interpreting Categorical and Quantitative Data.**

24. B. The correct solution is 35. The data set in order is 31, 32, 33, 33, 34, 35, 35, 36, 37, 37, 38, 39, and the middle numbers are both 35. Therefore, the median is 35. **See Lesson: Interpreting Graphics.**

25. A. The correct solution is A. There are 4 employees who have 10 minutes and 50 minutes, 5 employees who have 20 minutes, 6 employees who have 30 minutes and 40 minutes, and 1 employee who has 60 minutes. **See Lesson: Interpreting Categorical and Quantitative Data.**

26. B. The correct solution is 510 items because the three largest classes collected 180, 170, and 160 items. **See Lesson: Interpreting Graphics.**

27. D. The correct solution is 38. The difference between the highest value of 65 and the lowest value of 27 is 38. **See Lesson: Interpreting Graphics.**

28. B. The correct solution is 440. Substitute the values into the formula and simplify using the order of operations, $V = \frac{1}{3}Bh = \frac{1}{3}lwh = \frac{1}{3}(10)(11)12 = 440$ cubic inches. **See Lesson: Measurement and Dimension.**

29. B. The correct solution is 9 millimeters. Substitute the values into the formula, $972\pi = \frac{4}{3}\pi r^3$, then multiply by the reciprocal, $729 = r^3$, and apply the cube root, $r = 9$ millimeters. **See Lesson: Measurement and Dimension.**

30. A. The correct solution is 8. Substitute the values into the formula, $800\pi = \pi 10^2 h$, and apply the exponent, $800\pi = \pi(100)h$. Then, divide both sides of the equation by 100π, $h = 8$ centimeters. **See Lesson: Measurement and Dimension.**

31. A. The correct answer is $\frac{20}{43}$ because $\frac{5}{3} \div \frac{43}{12} = \frac{5}{3} \times \frac{12}{43} = \frac{60}{129} = \frac{20}{43}$. **See Lesson: Multiplication and Division of Fractions.**

32. C. The correct solution is $\frac{3}{5}$ because $\frac{6}{7} \times \frac{7}{10} = \frac{42}{70} = \frac{3}{5}$. **See Lesson: Multiplication and Division of Fractions.**

33. B. The correct solution is 2 because $\frac{16}{5} \times \frac{5}{8} = \frac{80}{40} = 2$. **See Lesson: Multiplication and Division of Fractions.**

34. A. The correct solution is $25x^2 - 9$.

$$(5x-3)(5x+3) = 5x(5x+3) - 3(5x+3) = 25x^2 + 15x - 15x - 9 = 25x^2 - 9$$

See Lesson: Polynomials.

35. D. The correct solution is $2x^2 + xy + y^2$.

$$(-3x^2 - 2xy + 4y^2) + (5x^2 + 3xy - 3y^2)$$

$$= (-3x^2 + 5x^2) + (-2xy + 3xy) + (4y^2 - 3y^2)$$

$$= 2x^2 + xy + y^2$$

See Lesson: Polynomials.

36. A. The correct solution is $(x+5)(x^2-5x+25)$. The expression $x^3 + 125$ is rewritten as $(x+5)(x^2-5x+25)$ because the value of a is x and the value of b is 5. **See Lesson: Polynomials.**

37. C. The correct solution is $\frac{x^{25}}{y^{25}}$ because

$$\left(\frac{x^3y^{-2}}{x^{-2}y^3}\right)^5 = \left(x^{3-(-2)}y^{-2-3}\right)^5 = \left(x^5y^{-5}\right)^5 = x^{5\times5}y^{-5\times5} = x^{25}y^{-25} = \frac{x^{25}}{y^{25}}.$$

See Lesson: Powers, Exponents, Roots, and Radicals.

38. D. The correct solution is 15 because the first athlete's salary is about \$30,000,000 and the second athlete's salary is about \$2,000,000. So, the first athlete's salary is about 15 times larger. **See Lesson: Powers, Exponents, Roots, and Radicals.**

39. A. The correct solution is –6 because the cube root of –216 is –6. **See Lesson: Powers, Exponents, Roots, and Radicals.**

40. C. The ratio is 23:35. The first part of the ratio is the number of people in group Y, which is 230. The second part is the number of people in either group, which is the sum 120 + 230 = 350. The ratio is therefore 230:350 = 23:35. **See Lesson: Ratios, Proportions, and Percentages.**

41. C. The fraction $\frac{22}{54}$ is 41%, meaning 22 is 41% of 54. **See Lesson: Ratios, Proportions, and Percentages.**

42. C. There are 300 cattle in the herd. Because the herd is only Ayrshire or Jersey, it is 65% Jersey. The equivalent decimals are 0.35 Ayrshire and 0.65 Jersey. Set up a proportion that relates these decimals to the number of cattle of each type:

$$\frac{0.35}{0.65} = \frac{?}{195}$$

One approach is to divide 195 by 0.65 to get 300, then multiply by 0.35 to get the number of Ayrshires: 105. Add 195 and 105 to get the total number of cattle in the herd. **See Lesson: Ratios, Proportions, and Percentages.**

43. A. The correct solution is 30. Substitute the values into the formula and simplify using the order of operations, $A = \frac{1}{2}ap = \frac{1}{2}(2)(6(5)) = 30$ square inches. **See Lesson: Similarity, Right Triangles, and Trigonometry.**

44. B. The correct solution is 5. Substitute the values into the formula, $150 = 30h$. Divide both sides of the equation by 30, $h = 5$ inches. **See Lesson: Similarity, Right Triangles, and Trigonometry.**

45. D. The correct solution is (115, 30) because 100 can be added to the x-coordinate, 15 + 100 = 115. **See Lesson: Similarity, Right Triangles, and Trigonometry.**

46. D. The correct solutions are $1 \pm \sqrt{38}$.

$x^2 - 2x = 37$	Add 37 to both sides of the equation.
$x^2 - 2x + 1 = 37 + 1$	Complete the square, $(\frac{2}{2})^2 = 1^2 = 1$.

Add 1 to both sides of the equation.

$x^2 - 2x + 1 = 38$	Simplify the right side of the equation.
$(x-1)^2 = 38$	Factor the left side of the equation.
$x-1 = \pm\sqrt{38}$	Apply the square root to both sides of the equation.
$x = 1 \pm \sqrt{38}$	Add 1 to both sides of the equation.

See Lesson: Solving Quadratic Equations.

47. B. The correct solutions are –10 and 5.

$(x + 10)(x–5) = 0$	Factor the equation.
$(x + 10) = 0$ *or* $(x–5) = 0$	Set each factor equal to 0.
$x + 10 = 0$	Subtract 10 from both sides of the equation to solve for the first factor.
$x = –10$	
$x–5 = 0$	Add 5 to both sides of the equation to solve for the second factor.
$x = 5$	

See Lesson: Solving Quadratic Equations.

48. A. The correct solutions are –15.73 and –1.27. The equation can be solved by the quadratic formula.

$x = \frac{-17 \pm \sqrt{17^2-4(1)(20)}}{2(1)}$	Substitute 1 for *a*, 17 for *b*, and 20 for *c*.
$x = \frac{-17 \pm \sqrt{289-80}}{2}$	Apply the exponent and perform the multiplication.
$x = \frac{-17 \pm \sqrt{209}}{2}$	Perform the subtraction.
$x = \frac{-17 \pm 14.46}{2}$	Apply the square root.
$x = \frac{-17 + 14.46}{2}$, $x = \frac{-17-14.46}{2}$	Separate the problem into two expressions.
$x = \frac{-2.54}{2} = -1.27$, $x = \frac{-31.46}{2} = -15.73$	Simplify the numerator and divide.

See Lesson: Solving Quadratic Equations.

49. A. The correct solution is –520 because $-8 \times 65 = -520$ points. **See Lesson: Solving Real-World Mathematical Problems.**

50. D. The correct solution is 73. The estimated weights are 20, 15, 21, and 17 pounds, and the total weight is about 73 pounds. **See Lesson: Solving Real-World Mathematical Problems.**

51. B. The correct solution is –1 because the sum of the scores is –10. The average is –10 divided by 10, or –1 point. **See Lesson: Solving Real-World Mathematical Problems.**

52. C. The correct solution is 0.015 metric ton. $15{,}000 \text{ g} \times \frac{1 \text{ kg}}{1{,}000 \text{ g}} \times \frac{1 \text{ t}}{1{,}000 \text{ kg}} = \frac{15{,}000}{1{,}000{,}000} = 0.015$ t. **See Lesson: Standards of Measure.**

53. D. The correct solution is 1500. Add 1200 to the time, 1200 + 300 = 1500. **See Lesson: Standards of Measure.**

54. D. The correct solution is 2:35 p.m. Subtract 1200 from the time, 1435 – 1200 = 2:35 p.m. **See Lesson: Standards of Measure.**

55. B. The correct solution is ten-sided number cube and use multiples of 2 because there are 4 results out of 10 that would match the probability of the actual event. **See Lesson: Statistical Measures.**

56. A. The correct solution is all eligible voters in the town because this is the population for the entire survey. **See Lesson: Statistical Measures.**

57. B. The correct solution is attendance every day because data is collected from every class every day. **See Lesson: Statistical Measures.**

58. B. The correct solution is 60% of gaining \$1 million and 40% of losing \$2 million. The expected value is $0.60(1) + 0.4(-2) = 0.6 + (-0.8) = -0.2$. **See Lesson: Statistics & Probability: The Rules of Probability.**

59. D. The correct solution is $\frac{1}{2}$. There are 3 S's and 2 T's in the word SUBTITUTE out of 10 letters. The probability is $\frac{3}{10} + \frac{2}{10} = \frac{5}{10} = \frac{1}{2}$. **See Lesson: Statistics & Probability: The Rules of Probability.**

60. C. The correct solution is $\frac{9}{20}$. There are six multiples of 3 and four multiples of 5. The overlap of 15 is subtracted from the probability, $\frac{6}{20} + \frac{4}{20} - \frac{1}{20} = \frac{9}{20}$. **See Lesson: Statistics & Probability: The Rules of Probability.**

Section III. Reading

1. A. The index tells which subtopics are covered on which pages of a book. **See Lesson: Evaluating and Integrating Data.**

2. C. The main point of this paragraph is that science fiction often depicts a particular kind of post-apocalyptic survival scenario that would not work in fact. The title of the passage should reflect this idea. **See Lesson: Evaluating and Integrating Data.**

3. C. The author argues that the New York City subway system would not be a good place to take refuge after a major weather event if nobody were working to pump the water out. Information about the water would help illustrate that point. **See Lesson: Evaluating and Integrating Data.**

4. C. Sidebar information should be peripheral to the text. That means it's clearly related and interesting to the same audience. Here, the list of sci-fi novels would be the best option. **See Lesson: Evaluating and Integrating Data.**

5. C. Writers can eliminate gender bias by replacing a pronoun with *one, he,* or *she*, or an article (*a, an, the*). **See Lesson: Facts, Opinions, and Evaluating an Argument**

6. D. The line about "gated retirement communities" suggests that CAT News viewers are wealthy and elderly. **See Lesson: Facts, Opinions, and Evaluating an Argument.**

7. B. The criticism of CAT News in the opening sentence is suspicious because it states that a subjective position is a fact. **See Lesson: Facts, Opinions, and Evaluating an Argument.**

8. D. The passage says CAT News stories "dupe naïve viewers"—a clear indication that the viewers are unintelligent and out of touch with reality. **See Lesson: Facts, Opinions, and Evaluating an Argument.**

9. B. A birthday party. It is an informal setting with friends and family. **See Lesson: Formal and Informal Language.**

10. C. Blonde hair is often associated with silliness. The sentence is the most formal because it does not use pronouns and has more formal vocabulary. **See Lesson: Formal and Informal Language.**

11. B. I won't do it. It is the most informal sentence because it has a contraction. **See Lesson: Formal and Informal Language.**

12. D. At a Parent-Teacher meeting. It is best to use formal language with a child's teacher to show respect. **See Lesson: Formal and Informal Language.**

13. C. Although the paragraph mentions obesity, the topic of this paragraph is narrowly focused on the fad diets people use as they try to control their weight. **See Lesson: Main Ideas, Topic Sentences, and Supporting Details.**

14. A. The first sentence of this paragraph leads the reader toward the main idea, which is expressed next in a topic sentence about the harmfulness of fad diets. **See Lesson: Main Ideas, Topic Sentences, and Supporting Details.**

15. C. A description of a failed experience with fad diets would function as a supporting detail in this paragraph about the negative consequences of fad diets. **See Lesson: Main Ideas, Topic Sentences, and Supporting Details.**

16. B. Although this description of the paragraph would be valid in an opinion response, it is not merely a statement of the main idea because it adds the reader's judgment about the paragraph. **See Lesson: Main Ideas, Topic Sentences, and Supporting Details.**

17. A. Although a statistic about early childhood obesity might belong in a passage focusing on obesity rates, it would be off-topic information in this paragraph on the harm of fad dieting. **See Lesson: Main Ideas, Topic Sentences, and Supporting Details.**

18. C. Labels name parts of the diagram and indicate them with lines pointing to the part of the picture to which they correspond. The small, root-like part of the neuron on the top right is a dendrite. **See Lesson: Summarizing Text and Using Text Features.**

19. B. A diagram illustrates what complex things look like and provides information about their parts. It cannot explain exactly what things do. **See Lesson: Summarizing Text and Using Text Features.**

20. D. The pie chart indicates the amount of time students of different genders contribute to discussions. The larger wedge for male speaking indicates that 70% of class discussion time is dominated by male speakers. **See Lesson: Summarizing Text and Using Text Features.**

21. B. If you read the labels carefully, you will see that the bar graph shows how many times students of each gender *are interrupted* during class discussions. The graph shows that students are interrupted more often than male students. **See Lesson: Summarizing Text and Using Text Features.**

22. B. The data in the chart and graph could help show that male students are receiving more chances to speak in class discussions, and that it would be a good idea to increase gender parity. **See Lesson: Summarizing Text and Using Text Features.**

23. B. The tone of this letter is hostile and arrogant as the author openly assumes her wealth and influence will secure a good chemistry grade for her daughter. **See Lesson: Tone, Mood, and Transition Words.**

24. C. The author of the letter uses mostly polite language to make her arrogant request, but her language becomes openly hostile when she calls grading practices "petty" and accuses Dr. Rodriguez of being "incompetent." **See Lesson: Tone, Mood, and Transition Words.**

25. A. A teacher receiving a note like this would likely feel furious. **See Lesson: Tone and Mood, Transition Words.**

26. C. The phrase "in fact" adds emphasis to the writer's implicit point that she intends to make sure her daughter unfairly receives a high chemistry grade. **See Lesson: Tone, Mood, and Transition Words.**

27. C. The paragraph is meant to convince the reader to pay for or otherwise help with the cleanup of Fly Lake. This makes it a persuasive text. **See Lesson: Types of Passages, Text Structures, Genre and Theme.**

28. B. The paragraph points out a problem at the beginning and offers a solution. In between, it describes the environmental problems at Fly Lake in a logical order. **See Lesson: Types of Passages, Text Structures, Genre and Theme.**

29. A. The author of this text is expressing a point of view in a short-form piece. This is most likely an essay. **See Lesson: Types of Passages, Text Structures, Genre and Theme.**

30. B. When finding a theme, steer away from options that only reflect a sentence or two, and from options that are not fully supported by the whole text. The entire passage makes an argument for cleaning up a polluted site because it would benefit everyone. **See Lesson: Types of Passages, Text Structures, Genre and Theme.**

31. A. From phrases like "your child," you can infer that the intended audience of this passage is parents. **See Lesson: Understanding Primary Sources, Making Inferences, and Drawing Conclusions.**

32. A. The author makes several references to time constraints but assumes that parents want their children to be well educated. **See Lesson: Understanding Primary Sources, Making Inferences, and Drawing Conclusions.**

33. D. The author of this article assumes that all children should grow up to become mindful world citizens. **See Lesson: Understanding Primary Sources, Making Inferences, and Drawing Conclusions.**

34. D. The author does not suggest that STEM instruction is unimportant. The article says only that increased time spent on STEM instruction is often made at the expense of other subjects, like social studies. **See Lesson: Understanding Primary Sources, Making Inferences, and Drawing Conclusions.**

35. B. The line about online library databases shows that the author understands that parents may need a convenient way to follow the article's advice. **See Lesson: Understanding Primary Sources, Making Inferences, and Drawing Conclusions.**

36. C. This is an advertisement. Although it includes some information its primary purpose is to convince you to buy something. This makes it a persuasive text. **See Lesson: The Author's Purpose and Point of View.**

37. D. It is difficult to know much about the true feelings of advertising writers because it's their job to sell products, not say what they believe. However, it is a fair bet that advertising writers believe people will pay money for products presented the way they describe. **See Lesson: The Author's Purpose and Point of View.**

38. C. Much of the information in this advertisement is not verifiable, but the fact that the clothing tracks the body's signals with sensors is a fact. **See Lesson: The Author's Purpose and Point of View..**

39. C. The advertisement highlights several aspects of WiseWear gear, such as the comfort and ease of use, that suggest the potential customer will feel good using the products. These details appeal to the emotions. **See Lesson: The Author's Purpose and Point of View.**

40. D. Celebrity endorsements in advertisements appeal to the emotions by associating a product for sale with a person who is widely admired. **See Lesson: The Author's Purpose and Point of View.**

Section IV. Science

1. C. There are seven classification systems in the classical Linnaean system: kingdom, phylum, class, order, family, genus, and species. **See Lesson: An Introduction to Biology.**

2. D. Because a cell membrane is selectively permeable, only certain molecules are allowed to enter. For molecules such as sodium ions to enter, they have to travel through specialized channels. **See Lesson: Cell Structure, Function, and Type.**

3. D. Ribosomes are organelles that play a role in the synthesis of proteins such as enzymes. **See Lesson: Cell Structure, Function, and Type.**

4. D. The ATP provides the reducing power to make carbon dioxide into sugar. **See Lesson: Cellular Reproduction, Cellular Respiration, and Photosynthesis.**

5. A. Glycolysis involves the breakdown of glucose into pyruvate. Per one glucose molecule, this metabolic reaction yields a net of two molecules of ATP, two molecules of NADH, and two molecules of pyruvate. **See Lesson: Cellular Reproduction, Cellular Respiration, and Photosynthesis.**

6. B. The G2 phase prepares for the M (mitotic) phase by making tubulin for microtubules. These microtubules, with the help of spindle fibers, separate chromosomes during mitosis. **See Lesson: Cellular Reproduction, Cellular Respiration, and Photosynthesis.**

7. B. A barometer is used to measure air pressure in an experiment. **See Lesson: Designing an Experiment.**

8. D. The variable that is manipulated, or what is administered to a group as a treatment, is called the treatment group. **See Lesson: Designing an Experiment.**

9. C. Peptide bonds connect amino acids together to form a protein. **See Lesson: Genetics and DNA.**

10. C. In a DNA molecule, cytosine can only pair with guanine. **See Lesson: Genetics and DNA.**

11. C. The only haploid cells are gametes, which are egg and sperm cells. **See Lesson: Genetics and DNA.**

12. A. Lipids are a class of biomolecules that provide a long-term storage solution for energy in living things. Examples of lipids include fats, steroids, and oils. **See Lesson: An Introduction to Biology.**

13. B. A weak base is a substance that partially dissociates in solution. Ammonia is an example of a weak base because it weakly dissociates to ammonium ions in solution. **See Lesson: Acids and Bases.**

14. D. When a Brønsted-Lowry base dissociates in an aqueous solution, it accepts hydrogen ions and increases hydroxide ion concentration. **See Lesson: Acids and Bases.**

15. A. Group 1 elements all have one valence electron, and the number of valence electrons increases going across the periodic table, from left to right, to the group 18 elements, which all have eight valence electrons. **See Lesson: Chemical Bonds.**

16. C. Zinc is a metal and will transfer electrons to a nonmetal, such as sulfur. **See Lesson: Chemical Bonds.**

17. C. Chlorine is in group 17 and has seven valence electrons, which means it must gain one electron to become stable. After it gains that electron, it will be an anion because it will have a negative charge. **See Lesson: Chemical Bonds.**

18. A. The substance inside of the bubbles must be a gas. The only gas in the reaction is the product carbon dioxide (CO_2), which is indicated by the *(g)* next to the formula in the equation. **See Lesson: Chemical Solutions.**

19. D. All combustion reactions begin with a fuel that contains carbon and hydrogen, which reacts with oxygen in the air. Carbon dioxide and water are always produced. **See Lesson: Chemical Solutions.**

20. C. In this reaction, two elements are trading places. In the reactants, lead and nitrate ions are together, and potassium and iodide ions are together. In the products, lead and iodide ions are together, and potassium and nitrate ions are together. **See Lesson: Chemical Solutions.**

21. D. Unable to cross the membrane, the polar solute particles would form hydrogen bonds with the water molecules surrounding them. **See Lesson: Properties of Matter.**

22. D. In a polar molecule, one end of the molecule is slightly negative, and the other end is slightly positive. **See Lesson: Properties of Matter.**

23. C. The atomic number of an element is determined by its number of protons. Lithium has an atomic number of 3, which means that if an atom has 3 protons, it is an atom of lithium. **See Lesson: Scientific Notation.**

24. A. All choices are written in scientific notation and have negative exponents, which means the decimal place moves to the left when converting to standard notation. Because its decimal place moves to the left more spaces than the others, answer A has the smallest magnitude. **See Lesson: Scientific Notation.**

25. D. In a solid, particles have the least amount of energy and do not move as much as they do in other states of matter. The strong cohesive forces between the particles keep them close together. **See Lesson: States of Matter.**

26. C. A substance has more energy as a plasma than in any other state of matter. **See Lesson: States of Matter.**

27. B. There are 1,000 grams in 1 kilogram. This means 1,800 grams divided by 1,000 grams yields 1.8 kilograms. **See Lesson: Temperature and the Metric System.**

28. D. One liter of solution is equivalent to 1.06 quarts. Multiplying 5 liters by 1.06 yields a total of 5.3 quarts of saline. **See Lesson: Temperature and the Metric System.**

29. B. The sum of currents going into a node must equal the sum of currents going out of the node. In this case, 3 amps are going in on one wire and 1 amp is going out on another. For the total in to equal the total out, the third wire must carry 2 amps out of the node. **See Lesson: Electricity and Magnetism.**

30. C. If a voltage source is connected to only one electrical component, the entire voltage is dropped across that component. Recall that when going in a particular direction around any loop in a circuit, the sum of the voltages must be zero. **See Lesson: Electricity and Magnetism.**

31. B. To slide the block, the minimum applied horizontal force must be at least the friction force. Because the friction force is horizontal in this case and opposite to the applied force, it is equal to the minimum applied force to slide the block. Multiply 0.050 by 230 to get that force in newtons: the result is 12 newtons. **See Lesson: Friction.**

32. B. An object in uniform circular motion has a centripetal acceleration equal to $\frac{v^2}{r}$, where v is its velocity and r is its distance from the center. If a satellite is in a circular orbit, its centripetal acceleration is equal to the acceleration due to gravity. Also, r is its distance to the center of Earth. Solve for v:

$$a_c = \frac{v^2}{r}$$

$$v^2 = ra_c$$

$$v = \sqrt{ra_c} = \sqrt{(6.7 \times 10^6\ m)(9.8\ m/s^2)} = \sqrt{6.6 \times 10^7\ m^2/s^2} = 8.1 \times 10^3\ m/s$$

See Lesson: Friction.

33. C. The angular frequency ω is $\frac{2\pi}{T}$, where T is the period. Thus,

$$T = \frac{2\pi}{\omega}$$

The velocity is the circumference of the circle ($2\varpi r$) divided by the period.

$$v = \frac{2\pi r}{T} = \frac{2\pi r}{2\pi/\omega} = r\omega = (42\ m)(0.29\ Hz) = 12\ m/s$$

See Lesson: Friction.

34. B. Use the potential energy formula to solve for *m*. Then, plug in all known variables and calculate.

$$PE = mgh$$

$$\frac{PE}{gh} = m$$

$$\frac{1900\ J}{9.8\ \frac{m}{s^2}(3.0\ m)} = m$$

$$65\ kg = m$$

See Lesson: Kinetic Energy.

35. D. Climate patterns include any regular cycle that occurs within climate over a period of time. **See Lesson: Meteorology**

36. B. Because velocity is squared in the kinetic energy formula, a change in velocity by a factor of 2 results in a change in kinetic energy by a factor of 4. **See Lesson: Kinetic Energy.**

37. B. Main sequence stars are stars that are in their longest stage of life. **See Lesson: Astronomy.**

38. B. Newton's first law is that an object's velocity remains fixed as long as no net force acts on that object. In this case, the ball on an ideal flat surface experiences no net forces, meaning its velocity will not change. **See Lesson: Nature of Motion.**

39. B. The amplitude of a wave is half the distance between the crest (or peak) and the trough. **See Lesson: Waves and Sounds.**

40. C. The biosphere contains all of the living organisms on Earth. **See Lesson: Geology**

CPSIA information can be obtained
at www.ICGtesting.com
Printed in the USA
JSHW031722280121
11322JS00006B/18

9 781949 147018